Listening In

Eric Prieto

Listening In:

Music, Mind, and the Modernist Narrative

University of Nebraska Press

Lincoln and London

Publication of this book was assisted by a grant from
The Andrew W. Mellon Foundation.

Earlier versions of chapters 2 and 3 were previously
published as "Recherches pour un roman musical," *Poétique* 94 (1993): 153–70, and "La musique et
la mimesis du moi," *Poétique* 104 (1995): 483–501,
respectively, and are reprinted by permission.

A portion of chapter 5 was published in "Caves:
Technology and the Total Artwork," *Mosaic* 35.1
(March 2002): 197–213, and is reprinted by permis-
sion. Figures 4 & 5 are supplied & reproduced by kind
permission of Südwestrundfunk, Stuttgart
(Germany), 2001.

Library of Congress Cataloging-in-Publication Data
Prieto, Eric, 1966–
Listening in: music, mind, and the modernist narra-
tive / Eric Prieto.
p. cm. – (Stages (Series); v.19)
Includes bibliographical references (p.) and index.
ISBN 0-8032-3732-4 (cloth: alkaline paper)
1. Music and literature – History – 20th century.
2. Music – Philosophy and aesthetics. 3. Modernism
(Literature) I. Title. II. Series.
ML3849 .P74 2002   780'.08–dc21   2002004334

Contents

Acknowledgments

Research for this book was supported in part by a Bourse Chateaubriand and by grants from New York University and the University of California, Santa Barbara. I would like to thank the mentors and colleagues without whom this book would have never come about: Gérard Genette, who first encouraged me to pursue this topic; Michel Beaujour, Tom Bishop, and Richard Sieburth, who read early versions of the manuscript; Ernest Sturm, whose advice was invaluable in the final stages; and Monika Laskowski-Caujolle, who, with a mathematician's rigor, helped prepare the final manuscript. I would also like to thank William Kraft, who shared his composer's insights with me, and James Knowlson, and Michael Bott, who introduced me to the riches of the Reading Beckett Archives. Out of the many friends who discussed these ideas with me, I would like to mention Michael Sohn, Patrick Degroseillers, Jean-Louis Pautrot, Sydney Lévy, and Porter Abbott. And thanks above all to my wife, Kim, who worked the day shift.

Introduction

When Philip Quarles speculates about the possibility of writing a musical novel in Aldous Huxley's *Point Counter Point*, he takes care to distinguish the specifically narrative scope of his project from the more traditional, poetic use of music as a source of prosodic metaphors. What interests him is not the subordination of sense to sound (which he derides as "mere glossolalia") or the use of musical thematics but the possibility of using music as a model for narrative "on a large scale, in the construction" (Huxley 301). This desire to incorporate musical principles into the construction of the narrative text has been a recurrent preoccupation of storytellers over the course of the twentieth century. Beginning with symbolist writers such as Mallarmé and Edouard Dujardin, continuing with what has been called the first generation of musical novelists (Proust, Joyce, Mann, Woolf, and Gide), through the work of the French New Novelists (Robbe-Grillet, Butor, Duras, Pinget), and on to more recent writers such as Anthony Burgess, Thomas Bernhardt, Milan Kundera, and Pascal Quignard, music has served not only as a theme for modernist storytellers but also as a model for the semiotic functioning of the narrative text, affecting the ways their narratives make and communicate meaning.

This specifically narrative use of music is unprecedented in literary history. It is true, of course, that poets and bards have, from time immemorial, looked to music as a way to reflect upon or supplement their own art (the interrelations of music and poetry go back to the very origins of the two arts), but it is only toward the end of the nineteenth century that music begins to be used as a model for narrative in its mimetic dimension. This development implies two distinct types of questions. First, given the long and venerable tradition that links music and poetry, why is it that music only gains influence as a model for narrative in the modernist era? Second, given the apparent heterogeneity of music and narrative (the abstract ordering of tones versus the semantic emphasis of literary representation), what is it that music can teach a novelist, playwright, or autobiographer about the art of telling stories? These are the questions around which this book is organized.

This modernist interest in music should be situated, I believe, with respect to the historical crisis in the mimetic function of literature that occurred toward the end of the nineteenth century. It is motivated by a growing mistrust of the conventions of nineteenth-century realism and by a desire to seek out techniques appropriate to one of the central quests of literary modernism: the ever more accurate representation of psychological states and processes. Music acts as a guide for reconfiguring the narrative text in such a way that it can better represent those elements of thought that had theretofore been considered to be ineffable, unrepresentable, or otherwise inaccessible to language. From the point of view of literary history, this development has its origins in the symbolist period, is intertwined with the rise of the stream-of-consciousness novel, and culminates in the work of the postwar avant-gardes before folding back into the ironic realism characteristic of much postmodern fiction. For those modernists more interested in the exploration of mental reality than in the representation of the physical and social realities of the outside world (the primary domain of narrative since at least Homer), music offers a set of formal, expressive, and referential principles that can be used in the attempt to better represent the inner space of consciousness. Notably, the musical emphasis on process and transformation has been seen as an alternative to the plot-based forms of traditional narrative. The literary means mobilized differ from author to author, but wherever a musical model is present, I argue, it always serves to further this inwardly directed mode of mimesis I call "listening in," where the primary object of representation is not the outside world but the subtly modulating interactions between consciousness and world.

The first part of chapter 1 is devoted to laying the groundwork for this historical explanation of the modernist interest in music. The historical explanation would be incomplete, however, without an investigation of the relations between the modes of symbolic functioning that govern the two arts. Musical works tend to subordinate semantic concerns to the abstract play of pitches and rhythms and the sensorial impact of sounds, whereas narrative is a mode of literature that has historically emphasized the semantic field over all else. How, then, can music serve as a model for narrative representation? What is it about music that encourages this turn to an art so far removed from the usual preoccupations of story-tellers? And how can the critic account for this use of music without simply falling back on the vague interart analogies that are often found in casual discussions of the arts but can have only limited heuristic value? My responses to these questions take up the bulk of chapter 1 and are presented in dialogue with some of the major narrative theorists of our day (Gérard Genette, Paul Ricoeur, Thomas Pavel, Peter Brooks), reconsidered in light of recent interdisciplinary attempts to understand the production of meaning in literature as it relates to the other arts (Nelson Goodman, Suzanne Langer, and Theodor Adorno in aesthetic philosophy; Jean-Jacques Nattiez, Joseph P. Swain, and Adorno in musicology). Nelson Goodman's *Languages of Art* has particular importance for my approach. Goodman's work, which attempts to describe the arts in light of cognitive skills and capacities that are not specific to any single art or the arts in general, has proven extremely useful for my attempt to isolate and analyze zones of semiotic overlap between music and literature. Rather than focusing on direct comparisons between musical and literary works, then, I seek to study them in light of the more general principles that subtend the relations between the arts, principles that Goodman groups under the headings of denotation, exemplification, and expression and that help to mediate between the concerns specific to each art.

This focus on mediating principles results in what I see as the primary methodological insight of *Listening In*, which is the importance of determining the proper logical status of the musical models studied. When an author claims to have written a narrative that is musical in some sense, she or he is making an inherently metaphorical gesture. Most previous studies on this subject have tended either to underestimate the fundamental heterogeneity of the two arts (taking these interart analogies too literally) or, conversely, to draw overly pessimistic conclusions about the heuristic value of such analogies (dismissing them as "mere" metaphors). My approach, grounded in the kind of comparative study of the arts enabled by Goodman's theory of symbols and by W. J. T. Mitchell's work on text and image, emphasizes the importance of taking these interart analogies not as ends in themselves but as clues that point to the under-

lying principles that govern the relationship between the arts. This focus
has two significant advantages. First, it helps to elucidate certain recurrent features of modernist narratives that have been particularly resistant
to the tools of more traditional literary criticism. Second, it makes possible a comprehensive, truly interdisciplinary understanding of the relationship between music and literature, one able to account for this relationship in terms that apply literally to both arts without neglecting the
semiotic specificity of either. These are crucial considerations for any
critic who seeks to describe this kind of semiotic boundary crossing
between music and literature.

The broader historical and theoretical arguments of chapter 1 give way
in the central chapters to detailed textual analyses of works that exemplify
the primary ways in which music has been used as a model for literature:
as a *formal* model, as an *expressive* model, and as an *essentialist* model of
nonconceptual communication. Each successive chapter focuses on a
single type of musical model (formal, expressive, essentialist), on a single, particularly noteworthy practitioner of that model (Robert Pinget,
Michel Leiris, Samuel Beckett), and on the narrative genre with which
that author's use of music is most closely associated (novel, autobiography, theater). Out of the multitude of available musical styles, and out of
the inextricably complex series of phenomena that occur while listening
to a piece of music, each of these authors finds himself drawn to certain
styles of music and discovers in them a specific set of attributes helpful in
addressing the problems posed to him by the genre he practices. Thus
Robert Pinget (chapter 2) favors baroque music and finds in the musical
theme-with-variations format a model for replacing the traditional plot-
bound linearity of the novel with a form able to depict the fleeting
instants of thought in its temporal dimension. Michel Leiris (chapter 3)
refers primarily to jazz and opera and is inspired by the expressive power
of song to develop a number of rhetorical devices helpful in achieving the
type of *communication entière* (total communication) he seeks to integrate into his autobiographical texts. As for Samuel Beckett (chapter 4),
his interest in Schopenhauerian idealism and the music of Beethoven and
Schubert manifests itself most notably in radio and television plays such
as *Words and Music*, *Cascando*, *Ghost Trio*, and *Nacht und Träume*, in
which he stages confrontations between music and text in order to suggest a mode of interpretation that works not on the level of "the plane of

the feasible," as he calls it, but on one that approaches the noumenal plane of Kantian essences.

In each of these chapters, my goals are, first, to show how the use of musical models affects the symbolic functioning of the narrative text and, second, to use that analysis as a springboard for an examination of the more general concerns that have made music such an important catalyst for narrative innovation throughout the twentieth century. Finally, in a conclusion titled "Music, Metaphysics, and Moral Purpose in Literature," I seek to tie together these various uses of music by relating them to the principal intellectual currents of the period. Claude Lévi-Strauss's writings on music in *Mythologiques* and the phenomenology of Edmund Husserl make useful points of reference here. It is, I believe, a worldview influenced by both the structuralist emphasis on relationality and the phenomenological emphasis on the temporal and perceptual structures of consciousness that makes music such an essential reference for the writers of this generation.

Listening In

1

Music, Mimesis, and Metaphor

In order to understand the issues raised by the modernist use of musical models studied in this book, it will first be necessary to understand the historical developments that made it possible. This type of relationship between music and literature—where music acts as a model for a literary mode of creation—is, historically speaking, a relatively recent development and one that depends on specifically modern definitions of both music and literature. Music could not have become available as a metaphor for literature in the first place if it were not for the fact that the traditional relationship between the two arts, in song, had begun to erode. This erosion is itself the result of a long history of increasing specialization that can be linked to the advent and spread of writing and print technology. A brief overview of this evolution is in order here.[1]

It is important to note that the modern Western distinction between music and poetic language is not universally recognized. In some cultures, it is the fundamental unity of these arts that is stressed. This unity was, for example, apparent to the ancient Greeks, who grouped music and poetry together, along with dance, under the heading *mousike*. This tendency to stress the unity of the various performance arts still has currency today in many oral cultures, both within the Occident (as in popular and folk music, where the singer-songwriter-musician unit is a central fixture) and outside of it, wherever a viable oral tradition has been maintained. For the purposes of this study, the Greek example provides the most useful starting point.

We know that the Homeric epics were originally sung or chanted, were based on a large body of shared histories and legends, and were not committed to writing until long after their creation. As specialists of

1

orality have often pointed out, music, along with such musico-poetic devices as rhythm, meter, and motivic repetition, played an important role in helping performers remember and pass on the traditional tales that constitute the primary repositories of historical and cultural memory in oral communities.[2] As writing gains currency in a culture, however, as it did in fourth-century Athens, it provides a new means for preserving cultural memory, obviating the need for oral performance in most situations. This affects the relationship between poetry and music and modifies the cultural role of poetry itself. Some of the traditional oral techniques will survive in more or less vestigial forms, but music and poetry will both gain a measure of autonomy that will make them available for other cultural tasks. Thus by the time of the Athenian golden era, the traditional unitary relationship between music and poetic language had been disrupted. And if we take such texts as Plato's *Phaedrus* as documents of this development, it appears to have been accompanied by a fair amount of uncertainty and anxiety about the true and proper relationship between thought and language, performance and writing.[3]

This question of the proper relationship between thought, language, performance, and writing is one that will be taken up again and again in debates over philosophy, rhetoric, the arts, and human expression in general. It concerns us here to the extent that poetry (and, more generally, all forms of poetic or literary language) seems able to switch sides, sometimes invoked as a performance art naturally allied with music, sometimes as a form of thought allied with philosophy. The historical advent of writing helps to complicate this relationship by driving a wedge between performance and the language arts, that is, by enabling thought to be isolated from performance. Once the human voice is no longer the requisite vehicle for the transmission of verbal knowledge, the traditional link between poetry and music in song begins to unravel. Words, which no longer need to be performed out loud, can be conceived independently of their performative aspect. Thus literature becomes possible as letters, a specifically written art, while instrumental music becomes possible as an autonomous art form, independent of its traditional link with words. This newfound freedom also entails certain risks, however, for both poetry and music; some worry that poetry, relegated to the page, will lose its voice, while music, cast adrift from its traditional verbal and contextual meanings, will stop making sense.

Following the logic of increasing specialization that seems to govern Occidental history in general, the paths of these arts in the Western high-art tradition have continued to diverge. This has not, of course, been a smooth, steady progression. As with all such broad cultural trends, the relations between music and literature vary considerably from milieu to milieu and from era to era. As a general rule, though, the distance between the two arts in any given community will increase in proportion to the importance of writing in that community. The European Middle Ages, for example, followed a path similar to that of Greek antiquity. The Arthurian romances and the chansons de geste began as oral genres that linked music to narrative in much the same way that the Homeric epics must have done. Music provided a valuable, and valued, link between the poet and his audience, whose literacy could not be assured. Even for the elite aristocratic audiences of the troubadours, music had an important phatic role to play, helping to guarantee the contact between poet and audience. On the other hand, in the Scholastic, Latin-speaking (and writing) milieu of the church and the university, the split between music and literature appears to have widened steadily. The rise of medieval polyphony, for example, contributed to a decline in the comprehensibility of the sung texts. As this music evolved, textual settings became less and less transparent (especially when texts in two or more languages were sung simultaneously), and vocal parts, beginning with the cantus firmus, were increasingly replaced by instruments. In this way, medieval polyphony played a large role in institutionalizing the division between music and text. Thus, as important as the link between music and poetry still was for the great fourteenth-century poet-composer Guillaume de Machaut (the first to write single-handedly a complete polyphonic setting of the mass ordinary), his role in the spread of polyphony could also be understood as marking a new phase in the practice of music and poetry as two distinct art forms.

Many of the subsequent debates about the relationship between music and literature will be motivated by nostalgia for the utopic unity of the arts captured in the term *mousike*, which is often invoked to call to mind a kind of prelapsarian state, where pleasure and knowledge, beauty and instruction, form and function went hand in hand, and where the distinction between music and poetry had not yet been institutionalized. Thus, by the Renaissance, we begin to find a growing concern with reforming both music and poetry by bringing them back together. One of the major themes of the Pléiade poets in France was the search for a modern equivalent to the *mousike* of Greek antiquity. Reformist institutions like Jean-Antoine de Baïf's Académie de la poésie et de la musique were founded under the influence of Neoplatonist, Pythagorean metaphysics, with the express intent of promoting what Ronsard and the Pléiade poets called "l'union de la musique et de la poésie."[4] Later, on the other side of the Alps, the Florentine Camerata made its case for a return to a monodic style of composition by proclaiming the need for a new relationship between text and music. The birth of opera as a modern art form is announced by Monteverdi's injunction to "let the word be the master not the servant of the music."[5]

Within the erudite tradition of medieval church music, musical meaning had been guaranteed by the devotional context of the mass and/or a Neoplatonic appeal to the Pythagorean notion of the harmony of the spheres. The idea that musical proportions reflect the divine architecture of the universe was a mantra of the musical theory of the Middle Ages, and it remained a mainstay of the musical theory of the early Renaissance polyphonists. With the rediscovery of Aristotle's *Poetics* during the Renaissance, however, the concept of mimesis began to gain prominence in discussions of the arts. The *Poetics*, of course, is concerned primarily with tragedy (and, more generally, all forms of "imitation by language"). But Aristotle also makes it clear that all art is to be understood in terms of imitation, including music. Just as painting imitates objects and narrative imitates action, music involves the imitation of "character, emotion, and action."[6] This renewed emphasis on mimesis helps us understand the vogue of word painting in the Renaissance and baroque periods (see Winn, *The Pale of Words* 20–24), but in the absence of linguistic, visual, or contextual clues, musical meaning and imitation do not seem to be especially compatible. How are we to know what is imitated by, say, a Bach violin partita or a Rameau *concert de clavecin*? Or, as Fontenelle is said to have asked, "Sonate, que me veux tu?" Indeed, Aristotle himself was rather vague on the subject of how this mode of imitation might work.[7]

Given the difficulty of reconciling instrumental music with the mimetic imperatives of Aristotelian poetics, it comes as no surprise that opera—with its hybrid blend of music, poetry, and drama—plays a central role in defining the parameters of the debate over the relationship between music and literature throughout the seventeenth and eighteenth centuries. The various *querelles* over Italian music that occupied French literary salons and the Encyclopédistes focused obsessively on this question, and Rousseau, in his *Discours sur l'origine des langues*, went so far as to locate the very origins of language in song. The key to Rousseau's aesthetic hierarchy is the term *expression*, and his application of this category to music reveals an important transformation that had been brewing since the Renaissance and that would usher in the romantic period in the arts. Musical expression, as Rousseau defines it, is a form of representation that passes through the mediating consciousness of an observer: "The art of the musician consists in substituting for the insensible image of the object that of the movements that its presence excites in the heart of the observer. . . . It will not represent these things directly but will excite in the soul the same sentiments that one feels in seeing them" (132–33, my translation). This definition of musical expression, in which expression is understood in mimetic terms (i.e., as the imitation of the sentiments of a subject standing before a spectacle), remained a primary force in the aesthetic theory of the nineteenth century and had a particularly strong impact on musical theory. As a result, nineteenth-century composers often found themselves in a position symmetrically related to that of the writers discussed in this study: looking to literature as a model for music.

Nineteenth-century composers experimented with a variety of means for integrating literary impulses into music and had a marked tendency to justify music in mimetic-expressive terms. Many of the most important innovations in nineteenth-century instrumental music were in genres in which the music was understood to fulfill quasi-literary functions. This is true of program music and the tone poem and in a more general way in the increasingly chromatic harmonic language of the nineteenth century, which was seen as a way to represent emotional states with ever greater precision and force. Add to this the broadening palette of the nineteenth-century symphony orchestra, the invention of semantically determined structural procedures like the leitmotiv, and the dominance of sonata form (which had evolved into a forum for the resolution of dramatic conflict between opposed forces), and it becomes clear that much of the development of nineteenth-century music is best understood in terms of mimetically inflected expression.[8]

If the growing interest in the union of music and poetry since the

Renaissance was motivated by a desire to achieve more powerful expressive effects, then romantic opera came closest to actualizing this ambition. It is perhaps not surprising, then, that opera gained steadily in prestige until, by the middle of the nineteenth century, the opera house sat at the center of cultural and social life in cities throughout Europe. Paradoxically, however, even as operas presented audiences with powerful multimedia spectacles, they also served to institutionalize the very division between music and poetry that earlier proponents of opera like Monteverdi and Rousseau had sought to overcome. In a culture that demands a high degree of professionalism and technical perfection of its artists, the creation of a total spectacle entails an ever increasing division of labor. The production of an opera is a huge undertaking that requires the collaboration of dozens of specialists. By formalizing the division of labor between the composer (who writes the score) and the librettist (who composes the text) as well as all the others involved in the creation of the work (stage designers, choreographers, costumers, directors, performers, etc.), opera can be seen as marking yet another step in the progressive divergence of music and poetry. This institutionalized division of labor cannot help but have an impact on the type of spectacle offered, and in some cases this impact will be negative, harming the artistic coherence of the work. Opera had always been vulnerable to this criticism (much as today's special-effects blockbusters are), but the problem seems to have come to a head in the second half of the nineteenth century, with the Parisian "grand operas" of Meyerbeer, Auber, and others. Enormously popular with *le grand public* of their day, they were also criticized as disjointed, fragmentary works, more concerned with crowd-pleasing effects and easy entertainment than with a true melding of artistic means. It was the perceived fragmentation of the Parisian grand opera aesthetic that stimulated Wagner's desire to reform opera through his theory of the *Gesamtkunstwerk*. With Wagner we find, once again, a reformer holding up an idealized conception of antique drama and the Greek notion of *mousike* as his models and arguing for the necessity of reuniting all elements of the spectacle into a single organic unity.

THE SYMBOLIST MOMENT

The influence of Wagner reached far outside the domain of opera and was instrumental in preparing the way for the kind of musical modeling used by twentieth-century storytellers, notably through its influence on the symbolists and their successors. Some symbolists (Hofmannsthal, Maeterlinck) did work on the grand scale of operatic spectacles, but most emphasized the more intimate tradition of lyric poetry. What interested them was the totalizing vision that characterized Wagner's theory of "the artwork of the future." Allied with the Schopenhauerian idealism that was such an important influence on fin de siècle aesthetics, Wagner's music provided the impulse for a renewed interest in studying the relationship between music and literature. Baudelaire was among the first French proponents of what came to be called "le Wagnérisme" in France, and many of the poets allied with the symbolists, from Paul Verlaine to René Ghil, referred to music to explain their objectives, as in Verlaine's injunction to put "De la musique avant toute chose" (Verlaine, "Art poétique").[9]

It might at first seem possible to think of the symbolist movement as yet another reformist attempt to renew the kind of "union de la poésie et de la musique" sought by Wagner, Rousseau, Monteverdi, and the poets of the French Renaissance. The aims of the symbolists, however, differed in significant ways from those of their predecessors. By the end of the nineteenth century, the paths of music and literature had diverged so radically that the notion of a rapprochement between the two had begun to have a somewhat paradoxical allure. Ronsard had insisted on the importance of having his poems set to music, but for the symbolist poets actual song, and even verbal performance, was no longer a priority. One thinks, for example, of the perhaps apocryphal jibe of Mallarmé, who, when asked what he thought about Debussy setting *L'après-midi d'un faune* to music, responded: "But I thought I had already done that!" (Sieburth 795). It is clear, moreover, that a text like *Un coup de dès*—with its careful spatialization of the page and its use of distinctive typefaces, font sizes, and alignments to advance the meaning of the poem—is better appreciated on the page than in performance. (Given the densely hermetic textures of so much of Mallarmé's output, in both prose and poetry, one might make the same argument for his oeuvre as a whole.) Thus, although Mallarmé argues strenuously in *La musique et les lettres* for an inherent link between music and literature, he does so in a way that has little to do with the Greek idea of *mousike*. Mallarmé uses the terms *music* and *letters* to designate not *actual* music and *actual* literature but, rather, the two opposing yet interdependent principles that make up "la face alternative . . . de l'idée" and that, faute de mieux, go by the names of music and letters.[10]

> Je pose, à mes risques esthétiquement, cette conclusion . . . que la Musique et les Lettres sont la face alternative ici élargie vers l'obscur; scintillante là, avec certitude, d'un phénomène, le seul, je l'appelai l'Idée. L'un des modes incline à l'autre et y disparaissant ressort avec emprunts.

> [I set forth, at great aesthetic risk to myself, this conclusion . . . that Music and Letters are the alternate sides, one expanding toward the obscure, the other scintillating, with certainty, of a phenomenon, the only one, which I called: the Idea. Each of these modes tends to the other and, disappearing into it, comes back with borrowings.] (*La musique et les lettres*, *Oeuvres complètes* 359, my translation)

This statement marks a critical juncture in the history of the relations between music and literature. At this point, the two are no longer considered to be linked through voice and performance but through the internalized, metaphorical voice that Mallarmé calls *l'Idée*. Music, in other words, has become available as a metaphor that embodies a type of thought, not a type of performance.

A large part of the value of music, in Mallarmé's account, is in its ability to signify without naming. What literature can borrow from music is not actual tones or rhythm or a model of poetic diction but a model of semantic autonomy, a mode of signification that does not limit thought to the denotata of words. "To *name* an object," as Mallarmé put it in an often-cited interview, "is to suppress three quarters of the pleasure of the poem, which consists in the joy of discovering little by little: to *suggest* it, that is the dream" ("Sur l'évolution littéraire," *Oeuvres complètes* 869, my translation). In this, he shows the influence of an aesthetic movement that was quickly building momentum in the second half of the nineteenth century. Both Schopenhauer and Pater put music at the top of their aesthetic hierarchies for precisely the same reason: music was not limited by the constraints of the concept. Not coincidentally, it is at about this point in time that musicians began to react against the romantic emphasis on mimetic expression and to proclaim the complete semantic autonomy of music. The view that musical meaning is immanent, having

nothing whatsoever to do with the semantic concerns of the representational arts, is usually dated back to the publication of Eduard Hanslick's
anti-Wagnerian treatise *On the Beautiful in Music*. It became a commonplace assertion of twentieth-century aesthetics

This idea of semantic autonomy particularly intrigued Mallarmé's disciple, Paul Valéry. Valéry regularly bemoaned the fact that poetry must
use the same words that serve as tokens in the day-to-day exchange of
information. In a letter to Matila Ghyka, Valéry writes of his desire to find
an intrinsic, mathematical basis for literary invention like those found in
music and architecture. The speculative literature that Valéry describes in
this letter explains a great deal about the attraction that music has exercised over literary minds in the twentieth century.

> On reading your book, I can't help but think of literature. This art
> has unfortunately lost ground to the others when it comes to the
> search for intrinsic relationships, the observance of proportions,
> and of formal conditions . . . No *Golden Section* there. I've always
> dreamed of constructing some work secretly armed with reasoned
> conventions and founded on the precise observation of the relations
> between language and the mind [*esprit*]. But I have always retreated
> before the excessive difficulty—the immense task of reformulating
> for oneself a conception of literature so clear that it would allow one
> to reason with it.—And anyway, what's the use in this day and
> age? . . . The equilibrium between knowledge, feeling, and power in
> the arts has been lost. Instinct can only provide bits and pieces. But
> great art must be in harmony with the whole man. (Ghyka 8–9)

What interested Valéry was not the observation of a real or imagined
world but the quasi-scientific observation of the relations between language and mind ("l'observation précise des relations du langage et de
l'esprit"). Valéry longed for a mode of literature justified not by semantic
content but by the search for "intrinsic relations" guaranteed by "rea-
soned conventions." This letter, printed as a preface to Matila Ghyka's
book on Pythagorean aesthetics, contains a fair bit of nostalgia for a lost
unity in the arts, but this unity is conceived not in terms of performance
or voice (i.e., *mousike*) but in terms of abstract principles that have as
their common denominator the adequation of a material (tones, language, building materials) and a thought structure. Valéry was interested
in the possibility of using literature as a tool for discovering the laws that

govern the ways the mind uses language, laws that would be as objectively verifiable as the acoustic laws that govern musical expression or as the golden section, which, as Ghyka maintains, governs the rules of classical architecture and painting.

What I have been trying to argue here is that by the end of the nineteenth century voice was no longer a necessary element of the relationship between music and literature: a new link between the two had been found, and that link was thought. Whereas the traditional relationship between poetry and music had been conceived in terms of vocal performance (whether real or virtual), it was in the context of literature as a written medium that this relationship was conceived by the symbolists. The mode of performance was no longer the issue but, rather, the mode of thought. This symbolist understanding of the relationship between music and poetry dominated modernist poetics in the first part of the twentieth century. T. S. Eliot, for example, makes a point of emphasizing the mentalist orientation of this understanding of music in his essay "The Music of Poetry": "a 'musical' poem . . . has a musical pattern of sound and a musical pattern of the secondary meanings of the words which compose it, *indissoluble and one*. And if you object that it is only the pure sound, apart from the sense, to which the adjective 'musical' can be rightly applied, I can only . . . [respond] that the sound of a poem is as much an abstraction from the poem as is the sense" (*Selected Prose of T. S. Eliot* 113, my emphasis). By stressing the indivisible relationship between sound and sense, Eliot explicitly rejects the more traditional metaphors that related music to poetic diction in terms of sound (i.e., "la musique du vers" and "imitative harmony"). Instead, he considers the linguistic sign as constituting an indivisible whole in the mind.[11] It is not, then, the sounds themselves that are musical for Eliot but, rather, the type of logic that governs those sounds. Eliot allies music with the concept of pattern in order to oppose it to the normal syntactic ordering of words in linguistic propositions. A "musical poem," in Eliot's sense, uses pattern to superimpose a supplementary layer of meaning over whatever direct, literal meanings the words may have. Needless to say, this type of logic can only be considered musical in a metaphorical sense, and Eliot is fully aware of this fact. He uses the term *music* as an oppositional term, a kind of catachresis that helps him to label a mode of thought for which he can find no adequate name but that has something to do with pattern and connotation (i.e., "the secondary meanings of the words").

It is this metaphorical use of music, allied with the notion of pattern and applied to thought rather than to prosody and performance, that governs the twentieth-century use of musical models in literature. Music, in this sense, refers to a mode of thought that owes little to actual musical composition apart from the abstract principles of pattern and proportion, which are taken to be in competition with the grammatical and semantic rules that govern normal linguistic statements.[12] It is this post-symbolist use of music, one that emphasizes pattern and thought, that makes music available for use as a model for the narrative genres.

MUSIC AND THE MODERN NARRATIVE

I have ascribed the historical divergence of music and letters to the advent of writing and the spread of printing technology. Within this first divergence, it is possible to trace another, equally important distinction between poetry (in the modern, restricted sense of the word) and narrative. This further distinction, which coincides roughly with the rise of the novel as a distinct art form, implies a further functional specialization, this time within the written context that frames the modern literary genres. Unlike the novel, modern poetry has often continued to identify itself, albeit in an increasingly metaphorical, nostalgic sense, with music and performance. When we speak of lyric poetry, we are usually referring to written poetry, but the qualifier "lyric" implies a claim for the vestigial link between poetry and song, as do many of the traditional set forms of poetry (e.g., rondeau, ballade, ode, canto, etc.), which remind us that poetry was originally a performance art linked with music. This may help to explain why music has remained active as a prosodic and expressive model for poetry, even where that poetry is no longer sung.

The modern narrative genres, on the other hand, have tended to identify themselves increasingly with writing and to forget or even actively repress the links that had traditionally bound narrative to music and performance. The novel provides the paradigmatic example of this tendency. The ancient epics, like the medieval chansons de geste, were certainly sung or chanted, but novelists have consistently downplayed this historical link between narrative and performance in order to focus with ever greater exclusivity on problems of representation, referentiality, and the mimetic illusion. Thus novelists have tended to emphasize the denotative function of language over all else, subordinating the linguistic performance to the objects and events to which they refer. The novelist may tend to treat the words on the page as if they were (or as if he or she wished they were) invisible and inaudible: the better the mimetic illusion, the less the reader is aware of the physical act of reading one word after another. This tendency is especially clear in the mass-market novel from, say, Dickens and Balzac to Stephen King and John Grisham. But even in those novels where the words that make up the text are considered to have an important role to play—as in the dual inscription of the epistolary novel or in the carefully sculpted sentences of a prose master like Flaubert—this function is always justified with respect to the representation.[13] In their preoccupation with issues like realism and the mimetic illusion, novelists have tended to turn away from music and toward the other representational arts for their models. Thus painting has provided the standard references for situating objects in space (tableau, portrait, perspective, etc.), while drama (via the Aristotelian *muthos*) has provided the standard model for ordering events in time. Music, of course, has always had its place in the novel, but always as a theme, source of inspiration, or object of representation, not as a model for the processes and structures of literary mimesis. Thus although there have been many literary narratives about music and musicians (Hoffmann's *Kreisleriana*, Diderot's *Neveu de Rameau*, Balzac's *Gambara* and *Massimila Doni*, etc.), there have been few before the twentieth century that claim to use music in ways that impinge directly on what Huxley called "the construction" of the novel. One notable exception to this rule is Thomas De Quincey's *Dream Fugue*, but even this significant precursor tends, upon closer analysis, to confirm the rule: De Quincey turns to the musical model of the fugue as a marker of *incoherence*, the confusion of a mind under the influence of opium. The idea that music might provide generalizable models for the production of literary narratives was of little interest to the novelists of the eighteenth and nineteenth centuries.[14]

The use of music as a generative model for the narrative text was an idea that only began to attract significant attention in the symbolist era. It was a phenomenon that coincided with the origins of twentieth-century modernism, and it would have been unthinkable without the historical shift in relations between music and literature that I have been describing, where music is defined as a mode of thought rather than a mode of performance. This shift in attitude coincided with the growing interest of twentieth-century writers in representing reality through the focal lens of a perceiving consciousness. Influenced in this by the symbolist poets, an increasing number of writers turned to music as a source of models useful for more accurately representing thought. It is no coincidence, then, that music was linked from the outset to the interior-monologue or stream-of-consciousness technique, one of the major innovations in the modern psychological novel. This link can be traced back to the person who is usually credited with inventing the interior-monologue technique: Edouard Dujardin.[15]

Dujardin, a disciple of Wagner's music and founding editor of *La revue wagnérienne*, claimed to have been inspired by Wagner's music when writing what is widely regarded as the first interior-monologue novel, *Les lauriers sont coupés* (first published in 1888). Decades later, in a lecture on the interior-monologue technique, Dujardin formulated the link between music and the interior monologue in this way:

> I'll tell you a secret: *Les lauriers sont coupés* was undertaken with the rash ambition of transposing into the literary domain the Wagnerian procedures that I defined for myself in this way: the life of the soul expressed by the incessant surfacing of musical motifs coming to present, one after another, indefinitely and successively, the "states" of thought, sentiment, or sensation and that materialized, or tried to materialize, in the indefinite succession of short phrases, each of which would give one of these states of thought, without logical order, in the form of breaths wafting up from the depths of being, today one would say of the unconscious or subconscious. (258, my translation)

Music represents for Dujardin an alternative to the "logical order" that governs traditional literary forms. For Dujardin, the primary characteristics of Wagner's music are its lack of "intellectualized development" and its use of short, undeveloped motifs, which he takes to be linked together according to a "purely emotional order." This, it must be admitted, is a somewhat tendentious reading of Wagner's music. Although the logic that governs Wagner's ordering of musical motifs is different from that found in the more conventional music of his day, it seems unlikely that a composer would agree with Dujardin when he asserts that Wagner's motifs follow each other "without logical order." In order to understand how Dujardin arrives at this understanding of music, we need to understand that he is not reasoning on the music itself but on his largely impressionistic experience of that music.[16] Nevertheless, this evaluation (which is a positive one in Dujardin's eyes) tells us quite a bit about what Dujardin sees in Wagner's music and how he hopes to transpose it into narrative terms.

The "purely emotional order" that Dujardin saw in Wagner's music is much like the "musical pattern" of sound and sense that Eliot detected in musical poetry: in both cases, the literary manifestation designated as musical has less to do with actual music than with a form of logic that can be opposed to the rules that govern conventional literary discourse. And, as Dujardin's oblique reference to psychoanalysis suggests, the logic that interests him is the logic of free association. The unity of Dujardin's novel does not depend on its plot, that is, "the imitation of an action that is complete and whole and of a certain magnitude" (Aristotle), but on the associations that link each successive thought with those that precede. *Les lauriers sont coupés* is to be taken as the written record of a series of thoughts, "a succession of undeveloped motifs," linked syntactically by the analogical relationships that lead from one to the next.

Whatever the objective value of Dujardin's description of Wagner's music, its value for the history of the modern novel is immense, because it is through Wagner that Dujardin justifies his decision to abandon the more strictly hierarchical logic of causal and sequential concatenation that governs discourse in traditional novels. One has the sense that without the example of Wagner's music, Dujardin would not have had the courage to attempt such a radical departure from the traditional forms of narrative. Dujardin credits Wagner with the invention of the interior-monologue technique, just as Lévi-Strauss, half a century later, named Wagner "the undeniable originator of the structural analysis of myths" (*The Raw and the Cooked* 15).[17] These are grandiose claims, but what is sure is that Wagner's new mix of music, myth, and drama was understood in fin de siècle literary circles as signaling an important new development in the analysis of thought and thought processes. Beginning with Dujardin and the symbolists, Wagner's music had enormous influence on writers and especially on novelists. In fact, it might be possible to paraphrase Lévi-Strauss and suggest, with Dujardin, that Wagner was the founding father of the narrative use of musical models.

One might wonder why it is Wagner's music and not that of other revered composers like Liszt, Chopin, and Beethoven (who was still the model of the heroic composer at the end of the nineteenth century) that has had this enduring influence on literary practice. It is true, of course, that Wagner's harmonic language and tonal innovations were perceived as being resolutely modern and as offering important new resources for exploring the aesthetic and psychological concerns of the day. This literary influence is also due, at least in part, to the vogue of Schopenhauerian thought, with which Wagner's music was linked and which had worked its way into the discussions of artistic and literary circles across the continent. But it is possible to go further and argue that if Wagner's music was of such interest to writers, it is because that music itself was the product of a literary mind. The Wagnerian revolution was not only a revolution in the tonal language of music (i.e., the final blow to the traditional, hierarchical tonality of Western music, as it is sometimes called), it was a revolution motivated by essentially literary goals and that only found its full expression on the stage. Nietzsche's scathing attacks on Wagner in *The Case of Wagner* (and other texts from the post-Schopenhauerian, anti-essentialist phase of Nietzsche's late work) insist on the literary nature of Wagner's music.

> Wagner begins from a hallucination—not of sounds but of gestures. Then he seeks the sign language of sounds for them . . . As a matter of fact, he repeated a single proposition all his life long: that his music did not mean mere music. But more. But infinitely more.— "*Not mere* music"—no musician would say that . . . he remained an orator even as a musician—he therefore had to move his "it means" into the foreground as a matter of principle. "Music is always a mere means": that was his theory, that above all the only *practice* open to him. But no musician would think that way. (170, 177)

Although we need not agree with Nietzsche's negative evaluation of this approach to composition, his analysis of Wagner's innovation seems to me entirely accurate. Wagner's operas did not simply place music at the service of poetry, as Monteverdi had claimed to do some two and a half centuries earlier. They made music a means for advancing the narrative, for telling the story on its own.

Of all the techniques associated with Wagner's style (chromaticism, continual development, etc.), it is that of the leitmotiv that has had the most influence in literary circles. It is possible, though, to argue that if the leitmotiv has been used by novelists more than any other musical analogy, it is precisely because the leitmotiv is, at bottom, not a musical technique at all but, rather, a literary technique. Borrowed from drama and dependent on that eminently linguistic procedure, the attribution of a referent to a sound symbol, its usage is entirely determined by dramatic considerations: all occurrences of a leitmotiv have dramatic consequences, establishing a relationship between the current dramatic situation and the concept or name to which the leitmotiv is affixed. Literary techniques inspired by the leitmotiv, then, may refer us to a musical effect, but that musical effect is itself derived from a dramatic convention. This does not of course mean that the leitmotiv offers nothing new to literature (I argue the contrary in chapter 2), but it does suggest that the literary critic should exercise caution when referring to such terms as a way of arguing for the musicality of a literary text. Use of such a musically inspired technique does not necessarily indicate any modification in the literary status of the text: as with all musical models for literature, techniques such as the leitmotiv can only be considered musical in a metaphorical sense.

What, then, does the use of such musically inspired devices as the leitmotiv tell us about the relation between text and music? This is a crucial question, indeed, the central question for those engaged in the study of the literary use of musical models. Having brought this history to the cusp of the twentieth century, it will be useful to pause here and turn to some of the theoretical problems involved in studying the use of music as a model for narrative.[18] Wagner's music and its literary associations will serve to introduce the thorny methodological problem of how best to accommodate the inherently metaphorical status of this type of musical model. The solution proposed here entails focusing on questions about the logical status of musical models within the literary text, their impact on the semiotic functioning of the text, and the tools at the disposal of the critic who seeks to decipher the meaning of such metaphors.

BEYOND "MUSICO-LITERARY" STUDIES

How can the literary critic determine the conditions under which musical predicates may be applied correctly to a work of literature? How does one establish the appropriateness of a musical metaphor? Are there criteria that can be invoked to guarantee both the necessity and the sufficiency of such models? Is it possible to justify the use of common analogies like leitmotiv, counterpoint, fugue, sonata form, and "la musique du vers" in a way that would satisfy a composer? These are some of the questions that have preoccupied literary critics studying the relationship between music and literature, and the answers given will have important consequences for the methods used by the critic.

I start with the conviction that the question of appropriateness, the search for some deciding criterion of musicality, has been seriously overemphasized in the majority of scholarly attempts to account for and explain the musical claims of literary texts. For no matter how constantly all the arts, as Pater would have it, aspire to the condition of music, there can be no literal contact between music and literature short of the actual superimposition of the two, as in song, opera, and the like. Barring this situation of mutual supplementarity, the only relationship that can obtain between music and literature is a metaphorical one.

Unease about the metaphorical status of musical models for literature is responsible for many of the most persistent problems critics have had in working with them. Anyone who has grappled seriously with this aspect of the relations between the two arts or has read through the abundant critical literature on the subject knows that there are two risks inherent in the study of music-and-literature: the temptation to seize on musical metaphors and use them indiscriminately, as if they had some kind of magical explanatory power, and the temptation to become so preoccupied with the uncertain status of such metaphors that it becomes impossible to make any significant determinations about the texts they are meant to describe.

It is common to find critics so bewitched by the introduction of a musical metaphor into a literary text—especially if the metaphor seems to govern the entire text, as in Célan's "Todesfuge," Strindberg's *Ghost Sonata*, Eliot's *Four Quartets*, or Huxley's *Point Counter Point*—that they content themselves with merely enumerating the points of comparison between the piece and its musical intertext, often without sufficient regard for the semiotic specificity of the two arts. The problem with this direct approach (i.e., the direct comparison of a literary text and its musical intertext) is that all attempts to apply musical terms to literature are of necessity metaphorical in nature. Is Huxley's *Crome Yellow* a rondo? Of course not. Is it *like* a rondo? Well, it could be said to have an ABA form (see Cupers 72). Is Joyce's "Sirens" episode a fugue? By no means. Is it *like* a fugue? Well . . . (see Wolf, "Can Stories Be Read" 228). Close analysis shows that even expert comparisons between literary texts and their musical references are often founded on analogies that simply cannot justify the need for a specifically musical intertext. When stripped of their metaphorical coverings, such extended comparisons often reveal themselves to depend on assertions of the type: "this piece is like a rondo in that it is divided into three parts," or "this piece is like a fugue in that there are several distinct voices." These are pertinent points; they are *necessary* parts of the definition of the musical form in question, but they are not *sufficient*. Indeed, the fact is that there is no criterion of musicality that would allow us to account for a literary text in musical terms without sacrificing the specificity of both arts.

Most critics who have devoted serious energy to the study of music-and-literature are well aware of the pitfalls of this naive, direct approach. But even caution and a resolutely critical stance may not be enough to clear up all of the misconceptions that the problematic relationship between the two arts seems to encourage. Some musically oriented critics become so troubled by the metaphorical status of the models they purport to study that their essays become studies of metaphoricity itself. These critics err on the side of caution; they risk losing sight of the larger goals of interdisciplinary criticism in a kind of methodological bait-and-switch. This becomes clear if we follow the progress of the metacritical literature the subject has inspired, which, for the sake of convenience, we can group around the heading of "musico-literary studies." This label, coined by Calvin S. Brown (whose 1948 study, *Music and Literature: A Comparison of the Arts,* is often cited by like-minded critics as a founding text), has been adopted by a variety of critics who attempt to regulate critical discourse about the music-and-literature question. For the most part these are critics who, having attempted to study literary texts in relation to music, recognize the need for a coherent system of guiding principles. To the extent that it exists as a field, then, musico-literary studies can be defined as an attempt to develop a methodology for the study of the relationship between literature and music. This is, needless to say, a highly desirable goal, a necessary step in the development of the field, but a viable methodology has not yet emerged.

Up till now, the activity of this type of critic has all too often been limited to wondering about whether this kind of discourse is even possible, whence interrogative titles like "How Meaningful Is 'Musical' in Literary Criticism?" (Scher) and "Can Stories Be Read as Music?" (Wolf), as well as cautionary subtitles like "Essai de réflexion méthodologique" (Cupers). Most metacritical essays of this type tend to follow a similar pattern. They begin with the following observations: (1) there is a lot of free-lance musical description of literary texts out there, on the part of both writers and critics; (2) most of it fails to do more than bandy about the same set of familiar clichés; (3) there is, therefore, a need for a more rigorous, scientific approach to musico-literary studies. They then set about establishing guidelines designed to restrict and regulate the application of musical terms to literature. This is usually accompanied by a demonstration of these principles on a literary example, but, more often than not, the results are disappointing, and the critic ends up falling back on optimistic speculation about the future of the discipline. We find this pattern repeated throughout the history of the field, from Brown's 1948 opus to some of the most recent contributions to the field, such as Werner Wolf's *The Musicalization of Fiction: A Study in the Theory and History of Intermediality* (1999) and a volume of essays, also published in 1999, edited by Walter Bernhart, Steven Paul Scher, and Werner Wolf, which, significantly, still bears the cautionary subtitle *Defining the Field*.

Why is it that after fifty years of musico-literary studies critics still feel uncomfortable with the available definitions of their field? What is it about the relationship between music and literature that makes it so difficult to stabilize and work with musical metaphors in literary texts? As I see it, the primary problem with the musico-literary approach is that, having correctly diagnosed a common source of critical error, the loose metaphor, these critics allow the question of metaphoricity to dominate their analyses to the exclusion of all other considerations. They mistake the effect (metaphors) for the cause (the irreducible heterogeneity of music and literature). By limiting themselves so exclusively to consideration of questions of appropriateness (e.g., "When does it make sense to speak of a 'musicalized fiction'?" [Wolf, "Can Stories Be Read" 213]), they neglect other fundamental questions about the meaning of the musical metaphors they have before them. What motivated this writer's turn to music in the first place? How does the use of such and such a model affect the semiotic functioning of the text? What consequences does the use of this model have for our interpretation of the text? What are its implications for the study of literature (and music) in general? Instead, all too much of the work of musico-literary critics is devoted to the problem of how much breadth to allow a metaphor before ruling that it is too distant and therefore inapplicable.

As these critics describe it, the problem is simply that most of us fail to use enough rigor in our use of musical metaphors: we use our terms inconsistently and are therefore unable to decide when a given metaphor is appropriate. So they set out to search for a standard that would allow musical metaphors to be used with precision, only to discover that no surefire set of standards is to be found. Wolf, for example, after listing four groups of criteria designed to "help to identify the musicalization of a given text of fiction," finds himself constrained to add that "it goes without saying that none of these (groups of) criteria has a decisive value individually. Their significance rather depends on a cumulative effect. Yet even then one has to admit that a certain skepticism concerning the idea of reading stories as music cannot be wholly dismissed" ("Can Stories Be Read" 216).

We see a similar preoccupation with the logical status of the musical metaphor in many of Calvin Brown's texts, as in the following passage, in which he asserts that "in discussions of the relations between music and literature," the application, even casual, of metaphors like leitmotiv and counterpoint to literary texts is dangerous because "they imply real analogies which are not actually applicable, and thus make for confusion" ("Musico-Literary Research" 6). In the same essay, he protests against the tendency "to apply musical metaphors to poetry as if they were analogies" (20). This distinction between metaphor and analogy is a disturbing one and not fully explained by Brown. He seems to attribute more authority and a greater degree of literality to analogies than to metaphors, limiting the use of the term *analogy* to the designation of predicates that are "actually applicable." In other words, for Brown, the crux of the musico-literary dilemma is in the imprecision of metaphors; and his proposed solution is to use *more precise* metaphors (which he distinguishes by calling them analogies) in order to find the point where a metaphor becomes "actually applicable."

This desire for precision leads inevitably to the stipulation that everyone always speak literally, an untenable notion in itself but especially troubling when applied to a field like music, where even the technical vocabulary of composers and musicologists is suffused with metaphoricity. Symptomatically, the conclusion of Brown's *Tones into Words* includes the statement that "poems dealing with music in any but specifically musical terms are unsatisfactory, and the use of musical terms to produce effective poetry is extremely difficult" (cited in Cupers 68). Brown's critical dilemma, it seems, brings him to the point of requiring that the poets themselves speak of music in literal terms. The problems with this approach are clear: critics have neither the right nor the means to require more of a metaphor than its author intended (although they may very well, in certain circumstances, *find* more than the author intended). But Brown is not the only musico-literary critic to make mistakes of this kind. Consider the following statement on Eliot's *Four Quartets*: "Eliot does not seem to realize, nor do the critics who take his clues, that [the relationship between these two passages] is in no way contrapuntal" (Barricelli 5). In order to take Eliot to task for the metaphoricity of the counterpoint metaphor, the critic conveniently ignores that Eliot had made no claim for literality. The critic blames the poet for his own misuse of the metaphor.

This kind of error is a by-product of the great myth of musico-literary studies, which is that careful study will eventually allow the critic to establish a set of fixed rules governing the use of musical models. Musico-literary critics, in other words, attempt to *legislate*, to decide once and for all what does and does not constitute an appropriate musical metaphor. And some, frustrated by their inability to turn metaphors into concepts (an evolutionary process that requires the tacit or overt participation of an entire linguistic community), attempt to impose by fiat their own set of criteria, only to find themselves in conflict with other critics and sometimes even with the very texts they purport to study.

It is interesting to note that none of the musico-literary critics devotes much space to more traditional metaphors like "imitative harmony" and "la musique du vers." It might seem surprising, at first glance, that a critic like Brown, intent on developing a clear set of rules for the use of musical metaphors, devotes so little attention to a set of musical metaphors that is readily understood and accepted by pretty much the entire literary community. Steven Paul Scher even goes so far as to exclude such prosodic metaphors specifically from the field of musico-literary studies. He concludes (with a symptomatic amount of hedging) that "only in the case of [large-scale structural analogies] are we dealing with literary techniques which can be proven on occasion to be more or less analogous to certain techniques in actual music" ("How Meaningful" 56). Why go so far as to exclude these traditional metaphors from the field under consideration? An important clue comes from Northrop Frye. Frye does study the question of musical metaphors for prosody, but he does so in a deliberately paradoxical manner. For Frye, "the literary meaning of musical *is* unmusical" ("Music in Poetry" 178). The primary intention of this definition, Frye tells us, is to counter the "sentimental fashion of calling any poetry musical if it sounds nice" (*Anatomy of Criticism* 255). Frye makes a point of emphasizing the counterintuitive nature of his definition: "When we find sharp barking accents, crabbed and obscure language, mouthfuls of consonants, and long lumbering polysyllables, we are probably dealing with *melos*, or poetry which shows an analogy to music, if not an actual influence from it" (*Anatomy of Criticism* 256). He emphasizes that "musical diction," defined his way, "is better fitted for the grotesque and horrible, or for invective and abuse," than for soothing, pleasing poetry (*Anatomy of Criticism* 256–57). Polemical value aside, his whole argument rides on a definition of musicality that seems no more able to serve as a basis for a description of the relationship between music and poetry than the sentimental one it is supposed to supplant. Frye asserts: "When in poetry we have a predominating stress accent and a variable number of syllables between two stresses (usually four stresses to a line, corresponding to 'common time' in music), we have musical poetry, that is, poetry which resembles in its structure the music contemporary with it" (*Anatomy of Criticism* 255). Frye correctly maintains the metaphorical distance between the two arts, but it is significant that he seems unable to come up with more than arbitrary distinctions between musical and nonmusical diction. Why, for example, should a four stress line, which he identifies with common time in music, be more musical than, say, a three stress line, where one could with equal legitimacy find an equivalent of "waltz time"? And why insist on such a paradoxical definition of musical poetry, where melody is described in terms of "barking" and "the grotesque and horrible" and where the musical is defined in terms of the *un*musical?

I believe that Frye approaches the question this way for the very same reason that Scher excludes such prosodic metaphor from consideration in the first place. If Scher prefers large-scale structural analogies to prosodic metaphors, and Frye prefers a paradoxical definition of musical verse, it is precisely because they are problematic, because they still require commentary and analysis in order to be understood. The traditional prosodic metaphor, in its standard acceptation, is now a dead metaphor: used indiscriminately in layman's discussions of poetry, its status has, to a great extent, congealed. But the formal analogies preferred by Scher (as well as the other types of metaphors considered in this study, i.e., expressive and essentialist) are still living metaphors; they speak to us because they still require a cognitive leap in order to be understood. For Aristotle, the value of metaphor was in its ability to instruct, to teach us something new about the relation between two objects.[19] And this applies to musical metaphors as well. The test of a good musical metaphor should never be one of "appropriateness," defined as the degree to which it approaches literality, but the same test that applies for any other kind of metaphor: the quantity and quality of information imparted, the extent to which the metaphor affords new ways of seeing. The question is not whether a metaphor is appropriate or not but where it can take us, how much it can teach us.

It is, then, their very novelty, their very paradoxicality, that explains why musical models for narrative have generated such interest in the twentieth century among both creators and critics. This is the crux of the matter, the point on which the entire interest of musico-literary studies depends. The traditional poetic metaphors of diction and prosody either have achieved quasi-conceptual status and pass almost unnoticed or have degenerated into clichés. They have interested twentieth-century poets primarily to the extent that they recall the days of the poet-composer (see Ezra Pound's work on the Provençal poets and Jacques Roubaud's *La fleur inverse*). The use of musical models for narrative, on the other hand, is a relatively recent development and one that has not yet been well understood. It was not until Wagner's new mix of music, myth, and drama, regulated by leitmotivs and the principle of "continuous melody," that music came to be seen as an exciting realm of exploration for storytellers. The authors studied in the central chapters of this book, inheritors of the Wagnerian, postsymbolist musical legacy, make excellent case studies for a new kind of musically oriented criticism because the musical models they use, and the ways they use them, shed an exceptionally great amount of light not only on the shape and meaning of their own texts but on their more general artistic aims and, finally, on the means and ends of literature itself. This is why it is so important for the proponents of the musico-literary approach to lay to rest their distrust of metaphors. By focusing so exclusively on the need to regulate the use of musical metaphors, to decide when it "makes sense to speak of" music, the musico-literary critics allow their attention to be deflected away from more interesting questions involving the semiotic functioning of the two arts and the relations between them.

The main point here is that the inherently metaphorical status of these claims for musicality should not be perceived as an obstacle to critical analysis. On the contrary, the very fact that there is a need for such metaphors provides an important clue as to what the task of the musico-literary critic should be, which is to isolate and explain these metaphors in a way that sheds light on those features of literary language that would not be apparent from within the narrower perspectives of more traditional literary criticism. By reflecting upon the underlying principles that govern this use of musical metaphors and by considering the aesthetic concerns that motivated their use in the first place, the critic can help integrate the study of literature into a more general theory of human expression, relativizing the traditional functions of literature rather than simply taking them as a given. This wider perspective can be especially helpful when studying the kind of avant-gardist, experimental literature produced by writers like Pinget, Leiris, Beckett, and their contemporaries, which defy many of the most widely accepted conventions of literary representation. Many of the traditional categories of literary criticism simply do not apply to this body of work in any illuminating way, and so music was invoked as a way of providing concepts that would help to fill, by catachresis, gaps in the vocabulary used to describe the theory and practice of literature.

In the event that a given metaphor is deemed worthy of closer study (not all of them are), the critic must first determine what has been done with the metaphor and then decide how to develop its implications. Determining the relevant points of comparison (i.e., this poem is like a fugue in that . . .) is only the first stage of this task. The real work of interpretation begins once that type of initial determination has been made. In order to bring to light the metaphor's significance, the critic must attempt to decode it, to explain how it is being *used*, in literal terms. This type of analysis requires, in turn, a conceptual shift to a level of greater generality, a set of concepts that will help to mediate between music and literature, showing what these two arts, as symbol systems, *can* share. For this it will be helpful to review how the relationship between the two arts has been approached in aesthetic philosophy. Aesthetics, which attempts to offer a general theory of the arts, provides concepts that help to relativize the forms and functions specific to music and literature, resituating them within a broader context. It helps to clarify what is at stake in the literary use of musical models by bringing to light the underlying principles that govern all relations between the two arts.

SOUNDS AND SYMBOLS IN MUSIC AND LITERATURE

If we restricted our analysis to the level of the signifier, it would become apparent that there is one point on which music and literature coincide precisely: like the musical score, the literary text determines a sequence of sounds ordered in time. This point has its importance: both music and literature are temporal arts that involve the manipulation of sound symbols, which is why, for example, they can be combined in song. But even at this basic level, it is the differences that predominate, since music and language organize the sound stream according to different criteria. Although we have become accustomed to hearing musical metaphors used to designate prosodic effects like euphony, assonance, alliteration, and rhyme, we must not forget their great imprecision: musical notation governs pitch and duration, while language governs phonological articulations. There are, of course, languages like Chinese, in which pitch marks important semantic distinctions, and even in English or French there is a small number of points on which pitch distinctions come into play (e.g., a rise in pitch at the end of a sentence signals a question). But the poverty of means that these conventions represent with respect to musical pitch is clear-cut, as is their relative marginality with respect to phonological articulations. For much the same reason, the correspondence between rhythm in music and poetry is quite limited: musicians can determine with great precision the relative duration of each unit (by subdividing the beat), but the variability of linguistic durations is quite limited and, for the most part, outside the control of the poet. Poets can choose their words but not the relative length of the syllables. And once they write them down, they can no longer even determine the speed at which their words will be read.

In short, even on the level of elementary sounds, the music/literature analogy has only limited applicability. Moreover, it quickly becomes apparent that limiting discussion to the level of the signifier would require bypassing the fundamental issue in the relationship between the two arts, which, to put it somewhat abruptly, is this: words denote, and notes do not. The literary text, like any linguistic utterance, determines sets of semantic correspondents that are utterly foreign to the musical score. Music, of course, can under certain conditions convey semantic effects: it can evoke states of mind and emotions; be linked to a particular idea, object, or character (as in the leitmotiv); and even, through a kind of onomatopoeic imitation, refer to sounds from the extramusical world (bird song, battles, trains, etc.). But musical structures, and this is true of even the most overtly programmatic tone poems, never depend on reference to the exterior world for their coherence as symbol systems. In linguistic terms, then, one might say that music is essentially a syntax. Music consists of a code for ordering sounds in time according to certain of their physical characteristics, but it has no codified semantic function. Musical syntax operates on tones (division of the octave into twelve equal intervals, usually organized hierarchically around the diatonic scale) and rhythms (multiples or divisions of the basic unit provided by the beat), not concepts.[20] Literature, on the other hand, uses language. And although language, like music, operates on certain physical characteristics of sound (phonetic oppositions), it orders them according to semantic criteria. This is equally true on the microscopic level (the only permissible combinations of phonemes are words), on the level of the sentence (grammatical categories like subject, verb, and object regulate semantic relations between concepts), and on the macroscopic level of arguments, stories, and descriptions. Linguistic syntax depends on and is determined by semantic categories. A work of literature may superimpose nonsemantic schemata over the semantic structure, as in rhyme, meter, and the fixed forms of poetry, but without the basic semantic mechanism of language—denotation—literature cannot exist. Thus, notwithstanding certain experimental forays into the domain of the nondenotative (like *Lettrisme* and Hugo Ball's poetry), there can be no such thing as "abstract literature," at least not in the sense that one speaks of abstraction in music or painting. A work of literature that didn't denote anything would not be abstract, it would simply be unreadable, in every sense of the word.

This issue of the relationship between the two-tiered linguistic sign and the "presentational" modalities of musical meaning has raised a number of questions for aesthetics. Instrumental music represents a problem for aesthetics because its mode of signification is difficult to reconcile with the semantically oriented theories developed to describe meaning in the representational arts. How does music manage to make meaning without referring to objects in the real world? Why does music matter even though it appears unable to address itself to the issues that concern us outside of the concert hall? In a sense, the question of meaning in music is the question of aesthetic value in its purest form. As Leonard B. Meyer put it in *Emotion and Meaning in Music,*

> the problem of musical meaning and its communication is of particular interest for several reasons. Not only does music use no linguistic signs but, on one level at least, it operates as a closed system, that is, it employs no signs or symbols referring to the non-musical world of objects, concepts, and human desires. Thus the meanings which it imparts differ in important ways from those conveyed by literature, painting, biology, or physics. Unlike a closed, non-referential mathematical system, music is said to communicate emotional and aesthetic meanings as well as purely intellectual ones. This puzzling combination of abstractness with concrete emotional and aesthetic experience can, if understood correctly, perhaps yield useful insights into more general problems of meaning and communication, especially those involving aesthetic experience. (vii)

A brief survey of the attempts that have been made to account for musical meaning will help us to appreciate the key role music has played in the thought of those working on what Meyer calls the "more general problems of meaning and communication." This is an essential step if we are to understand *why* a poet, prosateur, or playwright would seek models in an art that seems so far removed from the traditional concerns of wordsmiths. I will use Monroe Beardsley's search for a defensible account

of musical meaning as a way to frame the problem as well as the difficulties aesthetic theory has had in resolving it. I will then turn to Nelson
Goodman's *Languages of Art*, which offers an elegant solution to the
problem posed by Beardsley and uses it to formulate a comprehensive
theory able to address many of the "more general problems of meaning
and communication" alluded to by Meyer.

EXPRESSION, SIGNIFICATION, AND FORMALISM
IN BEARDSLEY'S *AESTHETICS*

Monroe Beardsley's *Aesthetics: Problems in the Philosophy of Criticism*
offers a good overview of the various theories that have been proposed to
explain how music makes meaning. Beardsley first runs through a variety
of "trivial theories" (music as the imitation of real sounds, as the evocation of words or places associated with that music, as the evocation of
impressionistic images in the listener), which he discards because they
only account for secondary components of musical communication. He
then turns to the three main theories of musical meaning that have
general currency today, which he calls the Expression Theory, the Signification Theory, and the "Formalist" Theory. Interestingly, Beardsley
adopts the third, "Formalist," theory even though, as he admits, he is
unable to fully defend it in logical terms. His reasons for making this
choice and for his inability to defend it will help us to understand the
primary point of contention among aestheticians on the question of
musical meaning. The "Formalist" Theory, as Beardsley formulates it,
consists primarily in "the denial of the proposition that music has a
meaning" (338). Beardsley is not entirely comfortable with it, but he
adopts this "entirely negative" theory anyway because he is unable to
discover how music could go about making meaning short of maintaining that it could somehow refer to the outside world like language. It is
this problem—the problem of *reference* or, rather, the apparent lack of
it—that leads Beardsley to discard both the Expression Theory and the
Signification Theory in favor of the "Formalist" Theory.[21]

The Expression Theory, as Beardsley describes it, treats music as an art
of the emotions: the primary purpose of the musical work is to convey
emotional and affective states. This theory seems plausible when applied
to the emphatically emotive content of, for example, much nineteenth-

century romantic music, but it falls short on several counts. First of all, music does not *only* express emotions. Every musical work has a significant cognitive, problem-solving dimension that cannot be accounted for in terms of emotion. This in itself would be enough to disqualify the Expression Theory as a general theory of musical meaning, but there are other problems with it as well. For instance, it is not clear what exactly the emotional content of a piece really tells us about that piece. Is Chopin's *Funeral March* sad because Chopin was sad when he wrote it or because it makes its listeners feel sad? Neither of these causal explanations stands up to close scrutiny. A happy composer could very well compose sad music, and a sad piece may not have that effect on all of its listeners. Indeed, having composed or listened to an excellent piece of tragic music could very well be cause for feelings of elation or exhilaration. There is, in other words, no necessary causal link between the emotional states of composer and audience and the emotions expressed in the piece. Perhaps, then, we need to choose an individual passage with a marked expressive character and look for some component of that passage that would express sadness (or triumph, or puckishness, or whatever other attributes it might be said to possess). Is there something inherently sad about the way the notes are organized? This immanent explanation of emotional content doesn't hold water either. No surefire rules exist, even by convention, that would allow us to predict the relationship between form and expression in music: there are sad passages in major keys, joyful passages in slow tempos, lazy passages full of thirty-second notes, and so forth. Affective predicates may be useful for describing a piece in general, impressionistic terms, but they do not account for the individual elements that make up the music in any predictable way. Emotion predicates are simply too imprecise to describe a piece or passage in any but the most general way. This is where Beardsley's Signification Theory seems to show promise.

According to the Signification Theory, music is a form of symbolism that depicts psychological processes, including, but not limited to, emotions. This theory, as Beardsley describes it, has the merit of accounting more completely for the cognitive complexity of music. Beardsley bases his account of this approach to musical meaning on Suzanne Langer's "semiotic" theory of music, as described in her *Philosophy in a New Key*, to which I now turn.

Langer treats music as a subset of her general theory of semiosis, or sign functioning, based on Wittgenstein's assertion from the *Tractatus* (later retracted in the *Philosophical Investigations*) that language creates a logical picture of the world. Langer extends this Wittgensteinian theory to music by proposing that music provides iconic signs of psychological processes. According to Langer, music provides "an implicit symbolism" (199), composed of "unconsummated symbols" (195) that reflect not individual feelings but "the forms of human feeling" (191). This approach marks a significant advance over the Expression Theory in that it doesn't imply a causal relationship to emotions (i.e., that a sad passage is caused by or causes sadness) and that it allows more nuanced interpretation of the details that make up a global effect. For Langer, "music is not self-expression, but *formulation and representation* of emotions, moods, mental tensions and resolutions—a 'logical picture' of sentient, responsive life . . . A composer not only indicates, but *articulates* subtle complexes of feeling that language cannot even name, let alone set forth; he knows the forms of emotion and can handle them, 'compose' them" (180, emphasis in original). In essence, Langer brings us back to a mimetic definition of music in the tradition of Aristotle and Rousseau: music formulates and represents emotions, moods, mental tensions, and resolutions. She places the onus of her demonstration on the Peircian notion of iconicity but has trouble explaining how music might refer to cognitive processes. How can there be an iconic relationship between sound sequences and the inaudible processes of mental activity? Langer counters this type of objection by emphasizing that the imitation happens on a metaphorical level, with the Wittgensteinian notion of the "logical picture" mediating between the auditive and the neuronal. As long as we remain clear about the fact that the relationship is a metaphorical one, this explanation seems to work fine. But here again, the question of reference causes a problem. This is where Beardsley takes Langer to task.

Beardsley sees no way to show that musical symbols, whether iconic or not, refer to extramusical realities. If there were a directly perceptible iconic relationship, as in painting, where the contours and colors of a representation and its real-world referents can be compared, the question of reference would pretty much take care of itself, and there would be no problem. But metaphorical iconicity has no such measurable referents. We need a key for decoding the metaphor if we are to translate sounds into emotions, and, as Beardsley points out, musical language has no means for providing us with such a key. Langer knows this too but sees no way out of the dilemma, which is why she resorts to paradoxical formulations like "unconsummated symbols" and "implicit symbolism." When a piece of music is accompanied by a text (as in song or program music, or when we have supplementary information like a programmatic title or the author's word), we can, in fact, begin the process of decoding as Langer describes it; but a piece of instrumental music does not necessarily give us the clues needed for this kind of interpretation. Moreover, this theory fails to account for more abstract music, like Stravinsky's neoclassical work, Webern's music, or that of the medieval polyphonists, all of which are highly resistant to "psychological" interpretations. Like the Expression Theory, this type of explanation is best suited to music with emphatic patterns of tension and release and/or explicit verbal scripts. Langer's theory clearly explains more than the Expression Theory (it offers an excellent explanation of the metaphorical process by which emotional significance can be attributed to music), but it doesn't cover the entire field of possible musical statements. Nor does it explain how musical tones can refer to anything outside themselves, and this, at bottom, is the problem that perplexes Beardsley.

Having rejected the Expression and Signification Theories for essentially the same reason (the apparent inability of musical tones to refer to the nonmusical world), Beardsley decides that he has run out of options and so falls back on this "entirely negative" formulation of musical meaning that he calls the "Formalist" Theory. Beardsley correctly notes that reference is a necessary component of any kind of signification (if it were not, then, à la limite, everything would symbolize everything else), but he sees no way in which music can refer to anything outside of itself in more than a trivial way. Consequently, Beardsley feels constrained to assert that music doesn't make meaning at all but is just there, as a mysteriously indifferent yet compelling object of thought: "To understand a piece of music is simply to hear it, in the fullest sense of this word, that is, to organize its sounds into wholes, to grasp its sequences of notes as melodic and rhythmic patterns, to perceive its kinetic qualities and, finally, the subtle and pervasive human qualities that depend on all the rest" (336).

The double entendre on the word "hear" is entirely uncharacteristic of Beardsley's usually explicit, matter-of-fact style and points toward the contradiction inherent in his "Formalist" Theory, the point that makes Beardsley himself uneasy and that forces him to qualify the theory as "entirely negative." On the one hand, he finds himself constrained to assert that music is incapable of making meaning, that it refers to nothing; and yet he also insists that music matters, that it demands to be followed with "exact and scrupulous and concentric attention": "Music, then, is no symbol of time or process, mental or physical, Newtonian or Bergsonian; it *is* process. And perhaps we can say it is the closest thing to pure process, to happening as such, to change abstracted from anything that changes, so that it is something whose course and destiny we can follow with the most exact and scrupulous and concentric attention, undistracted by reflections of our normal joys or woes, or by clues and implications for our safety or success" (338). Beardsley denies the symbolic value of music, asserting instead that music *is* process, which, I take it, is meant to suggest that music embodies process itself. "Human qualities," like emotions and ideas, are relegated to a secondary, almost incidental status. Music becomes a kind of cognitive lens that does not itself mean anything, acting simply as a catalyst for abstract (formal) thought but that still somehow manages to capture our "most exact and scrupulous and concentric attention." Beardsley has put his finger on one of the central problems of musical aesthetics: if he could discover the mode of reference that governed musical symbolism, he could explain this paradox, but the solution to the riddle remains elusive. That solution, or at least the most powerful solution attempted to date, will come from Nelson Goodman's *Languages of Art*, which introduces the concept of exemplification into aesthetics.[22]

EXEMPLIFICATION AND MEANING IN MUSIC

Using the concept of exemplification, Goodman is able to offer a theory of musical meaning that depends on neither resemblance, causal reference, nor denotation. If a work of pure music does not denote, resemble, or cause the things it is said to mean, then how does it get this meaning? Goodman's response to this question begins by reminding us that works of art are human artifacts, designed to act as symbols. This very fact makes them refer. A listener approaches a new work in an interpretative frame of mind, knowing that it is meant to signify, to refer to something.[23] So how do we know what a musical work refers to? Goodman's answer, loosely speaking, is that the meaning of a musical work is to be sought in that set of qualities of which it acts as an example.[24] This answer, banal, almost tautological in appearance, has important implications for the interpretation of both music and literature. It also offers a theory for the interpretation of nonrepresentational works in general by explaining how we manage to develop firmly held beliefs about the meaning of works even in the absence of verbal cues or other explicit indications as to how they are to be understood. It is superior to most previous attempts to explain "significant form" in art because it defines form itself as a mode of reference with a semantic dimension. In order to understand the significance of this concept, it will be necessary to understand its relationship to the other modes of symbolization used in the arts.

Goodman identifies three basic modes of symbolization: denotation, exemplification, and expression. They are common to all of the arts but have varying degrees of importance in each. Denotation plays the most prominent role in literature, since language is an inherently denotative medium, but it also plays a central role in all the representational arts, whether verbal, pictorial, or otherwise. For Goodman, representation, even nonverbal representation, works by naming the objects to which it refers. Take the example of a painting of a bowler hat. In the same way that the words "bowler hat" denote an object (or, rather, a *class* of objects, since many different objects—of varying size, texture, weight, and so forth—are picked out by the label "bowler hat"), a bowler-hat painting denotes that object (or class of objects) along with all the other objects that might be depicted in the painting. Similarly, a literary narrative can be thought of as a single, albeit complex, denotative symbol. A narrative denotes the story to which it refers (as well as all the other objects named in the text), sending the reader away from the artistic object itself (the sounds/printed marks that constitute the work) and into a world of concepts and classes that is not immanent to the work and that may vary noticeably for each receptor.

For Goodman, then, "denotation is the core of representation" (5). This thesis has sparked a great deal of controversy, especially when applied to pictorial representations, because it seems to neglect the importance of perception and resemblance in the recognition and appreciation of visual images. Goodman emphasizes instead the central role of convention and habit in the determination of what is represented. For Goodman, realism is not so much a product of conformity to reality as a matter of familiarity with the representational conventions in operation, a view that Goodman takes so far as to suggest that "representational customs, which govern realism, also tend to *generate* resemblance" (39, my emphasis). Realism, rather than being understood as a product of resemblance, as is usually thought, is understood here as the set of conventions that govern our perception of resemblance. Goodman's point, it seems, is at least partly polemical, meant to provide a stark contrast to the more traditional, naive, or pretheoretical theories of mimesis understood as a kind of mirror, simply held up to reality in an unmediated reflective gesture. Be that as it may, we need not go as far as Goodman in the direction of conventionalism to understand that his theory of representation offers two major advantages for a general theory of the arts. First, whether or not we fully endorse Goodman's use of the term *denotation* in this context, it does seem to capture something essential about what linguistic and pictorial representations have in common, despite the vastly different means at their disposal: denotation, as Goodman uses the term, is meant to suggest a *vector of attention* rather than a complete explanation of how representations are processed by their audiences. Second, Goodman's emphasis on denotation lays the groundwork for his explanation of musical meaning by preparing what is no doubt the most powerful innovation of his theory, which is the concept of exemplification.

Exemplification, in Goodman's system, is related to denotation but works in the opposite direction. When a symbol acts as an example of some quality, it is said to exemplify that quality. Baudelaire's poem "La musique," for example, exemplifies a variety of qualities: it is an example of a poem with the rhyme scheme of a sonnet, an example of a poem composed of alexandrines in alternation with five-syllable lines, and so forth.

Goodman, it should be noted, usually uses the term *label* instead of *quality*. To say that a symbol exemplifies a quality is also to say that it is denoted by or labeled by that quality.[25] The relationship between the two, in other words, is symmetrical: the exemplificational symbol is a member of one or more classes; the denotational symbol labels a class. This "difference in direction," as we shall see, is at the heart of Goodman's theory.

In the interests of clarity, I've only mentioned here a couple of simple, relatively uninteresting classes exemplified by "La musique." But a work of art, like any object, can be said to exemplify a potentially infinite number of classes. Some of these may be of primarily taxonomical interest (i.e., "sonnet"), while other categories may be so complex as to defy verbal designation. This latter attribute may even be considered a defining characteristic of great art: one speaks of the "indicible quality" or "subtlety" or "unclassifiability" of a masterpiece, which, in Goodmanian terms, means that the symbol exemplifies a quality for which we do not (yet) have an adequate label. That crooked, ambiguous, hard-to-describe smile of the *Mona Lisa* exemplifies a class of which it is the only member and for which there can be no adequate verbal predicate.

All works of art have an exemplificational dimension, but exemplification plays an especially crucial role in music: because music does not have highly developed denotational capacities, it must rely more exclusively on exemplification to create meaning. Music cannot denote efficiently, but it is quite able to refer to the qualities it possesses. It does so in much the same way that Baudelaire's poem is able to make its rhyme and verse structure signify and that the *Mona Lisa* is able to make a painted smile mean something more than just "a smile": by acting as an example of those qualities. Moreover, those qualities that are literally exemplified by a musical work can in turn be interpreted (metaphorically) in extramusical terms. This last point has particular importance for musical aesthetics because it allows Goodman's theory to bridge the gap between those purists who seek to maintain, as Stravinsky famously put it, that "music is, by its very nature, essentially powerless to express anything at all" (Stravinsky 53–54) and those "programmatic" listeners who insist, with equal legitimacy, that audiences always have and always will find it useful to attribute extramusical meaning to musical works. (This, as we recall, was precisely the problem that had confounded Beardsley: that of knowing how "extramusical" meanings can be attributed to works of "pure" music in other than arbitrary or trivial ways.)

Having proposed this mode of signification, it is important to recognize that exemplificational symbols pose considerable interpretative problems for the audience. If exemplification requires actual possession of an attribute plus reference to that attribute, then the audience must, in order to discover the meaning of a work, sort through the potentially infinite number of attributes possessed by a work and decide which of them are relevant to its meaning. For this reason, exemplification leaves much more room for indeterminacy and error in interpretation than denotation. This is precisely why describing musical meaning is so difficult. To be sure, anyone familiar with the conventions of musical syntax already has a vast arsenal of labels to aid in the sorting of musical symbols into signifying units—from basic terms such as cadence, modulation, inversion, and so on to the elaborate lexicons of harmonic language and compositional devices and *Affektenlehre* compiled by composers, theorists, and musicologists. Nevertheless, the question must be asked, How is one to know which attributes of a work are the relevant ones? Goodman responds to this concern by emphasizing the *institutional* dimension of art, stressing the centrality of convention, custom, training, and shared expectations in guaranteeing communication in all forms of artistic expression.[26] We learn to interpret works of art by comparing them to other works of the same or similar type. The novice might perceive very little, at first, of what is important about a given art form but will, with experience, come to recognize which elements reward attention and which do not. It is only then that true communication can be said to take place.

Ideally, the audience knows in advance what conventions are in effect and adjusts its expectations accordingly. We know, for example, that in a baroque concerto with continuo, the harmonic progression of the piece is considered crucial to its integrity, but the exact realization of the figured bass is not. Nineteenth-century orchestral scores left much less up to the imagination of the performers, making every detail of the orchestration a potentially crucial clue to the meaning of the work. In the repertoire of jazz standards, on the other hand, improvisation is not only allowed but taken to be a constitutive element of the work, which is identified more closely with the individual performance than with the melody and chordal structure of a tune. (John Coltrane's celebrated recording of "My Favorite Things" is a work of its own, not to be confused with the Rodgers and Hammerstein composition of the same name.) Finally, an aleatory piece by Berio, Cage, or Stockhausen is defined to such a great extent by the freedom it leaves to the performers that chance occurrences become part of the meaning of the piece. In all of these examples, the audience needs to know what conventions are in effect so that it will know what to listen for.

When an audience knows what to expect, it is in a position to judge a work qualitatively. Virtuosity, for example, can be defined in terms of exemplification, since a virtuoso performance exemplifies that extremely small class of elite performances that stand out against a background of mediocre or average performances by virtue of their skill, power, subtlety, or what have you. More generally, these conditioned expectations put the audience in a position to understand what is new and interesting about a work. Within any given piece, it is the novel element in an otherwise conventional context that signifies most strongly. The opening of Mozart's "Dissonance" Quartet (K. 465), which begins with a passage that contains all twelve notes of the chromatic scale, has great exemplificational value because it differs so radically from other openings of its kind. In Mozart's day, the mere fact of possessing such an opening made this quartet the only member of the class it exemplified, which gave it extraordinary signifying potential. This passage, therefore, has much greater significance in that piece than it would have in a Schoenberg twelve-tone piece, which might contain any number of combinations of all twelve notes.

On the other hand, in beginning his piece this way, Mozart took a great risk, because a piece can also contain too much novelty. When an audience does not understand the set of referential conventions at issue, it may lose interest, causing the communicative potential of the piece to decrease significantly, although it might pick up again at a later date, when the audience's ears have become accustomed to the rules that govern the work.[27] Every creator works against this background of convention, making sophisticated, although perhaps unconscious, judgments about what an audience expects, what it wants, and what the artist has to offer that is better than and/or different from what the audience has encountered in the past.

Before moving on to Goodman's third mode of symbolization—expression—we should note that he reserves the term *exemplification* to designate the formal and/or decorative characteristics of a work. In other words, exemplification only covers the classes to which a work belongs literally. Expression, Goodman's third mode of symbolic functioning, points in the same direction as exemplification (by reference to the classes of objects to which a symbol belongs), but expression functions by metaphorical reference. Thus, to say that a Beethoven symphony (or a Victor Hugo poem) expresses heroism is a way of saying that the work belongs to the class of objects that possess this property in a metaphorical sense.

The string of marks and/or sounds that make up a given text and/or performance could not normally be called heroic, but they can be taken to refer to this quality metaphorically. In this sense, Goodman's use of the term meshes nicely with that implied by Beardsley's discussion of the Expression Theory of musical meaning. A work can actually possess the metaphorical quality of heroism or sadness or sprightliness. It also covers the kind of "metaphorical iconicity" that Langer describes, music as the "'logical picture' of sentient, responsive life." But Goodman does not restrict expression to affective, psychological, or even human characteristics. A musical work can express springtime (or even all four seasons), a two-ton sculpture can express lightness, and a painting can express silence or harmony or cacophony). This aspect of Goodman's definition of expression is important, because it means that it can accommodate both those who think of music in psychological terms and those who emphasize the purity and abstraction of musical discourse.

As mentioned earlier, Goodman's theory, although powerful and highly influential, has not been exempt from criticism. It is most vulnerable, no doubt, in its seeming neglect of perception and in the radically constructivist nature of meaning in his work. Few theorists have trouble accepting the preponderant role of linguistic conventions in determining the objects of literary representations, but the idea that resemblance is neither a necessary nor sufficient condition for pictorial representation (Goodman 5) seems to contradict our most deeply held intuitions about the nature of pictorial representation. It should be pointed out, though, that Goodman does not deny that the perception of resemblance has an important role to play in representation; he simply isn't interested in it. For Goodman, the primary difference between verbal and pictorial representations is that the first uses a symbol system that is syntactically *disjoint* and *differentiated* (i.e., we can always distinguish one character from another), whereas pictorial symbol systems are syntactically *dense* and *undifferentiated* (meaning that between every two characters, a third can always be found) and relatively *replete* (every detail of the pictorial symbol, however minute, is constitutive of it as a symbol). This implies that perception plays a determinant role in the appreciation of pictures, because the viewer must pay careful attention to every detail of the image, much like a workman measuring a complexly organized space without preset units of measurement to aid him and, indeed, without knowing in advance precisely which measurements are the pertinent ones. In this sense, pictorial representations require prolonged scrutiny of a kind that is not necessary in verbal representations. Still, for Goodman, our perceptions are governed by our preconceptions: "the innocent eye is blind," and the perception of resemblance is subject to our familiarity with the representational conventions in effect in a given work.

It might be added that Goodman's primary distinction between verbal and pictorial representation has important applications for our understanding of music as well. The verbal arts, in Goodmanian terms, are *allographic* (syntactically disjoint and differentiated) while the pictorial arts are *autographic* (syntactically dense, undifferentiated, and replete). One way to understand this distinction is to remember that pictorial works can be forged, but literary works cannot. There is only one *Mona Lisa*. If I make a copy of it that is indistinguishable from the original, I have made a forgery. But if I make a copy of, say, the text of Baudelaire's poem "La musique," I have simply added one more inscription of the work to the world. The literary work itself has no fundamental link to any one of its physical manifestations. The same distinction could be made between musical scores and musical performances. A musical performance can be understood as just another instance of the work: whenever a work is performed it is the same work being performed. But if a performance is taken to have special value (i.e., such and such a performance of Bach's violin partitas by Schlomo Mintz), it is understood to be a nonrepeatable, autographic event. (This is why musical recordings can be copyrighted, even when the work performed is in the public domain.) This distinction helps to understand why, in jazz, it is the performance and not the composition that is the primary object of interest: the improvisational, spontaneous nature of jazz makes it an autographic, not allographic, style. Here again, though, Goodman's theory might leave us feeling somewhat disappointed, because his definition of the musical work, which is tied to the allographic nature of the score, has little to say about genres that are not so strictly bound to the score as the classical music of the Western art-music tradition. Goodman's relative neglect of the perceptual leaves his system ill equipped to deal with styles like jazz. His system does, to be sure, leave room for them (since all those elements of performance that cannot be understood in terms of musical notation can still be analyzed in the autographic terms of syntactic density and repleteness), but it has little of interest to say about them.

Goodman's neglect of perception, it should be noted, is related to a more general area of neglect in his work, which is the domain of the psychological, broadly speaking. Goodman gives little attention to what creators and appreciators do, psychologically, when they are involved with a work of art. Goodman's approach is resolutely cognitive, with cognitive defined in terms of basic skills like measuring, sorting, classifying, comparing, and labeling. Thus, for example, Goodman spends little time discussing the emotions. And when he does, he asserts that "in aesthetic experience the emotions function cognitively . . . Emotion in aesthetic experience is a means of discerning what properties a work has and expresses" (248). The advantage of this approach is that it opens up for analysis aspects of art that had often been relegated to the unanalyzable spheres of intuition, inspiration, genius, ecstatic experience, and the like. As Howard Gardner has put it, Goodman's system is part of "an effort to demystify the arts, to construe them as involving the same kinds of skills and capacities as are involved in other domains and other disciplines" (247). As a result, Goodman intentionally downplays anything that might suggest that the arts should have an exalted, quasi-religious status in our society, preferring to emphasize what they do that can be analyzed in the more down-to-earth terms of familiar cognitive tasks.

To reiterate, Goodman's system does not exclude from consideration the specifically perceptual nature of aesthetic works. Nor does it exclude consideration of psychological and emotional factors in understanding the arts. But it does not develop those aspects of the arts in any detailed way. In this, Goodman's account of pictorial representation is typical of what critics have called his "minimalism" (McIver Lopes 227), his "prudente réserve" (Cometti 238), and the "abstract and schematic" nature of his system (J. Robinson 214). Goodman, as Jenefer Robinson puts it, "gets us to rethink such basic aesthetic concepts as representation without spelling out all the implications of his view" (214).[28] For those seeking prescriptions on what artists and audiences should or should not do, or for those seeking guidelines for the interpretation of specific works, this laconism will be a disappointment. But this approach has the advantage of allowing Goodman to develop his ideas without getting caught up in the familiar dead-end debates of aesthetics, like those concerning the difficulty of reliably evaluating subjective responses to art, or those involving questions of value and taste that would entail promoting any one set of aesthetic values over others.

After this excursus on the main points of Goodman's system, we can return to the more specific question that concerns us in this study: the significance of Goodman's theory of symbols for the relationship between music and literature. First of all, as we saw, the concept of exemplification provides an explanation of nonrepresentational meaning able to resolve the problem of musical reference that so troubled Beardsley. Second, if we agree with Goodman that "exemplification, like denotation, relates a symbol to a referent" (253), then it becomes clear that even "pure" music has a semantic dimension: musical meaning is not incommensurable with linguistic meaning, because denotation and exemplification follow the same referential path, albeit in opposite directions. Finally, and perhaps most importantly for the purposes of this study, having understood Goodman's distinction between exemplification and denotation and the fact that music works primarily through exemplification, it becomes apparent that the use of a musical model in a literary text implies an emphasis on exemplification. And indeed, all of the literary techniques that have been explained or justified in relation to music—from imitative harmony to Dujardin's leitmotivs to the polyphonic texts of Maurice Roche or Louis Zukofsky—are intended to shift the reader's attention away from an exclusive focus on *what* is being represented (denotation) and on to the matter of *how* it is being represented (exemplification).

The fundamental insight of Goodman's theory involves the "difference in direction" between exemplification and denotation. Goodman's analysis adds new life to the old debate over form and content because it makes clear why exemplification requires a kind of attention different from denotation. Writers who invoke music as a model for their work are telling readers to read backward, so to speak, that is, to decode the work by seeking out the types of representation exemplified in the text. Rather than reading from the representation down to the things represented and judging the success of the representation as a function of "the adequation of form and content," a reader's task is to read up from the representation, to ask what type(s) of representation are being exemplified (there may be many), which of these are pertinent in the present context, and what their significance is.

The first consequence of the literary use of musical models, then, is that it implies an emphasis on exemplification. And I would argue that the modernist interest in musical models for narrative is, in large part, a symptom of a more general interest in those kinds of communication that are resistant to denotation and facilitated by exemplification. At this point it is worth reiterating, in order to avoid any misunderstandings, that although the literary use of musical models implies an interest in exemplification, the reverse is not necessarily true. Indeed, to the extent that a literary work implies a certain amount of work on language, literature is always exemplificational. This helps to explain, for example, why Mallarmé's proposed hierarchy, with "Le vers" (equals maximal exemplification) at one extreme and "Journalism" (equals the exclusive preoccupation with denotation) at the other, includes the stipulation that "vers il y a sitôt que s'accentue la diction, rythme dès que style" [verse is present as soon as diction is accentuated, rhythm as soon as style] (*Crise de vers*, *Oeuvres complètes* 361). The kinds of exemplification invoked by the reference to music constitute only a small subset of the field of exemplification as a whole.

We will examine the kinds of exemplification invoked by music in chapters 2, 3, and 4, but it will first be necessary to complete this account of the semiotic relationship between music and literature with some more specific considerations on the semantic dimension of this relationship. Goodman gives a disappointingly minimal description of the literary work, defining it, simply, as "the text or script itself" (209), and he specifically refuses to attempt a description of literary semantics. His account of representation as denotation offers a helpful way to initiate the discussion, but he is more concerned with providing a theory of representation applicable to all the arts than with the issues specific to literature and music. It is clear, nevertheless, that the shift in emphasis from denotation to exemplification implied by the use of musical models requires a rethinking of the relationship between narrative syntax and semantics. For this reason, a brief foray into recent studies on the relationship between syntax and semantics in both literature and music is in order here.

MUSIC AND METAPHOR, SYNTAX AND SEMANTICS

Literary theorists have in recent years devoted renewed attention to the study of narrative semantics. Motivated in large part by a reaction against the "bracketing" of the semantic field typical of the structuralist criticism that had dominated literary theory in the sixties and seventies, these theorists proceed according to the conviction that literature matters to us because it is able to address those "issues of immediate human concern" (Pavel 10) that confront us in the real world. More surprising, perhaps, is the fact that musical theorists have also begun to show great interest in the field of semantics and that many of them have begun to look to linguistics and literary theory for clues about how to explain the ability of music to address issues of "human concern." In order to understand this renewed interest in the semantic features of music and narrative, it will be necessary to understand how the notion of meaning itself has been defined in these two independent but interrelated bodies of research.

In *Fictional Worlds*, Thomas Pavel embarks on an investigation of narrative semantics enriched by both the structuralist emphasis on the "mechanics" of plot and by the semantic theory of Anglo-American philosophy in the analytic tradition. He is concerned with defending the semantic value of fiction against both structuralist formalism (which studies not the relation between text and world but the inner logic of the text) and philosophical "segregationism" (the tendency of some philosophers to undervalue the truth value of fictional statements with respect to the more directly referential declarations characteristic of philosophy). Pavel emphasizes the importance of the "ineliminable intuition . . . that literary artifacts often are not projected into fictional distance just to be neutrally beheld but that they vividly bear upon the beholder's world" (145). Central to his investigation is the apparent paradox of fiction: the fact that texts made up largely or even exclusively of false statements (i.e., for which there is no real-world correspondent) can be judged to be true as a whole: "their truth as a whole is not recursively definable starting from the truth of the individual sentences that constitute them" (17). He seeks to resolve this paradox by emphasizing the role of what he calls salient worlds, that is, the imaginary discursive worlds of fictional texts, which have value, in his estimation, precisely because their logical congruence with the real world is only indirect and partial. He points out that it is "useless to set up procedures for assessing the truth or falsity of isolated fictional sentences, since their micro-truth value may well have no impact on the macro-truth value of large segments of the text or on the text as a totality" (17). In this way, he shifts the burden of truth off of the individual sentences that make up the text and places it onto the text taken as a whole, as a single symbol that is to be interpreted meta-phorically (i.e., as partially congruent with the real world, but only par-tially). Pavel sees fiction as a way for ordinary people to think about their practical lives, to use the indirect predication of fiction as an aid in the discernment of important features of the real world that would not otherwise become apparent. This view of the value of fiction, it should be noted, is entirely consonant with Goodman's. For Goodman, as for Pavel, the primary function of art is to provide us with new ways to think about the world around us, to serve what he calls "the cognitive purpose." According to Goodman, any symbolic system, whether scientific or aes-thetic, should be judged according to "the delicacy of its discriminations and the aptness of its allusions; by the way it works in grasping, explor-ing, and informing the world; by how it analyzes, sorts, orders, and organizes; by how it participates in the making, manipulation, retention, and transformation of knowledge" (258).

Paul Ricoeur also adopts a semantically derived explanation of literary value in *The Rule of Metaphor* and *Time and Narrative*, although he frames his explanation in the terms of an ontological quest rather than in the more pragmatic, down-to-earth terms of Pavel's study or in the aus-terely analytical terms of Goodman. In *The Rule of Metaphor*, Ricoeur argues that a good metaphor refers to the real world with as much potency as a literal description. In fact, because metaphors refer indi-rectly, they are able to describe aspects of reality that remain inaccessible to the literal, directly descriptive mode of philosophy. The hypothetical relationship between metaphor and existential reality enables it to carry out a function as important as the direct predication that characterizes philosophy.

> In the *Rule of Metaphor* I defended the thesis that the poetic func-tion of language is not limited to the celebration of language for its own sake, at the expense of the referential function which is pre-dominant in descriptive language. I maintained that the suspension of this direct, descriptive referential function is only the reverse side, or the negative condition, of a more covered over referential func-tion of discourse, which is, so to speak, liberated by the suspending of the descriptive value of statements. In this way poetic discourse brings to language aspects, qualities, and values of reality that lack

access to language that is directly descriptive and that can be spoken only by means of the complex interplay between the metaphorical utterance and the rule-governed transgression of the usual meanings of our words. (*Time and Narrative I* x–xi)

Both Ricoeur and Pavel are in agreement with Goodman in placing supreme value on art's ability to reconfigure real-world problems in such a way that their salient features stand out with more clarity than they do in other modes of predication. This hypothetical relationship between work and world is part of the privilege of art, that which makes it more than just an idle game. Literature (and, by extension, all representational art) is that domain of human expression that has specialized in the hypothetical mode of predication known as metaphor. Only a tool in the normal, pragmatic use of language, metaphor is the very vocation of literature and determines its referential function, which is indirect.[29]

Musicologists have also been attracted to the field of literary semantics as a way of explaining musical meaning. As in literary theory, this work has focused on a reappraisal of the relationship between denotation and the global meaning of a work. The goal is to find a common ground where meaning in music and the language arts can be reconciled. Thus, for example, Jean-Jacques Nattiez's *Music and Discourse: Toward a Semiology of Music* opens with a critique of Saussure's definition of the linguistic sign. Nattiez uses Peirce's notion of the interpretant to undermine the strict one-to-one relationship between signifier and signified of the linguistic sign as described by Saussure. He does not go so far as to deny the existence of the bond between signifier and signified, but he takes care to distinguish meaning, be it musical or literary, from denotation. In a gesture that recalls Frege's distinction between *Sinn* and *Bedeutung*, Nattiez invokes Peirce's notion of the interpretant to describe this difference and to argue that meaning is situated not in the text but in the experience of the individual.

> Peirce's first and greatest original idea is his notion that the thing to which the sign refers—that is, the interpretant—is also a *sign*. Why? Because . . . the process of referring effected by the sign is *infinite* . . . For each reader, the word ["happiness"] will instantly "make sense." But what happens if we try to explain its content? In attempting to do this, a series of new *signs* occur to us—"bliss," "satisfaction," "contentment," "fulfillment," and so forth—*signs that vary from one*

reader to the next, according to the personal experiences of each. (*Music and Discourse* 7, emphasis in original)

Meaning, defined in this way, is fundamentally incommunicable. All the literary (or musical) text can do is provide signs that will instigate a search for meaning and orient that search in a certain direction. The search itself takes place in the private sphere of the subject: "An object of any kind takes on meaning for an individual apprehending that object, as soon as that individual places the object in relation to areas of his lived experience—that is, in relation to a collection of other objects that belong to his or her experience of the world" (Nattiez, *Music and Discourse* 9). Both music and language, according to Nattiez, proffer signs that will be used in a personal search for meaning. Denotation, in this view, plays a merely auxiliary role. His goal in handing this demotion to denotation is to bring language one step closer to music, placing the emphasis on indeterminacy. Later on in his book, he will seek to return the favor, bringing music closer to literature, by citing Adorno's assertion that music is "a narrative that narrates nothing" and proposing that "music is not a narrative, but an incitement to make a narrative, to comment, to analyze" (Nattiez, *Music and Discourse* 128). Here again, meaning is not to be located in the musical sign but must be sought in the referring process that takes place within the consciousness of the apprehending individual.

Nattiez's argument, then, has two basic components. By projecting the referential moment of language into an inaccessible future (using Peirce's notion of the interpretant), he tries to suggest that linguistic communication is not as direct as is usually thought, that, in fact, the moment of reference is deferred indefinitely, that linguistic reference is ultimately an infinite process. He then insists on music's ability "to elicit narrative behavior" (praising, incidentally, Langer's notion of the "unconsummated symbol") in order to bring musical meaning one step closer to the realm of linguistic meaning. The general strategy of this mode of explanation is to constantly nudge language toward the indeterminacy of music while at the same time lending music ever more precise powers of evocation.

The shortcomings of this approach to the relationship between music and language are fairly evident. In order to identify linguistic communication with musical communication, Nattiez finds himself trying to gloss over the single most important element of the definition of the linguistic sign: its denotative function. His appeal to the private, unanalyzable sphere of individual consciousness as the location of all meaning (i.e., *Sinn*, in Frege's sense) corresponds in some respects to the kind of meaning described by Ricoeur and Pavel. But Ricoeur and Pavel were concerned with describing those kinds of secondary meanings that depend on the indirect reference characteristic of metaphor and fiction, whereas Nattiez seems intent on making this kind of indeterminacy part of the very definition of language. It is true that Peirce's notion of the interpretant captures an important aspect of the ontological lack that characterizes linguistic communication, but the fact is that in most real-world situations, including those most characteristic of literature, communication takes place relatively untroubled by this deferral of reference. Pragmatic language users factor this loss into their calculations and are able to communicate with a high, albeit far from perfect, success ratio. If the semantic dimension of language were really as unstable as Nattiez seems to suggest, then the fact that humans manage to exchange information at all would begin to take on a quasi-miraculous aura.

Another linguistically oriented musicologist, Joseph P. Swain, tries a different approach to the question of semantic indeterminacy. In his essay "The Range of Musical Semantics," Swain begins with the observation that, as pragmatic linguistics and speech-act theory have shown, dictionary definitions help to orient us in the decoding of individual words, just as the rules of syntax help to determine the logical relationships between those words. But the act of interpretation depends on a variety of intuitive processes and situational conventions that are not strictly codified. Meaning circulates between the words that make up an utterance in ways that cannot always be predicted by someone standing outside of the functional context in which they are used. Meaning is situational, determined by context and a set of shared conventions. Like Nattiez, Swain emphasizes the fluid circulation of meaning in language in order to argue that music may have a semantic dimension comparable to that of language. The primary difference between musical and linguistic semantics, he suggests, is simply that "the greater, less precise semantic range of a musical gesture requires that interpretation stem from syntactic effect in a way that is unnecessary in language" (Swain, "The Range" 150).

One of the primary improvements of Swain's theory is his insistence on the importance of syntax. (This is an issue to which we will return shortly.) But Swain's argument suffers from the same basic problem as that of Nattiez: both overplay the semantic indetermination of linguistic propositions. Nattiez's argument rests on an appeal to the interpretative role of subjective experience, while Swain emphasizes the importance of context, situation, and convention, but both attempt to disguise or minimize the essential difference between linguistic and musical communication, which is that the first depends primarily on denotation while the second depends primarily on exemplification. It is interesting, in this regard, to note that we find these musicologists in a position symmetrically related to that of the musico-literary critics: both, in their eagerness to find common ground between music and language, set up a metaphorical equivalency between the two but have trouble regulating the mediating principles that make the comparison possible.

This linguistic approach to musical semantics, then, cannot be said to resolve the problem of musical meaning. It does, however, have interesting implications for literature in that it suggests an argument for dilating the semantic sphere of the text—not by deconstructing the linguistic sign itself but by placing metaphoricity at the heart of the literary project. It is in the realm of indirect reference, which is the realm of metaphorical language and fiction, that the arguments of Nattiez and Swain meet up with those of Pavel and Ricoeur. If the goal of Nattiez and Swain is to provide a definitive explanation of musical meaning in terms of language, then their arguments fall short. But they do succeed in suggesting a way to align music with literature, which is by way of the mediating notion of metaphor. Indeed, it is possible to use Swain's notion of "semantic range" to suggest that music is not an *other* of literature but, rather, a semantic horizon of literature, that point at which literary statement, having traded directness and literality for an ever increasing semantic range, gains access to meanings completely inaccessible to direct verbal predication. This approach, as it turns out, coincides with what I have been calling the essentialist argument for the use of musical models.

ESSENTIALIST, EXPRESSIVIST, AND FORMALIST USES OF MUSICAL MODELS

There may be a point, the essentialist argues, at which the purely aesthetic ambition of art for art's sake or the Flaubertian idea of a *livre sur rien* meets up with the quasi-theological pretension to maximal, transcendent meaning. If semantic range and literal applicability are inversely related, if the descriptive value of poetic statement declines as it makes an asymptotic approach to maximal meaning, then music can be taken as a figure of that point at which metaphor spills over into the ineffable. The apparent semantic muteness of music, in other words, can also be interpreted as a sign of profundity, a sign of infinite semantic potential and access to anagogic meaning. The symbolists, following Schopenhauer, refer to music in this way. This is also how Beckett uses music: as a model for the communication of meanings that remain hidden to the normal modes of conceptual thought. Roland Barthes, who subscribes to this approach to musical meaning, defines music in terms of metaphor in *L'obvie et l'obtus*.

> Music, like *signifiance*, is governed by no metalanguage but only by a discourse of value, of praise: an amorous discourse. Every "successful" relation—successful in that it manages to express the implicit without articulating it, to go beyond articulation without falling into the respectful silence of desire or the sublimation of the indicible—such a relation can properly be called *musical*. Perhaps a thing has value only through its metaphorical force; perhaps that is the value of music: to be a good metaphor. (252, my translation)

Music provides a model for that aspect of literary semantics identified not with denotation or direct predication but with *signifiance*, with the secondary meanings of larger syntactical units that cannot be analyzed in terms of the denotative values of the individual words that make up the text.

This identification of music with semantic range and *signifiance* provides an interesting literary counterpart to what might be called the "programmatic" approach to music. When listeners interpret a piece of music by attaching semantic values to it, they are essentially treating it like a metaphor. It is a fact, although often decried by musical purists, that for many listeners the interpretation of a musical piece amounts to an attempt to decode the piece semantically—to interpret sonatas as stories, to attach visual images or emotions to musical passages, or to discuss a piece in terms of moods and *états d'âme*. This programmatic approach to the interpretation of music, linked to the nineteenth-century vogue of program music and the symphonic poem, has been dismissed as a romantic excess. But the urge to orient musical interpretation semantically is as old as music itself. Moreover, composers themselves tend to encourage us in this habit. The association of a musical piece and an extramusical idea can be sparked not only by extensive program notes or by lyrics but also by marginal notes in the score (i.e., Beethoven's famous "Muß es sein?—Es muß sein!"), a thematic title ("Le ranz des vaches"), the social context of the piece (liturgical, military, celebratory), or even a general genre title or tempo marking (ballade, *con brio*). As Anthony Burgess, in a sly reference to Gide's quip about one-handed literature, once remarked: "One word will be enough to call the music down from the sky of generality to the wrist of the particular" ("Meaning Means Language," *This Man and Music* 89).

The programmatic approach to music, then, is a kind of reverse image or negative of the essentialist approach to literature. Anthony Burgess, a self-described programmatic listener, feels uncomfortable with the indeterminacy of music and so feels the need to translate it into words. Indeed, Burgess claims in *This Man and Music* that it was his conviction that "Meaning Means Language" that convinced him to abandon his ambition to become a composer and take up literature. The vestiges of this belief can be found in his ambitious literary pastiches of Beethoven (*Napoleon Symphony*) and Mozart (in *Mozart and the Wolf Gang*), which attempt to translate music into language in the most literal way. For essentialists like Mallarmé, Schopenhauer, and Beckett, on the other hand, it is precisely the indeterminacy of music that has value: they use music to argue for the possibility of dilating the sphere of the concept, for making language a tool of suggestion and hidden semantic portent rather than for the pragmatic exchange of information.

The expressivist, like the essentialist, tends to insist on music's hidden referential capacity but is more likely to explain this function in affective rather than cognitive terms and to assert that musical symbols are somehow more natural, powerful, or direct than linguistic symbols. This is how Leiris, with his desire to engage the reader in an act of full communication ("une communication entière"), refers to music. Music, the expressivist argues, has the ability to bypass the intellect and appeal directly to the senses. Unlike a linguistic utterance, the significance of a simple musical utterance, say, a cadence, can be *felt*.

This expressivist explanation of musical signification has its merits. At

1. Helmholtz's Place Theory of Sound Perception. Diagram by Jack Mohr.

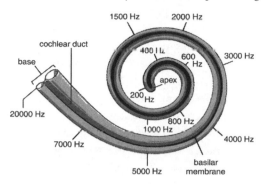

the most obvious level, music has the ability to make use of effects that provoke a massive physiological response—the deafening volumes and crushing rhythms of highly amplified rock and roll, or the high-note, heavily vibratoed climaxes so common in opera arias and big-band jazz arrangements. These are special cases, but they are generalizable. Indeed, it is not an exaggeration to say that the sensual appeal of music is at work on every level of musical interpretation. The most basic principle of musical communication, the controlled manipulation of tension and release, is rooted in a physiological mechanism. This mechanism was first described in the nineteenth century by Hermann Helmholtz, in *On the Sensations of Tone*, as the "place theory" of sound perception.[30] This speculative theory was subsequently documented in the Nobel prize–winning experiments of Georg von Békésy. According to the place theory, the perception of qualitative differences between harmonic relationships results from the fact that sounds of different frequency are received at different locations along the length of the cochlea and transmitted to the brain via different neural routes.

The implications of this discovery are enormous. We can physically feel the difference between a dissonance and a harmony (or different types and degrees of dissonance and harmony) because the information pertaining to different bands of sound frequencies is transmitted to the brain along different nerve pathways. In other words, unlike the phonetic articulations that define language, which must be sorted in the cortex, musical pitches arrive in the brain already sorted to a great degree. Linguistic relationships must be decoded at a level just below that of conscious decision making, but atomic musical relationships are sorted at a level much closer to that of the act of perception; they are overdetermined in the ear by a precise physiological response to pitch stimuli.[31]

It is this physical and physiological ground for musical interpretation that explains the truth in the cliché about music as a universal language. There are, needless to say, differing standards for what is considered consonant/dissonant, pleasant/unpleasant, interesting/uninteresting, and so on, and these criteria vary from culture to culture and person to person. But there are, nevertheless, indisputable universals that can be explained by reference to the harmonic series and the physiological makeup of the ear. Every culture knows the octave, the perfect fifth and fourth, the wavering quality of dissonant pitches played simultaneously, and so forth. Cultural difference only comes in at the level of how these realities will be exploited and how the "effects" that can be created will be organized. The history of Western art music tells the story of an increasingly artificial relationship to the physics of sound, at ever greater removes from the basic relationships of the harmonic series (from "real" tuning, to proportional tuning, to the adoption of the tempered scale, to the abandonment, in some circles, of the diatonic scale), but no music could subsist without some knowledge, however intuitive, of acoustics and the physiological perception of tones. Even Anton Webern, who participated in one of the least "natural" attempts to revolutionize musical syntax, called music "natural law as related to the sense of hearing" (11, passim) and described his place in music history as yet another step in the ongoing "conquest of the tonal field" (32, passim).

Language, on the other hand, has no such grounding in the physical world. Spoken words, of course, have acoustic profiles, just as musical notes do, but their acoustic properties are of a sort that cannot be regulated by mathematical proportions.[32] Language, as Valéry lamented, does not have the luxury of being objectively quantifiable or acoustically overdetermined. On the other hand, it is probably just this lack of acoustic overdetermination that makes language such an efficient communicational tool. Without the arbitrary relation of signifier and signified, language would not have the semantic mobility necessary for the efficient communication of concepts. What spoken language concedes to music in acoustical richness and sensual appeal it makes up for by the ease with which it can refer to extralinguistic realities.

These considerations help to explain the appeal of musical models for the literary expressivist: if musical tones are able to elicit such strong affective responses from listeners, if music is so universally identified with the emotions and with performance, it is because musical tones interact with the organism in more direct ways than linguistic signs. These interactions can be harnessed and used to exemplify the shifting patterns of tension and release, conflict and concord, that relate, metaphorically, to more specifically human, "real-world" concerns. Of course, having recognized this, we must immediately concede that it is precisely this aspect of musical meaning that cannot be exploited in the literary text. Given the relative poverty of means at their disposal, lyric poets and writers like Leiris can only admire this intrinsically sensual aspect of musical communication from a distance: the precise distance that separates poetry from song. Short of becoming composers or taking up singing, poets cannot turn their words into tones. They can only borrow certain elements of musical syntax from music, as mediated by more general concepts like that of pattern. This is all the more true for novelists and brings us to consideration of the role of syntax in the formalist approach to the use of musical models.

Whether justified in terms of expression or semantic essentialism, no understanding of music can be complete without reference to syntax. Musical language, as I have had occasion to suggest, having no codified semantic dimension, is essentially a syntax. Writers, and particularly novelists, have seized on this fact in their use of musical models. For them, music serves to demonstrate the importance of form as a determinant of the semantic content of a work, and they have been willing to exploit music as a kind of repository for alternative syntactical models for literature. Here again, Ricoeur's work, although not specifically concerned with music, can be useful for understanding the relationship between narrative syntax and semantics.

Ricoeur's *Time and Narrative* builds on his earlier work in *The Rule of Metaphor* by making a case for the determinant role of syntax in the narrative production of meaning. Like the isolated metaphor, the literary narrative has value by virtue of its metaphorical relation to the empirical plane. But for Ricoeur, narrative is more specifically concerned with that dimension of human experience that has most successfully resisted the explanatory powers of philosophical speculation: the temporal. It is,

Ricoeur argues, the reconfiguring power of narrative syntax, which he identifies with the Aristotelian *muthos*, that enables narratives to further our understanding of the world around us:

> The mimetic function of plots takes place by preference in the field of action and of its temporal values. . . . I see in the plots we invent the privileged means by which we re-configure our confused, unformed, and ultimately mute temporal experience. "What, then, is time?" asks Augustine. "I know well enough what it is, provided that nobody asks me; but if I am asked what it is and try to explain, I am baffled." In the capacity of poetic composition to re-figure this temporal experience, which is prey to the aporias of philosophical speculation, resides the referential function of the plot. (*Time and Narrative I* xi)

Because the *muthos* takes a mere succession of events and shapes them into a single unified whole, it is able to offer—through the binding power of narrative syntax—an understanding of time that can only elude the descriptive, declarative mode of philosophy. In other words, rather than trying to describe time, to name it, narrative exemplifies it; narrative makes time cognizable by offering us a rationalized path through time. In this way, the logical reconfiguration of time carried out by the *muthos* enables narrative texts to offer insights into temporal existence that remain inaccessible to philosophy in its descriptive mode.

Ricoeur's work, then, provides an important first clue in understanding why models borrowed from music might have special appeal for storytellers: music, like narrative, is an art of time. If narrative syntax can help us to understand the temporal nature of human experience, then musical syntax should also further our understanding of the human experience of time. But Ricoeur's thesis can only take us so far. First of all, Ricoeur seems to neglect the fact that narratives are rarely concerned exclusively with temporal experience. Certainly, time will always be present, at least as a "deep" or unconscious theme, by virtue of the fact that narrative organizes experience into temporal sequences. But narratives have much to offer besides, including understanding of social relationships, psychological states, and any number of other areas of human concern. Second, it seems equally plausible to suggest, with John Tooby and Leda Cosmides (proponents of evolutionary psychology), that narratives appeal to us because "stories are told in a way that mimics the format in which experienced events are mentally represented and stored in memory, in order to make them acceptable to the machinery the mind uses to extract meaning from experience" (24). The apparent universality of the *muthos*, in other words, may have as much to do with the architec- ture of the mind and its storage devices as with the temporal nature of subjective experience.

Apart from these two objections, there is another limitation to the usefulness of Ricoeur's study for our purposes, which is that Ricoeur's theory applies primarily to narratives that respect the traditional plot- bound structures of the Aristotelian *muthos*. This is, however, precisely the structure that is called into question by the writers of the postwar Parisian avant-gardes. If Pinget, Leiris, and Beckett appeal to musical models for their work, it is, in large part, because they seek models for expressing realities that do not fit into the traditional narrative syntax of the *muthos*. We will need, therefore, to push farther afield in order to develop the insights offered by Ricoeur. Peter Brooks's *Reading for the Plot* will help us make the next step.

Brooks, like Ricoeur and Pavel, is interested in the predicative function of narrative and the relations between narrative syntax and semantic import. But he is less concerned with the conventional syntax of the Aristotelian *muthos* than with "the temporal dynamics that shape nar- ratives in our reading of them, the play of desire in time that makes us turn pages and strive toward narrative ends" (Brooks xiii). Brooks ap- peals to the Freudian category of desire and translates it into narrative terms by focusing on the reader's desire for an ending. It is the constitu- tive function of desire that, in Brooks's opinion, enables the act of plot- ting to make sense of the temporal aspect of human experience. Like Ricoeur, Brooks devotes the majority of his book to the study of tradi- tional novels that do not violate in any serious way the norms of the Aristotelian *muthos*. His study focuses primarily on novels in the tra- dition of nineteenth-century realism. But he does devote a short, con- cluding chapter to the nontraditional forms pioneered by the postwar avant-gardes. And significantly, when he does finally broach the issue of nontraditional narrative forms, he turns to music as the paradigmatic alternative model, using the well-known musical *mise en abyme* from Robbe-Grillet's *La Jalousie* as an emblem of the *nouveau roman*: "No doubt it is always the same song that goes on. If sometimes the themes blur, it is only to come back a little later, more marked, very close to identical. Nonetheless, these repetitions, these minute variants, these elisions, these turnings back, can produce modifications—moving eventually quite far from the point of departure" (as quoted in Brooks 316). For Brooks, the patterns of repetition and variation that characterize the *nouveau roman* invite the reader to participate in the creation, as opposed to the passive reception, of plot. But Brooks's explanation is far from exhausting the implications of the use of music as a formal model for fictional discourse, and so it is to this question that I now turn by way of introduction to chapter 2, which explores the subject in greater depth.

We've already seen how Dujardin reads Wagner's music in terms of free association. This link between musical syntax and associative syntax will hold fast over the course of the twentieth century. Novelists tend to see in music a model for associative progression. This identification of music with associative syntax makes sense if we remember that writers tend to reason about music from the point of view of musical consumers. Because of music's inability to denote efficiently, listeners can only follow a musical argument to the extent that they are able to recognize its themes and motifs in their successive transformations. The musical principles of development and variation require that themes remain recognizable in each of their successive appearances, even as they are transformed over the course of a piece. This, of course, should not be taken to imply that the *composer* proceeds by a process of free association (although the improviser might). Nor does it imply, as Schopenhauer asserted, that music presents itself as effects without causes. (On the contrary, a musical piece would only be interpreted in this way by someone who, ignorant of the conventions that govern that piece, did not know that such and such a passage was designed to be a modulation, or a sequence, or a cadence, and so on.) Nevertheless, listeners, even knowledgeable listeners, when faced with a new piece of music, may find themselves forced to depend on associative procedures, to interpret by reasoning from the audible resemblances between passages to the musical logic governing them. Listeners only discover the relationship between, say, the antecedent and the consequent of a fugue subject once they have noticed that they bear a close physical resemblance to each other (i.e., the same melodic contour at the interval of a fifth). The same holds true for all the means of thematic transformation: transposition, inversion, augmentation, diminution, retrograde movement, and so on. All of these depend on the subsistence of at least one analogous element, preferably a clearly perceptible one. Every new transformation or variation of a theme or motif must remain recognizable, at least in a theoretical sense, which is why it is possible to agree with Anton Webern when he asserts that "development is also a kind of repetition" (27). Unexpected or even incongruous elements may be brought into the piece in a punctual manner, but as soon as the elements of disjunction overwhelm the elements of continuity, the piece begins to lose its ability to communicate. This is one of the reasons exact repetition plays such an important role in music: a theme must be constantly recalled to our attention so that we can follow it in its successive transformations. The perception of musical form depends on audible resemblances.

This analogical form of development contrasts entirely with the causal and sequential rules that have traditionally governed narrative form in literature, helping to explain why the formalist use of musical models has tended to result in narratives that progress associatively. To the narrative mind, development by analogical association, as opposed to causal and sequential concatenation, resembles the progressive unfolding of themes in musical development. In music, this progression necessarily takes place on the level of audible resemblances, but in literature, by virtue of the properties of the two-tiered linguistic sign, analogical progression may take place either on the level of the signifier (via the principle of paronomasia), on the level of the signified (via metaphorical substitutions, as in the association of ideas), or between the two levels (punning, "imitative harmony"). It is this issue of associative syntax that I will study in the following chapter, along with the corollary issues of repetition and variation. My primary goal will be to show how the musically motivated divergence from the traditional plot-based forms of narrative affects the text in its mimetic dimension and how this modification affects in turn the referential functioning of the text.

2

Robert Pinget and the Musicalization of Fiction

MUSIC AND THE NOVEL FROM DUJARDIN
TO THE *NOUVEAU ROMAN*

"The musicalization of fiction," to borrow Aldous Huxley's phrase, is a twentieth-century phenomenon, a specifically modern attempt to expand the novel's expressive capacities by seeking new models in an art that had traditionally seemed remote from the novel's primarily mimetic vocation. The most visible consequence of the twentieth-century interest in the relationship between music and the novel has been an emphasis on direct formal analogies. Numerous attempts have been made to organize narratives along the lines of musical forms like the fugue (the "Sirens" episode from *Ulysses*), sonata form (Anthony Burgess's *Napoleon Symphony*), and the theme with variations (Queneau's *Exercices de style*), and there has been sustained interest in finding literary equivalents for such musical procedures as counterpoint (Joyce, Gide, Huxley, Kundera, etc.) and the leitmotiv (Dujardin, Mann, Proust, etc.). It is important to stress the formal, structural focus of this use of music: twentieth-century novelists, when they turn to music, tend to see in it a source of models for rethinking the plot-based forms that have traditionally governed the novel.

In order to understand the specifically narrative dimension of this use of music, we'll need to dismiss two of the more common categories used to explain the presence of musical models in literature: prosody and abstraction.

1. Prosody. The primary thrust of this trend is not prosodic, that is, not motivated by problems of oratorical and poetic elocution traditionally linked to music via such metaphors as "la musique du vers." For novelists like Huxley, prosodic considerations are specifically excluded: "The musicalization of fiction. Not in the symbolist way, by subordinating sense to

sound. (*Pleuvent les bleus baisers des astres taciturnes.* Mere glossolalia.) But on a large scale, in the construction" (301). This does not, of course, mean that novelists never invoke such ideas as "imitative harmony," but even those novelists who incorporate prosodic work into their concept of musical fiction do so as part of the large-scale work on form. Joyce, for example, made widespread use of the type of phonetic and rhythmic effects that have traditionally been associated with music, but always within the larger context of his experiments with the interior-monologue or stream-of-consciousness technique and the representation of consciousness in general. Joyce's puns, alliterations, and word games are never exclusively motivated by prosodic or ludic concerns; they always give crucial information about narrative structures and intentions, usually by conveying information about the psychological state of the narrative consciousness.

2. Abstraction. "Musicalization" does not imply abstraction. In the 1960s and 1970s there was much discussion about the possibility of supplanting the traditional representational justifications of fiction with an antimimetic theory that emphasized "production" and *écriture* over representation and literature. The writers grouped around Philippe Sollers and the journal *Tel Quel* were particularly committed to a postrepresentational justification of literature, and Gilles Deleuze had gone so far as to argue that representation was inherently oppressive.[1] It might seem in this context that music, as a nonmimetic art, would make a natural reference, but, as it turns out, those novelists most interested in music were also committed to fundamentally mimetic projects. What the musicalization of fiction does entail is an attempt to rethink the form of the novel, its large-scale syntax, in terms other than those of the objects and events represented: not to do away with content but to envisage content as a function of form. Traditionally, the reverse has been true: the novel has been defined by its mimetic function, and novelists have tended to speak of narrative form as if it were an almost incidental by-product of content. This is already true of Aristotle's definition of the *muthos* as "the organization *of the events*."[2] But when a novelist turns to a model like counterpoint or the leitmotiv, it is to subvert the chronological and causal ordering called for by the *muthos* by appealing to principles of organization that are not dramatic (i.e., plot-bound) in nature.

This last point raises an important question: why would these novelists want to organize the representation along the lines of an extraliterary model when they already have, in the form of the *muthos* (and related substructures like dialogue, description, etc.), such a powerful model at their disposal, a model that has proven its worth over the course of centuries? As I suggested in chapter 1, I believe that this turn to musical models for narrative should be understood as a response to our growing awareness in the twentieth century of the extent to which all literary representations of reality depend on mental and linguistic structures that have no direct relation to the objects represented. The musicalization of the novel participates in a more general movement away from the nineteenth-century mimetic ideal of objectivity and omniscience (with the novel modeling itself on history and focusing on primarily social themes) and toward a more specifically twentieth-century mimetic project that replaces the ideal of objectivity with an increasing awareness of and interest in the factors that overdetermine our representations of the world. Many of these can be linked to twentieth-century developments in the sciences, such as the role of the point of view of the perceiving subject (the theory of relativity, phenomenology), of cultural conventions (anthropology), of semiosis (structuralist linguistics), of the unconscious (psychoanalysis), of ideology and entrenched power structures (Foucault, Marxian criticism, postcolonial criticism), and so forth, and all of them have influenced the way novelists view their craft. Within this general trend away from the illusion of objectivity, the description of the mental life of the subject becomes a major preoccupation in its own right, equally well represented in philosophy (Bergson, Husserl, James), the sciences (from neurology and cognitive science to cybernetics and artificial intelligence), and literature (the stream-of-consciousness novel, the interior monologue, and parallel trends like the surrealist emphasis on "le fonctionnement réel de la pensée" [thought as it truly functions]).

Essentially, then, music acts as a metaphor for mind. Since at least Aristotle, theorists of narrative have advocated an emphasis on showing (mimesis) over telling (diegesis), and the most significant attempts to "musicalize" the novel have been coupled with strategies designed to show the mind in action rather than simply telling us about the results of that action. This link between music and mind stretches back to the symbolist, Wagnerian 1880s, runs through the literary generation of Joyce and Proust, and is inherited by the *nouveau roman* and the author I will focus on in this chapter, Robert Pinget. It seems that, having no existing literary forms capable of adequately representing thought in its temporal dimension, these novelists needed new forms and turned to music as a model capable of mediating between thought and narrative. As I suggested in chapter 1, a useful place to begin the exploration of this trend is Edouard Dujardin's 1888 novel, *Les lauriers sont coupés*. Dujardin bases his analogy between the Wagnerian leitmotiv and the interior-monologue technique on a simple empirical observation: the substance of thought is, like the sound stream of a melody, unidirectional (i.e., running continuously in time), but the content of thought is full of motivic recurrences. Thus, in *Les lauriers sont coupés*, a few thoughts that preoccupy the hero recur regularly throughout the narrative, and an overheard tune keeps surfacing in the hero's consciousness.

Joyce, building on Dujardin's theory of the interior monologue, also equates music with thought processes when he invokes the model of musical counterpoint for the "Sirens" chapter of *Ulysses*. The counterpoint analogy, like Dujardin's leitmotiv analogy, depends on a basic empirical observation, that of the mind's ability to operate on several stimuli at the same time. Just as the audience of a Bach organ fugue may hear a single organist simultaneously perform several complex melodic lines, we observe Bloom simultaneously eating his lunch, listening in on an impromptu concert, thinking about his wife's infidelity, and concentrating on various other stimuli, both internal and external, with varying levels of conscious and subconscious clarity. Of course, limited by the inability of the prose text to present more than one thought at a time, Joyce must translate the musical technique of counterpoint into literary terms, which he does by equating contrapuntal simultaneity with the juxtaposition and rapid alternation of narrative strands.

In *Finnegans Wake* Joyce will push this technique even further, recombining and fusing words in order to suggest the simultaneous presence of more than one thought. Joyce once described *Finnegans Wake* as "pure music," a claim justified, presumably, by the radical evacuation of traditional narrative content, which is replaced by an exclusive concern with the narrating consciousness itself. Not even in such a "pure" (read: extreme) text, however, is it possible to argue for an "abstract" use of language. On the contrary, *Finnegans Wake* represents a kind of apotheosis of the interior-monologue technique, where not only is the representation of events governed by the associational logic of the stream of consciousness, but the words themselves are subjected to a process of recombination and permutation designed to render the even greater flux of the dreaming or half-dreaming state of the hero.[3]

Proust did not share Joyce's interest in representing the stream of consciousness per se. In fact, if, as I suggested at the outset of this chapter, novelists typically turn to music in search of formal models, then Proust provides an exception to the rule. Nevertheless, his emphasis on memory and the temporal dimension of thought, as well as his theories of metaphor and style, are founded on a closely related concern with the mental act as the primary criterion of truth and lead him to music for similar reasons. For Proust, artistic truth does not reside in the depiction of discrete objects but in the depiction of acts of cognition. Analogy plays a key role in this theory of representation: "Truth will be attained by [the artist] only when he takes two different objects, states the connexion between them . . . and encloses them in the necessary links of a well-wrought style" (*Remembrance of Things Past* 3:925). The relationship between this theory of knowledge and music is developed sporadically throughout Proust's *Remembrance of Things Past*. The *moment privilégié* and the *impression*, for example, are both described in relation to music.[4] Moreover, Proust's concern with representing mental functioning is related to the length and sinuosity of his sentences, which are designed "symphonically," as Edmund Wilson put it in his study of Proust in *Axel's Castle*, in order to unite as many of the various elements of a given experience as possible within the "indestructible bond" of a single sentence. None of these remarks should be taken to imply that the formal makeup of the *Remembrance* bears any direct resemblance to musical form, but Proust repeatedly links his prose to music through the more general notions of style, metaphor, and thought and demonstrates the relationship between music and the kind of thought that interests him in his wonderfully evocative descriptions of Vinteuil's music.[5] Whereas Joyce applied his musical analogies in ways that have a direct impact on narrative syntax, Proust, influenced in this by Schopenhauer, emphasizes above all music's ability to reveal intemporal essences. Marcel and Swann repeatedly express their admiration for the ability of Vinteuil's music to communicate a sense of those intemporal essences, and it is in their experience of Vinteuil's music that one finds the clearest examples of the kind of meaning Proust sought to integrate into the sinuous phrases and densely metaphorical language of the *Remembrance.*

It is possible, mutatis mutandis, to make the same kind of argument about the musical models found in the novels of Thomas Mann, André Gide, Virginia Woolf, and Aldous Huxley. For all these writers, music suggests ways to bring narrative form into line with a search for truth that relies on perfecting the representation of thought. For Mann, the principles of counterpoint and the leitmotiv seemed especially helpful for resolving the conflict between "the emotion and the idea" in fiction. This notion is present in the form of his early works, which clearly display the influence of Wagner, but finds its most powerful expression in *Doctor Faustus*, which aspires to a reconciliation of "harmonic subjectivity" with "polyphonic objectivity."[6] Similarly, André Gide's alter ego in *Les faux monnayeurs* sees Bach's *Die Kunst der Fuge* as a model for a mode of narrative that would emphasize the "life of ideas" over the lives of men (187). Even Aldous Huxley—despite his penchant for the conservative, realist style characteristic of the novel of ideas—links music to the representation of his characters' mental lives. Thus, the passage on the musicalization of fiction that justifies the title of *Point Counter Point* (300–03) is presented in the novel as a response to a discovery about "how one's mind naturally works." Philip Quarles—who acts in *Point Counter Point* as Huxley's spokesman on literary issues—describes how the sight of Lucy Tantamount's mouth, opened in laughter, calls forth, in a spontaneous association of ideas, the incongruous image of crocodiles feeding. This initial association of ideas, he tells us, then unleashes a host of memories, none of which have any direct logical link with Lucy's laughing mouth. Quarles qualifies this experience as a revelation ("Well, well. But what a windfall for my novel! I shall begin the book with it"), and, in the passage on music that follows, he links this experience to counterpoint (the simultaneous presence of two images) and musical development (the rapid succession of ideas related in more or less perceptible ways). Again, neither of these techniques bears any strict relation to musical techniques (especially not in the manner in which Huxley deploys them in this flatly didactic novel of ideas), but he sees a link there, and it is the nature of this link that interests me.

Before turning to the textual analysis that will make up the bulk of this chapter, it will be necessary to make an important methodological point about the status of these analogies between musical and narrative form. All of the novelists mentioned above deal with the relationship between the two arts in metaphorical terms, and wisely so: attempting to discuss this type of relationship in literal terms would require speaking at a level of abstraction that is foreign to the mimetic project of their novels. Novelists, after all, are under no obligation to speak literally, and this type of metaphor has the advantage of communicating intentions rapidly to the reader. But for the critic attempting to explain the function of such analogies, it is essential to go beyond the metaphorical level. No matter how useful a given analogy might have been for the novelist (as a source of inspiration, guide for composition, or explanatory device), and no matter how much such an analogy may help the reader decode the text, this type of comparison will always fail to account for the specifically literary features that make a given work what it is. This brings me back to an argument presented in chapter 1: critics must not limit themselves to debating the appropriateness (or lack thereof) of a given analogy; instead, they should use such analogies as clues that point to the deeper semiotic principles invoked by such metaphors. The primary difficulty of this approach is that these principles are at once so basic and so intricately woven into the fabric of the two arts that they seem either to need no explanation or, conversely, to defy explanation. For this reason, these principles, which constitute the grain of truth that all such metaphors must contain, are most often either simply assumed or are mentioned only in passing, as a matter of course. This can become an obstacle for critics: it is only by *grounding* these metaphors, by considering them in light of the concerns that motivated their use in the first place, that critics can avoid the loose analogizing that has marred so much musically oriented criticism.

My analysis, then, will be guided by the search for this type of basic semiotic principle. And in the case of the formal metaphors that I propose to study in this chapter, these principles can be grouped in three general categories: repetition, analogy, and exemplification. I would argue that all formal metaphors between music and narrative—from the leitmotiv, to counterpoint, to large-scale structural analogies—imply an investigation of three basic issues: (1) the role of repetition and variation in the determination of narrative form; (2) the use of analogical, as opposed to causal, logic; and (3) the respective roles of denotation and exemplification in the novel. These claims need some explanation.

1. Repetition and variation. The novel has traditionally been a linear genre, both on the local scale of enunciation (prose, *prosa*: in a straight line) and on the larger scale of the story told, which, following the format of the Aristotelian *muthos*, progresses inexorably from beginning to end. On the level of the signifier, repeated elements are either completely incidental (e.g., the unavoidable recurrence of the same sounds/letters in different words and of the same words in different sentences) or employed as a function of the objects and events represented (repetition of character and place names, the necessity of self-quotation and reminders, etc.). Repetition is equally marginalized on the level of the story told. It is often possible to locate symbolic parallels between successive events, but exact literal repetition of a given event is extremely rare and used only in precise narrative situations (e.g., time travel) or to make a certain kind of doctrinal statement (about cyclical time, the eternal return, and so forth). As Anthony Burgess puts it, "repetition is what neither fictional nor historical narrative can accommodate—at least, not in the literal manner of music" (*This Man and Music* 183). This narrative aversion to repetition can best be explained, I think, in terms of semantic staying power. As Vladimir Jankélévitch argues, in discursive genres like the novel and philosophy, "what is said stays said, what is said is definitive: once is enough and any repeat is useless" (33, my translation). The semantic mechanism of denotation, it seems, has an anchoring effect; it lends utterances a permanence that obviates the need for literal repetition of the kind we find in music. The traditional musical forms, on the other hand, not only make use of repetition but are *defined* by it. This is true on the local level (i.e., motivic repetition) and on the global level, where all forms, from the simplest (binary, rondo) to the most complex (sonata, fugue), are defined by the patterns of repetition and variation that they use. When novelists turn to a musical form for their model, they are, in essence, seeking a way to use repetition and variation in order to break out of the linearity of plot-based form. All of the various musical structures and techniques that have been invoked (often rather confusedly) as alternatives to or supplements for the *muthos*—leitmotiv, sonata form, theme and variations, counterpoint and fugue, and so on—must, in the final analysis, be understood in terms of this opposition between linearity (*muthos*) and repetition (music). Even narrative counterpoint, which appears to depend only on the "simultaneity equals alternation" analogy,

can be explained in terms of repetition. If we made a simple diagram of a novel that developed, say, two narrative strands in "contrapuntal" alternation, it might look something like the following:

Theme 1   —   —   —

                                     etc.

Theme 2   —   —   —

In order to understand the contrapuntal relationship, readers must be able to discern the common element that links each successive development to either theme 1 or theme 2, that is, the common factor that allows readers to sort each development and place it on either the upper or lower level of the above diagram. The common (i.e., repeated) element may be highly abstract, as in Huxley's or Kundera's use of contrapuntally juxtaposed plots, or immediately perceptible, as in the bronze and gold alternation that Joyce uses in "Sirens." Either way, repetition is inseparable from the perception of contrapuntal alternation, which involves sorting through the elements that have been modified in order to find the repeated elements. This brings us to the next principle at issue: analogy.

2. Analogical transformation goes hand in hand with repetition. Repetition guarantees, in the absence of plot, the perception of form, but there must also be a principle of change. In traditional narrative, development is synonymous with sequential and causal concatenation. The musical novel, however, doubles or even supplants the causal logic of traditional narrative by developing analogical relationships. Huxley explains this shift in perspective in terms of counterpoint, modulation, and variation: "A novelist modulates by reduplicating situations and characters. He shows several people falling in love, or dying, or praying in different ways—dissimilars solving the same problem. Or, *vice versa*, similar people confronted with dissimilar problems. In this way you can modulate through all the aspects of your theme, you can write variations in any number of different moods" (301). For Huxley, the common element may be a concept (love, death, prayer) varied in the specifics of plot and character, or, conversely, the plots and characters may be identical, with the problems and themes being varied. Similarly in music, the common element may be a theme or motif varied through transposition, inversion, and so on, or a new theme might be introduced into an existing

harmonic/rhythmic/motivic context. What is important from the mentalist perspective of this study is the logical shift that is implied by the change from the linear, sequential, causal logic of the *muthos* to the analogical syntax of musically inspired narrative structures. In an important sense, analogy is the principle that underlies the perception of causality. From a psychological, developmental point of view, the perception of analogical relationships precedes and conditions the determination of causal connections. We learn about cause and effect by comparing situations that have a greater or lesser number of common elements: where there's smoke there's fire; or when Pavlov rings his bell, the dogs will salivate. This is why the interior-monologue novel and its avatars depend so heavily on analogical progression: if the perception of analogical relationships governs the determination of causal relationships, then analogy can be taken to embody the cognitive process itself. And it is this emphasis on cognitive process that links the interior-monologue or stream-of-consciousness technique to music.

3. We are now in a position to understand the third determinant of musical form in the novel, which is the stress on exemplification over denotation. This is a question of the primary mode of reference in the two arts. Historically speaking, the novel, in its overriding preoccupation with the representation of external reality, has tended to privilege denotation over all other modes of signification. But when novelists go out of their way to reorder the presentation of the events depicted, it is because that order has something important to tell us about the meaning of the representation. It is this nondenotational information, information that depends on the configuration of the text (on the order of the words on the page and on the patterns formed by those words), that I (following Goodman) have been calling exemplification. Now music, which has no codified denotational dimension, signifies primarily by exemplification, and it is the mystery of this mode of signification that has fascinated novelists, encouraging them to look to music as a model for those elements that can make a novel something more than ("just") a story well told.

Of course, the closer one looks, the more it becomes apparent that all three of these principles—repetition, analogy, and exemplification—are interrelated: form, logic, and content are inseparable; any modification in one will necessarily affect the status of the others. This is why I've chosen to focus in this chapter on a representative of the *nouveau roman*. Few literary movements have devoted so much effort to laying bare the conventions that have governed representation in the novel, exploring the implications of these conventions, and seeking out new forms and new models. The *nouveau roman*, as a group, dedicated itself to the idea that there is no such thing as an innocent form. Thus Robbe-Grillet, in his *Pour un nouveau roman*, attempts to show what links "Balzacian" realism with a specifically nineteenth-century ideology, arguing that realism does not imply the use of "natural" forms (i.e., bearing an iconic relationship to the world) but forms that are tied to a worldview that has general currency. And if the *nouveau roman*, as a movement, has been set on calling the traditional conventions into question, it is precisely because these novelists sought to express a new worldview. The *nouveau roman* inherited the mentalist legacy of Proust and Joyce and set about pushing farther along the path these earlier writers had opened. For the *nouveaux romanciers*, the job of the novel could no longer be to create the illusion of a stable external reality but to explore the essentially unstable nature of the interaction between self and world that takes place in consciousness. Their message—descended from Joyce, Woolf, and Proust but linked more directly to the phenomenological notion that no division of "subjective" consciousness and "external" reality is possible—required a new use of narrative and, consequently, a need for new models.

Music played an important role in this search for new models. Butor, Duras, Pinget, and Robbe-Grillet have all referred to music to explain their intentions, and some of them have expended considerable effort on the exploration of the relationship between music and literature.[7] Robert Pinget stands out in this group, not because he is the best or most successful *nouveau romancier* (although I would argue that his work, which has received little attention in the United States, is due for a reassessment) or even necessarily because he has placed the most emphasis on music, but because he is the one who has most single-mindedly exploited the resources of repetition and variation. My intention in this chapter is to study Pinget's 1969 novel, *Passacaille,* in order to determine exactly how the musical model that governs the syntax of the novel interacts with the denotational content of its parts and how this interaction modifies the meaning of the novel as a whole. Using the key concepts of repetition, analogy, and exemplification, I'll show how Pinget uses the theme-with-variations format borrowed from music as a guide that enables him to reverse the normal referential vector of the representation and focus the reader's attention not on the objects and events depicted but on the narrative consciousness implied by the representation.

PINGET'S PASSACAGLIA

Robert Pinget likes to explore that domain, somewhere between music and ordinary language, where content and form are indistinguishable. For him, "the co-existence or co-birth of form and content . . . is the only poetic reality."[8] Pinget thinks of his art as the search for a tone of voice— "un ton"—rather than as a story to tell: "To choose every time, for love of novelty, one tone out of the billions captured by the ear, that is my lot in life." Thus, if Pinget has said, "I am more of a poet than a novelist" and "the novel doesn't interest me," it is in the sense that he subordinates the telling of stories to the direct manipulation of language, to the search for this ever-evolving tone of voice: "All that one can state or signify is of little interest to me; it's in the way things are said" ("Une interview" 551, my translation).

Significantly, and somewhat paradoxically, Pinget does not describe this search for a tone of voice in the usual poetic terms of diction and prosody but in terms of formal construction: "It seems to me that the interest of work up till now has been the search for a tone. This is a problem of form and explains perhaps my inclusion in what has been called the *nouveau roman*" ("Pseudo-principes" 311–12, my translation). It is the relation between this "search for a tone" and the "problem of form" that we'll need to clarify in order to understand the project behind *Passacaille*.

The title of *Passacaille* already suggests this interplay of form and tone: the term *passacaglia* designates both the formal model of the text (a baroque-era subspecies of the theme with variations) and the discourse of its protagonist, which is described in the text as "a kind of passacaglia" (37, my translation). In music, the term *passacaglia* refers to a type of composition based on an indefinite number of free variations executed by the upper voices over a single reiterated progression in the bass (*basso ostinato*). It is this contrast between the unvarying bass and the freely developing variations that characterizes the musical form and that furnishes the analogy for Pinget's novel. The piece that seems to have served as Pinget's model is the Passacaglia in C Minor for organ (BWV 582) by J. S. Bach.[9] Pinget's novel translates the passacaglia principle into novelistic terms by elaborating a series of increasingly complex stories all based on the same theme, a single sentence enunciated near the beginning of the novel. The successive developments of this theme are interspersed with several short motifs that, following the principle of the *basso ostinato*, recur regularly (obstinately) over the course of the novel. The theme undergoes a series of ever stranger narrative metamorphoses, but the *ostinato* motifs ("le calme, le gris," "la pendule détraquée," etc.) stay the same, recurring over and over, lending structure to each variation, and integrating the individual variations into a single unified structure.

The fact that Pinget has chosen a baroque-era form as the model for his novel is no accident. It was baroque music, Pinget claims, that inspired his particular approach to the novel: "My attachment to the technique of the intermingling of themes and their variations is due to the admiration I have always felt for so-called baroque music. When I was very young I was already captivated by it, and for years I tried to exalt its spirit in rather imperfect poems. It was only later that I pursued the idea of taking inspiration from it in the novel" ("Robert Pinget" 148). The appropriateness of baroque music as a model for Pinget's search for "un ton" becomes especially clear when we compare it with that most narrative of musical forms, sonata form. Sonata form, also called sonata-allegro form, consists (in the most general terms) in the exposition, development, and recapitulation of two contrasting themes or sets of themes. It is the form that dominated serious Western art music from the eighteenth century to the beginning of the twentieth. Historically, then, it is more or less contemporaneous with the modern novel, and, like the novel, it has a markedly dramatic orientation in the sense that it involves the resolution of a musical conflict between the opposing forces of its two themes. Baroque music, on the other hand, makes little use of this kind of dramatic progression, which does not gain currency until after the baroque era, with Haydn and Mozart. The fugue, the theme and variations, and the various dance forms typical of baroque music may use effects of contrast, but they do not develop ideas in the dialectical, conflictual way that a sonata, with its development section, does. This is why modern musicologists often describe baroque music in terms of "mood" and "contemplation" and contrast it with the classical and (especially) romantic interest in conflict and dramatic resolution.[10]

Passacaille is not Pinget's first experiment with theme and variations. In fact, the principle of variation has governed his writing ever since his first novel, *Mahu ou le matériau*, in which the narrative material for a novel is worked and reworked but never coalesces into a finished product. Similarly, *Le fiston* consists primarily of a series of letters from father to son, none of which have been sent, and all of which relate different versions of similar events in what appears to be an unending series. To give one last example: in *Quelqu'un*, the hero/narrator tries to tell the story of a single day spent in search of a scrap of paper. However, hindered by his bad memory (among other things), he is forced to speculate and finds himself constantly telling revised versions of his story in hope of eventually hitting upon the right sequence of events. Each version differs noticeably from the others, and it very quickly becomes apparent to the reader (if not the narrator) that the narrator will never find the definitive version, because all he has to work with is the continually evolving story in his head. Finally, in case these examples do not provide sufficient evidence of the importance of repetition and variation in Pinget's work, we should note that he has gone so far as to classify his novels according to the types of recurrence they use ("Robert Pinget" 146–47).

What is particular about *Passacaille* is that it does away completely with the type of (pseudo)realist contexts that his previous novels had used to orient his readers in the text. The various stories of *Quelqu'un* and *Le fiston* are all inscribed in a larger diegetic context: we know who the narrator is, we know why he is telling us stories, and we know why variations and contradictions occur. *Passacaille*, however, like *Le Libera* (which was published one year earlier, in 1968), offers no diegetic context for the storytelling, as if the musical intertext obviated the need to explain or justify the use of repetition and variation.[11] This is precisely what makes *Passacaille* so interesting. Instead of presenting itself as a single unified story or a succession of similar but unrelated stories, *Passacaille* takes shape as an obsessive search for meaning that proceeds by incessantly reworking the same set of elements. Although the successive variations are often logically incompatible with each other (since they are all based on the same set of key terms but ordered by different spatial, sequential, and causal relationships), they are not organized disjunctively or paratactically—as in a musical suite, short story anthology, collection of poems, or Queneau's *Exercices de style*—but are integrated into a single organic structure. They overlap, intertwine, and modify each other, forcing the reader to try to account for and justify in narrative terms the incompatibilities and contradictions that occur.

Having suggested the basic principle of variations on a theme, the usefulness of the passacaglia analogy begins to wane, primarily because of the fact that the musical form is, by definition, a polyphonic form (the superimposition of the *basso ostinato* and the variations in the upper voices), while the novel can present only one voice at a time. The inherent linearity of the prose text makes true polyphony in the musical sense an impossibility. Thus, although we might be able to speak of a "polyphonic effect" in *Passacaille*, created by the constant alternation between the principal narrative discourse and the *ostinato* motifs, there is no way to fully equate this effect with polyphony in the strict musical sense. For this reason, I'll abandon this aspect of the passacaglia metaphor here, simply accepting the alternation equals polyphony convention as a given. We'll examine later some of the thematic implications of the *ostinato* metaphor, but it is important to begin by stressing the single element of the musical intertext that can be taken to have a direct, nonmetaphorical application in the novel: the principle of variation.

Pinget does not approach Bach's passacaglia as a kind of template, where the point is to find literary equivalents for each of the musical problems and solutions proposed in Bach's piece, but as a more general incitement to explore the use of variation as a mode of narrative development. The concept of variations on a theme suggests a set of novelistic techniques that, although not directly related to the techniques of musical composition, remain linked to music through the overarching principle of permutational development. This approach to the musical intertext has led to some confusion amongst critics, who, like Werner Wolf ("Can Stories Be Read as Music?"), expect the musicalization of a novel to involve term-for-term analogies between a work and its model. Wolf prefers a form of pastiche, in which, as in Anthony Burgess's *Napoleon Symphony*, the novelist sets forth an explicit musical intertext (i.e., Beethoven's Symphony no. 3 ["Eroica"]) and attempts to find literary equivalents for the principal features of the musical piece. Wolf dismisses Pinget's use of the musical intertext as inauthentic on the grounds that "the rough structure of theme and variation underlying this *nouveau roman* does not follow the pattern of the musical form announced in the title" ("Can Stories Be Read" 216).[12]

Wolf's preference for the pastiche is perhaps understandable: the game of locating equivalencies between a literary work and its musical intertext can be a stimulating one. Burgess has demonstrated the possibilities of this subgenre both in *Napoleon Symphony* and in his pastiche of Mozart's Symphony no. 40 in *Mozart and the Wolf Gang*. Moreover, as Wolf points out, by giving somewhat more latitude to the type of musical intertext imitated, both Proust's descriptions of Vinteuil's music and Joyce's "Sirens" chapter can also be evaluated as pastiches. (In the case of Proust, the piece imitated is imaginary; Joyce imitates not an individual piece but a set of characteristics borrowed from a generic definition of the fugue.) But any critic who favors this approach to the use of musical models is bound to misinterpret what Pinget and writers like him are up to. More important, such a critic risks marginalizing an important source of literary innovation: Pinget's goal is not to impersonate a passacaglia, to attempt to translate a certain number of musical effects into prose, but to use the musical model as a starting point for a reflection on the ways that a novel can use repetition and variation to make meaning. He borrows from his model the principle of variation, not a certain number of fixed traits. The music-literature analogy is not for Pinget a goal in itself but a means to an end that is neither strictly literary nor strictly musical but, rather, part of a more general exploration of the way the mind works.

Wolf's objection to *Passacaille* does, nevertheless, call attention to an important problem for analysis. If the principle of theme and variations is not specific to music but is common to all the arts, then the musical reference risks losing its relevance, becoming a merely ornamental metaphor for an object that could perhaps have been described more simply in another way. If musical analogies are to advance our understanding of the relationship between music and literature, they should contribute something to our understanding of the work that could not be explained as well in other terms. In other words, Wolf's objection forces us to pose the question of the *specificity* of the musical model: what makes the passacaglia a necessary and not merely sufficient reference for *Passacaille*.[13] In order to meet this requirement, we'll need to go beyond the more or less superficial formal analogy implied by the novel's title and search for those characteristics of the novel that make the musical metaphor more than just an embellishment. This is the task that will guide my analysis. The first step in this process will be to acquaint ourselves with the various procedures for variation used in the text.

VARIATIONS ON THE MYSTERY NOVEL

Passacaille, like much of Pinget's work (*L'inquisitoire*, *Clope au dossier*, *L'hypothèse*, *Autour de Mortin*), makes use of the conventions of the mystery novel, presenting the reader with the details that surround a crime and suggesting the existence of a mystery to solve. Although presented in an elliptical, hermetic manner that is foreign to the genre, the atmosphere of generalized suspicion that characterizes the mystery novel is established in the opening sequence of *Passacaille*:

> Le calme. Le gris. De remous aucun. Quelque chose doit être cassé dans la mécanique mais rien ne transparaît. La pendule est sur la cheminée, les aiguilles marquent l'heure.
>
> Quelqu'un dans la pièce froide viendrait d'entrer, la maison était fermée, c'était l'hiver.
>
> Le gris. Le calme. Se serait assis devant la table. Transi de froid, jusqu'à la tombée de la nuit.
>
> C'était l'hiver, le jardin mort, la cour herbue. Il n'y aurait personne pendant des mois, tout est en ordre.
>
> La route qui conduit jusque-là côtoie des champs où il n'y avait rien. Des corbeaux s'envolent ou des pies, on voit mal, la nuit va tomber.
>
> La pendule sur la cheminée est en marbre noir, cadran cerclé d'or et chiffres romains. (7–8)

> [So calm. So grey. Not a ripple in view. Something must be broken in the mechanism, but there's nothing to be seen. The clock is on the mantelpiece, its hands tell the time.
>
> Someone in the cold room must have just come in, the house was shut up, it was winter.
>
> So grey. So calm. Must have sat down at the table. Numb with cold, until nightfall.
>
> It was winter, the garden was dead, the courtyard grassy. No one would be there for months, everything is in order.
>
> The road up to it skirts some fields lying fallow. Crows fly up, or are they magpies, you can't see very well, night is about to fall. The

clock on the mantelpiece is made of black marble, it has a gold-rimmed face and Roman figures.] (7)[14]

This opening sequence corresponds to the presentation of the *basso ostinato* that always precedes the first enunciation of the theme in the musical passacaglia. These six paragraphs introduce all the elements that will be developed as recurrent motifs over the course of the novel (*le calme, le gris, la mécanique, la pendule, la maison, la table, le jardin, la cour, la route, les champs, les corbeaux/pies*). Presented here as simple elements of a décor, these objects provide the background, the setting for the beginning of a tale about the movements of a person ("quelqu'un") who may or may not have entered the house. The hypothetical status of the narrative, suggested by the conditional verbs and the indetermination of the pronoun *quelqu'un*, creates an atmosphere of mystery, the desire for an explanation. The reader should notice the present-tense verbs in paragraphs 1, 4, 5, and 6 that surround the conditionals and imperfects of paragraphs 2 and 3. They serve to incorporate the hypothetical miniature story of the center paragraphs into a descriptive context that implies the active presence of whoever is telling the story: someone may (or may not) have entered this shadowy house on some unspecified winter day in the past, but the clock on the fireplace and this broken mechanism are there *now*, in the present tense, as is this road that skirts the fields where there used to be nothing. By surrounding the past-tense narrative about this "quelqu'un" with the present-tense description of a room, the novel introduces the teller into the story told. But the identity of the speaker remains as mysterious as the identity of this "quelqu'un" whose movements he describes. In other words, the novel opens with not one but two mysteries: that of the story told and that of the story teller. For the moment, the story that concerns us has not yet taken place: "everything is in order."

As in the musical form, the presentation of the *ostinato* line serves to prepare the first statement of the theme, setting the mood and establishing the basic set of materials the piece will have to work with. And, as in the musical form, the first statement of the sentence that makes up the theme of *Passacaille* follows immediately. The theme sentence of *Passacaille* depicts an ambiguous image, a juxtaposition of victim, witness, and perpetrator. Situated in an indefinite time, it condenses the elements of a potential story—a body on a dunghill, a sentinel, a man in his house—into a single ambiguous sentence:

L'homme assis à cette table quelques heures avant retrouvé mort sur
le fumier n'aurait pas été seul, une sentinelle veillait, un paysan sûr
qui n'avait aperçu que le défunt un jour gris, froid, se serait ap-
proché de la fente du volet et l'aurait vu distinctement détraquer la
pendule puis rester prostré sur sa chaise, les coudes sur la table, la
tête dans les mains. (8)

[The man sitting at this table a few hours earlier found dead on the
dunghill, wouldn't have been alone, a sentry was on guard, a trusty
peasant who had seen no one but the deceased one cold, grey day,
must have gone over to the slit in the shutter and apparently distinctly saw him put the clock out of action and then sit there prostrate in his chair, elbows on the table, head in his hands.] (7–8)

All subsequent variations will elaborate upon this single sentence, each
one based on a different permutation of the relationships implied here
and using the same set of key words. We should notice that, semantically
speaking, this sentence is clearly situated in an "afterward" where the
incidents in question have already occurred, and everything is finished. It
is the interval between the "before" of the introductory sequence and the
"afterward" of the theme sentence that engenders the fiction. The lack
created by the absence of information about this interval, these "few
hours," serves as the catalyst for the work of variation by implying the
presence of a mystery to resolve. In this way *Passacaille* presents itself
from the beginning as a kind of quest for the truth. As in the mystery
novel, all of *Passacaille* can be read as an attempt to resolve the ambiguities of the initial situation. But if the mystery novel promises a solution
to the mystery that surrounds the crime, *Passacaille* closes with this mystery as deep, if not deeper, than ever. It invokes the format of the mystery
novel, its thematics of criminality and its obsession with the resolution of
enigmas, but only to displace the enigma from the story told to the telling
of the story.

The suggestive polysemy of the theme sentence makes it an excellent
generator of literary variations. How is one to read this statement? Although it begins and ends with a man in front of a table, it is as ambiguous syntactically as it is semantically. The circular construction of the
sentence makes it impossible to determine the relationships between the
man, the deceased, the peasant, and the sentry or the chronology of the
story it suggests. The sentry and the trusty peasant—are they the same

person? And "the man" from the beginning of the sentence—is he the deceased? Or might he be the trusty peasant? Even the chronological clue "a few hours earlier" is ambiguous: does it modify the clause that precedes it or the one that follows? Close reading shows that it is simply not possible to resolve the ambiguities of this sentence without some sort of supplementary information. And as we'll see, the response to all the questions posed here will be different in each variation. Pinget does not offer a single solution to any of them; rather, he uses all such questions to generate new ambiguities.

This image/sentence will be developed according to principles that do in fact owe as much to the exemplificational logic of music as to the denotational logic of the novel. Pinget treats the theme not only as a semantic unit but as a formal unit, a group of identifiable symbols that serves as the basis for composition. The theme does not give rise to a single story or conceptual line of reasoning but to a series of increasingly freer fantasies all built around the same set of key words. By making sure to incorporate the key words from the theme into each variation, Pinget ensures that it remains present as an audible and visible entity even as its logical, narrative identity undergoes the most unexpected metamorphoses. As such, it can be transformed and integrated into apparently unrelated semantic structures without losing its distinctive formal identity. The theme sentence, then, can be thought of as a theme both in the musical sense (like a melody, it constitutes a self-contained, recognizable set of symbols to be developed through the transformation of its material constituents) and in the literary sense (where a theme is above all a conceptual unit to be explored semantically). The theme sentence will engender a long series of new images and new narrative developments that may have little to do with the situation implied by the initial statement, but the links between each variation and the theme—which may be prosodic, semantic, syntactical, or any combination of the three—are there and can always be invoked to relate each successive development to the initial sentence.

In a sense, *Passacaille* is *about* the relationship of syntax and meaning. The architectonic unity of *Passacaille* is not dramatic; it does not depend on the unity of a single plot or argument but on this continual presence of the theme in its successive incarnations. This does not, of course, mean that Pinget refuses to tell stories. On the contrary, *Passacaille* is full of stories; the urge to narrativize seems irrepressible. But each new narrative development is made without any guarantee of logical continuity with those that precede. Readers, disoriented by the contradictions that accumulate from page to page, find themselves incapable of locating a stable diegetic universe, and even the narrator seems incapable of stabilizing the universe of the fiction. Thus the real verbal tense of the novel is the conditional, its modality that of the hypothesis.

> Qu'on aurait donc vu, ne m'interrompez pas, au petit matin un cadavre sur le fumier, il devait être cinq heures, et qu'on aurait pensé qu'il s'agissait du maître lequel s'était mis à boire, pas plus difficile, or rien n'autorisait à cette déduction . . . mais les choses s'installent dans l'esprit et plus moyen de les en déloger, d'ailleurs qui on, il fallait préciser, d'ailleurs pourquoi cadavre, ce pouvait être un corps qui se relèverait quelques minutes ou quelques heures après, une défaillance, ivrognerie pas indispensable non plus, une perte de conscience tout simplement. (86)

> [That they apparently saw, then, don't interrupt me, in the early morning a corpse on the dunghill, it must have been five o'clock, and it seems they thought it was the master because he had taken to drink, no more difficult than that, no there was nothing to justify this deduction . . . but things take root in people's minds and no way of getting them out again, anyway who's people, something more explicit was necessary, and anyway why corpse, it could have been a body which would get up a few minutes or a few hours later, a fainting fit, drunkenness not indispensable either, quite simply a loss of consciousness.] (61)

We know that there has been some sort of crime, "a perpetual crime, perpetrated for years in this cold house," but we also know that "the story will remain secret, with no visible flaws." The narrator does everything he can to give greater consistency to this image that, refusing to go away, "demanded its fill of flesh," but each new development creates more ambiguities, and before any of the stories can arrive at a satisfactory conclusion, new doubts have forced the process to begin again.

Each variation develops around a character—named variously "the other," "the storyteller," "the deceased," "the testator," and, in one of the last variations, "I"—whose identity will gradually stabilize around the title of "master." This identification comes about slowly. The novel's opening sequence, as we saw, refers only to a shadowy "quelqu'un." The theme sentence is only slightly more specific, mentioning "a man" in his house. The identity of this man remains hidden behind the anonymity of the pronoun "he" for several episodes, and the narrator seems to wonder himself about the identity of this "funny little guy" with his "inexplicable passions." It is not until about twenty pages into the novel that the word "master" appears for the first time, but once it appears, the title will stick, becoming the focal point of the novel. Almost all of the rest of the stories that make up *Passacaille* will, after this point, focus on the master. But the modalities of this identity remain complex: can we really be sure that from variation to variation the master is still the same person? To a certain extent, the text seems to imply, yes. In every variation the master is an aging writer who spends most of his time writing and pacing back and forth between his writing table and the clock on the mantelpiece. We always find him in the same little country house, with its garden, court-yard, and dunghill, located not far from the swamp, forest, and town that are all situated somewhere along the road that runs past the front gate. We also find the master surrounded by the same characters: the sentry mentioned in the theme sentence, an old goatherd, the neighbor with his wife and son, and the master's old friend, the doctor. But if these people and places guarantee a certain amount of continuity, helping to define the master as a character with a stable identity, their effect is more than counterbalanced by the contradictions between variations.

In every variation the master is linked to a cadaver and a dunghill (which we recognize from the "dead on the dunghill" motif from the theme sentence), but the nature of the relationship between master, ca-daver, and dunghill varies widely. In some variations it is the master himself who is discovered, dead, on the dunghill; in others the master discovers a body or gossips about the discovery of a corpse by someone else; in still others the master only hears, or overhears, or thinks he overhears, a story about the discovery of a body on a dunghill. Each variation begins from scratch, with the master in a different relation to the body on the dunghill. The contradictions suggest that there is not one single master, an individual with a unique identity, but a series of mas-ters, a set of anonymous actors that all have, as if by chance, the same title. In this way *Passacaille* destabilizes the traditional function of the fictional character, refusing to endow the master with the continuity of identity that, in a conventional linear novel, would be guaranteed by the simple anaphoric repetition of his title. The master, the central figure of the novel (and we cannot know here if we should take the word "figure" in its rhetorical or social sense), teeters on the fulcrum of his title; his status swings between that of the protagonist, capable of guaranteeing narrative coherence by the sheer fact of his nominal presence, and that of the motif, a signifier without signified, a mere textual effect.

This same uncertainty governs our relationship to all elements of the theme. The opening sequence and theme sentence introduce, as we've seen, the notion of a crime to solve. Accordingly, all of the variations involve a crime and focus on the problem of the identity of the perpetrator. In most of the variations, a dead body is discovered in suspicious circumstances. In the first variation, for example, the neighbor's son discovers a dead body on the dunghill and runs home to look for his parents, who, upon their arrival, drag the body inside the house. The father then sends away the mother and the son, closes the windows, and locks the door, and we are told: "this wasn't the first corpse he's had to cope with." This hint of foul play seems to be confirmed when the father, having locked the body inside, turns to take one last look at the house: "there'd been no witness and no one supposed to know that the owner had come back this grey winter's day to inspect the premises" (11). But the meaning of all this apparently suspicious activity is not clarified, and the novel passes on, without further commentary, allowing us to draw our own conclusions or, as seems more prudent, to withhold judgment in the hope that later information will clarify the situation. This is the first development of the crime motif, and, relatively straightforward, it seems to serve primarily as an introduction, preparing the way for the complexities of the later variations. In each successive variation, however, the nature of the crime and the identity of the suspects will change. Most will involve a murder, but the explanation of that murder will include everything from suicide to espionage, from drug running to voodoo curses and illicit sex. Then again, some variations will abandon the body-on-a-dunghill idea entirely. In these the crime in question involves, variously, the poisoning of a cow, the theft of a few sous by a child, the theft of the master's will and testament, an attack on the mailman by a gang of kids, and even the carving, or "massacre," of a duck at dinner.

The primary mode of presentation, as is appropriate for a text that claims to be a *roman* (*nouveau* or otherwise), is narrative. But the mode of thought in this novel is not exclusively or even primarily narrative. Each variation, it is true, offers a new incarnation of the theme, presented according to the sequential and causal logic of narrative, but the mechanisms that account for the transformations of the theme from one variation to the next work according to a different principle, and it is in this process of transformation that the real work of the novel takes place. In general, the transformations of the theme work by analogical substitution. Each successive variation is linked by at least one but usually several elements to the original theme sentence. These links may be purely semantic (e.g., metaphorical substitution) or purely formal (paranomastic, rhythmic, syntactical) or, as is most often the case, a combination of the two. Although too widespread and complex to analyze in detail, a few examples should suffice to give an idea of the ways in which the work of substitution takes place in *Passacaille*.

We've already begun to see how the theme sentence generates variations using the "crime" motif. But if we return to the theme sentence, we can see that every fragment of the sentence plays a part in controlling the variations. The fragment "dead on the dunghill," for example, gives rise to semantic variations that emphasize the idea of death by transforming it into everything from the cadaver of a chicken to a cow cadaver to carcasses in the swamp to an outright hecatomb. In some variations, the obsession with death spirals out of control, and the murder motif shifts into the register of the horror film: "suddenly the whole countryside disintegrates, corpses are strewn all along the meadows and roads." Still others transpose the death motif into the mechanical register of disabled machinery, giving rise to developments about the broken clock, a bogged-down tractor, and a bloody tow truck. The "dead on the dunghill" fragment also gives rise to variations that deemphasize the first syntagm—dead—in order to stress the second—on the dunghill. In these variations the dead man on the dunghill is replaced by other bodies, some living ("was it a cadaver?"), some dead ("the remains of an animal, legs in the air, gut opened"), and some in between (like the mailman, who is "*dead* drunk," the dy*ing* village idiot, with his "bloodstained trouser fly," or the master, fallen because of a "sudden swoon"). All of these, like the cruciform scarecrow that falls onto the dunghill in several variations, are nothing but simulacra, stand-ins for this essentially anony-mous scapegoat that must be found fallen "on the dunghill."

All the constituents of the theme sentence are subjected to this kind of ongoing transformation. The fragment "the man seated at this table," for example, is permuted in a variety of ways, becoming a "man collapsed on the table," an anonymous "dead reader" with his elbows on the table, the master writing at his table, the master in front of his table reading, and so on. Nevertheless, it is clearly the "dead on the dunghill" fragment that dominates this novel. It plays the most important role because it contains the greatest amount of narrative energy, generating the most highly charged sequences, those that, titillating or horrifying or simply strange, seem to demand the reader's attention.

This question of narrative energy is fundamental to our understanding of *Passacaille*. Pinget is a self-proclaimed improviser. He never works with an outline; instead, like a jazz soloist or a composer meditating at the keyboard, he allows ideas that come to him while writing to influence the subsequent development of the novel. Often, for example, the course of a narrative development will be altered by a single word or phrase. The variations tend to mutate into one another, and a particularly evocative word or turn of phrase will, once introduced into the texture of the novel, tend to recur, to become a motif that surfaces at more or less regular intervals. And if the motif contains enough narrative energy, it will even-tually take over, determining the course of an entire variation. This is the case with the mutilated cadaver/bloodstained trouser fly motif, which, with its lurid implications of sex crime and torture as well as the arche-typal resonance of castration myths, contains a particularly high amount of narrative energy. This motif is introduced early on in the novel (40) and recurs twice more in its initial form and once in a slightly varied form before taking over and playing a central role in what turns out to be the longest single narrative sequence, by far, of the novel. And yet, despite the precise connotations that this kind of image comports, the bloods-tained trouser fly motif can with the aid of hindsight be traced, both prosodically and semantically, back to the opening sequence of the novel and the theme sentence as an extension of the broken clock/pendulum motif, with intermediate stages like the bloodied tow truck and the refer-ence to a cow cadaver with its detached teat that immediately precedes the first occurrence of the motif.

Given the importance of this ongoing process of substitution, the most profitable way to approach the novel might be to attempt to trace the substitutive chains that generate the various images and stories. Every development, no matter how distant in appearance from the theme sentence, can be explained in terms of its relationship to the initial theme. The novel uses a process of free association whereby each variation can engender others in turn so that as the text progresses the links between each variation and the original theme become less and less apparent. Still, no matter how distant the reference, careful reading suffices to locate at least one element that can be traced back to the theme. Thus when, at one point, we read about someone's mother leaving in "the exile train," we can easily trace the mother (*mère*) back to the master (*maître*) phonetically and link the exile train to the original theme by a series of metaphorical substitutions that might be reconstituted something like this: broken clock/broken machine/broken motor/bogged-down tractor/bloody tow truck/train compartment/exile train.

This list of variational techniques could go on and on, but it is equally important to point out how well this novel coheres from a strictly prosodic point of view. Indeed, it is no accident that much of the critical attention Pinget's work has attracted has a decidedly anagrammatic slant. Pinget has interested critics influenced by the Saussurian theory that the development of a text is determined to a large degree by the dissemination of a small set of significant phonemes. Pierre Vidal, for example, suggests that the theme sentence of *Passacaille* (and, by extension, the entire novel) is generated by the phonemes of the first line of the text: "Le calme. Le gris. De remous aucun."[15] From this perspective, it seems significant that in the first variation, where the master (*maître*) has not yet been named, it is the mayor (*maire*) who comes to verify the death of the man, as if it were necessary to fill the phonetic gap left by the absence of the word *maître*. Other passages will substitute for the master a mother (*mère*), a flood (*marée*), a merchant (*marchand*), or a murmur (*murmure*). One might even say this is a novel in the key of m. The novel is full of "m" motifs like "Dans le matin sempiternel de sa manie" (67) and "la mort au moindre défaut de la pensée" (33, 118, 128), both of which are very close to being anagrams of the fragment from which the title of the novel is derived, "une manière de passacaille" (36). I don't think the anagrammatic explanation can provide on its own a sufficiently complete description of *Passacaille*, but it is clear that Pinget has gone to great lengths to assure the phonetic coherence of the novel. This is true not only of the repetition of the *ostinato* motifs but also within each variation, many of which are built around one or two phonemes (re- or ou) and incorporate phonetically linked couples like *orchis/iris*, Rodolphe/Momolphe, Edouard/Nanard, *chèvres/rêves*, and so on.

A complete accounting of the novel would also have to highlight the pervasive use of exact repetition. As we've seen, each successive variation is punctuated by the repetition of the *ostinato* motifs introduced in the first sequence of the novel, a procedure that helps to guarantee what Pinget calls the "surface unity" of the text. The first of these, "le calme, le gris" (repeated ten times), traverses the entire text and marks the moments of rest, what one might call the cadences of the text. Other motifs derived from the first sequence include "something broken in the mechanism" [quelque chose cassé dans la mécanique] (ten times) and "the broken clock" [la pendule détraquée] (eight exact repetitions, two slightly varied).[16] There is also a large number of other motifs that don't belong to the *ostinato* line but appear episodically within some of the variations. I have tried to cite as many occurrences of these motifs as possible, which is why many of my citations are followed by multiple page references.

Of all the repetitions in the text, the most important is, no doubt, the last. Pinget closes his novel with a procedure sometimes used in the theme and variation form in music (compare Bach's *Goldberg Variations*): a reprise of the original theme. Thus *Passacaille* ends with an (almost) exact repetition of the theme sentence, creating an effect of closure, of return to the novel's point of origin. In this way, the universe of the fiction, following the principle of the eternal return, closes in on itself. The narrative, subjected to the circular temporality of repetition, fades before the eternity of the image that generated it. And yet, although the restatement is clearly meant to recall the original enunciation of the theme, there are important modifications in the final enunciation of the theme that must be taken into account.

[L'homme] Assis à cette table quelques heures avant retrouvé mort sur le fumier [n'aurait pas été seul], une sentinelle veillait [un paysan sûr] qui n'avait aperçu que le défunt un jour gris, froid, se serait approchée de la fente du volet et l'aurait vu distinctement détraquer

la pendule puis rester prostré sur sa chaise, les coudes sur la table, la
tête dans les mains. (133)

[(The man) Sitting at that (this) table a few hours earlier, found
dead on the dunghill, (wouldn't have been alone), a sentry was on
guard, (a trusty peasant) he (who) had seen no one but the deceased
one cold, grey day, must have gone over to the slit in the shutter and
apparently distinctly saw him put the clock out of action and then sit
there prostrate in his chair, elbows on the table, head in his hands.]
(94)

This is the closing sentence of the novel. (The words in brackets appear in
the initial statement of the theme [page 8] but have been omitted from
the restatement; the *e* in italics appears in the latter but not the former.) A
comparison with the original statement of the theme sentence shows that
there is now one element less—the man who had been, up to this point, at
the center of each variation has disappeared. This occultation of the
masculine presence that had been at the thematic heart of the entire novel
suggests the possibility of a whole new series of variations that would take
place without the master. The theme sentence has already been unfolded
to reveal many of the myriad narrative possibilities contained in it, but, as
this last modification suggests, it could continue to generate stories infinitely. This is an important principle for Pinget, who has said, "My own
way of exalting nature has been to make people discover, or to try to make
them discover, its infinite variety. What I have called its potentialities,
which are all included in a given reality" ("Robert Pinget" 148).

Where the traditional novel demands a choice, the elaboration of a
single reality unified by a single overarching plot, Pinget's novel multi-
plies both realities and plots into the series of "these innumerable instants" (43, 70), held together only by the obsessive force of the image that
generates them. It would be useless (and absurd) to try to establish direct
equivalencies between the literary techniques of transformation that
Pinget uses (be they semantic, syntactical, phonetic, or otherwise) and
musical principles of transformation (transposition, inversion, augmentation, diminution, etc.). Music works in the realm of tones and proportional rhythm, while literature works in the realm of conceptual and
phonemic relationships. And just as music and literature each have their
own materials, they also have their own means of transformation: no
direct exchange is possible.[17] *Passacaille* makes no claim to bear any such

direct resemblance to its model. It is, rather, the principle of permutational transformation that *Passacaille* borrows from music. What counts in *Passacaille*, as in the musical variations on a theme, is that every variation must have at least one distinctive element in common with the theme, that it be possible, at least theoretically, to bring every element of a given variation back to the original theme, identifying the elements that have been retained.

The principle of permutational transformation requires that readers modify their interpretative strategies accordingly. The perception of form and meaning in *Passacaille* is not guaranteed by narrative concatenation but by the continual process of comparison between theme and variation that the reader must carry out in order to follow the novel's progress. To be sure, the reader of *Passacaille* must be able to decipher the individual stories, but this is only a preliminary task. The individual stories only take on full significance when considered in terms of the relationships between them. The essential interpretative act takes place during the process of comparison and depends on the perception of equivalencies at every level. Readers should be able to distinguish what is new in each variation and what has been retained from the original theme. Otherwise, mystified by the lack of dramatic continuity, they are bound to lose interest and abandon the book for more stimulating pursuits. As in the variation form in music, where a large part of the audience's pleasure derives from the composer's ability to surprise it without losing touch with the original theme, the reader's pleasure in *Passacaille* is in appreciating the dialectical intricacies of the relationship between the theme and its variations. In this way, using only conventional literary techniques, Pinget manages to build a thought structure that owes as much to music as to literature.

MUSIC, MIMESIS, AND THE MURMUR

Pinget's application of the principle of permutational variation to the novel brings about, as we've seen, a systematic transgression of one of the fundamental laws of traditional narrative: the principle of noncontradiction or internal coherence. Pinget's use of theme and variation rather than plot as the primary organizational principle makes the narrative chain constantly mutate into new sequences that do not correlate logically with the preceding sequences. This has the effect of completely destabilizing the mimetic illusion: *Passacaille* cannot be resolved in terms of a single, stable diegetic reality. This does not make *Passacaille* an "abstract" or "antimimetic" novel, as some have suggested, but it does radically modify the status of the representation.

Since at least Homer, storytellers have assumed the existence of a universe, real or imaginary, where the events narrated are considered to take place. This universe, even though it may differ significantly from the one we live in (as is the case in science fiction stories and fairy tales), is assumed to function like ours in several important respects: time is irreversible, every effect has its cause, and an event, once it has taken place, is considered to be inscribed indelibly in the history of this world. Thus, when the narrator of *The Odyssey* tells us that Odysseus has been gored by a boar, or when the narrator of *Le rouge et le noir* tells us that Mme de Rênal has been shot by Julien Sorel, we know that, barring exceptional circumstances (hidden identity, unreliable narrator, bad information, etc.), he or she will always bear the scar of that wound. Henceforth, every time the name Odysseus/Mme de Rênal appears in the text, it will denote a man/woman with a scar. The scar may later play an important role in the narrative (as it does in *The Odyssey*) or an insignificant one (as in *Le rouge et le noir*), but once the existence of that scar has been established by the text, it will remain part of the set of attributes of that character, available for use in any subsequent development, sequel, or retelling of the story.

The general trend of postwar avant-gardes like the *nouveau roman* has been to question this convention. Texts like Beckett's *Molloy* and Robbe-Grillet's *La Jalousie* carry out a frontal assault on it as part of their more general attack on the type of mimetic illusion traditionally sought in the novel. Molloy, for example, has a bad leg, but he can't quite remember if it's the left leg or the right leg, and he ends up deciding that in fact it doesn't matter. Molloy, in other words, is above all the person *telling* the story, not the person represented, and he imperiously asserts his right as narrator to modify his infirmity as necessary to fit the needs of the (purely discursive) situation in which he finds himself: if he suddenly changes his mind and decides that his left leg is the weak one, then it is. The narrator of Beckett's *Unnamable* will be even more direct: "But I just said I have spoken of me, am speaking of me. I don't care a curse what I just said. It is now I shall speak of me, for the first time" (*Three Novels*

303). Robbe-Grillet makes similar gestures in *La Jalousie*, in which, for example, the shape of this house, detailed by the narrator with maniacal precision, is nevertheless subject to inexplicable modifications over the course of the novel (disappearing rooms, changing dimensions) without explanation. In both *Molloy* and *La Jalousie*, this destabilization of the narrative illusion is reinforced in the accompanying metanarrative commentary. In the famous shift from *récit* to *discours* that marks the close of *Molloy*, we read: "Then I went back into the house and wrote, It is midnight. The rain is beating on the windows. It was not midnight. It was not raining" (*Three Novels* 176). And in the equally famous *en abyme* close of *La Jalousie* we find a similar narrative gesture: "The protagonist of the book is a civil servant for the customs office. The character is not a civil servant . . . The accounts of this company are in bad shape . . . The accounts of the company are very good. The protagonist—we learn—is dishonest. He is honest" (*La Jalousie* 216). In this way, using the simple mechanism of negation, Beckett and Robbe-Grillet denounce their own fictions. They insist on closing with a demonstration of the fact that fiction is, by nature, a string of lies, that the illusion of truthfulness in fiction (verisimilitude, plausibility) is simply an effect, a matter of assuring that no unexplainable contradictions occur.

The narrators of *Molloy* and *La Jalousie* confront this convention directly by refusing expressly to accept it, but Pinget's *Passacaille* takes a different route, one that is at once less contestatory and more radical: the principle of noncontradiction is not denounced in *Passacaille*, it is simply taken to be irrelevant, inapplicable, it is not even *considered*. The implications of this attitude are far-reaching. Although *Molloy* and *La Jalousie* both refuse the noncontradiction principle, they still make use of the convention on which it is founded, which is the diegetic or "world-making" assumption of traditional narrative. Both novels create the illusion that they do in fact describe part of a world, that the events of the novel, in other words, take place in a diegetic universe that predates, surrounds, and will outlast the events related in the novel. Both *Molloy* and *La Jalousie* try to break with this tradition by reminding us from time to time that their worlds are only invented, illusionary worlds of words and that we should not place too much faith in them or expect them to follow the rules we are accustomed to. But in fact, if Beckett's and Robbe-Grillet's narrators find they must denounce the mimetic illusion from time to time, it is precisely because the illusion is so strong.[18]

In *Passacaille* the situation is different. There, the constant metamorphoses of the narrative chain rule out the usual assumption of a place where the events described could be considered to have a real existence. The narrator tells stories but without ever postulating a single diegetic universe, and the reader is left with the puzzle of what to do with these irreconcilable bits of information, how to situate them with respect to each other. This is, on a first reading, the primary difficulty of the novel. It is only gradually that the reader comes to realize that the sole truth of the novel is situated in the interior of the depicting consciousness and not outside in some hypothetical real world. This narrative consciousness is completely identified with the words on the page: we know it, so to speak, from the inside; we share its perspective. For this reason, when we speak of representation in this novel, we must speak of the representation of the act of storytelling. *Passacaille* tells the story of a man listening to himself, of a man writing what he hears listening to himself:

> A tâcher de saisir ce murmure entre deux hoquets il s'était d'abord aiguisé l'ouïe tant que jeunesse durait puis la courbe dépassée la perdait progressivement pour aboutir peu avant l'époque dite à la surdité compacte, aux grésillements internes, aux vertiges et aux céphalées mais sa volonté aidant, tel un musicien de bazar, reconstituait une manière de passacaille. (37)

> [Through trying to catch that murmur between two hiccups he had at first managed to make his hearing more acute so long as youth had lasted but once he was over the bend it had gradually started to diminish and resulted not long before the aforementioned period in solid deafness, internal crackling, dizzy spells, and headaches but by exercising all his willpower, like a street-corner musician, he had reconstituted a kind of passacaglia.] (26–27)

The master—and it should be clear by now that the master is nothing other than a figure of the narrator, speaking of himself in the third person—lives only in his words: "the only history he would have now would be written, his only breath would be literary" (69). His sensory world reduced to almost naught by this "solid deafness" that envelops him, his only reality is made up of the "internal cracklings" of memory and imagination. His task is to attempt to "capture" the murmur he hears ("saisir ce murmure"), to "reconstitute" it in words. But the past becomes confused with the present, reality with imagination, and all are subject to distortion from his unreliable senses and bad memory: "it's hard to see" (7, 12), "it's hard to make it out" (132), "it was hard to hear" (19, 22, 34, 45, 50, 74, 78, 84), "it was hard to make it out" (43, 24, 46, 65, 69). The narrator, who complains regularly about his "failing source of information" (9, 25, 35, 99), seems to be losing contact with the outside world. *Passacaille*, then, is not about the crime or crimes that are so often named in the text, it is about the "murmur" that induces the master/narrator to name them, about his struggle to transcribe, capture, or seize the murmur that is so often mentioned in the text.[19] The concept of the murmur and the type of writing it implies can be better understood in relation to the "murmure géant" (giant murmuring) that Maurice Blanchot writes about in *The Space of Literature*:[20]

> To write is to make oneself the echo of what cannot cease speaking—and since it cannot, in order to become its echo I have, in a way, to silence it. I bring to this incessant speech the decisiveness, the authority of my own silence. I make perceptible, by my silent mediation, the uninterrupted affirmation, the giant murmuring upon which language opens and thus becomes image, becomes imaginary, becomes a speaking depth, an indistinct plenitude which is empty. (*The Space of Literature* 27)

The master does not invent from nothing, he is not simply making up stories; rather, he attempts to make himself the echo of the murmur, and his attempt to write the story of his own life and death is above all an attempt to transcribe or reconstitute the voice that he hears, which he does by writing a story, the story of his own death. And the results of this attempt to write his story—"imagined in detail, amplified over the years, tragic or touching according to the evening" (20)—make up both the text that the master calls his "testament" and the text that we readers have before us. The master's ultimate goal, it seems, is to silence the voice, "faire taire le murmure" (Pinget), "to silence it" (Blanchot), which he can only do by "capturing" the murmur (Pinget), by "echoing" it (Blanchot). But since the murmur, identified with consciousness itself, "cannot," in Blanchot's words, "cease speaking," the master cannot prevent his story from evolving, from mutating.

The text repeatedly describes the master's work as a "work on marginal notations" (18, 42, 97, 118), and it describes the master's output as notations "in the margin of a murmured phrase" (19, 74) or "in the margin of a meaningless sentence" (21, 35, 44, 52, 96). If we accept the hypothesis that the text described in *Passacaille* and the text *of Passacaille* are one and the same, it becomes evident that this "murmured sentence," this "empty phrase," is in fact what I've been calling the theme sentence of the novel. The task that the master has set for himself (or, rather, that has been set for him) is to seek out the truth behind the theme sentence, to reconcile it with the murmur, to *mediate* (in Blanchot's sense of the word) between the two.

It is this mediate relationship between the actualized text and the implied murmur that explains the *basso ostinato* metaphor and justifies its polyphonic implications. In the musical passacaglia, the *basso ostinato* runs continuously throughout the piece, but the listener, occupied for the most part with the melody, will usually only notice it during moments of relative rest or, exceptionally, when it is highlighted for some reason (as, for example, when one of the upper parts takes over the *ostinato* line in Bach's organ passacaglia). Similarly, the *ostinato* motifs only surface in Pinget's text at moments of rest, in the spaces or pauses between narrative developments. It seems that we're supposed to extrapolate, from the few bits that are written out, that these motifs continue in the background, as it were, even when not transcribed in the text. Since, according to an ineluctable law of written literature, it is impossible to read and understand two texts at the same time, this is the only path available for Pinget to communicate a sense of the continuity of the murmur. The logic of this approach becomes apparent if we imagine, for example, that Pinget had decided to configure his text as a kind of musical score, with two or more lines of prose, say, superimposed vertically or placed side by side in such a way as to suggest simultaneity. Writers like Roche, Kristeva, Derrida, and Zukofsky have done just this. But this solution proves to be inadequate in Pinget's case since it would place too much importance on the *ostinato* line. The point of the *basso ostinato* metaphor, its profound appropriateness, lies in the fact that it is always there but heard indistinctly, surfacing only intermittently when attention is not directed elsewhere. And yet, although the murmur cannot be silenced, it cannot be "seized" either. The very attempt to reach for it submerges it. The murmur, then, is above all that which makes writing an endless task.

The theme sentence might be thought of as an inaugural attempt to transcribe the murmur. But at once too vague (*creuse*) to have any meaning and too partial to capture the import of the murmured voice, it needs to be elucidated. The rest of the novel carries out this attempt at elucidation. But how does one clarify a partial transcription of a voice that is heard only indistinctly and that is in constant evolution? The master's solution is that of variation.

It is worth pointing out here that this solution bears an important resemblance to Lévi-Strauss's structural approach to the study of myth. Pinget's novel proposes a study of an individual consciousness that, like Lévi-Strauss's myth-oriented analysis of culture, compares all available variants of a story in order to find the Ur-myth that, it is presumed, is common to all of them. The Ur-myth is taken to be a fundamental, defining component of the culture or consciousness in question. The mere existence, it is argued, of so many variants seems to suggest the presence of an original or underlying structure that they would all have in common. But this original remains hidden from view; only simulacra appear. Pinget's master hopes to locate this Ur-myth, to find the original through a process of amplification, comparison, and elimination:

> Quelques images qu'il fallait amplifier, débarrasser de leurs scories, enténébrer jusqu'au moment où devenues interchangeables leur différence profonde ferait surgir un monde d'agressivité et de déroute, c'était la tâche qu'il s'était imposée à cette table même . . .
>
> Quelques images à débarrasser de leurs scories pour découvrir au fond de leur trame la déroute, la détresse, puis progressivement l'accalmie, que d'années de ce travail, ténèbres jamais assez denses, fantasmes à l'état de hoquets, la nuit ne surgirait qu'impromptu lorsqu'elle ne serait plus désirée. (17, 19)

> [A few pictures that needed amplifying, extricating from their dross, obscuring until the moment when, having become interchangeable, their profound difference would give rise to a world of aggression and rout, that was the task he'd set himself at this very table . . .
>
> A few pictures to extricate from their dross in order to discover beneath their weft disorder, distress, and then progressively a lull, so many years of this work, shadows never so dense, phantasms reduced to hiccups, night would only come impromptu when it was no longer desired.] (14, 16)

It is this search for an underlying structure that creates the need for the variation format. It is hoped that once all the extraneous particularizations, or dross (*scories*), of the Ur-myth have been eliminated, only the essential structure that the individual actualizations have in common will remain, revealing the forces that make the consciousness in question what it is. But the final stage of this process, that of interpretation, must wait for a reader. Indeed, if the master calls his text a "testament," it is precisely because he bequeaths its accumulation of contradictory stories to the reader. Meanwhile, the master, a "plaything of this farce named consciousness" (131), can only continue to make notations in the margins of this murmured sentence and wonder, as he often does, "what to do with these snippets" (39, 45, 83, 83). Pinget's master knows that he's repeating himself ("hundredth repeat" [22, 23, 38, 42, 44, 47, 77, 85, 123]), turning in circles ("turn, return, revert" [47, 49, 91, 121]), and that, master or not, he will never master the truth he seeks. Nevertheless, he still believes in the existence of this ideal form, still believes in the possibility of a totalizing statement that would permit him to capture, in a single sentence, the truth behind the sentence/image/story/myth that haunts him. Whence his dismay at the fact that "we haven't yet found a sentence . . . that would hold everything together" (117).

Again, to the extent that we can speak of mimesis in this novel we need to speak of the mimesis of a consciousness turned back upon itself, the representation of the process of inventing stories. The object to be represented in *Passacaille* is the narrative consciousness itself, not the outside world, object of consciousness. But consciousness—that is, what belongs to consciousness and not to the world, its object—cannot be named. This is a fundamental axiom of Husserlian phenomenology: consciousness is always "consciousness-of" something. It is not a substance that can be directly observed and described. How, then, might one go about representing something as intangible as the workings of a consciousness in action? Or, to pose the question more generally, how might one go about distinguishing consciousness from the objects of consciousness? Unable to offer his readers direct access to the structures that define consciousness (and, a fortiori, those of the unconscious), Pinget needs to find a literary equivalent of Husserl's *epoché*, a way to bracket content. But at this level, language—or, more precisely, the denotative function of language—begins to get in the way. Language, after all, shares the intentional structure of consciousness: just as there is no consciousness without something to be conscious of, there is no signifier without signified, no *récit* without its *histoire*, no form without content.

And this is where the variation format comes into play: the contradictions between the stories have the effect of annulling each of them as individuals, of bracketing their content. The reader, in order to make sense out of the novel, must understand this bracketing gesture, must turn away from the narrative content of the stories in order to focus on the narrative consciousness that reveals itself in the essentially contentless act of narrating. The principle of musical variation allows Pinget to create a form that is familiar enough to make his text intelligible without forcing him to rely on the *muthos*-based, content-oriented forms of the traditional novel. The initial germ of the theme sentence furnishes the point of departure for the novel and, dominating the representation with the obsessional force of a dream image, lends thematic unity to the text. Like the musical theme, it delimits a zone of exploration; it reduces the field of narrative possibilities to a manageable size, for the reader as well as the author. Conversely, the principle of variation obviates the need to choose a single narrative path, to opt for a single world. It allows a multiplicity of mental universes where logical contradiction—which, according to Pinget, is nothing more than "the simplest and most obvious form of variation" ("Robert Pinget" 150)—has its place in the novel alongside all the other procedures for literary transformation. Pinget has often insisted on the importance of contradiction in his work ("let me repeat that my work belongs to the domain of art, and that I use every artifice of language in it, among which contradiction is by no means the least" ["Robert Pinget" 150]), and it is contradiction—repetition with a negative coefficient—that provides the essential tool of the literary *epoché* by undermining the world-building tendency of traditional narrative.

MUSIC AND TEMPORALITY

Pinget characterizes his compositional technique as a form of improvisation, "automatic writing in complete awareness, that is, with immediate filtering of possibilities" ("Une interview" 554, my translation). He has always refused to use any kind of set method or system, preferring to entrust the work of variation to the spontaneous associations that occur during composition. This does not mean that Pinget is not interested in the structure of his novels but, on the contrary, that he wants their structure to reflect the process of inventing.

> [The reader must] realize that the book takes place in full view of the reader with all the doubts of the author, all his hesitations, passions, regressions, leaps forward. *Understand that we're talking about a literature opposed to that classical literature that formulated, or claimed to formulate definitively a kind of thought prepared in advance, a circumscribed situation, shored up, annotated, and ready for delivery . . .* The text that the reader has before him is that of an adventure that is taking place, that is being attempted, and not already lived and retranscribed. That's why I say that I never know what I'm going to say. I discover as I go along that I'm writing in *terra incognita*, word after word, and that I won't be able to see in its totality until the book is finished. ("Pseudo-principes" 317, my translation)

Fiction becomes a form of autobiography that is truer, paradoxically, than any attempt to set down the truth once and for all, precisely because, at least from the point of view of consciousness, it is the once and for all that falsifies. As Peter Brooks and Paul Ricoeur remind us, narrative communicates a particular kind of knowledge; it organizes experience into sequential and causal relationships, using the syntax of sequence to perform tasks that syllogistic logic cannot. But the traditional novel, with its linear, *muthos*-based forms, emphasis on denotation, and dependence on the aggregative logic of narrative concatenation, has an architectural tendency: it transforms human experience, which is fundamentally temporal in nature, into a logical, hence synchronic, edifice.[21] The *muthos*, that is, tends to objectify, to turn phenomena into objects that have a stability and permanence that they do not have in the "now" of consciousness. And if the *muthos* model has governed storytelling for thousands of years, this is because it offers a useful way for organizing the often enormous amount of information about a world that traditional narratives have tried to communicate. But when the type of knowledge sought is no longer that of making sense of the outside world of social relationships and historical events ("encompassing the complexity of existence in the modern world," in Kundera's phrase [*The Art of the Novel* 72]) but making sense out of the inner world of consciousness (where the term *event* has an entirely different meaning), the *muthos* loses its structural utility.

This brings us one step closer to understanding the necessity of the musical model in *Passacaille*. To the architectural ideal of semantic stability, *Passacaille* opposes the temporal flux of musical discourse. *Passacaille* tries to communicate a sense of the fleeting nature of thought, tries to reconstitute, in all their ephemerality, the chains of thought that flash before consciousness, only to be superseded by those that follow. This is the kind of thought that Husserl describes in terms of protension and retention, that Derrida critiques in terms of *trace* and *biffure*, and that constitutes for Pinget "un ton." In *Passacaille*, the succession of contradictory stories never simply negates those that precede because nothing is ever asserted definitively. It is not the denotational content of the statements that matters but the chains of thought exemplified by their passing. It is, I believe, this attempt to exemplify the passing of thought in its temporal dimension that provides the most profound explanation for Pinget's interest in music: *music is to consciousness in its temporal dimension what the linguistic sign is to consciousness in its intentional, synchronic dimension*. The fugitive relationships exemplified by music resemble those of consciousness in that, perceived only in time and not in space, they disappear as quickly as they are perceived, leaving only traces in the memory of the listener. It is the path of this trace, never definitive, always subject to modification, that Pinget's variations attempt to render. The theme-and-variations format provides a way to evoke the modalities of this narrating consciousness that, in search only of itself, is always ready to abandon its previous hypotheses in the knowledge that "other themes would emerge from this nervous distress" (97).

It should be clear by now how much *Passacaille* owes to the interior-monologue or stream-of-consciousness novel. Like the novels of Dujardin, Joyce, Faulkner, Woolf, and Simon, *Passacaille* constitutes an attempt to show (not tell) the mind in action, to create an effect of the passing of thought in its temporal dimension. But there is a crucial difference: unlike the interior-monologue novel, which still depends on the mimetic illusion and the world-making convention, *Passacaille* is concerned exclusively with the imaginative process. Direct perception of the outside world doesn't enter into the picture because the consciousness on display in *Passacaille* is no longer concerned with the outside world. Indeed, there is no outside world in *Passacaille*, no universe where any kind of action takes place; there is only the evolution of an idea in a consciousness, strictly identified with the stream of words on the page.

Contradiction—repetition with a negative coefficient—plays the crucial role in creating this effect, just as literal repetition, via the leitmotiv, played the crucial role in Dujardin's conception of the interior monologue. What the principle of variation brings to *Passacaille* is exactly what the leitmotiv technique brought to *Les lauriers sont coupés*: a new way to think about the ordering of narrative discourse based on repetition and variation rather than on linear, concatenational progression. It is as if Pinget and Dujardin needed music as justification for an intuition about the importance of repetition and variation. Or perhaps it is the novel in general that needs music, as a reminder that the traditional narrative forms—all based on some combination of plot, description, and argument—fail to account for critical characteristics of subjective experience. The primary utility of the traditional structures like argument and plot is in their ability to reorder thought, that is, to take brute thought and make it so that it can be communicated more efficaciously, making arguments more convincing, making the chronological, spatial, and causal ordering of facts more clear, and generally allowing discourse to work efficiently. But to the extent that plot and argument make thought content more easily communicable, they modify the status of that thought, making novels documents about the objects of thought rather than of thought itself.

The use of repetition that we find in *Les lauriers sont coupés* and *Passacaille* brings about an important modification in the referential vector of the narrative, swinging the focus of the novel away from the objects depicted and onto the consciousness that those depictions imply. The words that make up the narrative still refer to objects and events (they could hardly do otherwise), but the readers' understanding of the novel depends on their ability to subordinate the denotational content of the words to the mental processes that their ordering exemplifies. Readers are put into the role of detective: their job is to infer, from the ordering of the statements, what is going on in the narrative consciousness. This is why a novel by interior monologue can speak of the most banal events (shaving, going to the pub, etc.) and still fascinate: the perceiving mind is the primary focus of attention, not the objects perceived. Readers must actively involve themselves in the reconstruction not of a crime, not of the objects and events denoted, but of the perceiving mind. The mimetic "shock of recognition" in this type of novel has much less to do with the people, places, objects, and ideas denoted than with the order and manner in which they are noted.

I prefaced my analysis of *Passacaille* by insisting on the importance of locating the factors that make music a necessary and not simply sufficient reference. In my opinion, it is the temporality of the representation that provides the most definitive justification for the specificity of the musical intertext. As for Bergson, music serves here as a model for thought in its temporal dimension, opposed to the synchronic, spatializing dimension of the linguistic sign. No other art exists so exclusively in time, which is why Husserl, in his "The Phenomenology of Time Consciousness," uses music as the primary example of a "temporal object." This does not necessarily make Pinget's use of the musical model any less metaphorical than, say, Huxley's, but it does help to show why only music could have served as a model here. Literature is, like music and dance, a time art by definition. And narrative is that mode of literature that is most concerned with the temporal dimension of human experience. Nevertheless, few narratives are able to attain the powerful effect of passing thought that *Passacaille* achieves because in most novels the emphasis on world building and internal coherence has the effect of masking the fluid temporality of the verbal performance. But in *Passacaille* the adoption of the variation format allows the temporality of the representation to double that of the performance: the words on the page are completely identified with consciousness, with the evolution of an idea in consciousness. Thus, if, as I suggested, *Passacaille* can be understood as the search for a structure (in Lévi-Strauss's sense of the term), we must be clear about the fact that while structuralism purports to study intemporal (synchronic) structures, Pinget's novel shows that we only have access to mental structures as they appear in time. To the extent that the hypothetical Ur-myth sought by the master exists, it is a contentless myth, a process identified with the ongoing variations responsible for emptying the individual stories of their denotative value. And we must not forget the extent to which this effect of cognitive flux depends on the set of variational techniques we've examined, with contradiction playing a crucial role. It is only by replacing the aggregative, concatenational logic of plot-based narrative with the permutational, differential logic of the variation technique that Pinget is able to create a situation in which the fluidity that characterizes both thought and music supersedes the architectural tendency of the traditional plot-making impulse. Form here is, strictly speaking, identical with content because the analogical relationships between variations replace the denotata of those variations as the primary focus of the representation. This is why, despite the best efforts of the master, there can be no "sentence that would hold everything together." Without the process of continual variation that links the first and last statements of the theme sentence, it would remain inoperative, having no significance in its own right. The moment of arrival means nothing without the voyage that makes it possible.

3

Music and Autobiography (Leiris *lyrique*)

Song is the superimposition of two logical orders: the human order of language and the order of music, which, unconcerned with the semantic categories that determine the shape of linguistic propositions, functions in a way that is in a certain sense inhuman. This, at least, is how Michel Leiris describes song, as the superimposition of two logical orders, the double organization of words, and it is this understanding of song that guides him in his attempts to model his writing on musical communication. The radical transformation in the nature of linguistic communication brought about by the addition of music and the fundamental alterity of the logic that governs music are the two most striking features of Leiris's descriptions of song. Leiris may associate music with "a world outside our laws" or with the subterranean world of "Persephone" (the title of a key chapter in *Biffures*), or he may describe it as a "peace pledge" between the subject and the outside world, but in all cases he treats it as a kind of emissary from the outside, capable of mediating between the human and the inhuman, between the familiar interiority of subjective experience and the ineradicable otherness of objects and the outside world in general.

It is this ability of song to mediate between inside and outside that makes it one of the most enduring themes in Leiris's work. Leiris began his literary career under the sway of surrealism; he then made his presence felt as the author of *L'âge d'homme*, an autobiographical text that put forth the bull's horn as a symbol of the existential peril of autobiography as Leiris practiced it. But these components of Leiris's literary aesthetic quickly faded in importance. Music never did. Both in private and in his public works, Leiris consistently turned to music to explain the kind of communication he sought to establish and to justify the techniques he used. It is significant in this regard that both the first and last legible entries in his *Journal* relate to music. The first, a beautiful homage to Stravinsky from 1922, has particular importance as it focuses on music's power to mediate between the human subject and the inhuman realm of nature.

> Avec Stravinski, l'orchestre est un animal dont le coeur bat, dont les poumons respirent. Il marche, il court, il s'arrête, et son pouls s'accélère ou se ralentit suivant le rythme de ses évolutions. Peu à peu, par suggestion, nous devenons l'animal, et mentalement nous remuons, nous nous endormons ou nous faisons l'amour. Le sang afflue à notre visage, puis, brusquement, il se retire pour aller se confiner dans la paume de nos mains et la plante de nos pieds. Nous respirons difficilement, forcés que nous sommes de suivre le rythme haletant de l'orchestre. Parfois une mélodie plus précise nous rappelle des mysticismes lointains et c'est l'éveil de la bête à la conscience humaine. Et quand l'orchestre s'arrête, nous sommes étonnés de ne pas mourir par la cessation brusque de toutes nos fonctions.

> [With Stravinsky, the orchestra is an animal whose heart beats, whose lungs breathe. It walks, it runs, it stops, and its pulse speeds up or slows down according to the rhythm of its developments. Little by little, by suggestion, we become the animal, and mentally we move about, we fall asleep, or we make love. Blood flows to our face, then, suddenly, it withdraws and flows to the palms of our hands and the soles of our feet. We breathe with difficulty, forced as we are to follow the breathless rhythm of the orchestra. Sometimes a more precise melody reminds us of distant mysticisms, and we find ourselves at the dawn of human consciousness. And when the orchestra finishes, we are astonished not to have died from the brusque cessation of all our functions.] (*Journal* 27)[1]

This apparent description of Stravinsky's *Rite of Spring* places music at the threshold between animality and human consciousness, emphasizing music's extraordinary powers of suggestion. The expressive power of music as it is described here is such that it is able to take over the mental and physiological functions of listeners, enabling them to step outside of the usual limits of human experience. This is an idea that dominates much of what Leiris has to say about music, from his remarks on jazz in *L'âge d'homme* to the important preface to Gilbert Rouget's *La musique et la transe*, in which Leiris argues for an inherent link between music and ritual, to *A cor et à cri* and "Musique en texte," two of the last texts published during his lifetime. Jazz continued to play an important part in Leiris's writings on music, but it is opera that furnished the primary metaphors for his theoretical discourse on the relationship between music and literature. Opera puts in an appearance as early as *L'âge d'homme*, along with jazz, and then comes to the forefront in Leiris's four-volume autobiographical project, *La règle du jeu*, as well as in his book-length study of opera, which, unfinished at his death, was published posthumously in 1992 as *Operratiques*. Two texts, *A cor et à cri* and "Musique en texte," published in 1988 and 1985, respectively, have particular importance for the subject of this book, since it is in them that Leiris makes the most significant attempt to fully integrate his view of musical communication into a theoretical justification of his poetic practice.

One might justifiably ask why it is music that comes to play such an important role in Leiris's poetics rather than, say, painting. After all, Leiris's art world credentials are impeccable, while his understanding of music has been subject to skepticism. An active art critic, he was deeply involved in the art world not only through his writing on art and artists but also through his wife's gallery and his circle of friends, which included prominent figures like André Masson, Francis Bacon, Henri Kahnweiler, and his next-door neighbor, Pablo Picasso. Nevertheless, after *L'âge d'homme* (in which Leiris deals extensively with questions of pictorial iconography), references to painting drop out almost entirely from his autobiographical work, while music begins to take over.[2] This happens despite the fact that he had no special aptitude for music. Leiris, as he himself reminds us in *Operratiques*, was not a musician at all but "a simple amateur." Moreover, his notes for *Operratiques* make it clear that opera attracted him first and foremost as a form of theater, not as a form of musical expression. He regarded music in opera as more of an enhancement for drama and poetry—as a "vibratory space" or "sonorous space"—than as an object of study in its own right.[3]

Some clues for understanding Leiris's abiding fascination with music can be found in the opening chapters of *Biffures*, the first volume of his four-volume autobiography, *La règle du jeu*. These chapters emphasize the extent to which music had a shaping influence on Leiris's view of language during the formative years of his childhood. The difference between music and language for the young Leiris is, simply put, that between pleasure and pain: the pleasurable experiences linked to song in the early chapters of *Biffures* ("Chansons," "Habillé en cour," and "Perséphone") mark a vivid contrast with the dysphoric episodes of verbal apprenticeship recounted in chapters such as "Alphabet." Throughout these introductory chapters, the aural, sonorous, intuitive world of music appeals to the young Leiris as an enclave of mystery and freedom. Compared with the painfully slow mastery of concepts and the discipline of the written word described in "Alphabet"—"the cruel conquest of this *I*, which first had to become expert in the art of naming things" (*Scratches* 46)—music stands out as a realm of freedom and pleasure. In a sense, music occupies the place in Leiris's childhood that poetry and literature will occupy in the life of the adult, that of an affective enclave, an escape from the utilitarian servitude of work and the oh-so-reasonable reasonableness the French call "la raison raisonnante."

The affective importance of music for the young Leiris certainly helps to explain the prominence of music as a theme in *Biffures*, but what Leiris emphasizes in *Operratiques* is his theoretical interest in music: "cet amateur . . . est un écrivain et se pose donc des problèmes esthétiques que de telles réflexions—bien que portant sur un acte qui n'est pas le sien—peuvent l'aider à résoudre" [this amateur . . . is a writer who asks himself, therefore, aesthetic questions that such reflections—although not relating directly to his own art—can help him to resolve] (11). It is this theoretical interest in music that needs to be explained—and justified—if Leiris's work is to teach us anything useful about the relationship between music and the art of autobiography. I will be concerned, in the rest of this chapter, with exploring the implications of Leiris's turn to music as a poetic paradigm. But before continuing, there are three preliminary issues that need to be clarified. The first has already been mentioned.

First, Leiris has no real interest in "pure" music (i.e., nonprogrammatic instrumental music) or in the semiotic functioning of music as a distinct art in its own right. Apart from a few isolated references (the Stravinsky *Journal* entry previously mentioned, an article on Schoenberg republished in *Brisées*, a few brief references to jazz), Leiris always thinks of music as linked to a text and/or a dramatic situation. This is as true of Leiris's writings on opera as of his theoretical use of music as a model for writing. Leiris is precisely the kind of *mélomane*—uninterested in "structural" listening—criticized so often by Adorno. Leiris is interested in the effect music has on the reception of language in song, and it is this fundamentally mixed form—song—that serves as his primary model.

Second, Leiris's entire attitude toward music and song is marked by a certain confusion due to the shift in perspective of a writer thinking about literary production from the point of view of a listener. He reasons about his creative goals through the filter of his experiences listening to music. He never places himself in the role of the musical composer, even when describing his own compositional techniques. Rather, he uses music to justify and explain his own practices by describing the effects that music has on him as a listener.

Finally, Leiris uses music primarily as a rhetorical model, as a model of ideal expressive force. This means that the kind of formal analysis that enabled us to describe Pinget's novel in musical terms will be less useful for Leiris's work. Whereas Pinget uses the musical principle of theme and variations as a formal model for structuring his narrative developments, Leiris attributes no precise formal characteristics to song. Of course, any concern with expression and communication will have important consequences for the form of a work, but form is only an incidental concern of Leiris, who studies music, rather, as a model of "full communication."

In order to fully understand the role of music and song in *La règle du jeu* and the reasons for Leiris's interest in this type of extraliterary modeling, we'll need to situate music in relation to the triple imperative that governs Leiris's autobiographical project. Leiris seeks a complete mode of expression, one able to reconcile the private concerns of the individual with the public concerns of social life and the aesthetic imperatives of art. This desire is stated most explicitly in a crucial passage of *Biffures*, well worth quoting at length.

> Plus fort est mon désir de rompre toutes entraves vers une communication entière (aider autrui à vivre par ce que je lui dis, m'aider moi-même par ce partage de paroles avec autrui), plus dures deviennent aussitôt, plus desséchantes et vétilleuses les exigences auxquelles je souscris pour arriver, d'une part, à un discours capable d'émouvoir ou de séduire et, d'autre part, à une figuration de ma pensée suffisamment ressemblante en même temps que conforme à une démarche dont je veux qu'elle progresse avec toute la rigueur d'une argumentation logique. Et sans doute est-ce par-là que mon

but se révèle mouvement perpétuel, pierre philosophale ou quadra-
ture du cercle: comment puis-je, en effet, concilier le goût que j'ai
pour ce qui fait image, mon souci d'aboutir à une formulation
authentique, ma volonté enfin de me construire une sorte de système qui ait une validité selon les normes et non seulement pour
moi? Comment pourrais-je, sans que ces trois composantes mutu-
ellement se neutralisent, les faire converger en un écrit dont je voudrais follement qu'il fulgure alors que je ne puis que, bribe par bribe,
et non sans d'infinies précautions, le tirer de la grenaille de mes
fiches? (*Biffures* 292–93)

[The stronger my desire to break down all obstacles to complete
communication (and say something to someone else that helps him
to live, help myself by sharing these words with someone else), the
harder, the more finicky and paralyzing become my requirements
for achieving both a discourse capable of moving and beguiling others and a sufficiently accurate portrayal of my thought carried out
according to a rigorous, logical procedure. And no doubt this shows
that what I'm really after is perpetual motion, or the philosopher's
stone, or the squaring of the circle. How can I, in fact, reconcile the
delight I have in vivid images, my concern for achieving an authentic formulation, and my desire to build myself a sort of system that
would have some validity by general standards? How might I make
these three components converge, without their neutralizing one
another, in one work that I would foolishly love to see flash like
lightning, whereas I can only pull it, scrap by scrap, and not without infinite precautions, from the tailings of my slips of paper?]
(*Scratches* 250)

The desire for "complete communication" means that Leiris's text
must function poetically as an aesthetic object ("a discourse capable of
moving and beguiling others," with "vivid images") while fulfilling its
double function as an authentic document of the self ("a sufficiently accurate portrayal of my thought," "an authentic formulation") and an
objectively valid system (a system "that would have some validity by general standards" and would be "carried out according to a rigorous, logical
procedure"). These criteria for "complete communication" receive many
different formulations throughout Leiris's autobiographical work but always involve the requirement that this communication be able to recon-

cile self-expression with social utility and objectively verifiable standards of truth and beauty.[4] Caught in the pull of two equally attractive but contradictory idealisms (the narcissistic, aristocratic ideal of *otium* and self-contemplation and the political, ethical ideal of civic utility and full participation in the life of the community), Leiris spends his entire literary career trying to forge a style capable of reconciling them poetically, to mediate between the inward movement of self-contemplation and the outward movement toward the community. This tension between the public and private, summed up by Gérard Genette in terms of the ancient debate between Cratylus and Hermogenes and by Michel Beaujour as a conflict between the desire for self-expression and the inescapability of the public determinations of rhetoric, controls the various antinomies that traverse Leiris's work: free play and functionality, self and community, subjectivity and objectivity.[5]

Opera and song play a central role in Leiris's attempts to make this tension productive by providing him with the model of an art that seems to overcome the apparent incompatibility of self-expression, social responsibility, and beauty. Song seems to Leiris to resolve a whole series of conflicts implied by the tension between the public, private, and aesthetic spheres, and so he repeatedly formulates his desire to achieve the goal of full communication in terms of a metaphor with song.

> Mais quelles montagnes à remuer pour que, éloigné tout autant de la bouche hermétiquement cousue (reine du quant-à-soi) que de celle qui dévide intarissablement son monologue, j'en arrive à formuler un chant qui fasse son chemin hors de moi et soit comme ces airs dont furent accompagnées certaines minutes de ma vie que j'estimai cruciales! (*Biffures* 291–92)

> [But what mountains have to be moved if I, who am just as unfamiliar with a mouth that is hermetically sealed (supreme dignity) as with a mouth that pours forth its monologue and never runs dry, am to succeed in composing a song that may find its way out of me and resemble those tunes that accompanied the moments of my life that I believe were crucial.] (*Scratches* 249)

Leiris defines *chant* as an attempt to affirm individuality in the public sphere without falling into the full but uninviting *quant-à-soi* of hermeticism or the meaninglessness of endless monologue, an attempt to resolve the inherent conflict between the desire for a purely private mode of expression and the need for a public language.[6] The striving toward song requires a monumental effort to imbue words with the pneumatic force of melody, enabling discourse to make its way out into the world and be understood.

Leiris's descriptions of song emphasize his belief that the addition of music to language enables song to make up for the qualitative lack that characterizes written language. Language, on its own, is "incapable . . . de nous conduire jusqu'à nos derniers recoins" [incapable . . . of taking us to our remotest recesses] ("Musique en texte" 113–14). It cannot provide access to thought in its plenitude. In song, music complements the denotational function of the linguistic message with its more fully developed exemplificational and expressive capabilities. This is a familiar view of song's place in the arts and one that may help to explain the apparent universality of song throughout history and across cultures. Nicolas Ruwet, for example, formulates this view of song's function in terms that correspond well to Leiris's.

> "Language is truer," Hegel liked to say, but language separates, isolates, displaces, and in the end I always want something other than what I say. "Music expresses pure interiority," says Boris de Schloezer, but it is unable to name. One can easily see then what is so seductive about an enterprise that, in combining the two in an intimate fusion, through the intermediary of their shared medium, voice, attempts to give the illusion that the lack at the heart of one will be compensated by the other, and vice versa. ("Fonction de la parole dans la musique vocale," *Langage, musique, poésie* 68)

Music and language complete each other in song, enabling the words to communicate at a deeper level. How else, Leiris asks, to explain the affective force of the often mediocre texts used in opera arias? Hesitating to use a nebulous term like *indicible* ("qui ne suggère l'infini que par sa vacuité même" [which only suggests infinity by its very vacuity]) to describe musical communication, Leiris attempts to formulate a description of the exemplificational function of music: "la chose à dire est expressément dite, mais l'est par la Musique avec les sons pénétrants—qu'aucune entente seconde n'émousse—de son langage à elle" [the thing to be said is said explicitly, but by the music with the penetrating sounds—undisturbed by any secondary understanding—of its own language] ("Musique en texte" 113–14). This penetrative, exemplificational power of music allows it to fill up the gap between language and thought; this is music's role: "combler la carence du langage" [to make up for the shortcomings of language]. But how does one go about integrating this supplemental function of music into a written text? It is not yet clear what, if anything, *chant* as a form of writing might involve or what it could share with song in the strict sense. Clarifying this point will be the first task of analysis.

Leiris relates his own literary practice to music in two distinct ways. On the one hand, he understands music as something that is fundamentally opposed to language, that has a kind of metaphysical purity that allows it to escape from the prosaic limitations of linguistic communication; on the other hand, music is sometimes described as a supplement to language, a way to make speech more expressive. The polarity between these two conceptions of music becomes clear in two of Leiris's latest texts—*A cor et à cri* (1988) and the piece in *Langage tangage* titled "Musique en texte et Musique anti-texte" (1985). These texts provide an excellent introduction to the study of music in Leiris's work because they show Leiris attempting for the first time to untangle the sometimes confusing web of musical metaphors that run through *La règle du jeu*. Although published within three years of each other (a relatively short time given Leiris's habitual rhythm of publication), they describe the relationship between music and literature in two very different, if not contradictory, ways: "Musique en texte" opposes music and normal language, using music as the model of a "language of the other world," while *A cor et à cri* treats music as a supplement to language, as an elusive poetic element that, when united with words, results in the superior form of communication Leiris names *chant*. If these approaches appear contradictory, it is because they work on two entirely different levels. In both cases music acts as an expressive model for literature, but in "Musique en texte," music represents a set of compositional techniques (tropes), whereas in *A cor et à cri*, music helps Leiris to give his own formulation of the expressive goal to which all rhetorics aspire: that of maximizing language's potential as a form of power.

MUSIC AND/ANTI TEXT

"Musique en texte et Musique anti-texte," although written at the very end of Leiris's career, must be considered in relation to one of his earliest poetic texts, *Glossaire: J'y serre mes gloses*. This poetic "glossary" was organized alphabetically, like a dictionary. It consisted of a series of key words, each of which was "defined" by a short poetic text that worked according to the principle of paronomasia, by embroidering a series of playful puns around the key word. "Musique en texte" is, among other things, an attempt to justify the validity of this technique, which might, Leiris fears, be interpreted as a merely frivolous exercise. His defense of the technique depends in large part on an appeal to music. Leiris hopes that by stressing the *Glossaire*'s affinity with music, an art that manipulates pure sound in demonstrably significant ways, he will be able to justify his lifelong fascination with the palpable material of language. The *Glossaire*, Leiris asserts, is a product of his desire to discover ways of manipulating language that are unrestrained by the limiting conventions of ordinary discourse, and able, therefore, to bypass the normal communicative goals of literature altogether in order to found an entirely different order of language.

Leiris's earlier prefaces to the *Glossaire* had tried to defend this practice without really justifying it; they sought to obtain the adherence of the reader by using such combative tactics as declaring that standard usage is nothing more than "une monstrueuse aberration" [a monstrous aberration] and affirming in quasi-mystical fashion the oracular power of such techniques, where "le langage se transform en oracle . . . pour nous guider dans la Babel de notre esprit" [language becomes an oracle . . . so as to guide us in the Babel of our mind] (*Brisées* 11, 12).

"Musique en texte" instead uses the comparison with music as a strategy for asserting the seriousness of the apparently frivolous practice of punning and wordplay. In the process, it gives an autobiographical account of the form Leiris's life and work have taken, opening up a theoretical reformulation of Leiris's entire literary project in terms of music. Indeed, this essay can be seen as a retrospective distillation of Leiris's oeuvre: it presents, in compact form, not only a fairly complete sampling of the techniques and themes used throughout his career, with all that is most intriguing (and at times irritating) about them, but also a broad analysis of what he perceives to be the successful and unsuccessful elements of his work, all under the controlling musical metaphor. We find Leiris at the end of his career and willing to distance himself from, perhaps even renounce, the artistic credo of some of his earlier work; thus he opens with a gesture of Faustian regret: "I'll burn my books." This strategy engenders a back and forth movement between the exposition of beliefs and justifications, on the one hand, and attempts to give a critical analysis of what these beliefs are founded on, on the other. The title of this little "mémoire" as well as Leiris's decision to treat his text "allègrement... comme une pièce de musique" [light-heartedly... like a piece of music] (back-cover matter) make it clear from the outset that Leiris intends to explore the limits as well as the utility of the music-text metaphor. This back and forth movement, which is so characteristic of Leiris's work, is already present in the work's full title, "Musique en texte et Musique anti-texte."[7] The anagrammatic progression from "en texte" to "anti-texte" first suggests the identification of music and text before immediately opposing the two terms antonymically (*anti*-text), giving all the while an inaugural example of the form of verbal play that Leiris will try to define as musical.

Leiris's first line of defense has a distinctly aestheticizing tendency. He starts by noticing that music depends on pattern rather than denotation for its meaning and sees this as a liberation from the utilitarian obligations of discursive communication. According to Leiris, music's status as patterned sound takes it out of the realm of the useful and places it necessarily in the aesthetic realm of art for art's sake. Thus music offers to literature the model of an art that can escape from language's utilitarian servitude to the representational function of language, that "besogne asservissante" [servile chore] (135) of ordinary language. In fact, Leiris asserts, if there is a danger, it is in taking poetry out of the domain of the purely aesthetic, "à l'affubler d'un vêtement d'utilité . . . alors qu'elle devrait être traitée . . . en beauté si ensorcelante qu'elle peut entrer partout sans avoir à justifier sa présence" [dressing it up in the clothes of utility . . . when it should be treated . . . as a beauty so entrancing that it can enter everywhere without having to justify its presence] (158). Poetry must stay free of any utilitarian or therapeutic function: "Peu importe même qu'elle ait un sens autre que la joie particulière qu'elle nous dispense . . . inutile comme la beauté, elle déroge et perd de son pouvoir de subjuguer si, par force, elle est pliée à un métier, fût-il le plus honorable" [It is of no importance that it even have a sense other than the particular joy it can dispense to us . . . as useless as beauty itself, it breaks with and loses its ability to subjugate if, by force, it is bent to a trade, no matter how honorable] (159–60).

Leiris then uses this aesthetic argument as a basis for a defense of the *Glossaire* in metaphysical terms by asserting that music's freedom from the semantic burden of language endows it with a kind purity, an absolute status that ordinary language does not have. Music operates on a different level from that of our day-to-day concerns and real-world preoccupations, and Leiris wants his literary language to operate on this absolute level, which he locates alternatively above ("au-delà") or below ("en-deçà") normal uses of language. The language of the *Glossaire* project gets several different types of "absolute" predicates in "Musique en texte": "langue de la mort" [language of death] (144), "langue d'ailleurs" [language from beyond] (176), "pépiement émanant d'une autre sphère" [chirping from another sphere] (184), "sorte de langage des oiseaux et donc langage d'innocents" [a kind of language of birds and therefore of innocents] (184), and so forth. It is also linked to the cratylic idealism of "une langue moins arbitraire, en connexion authentique avec les choses" [a less arbitrary language, having an authentic connection to things] (178) and is repeatedly described in terms of death: Leiris argues that his project demands a kind of total absorption that is variously understood as a form of protection against, a diversion from, or a cathartic incorporation of the metaphysical preoccupation with death.

These first two arguments—aesthetic and metaphysical—work by opposing music to ordinary language. The mode of poetry used in the *Glossaire*, as a "langue d'ailleurs," is musical precisely to the extent that it escapes the functions assigned to words in normal discourse. Leiris returns over and over to these arguments in "Musique en texte." They attract him because they enable him to argue that although the particular form of poetry practiced in the *Glossaire* may appear frivolous, it participates in fact in the kind of serious mission attributed to music by such thinkers as Pythagoras and Schopenhauer.

But Leiris also mounts an expressive justification of the *Glossaire* that amounts, in essence, to a rhetorical defense of literature, where it is understood above all as a communicative art, a form of power. This argument flies in the face of the first two arguments, but Leiris, upon reflection, realizes that the kinds of music he actually likes all have a primarily expressive, affective function. And this, ultimately, is the effect he seeks in his writing. The disadvantage of this rhetorical version of the expressivist argument for Leiris is that it has none of the absoluteness of the first two. Once it is introduced into "Musique en texte," Leiris's problem becomes that of differentiating his "musical" techniques from the bundle of conventional ornaments associated with the more traditional forms of rhetoric that Leiris abhors. It takes Leiris out of the realm of the absoluteness of "pure" music and forces him to acknowledge the mixed status of poetic language—somewhere between pure play and ordinary, utilitarian discourse. The introduction of the expressive argument into "Musique en texte," then, poses problems for Leiris because it seems to contradict his other arguments. But this is also the domain of *La règle du jeu* and of the great majority of Leiris's texts. Without the rhetorical argument, Leiris cannot adequately account for the characteristics of his autobiographical work. It is not until three years later, with *A cor et à cri*, that Leiris fully resolves this apparent contradiction. There communication becomes the primary concern, and the overarching metaphor is song, with music acting as a supplement to language, helping it to communicate better. In this sense, *A cor et à cri* can be read as a complement to "Musique en texte," as the logical conclusion of an argument left dangling at the end of "Musique en texte."

FROM "MUSIC" TO *CHANT*

A cor et à cri is concerned not with justifying a technique, as in "Musique en texte," but with defining a mode of communication. Song in *A cor et à cri* does not constitute a practical model for composition or a set of techniques that can be easily defined and applied to writing; it is understood instead as the ideal point to which poetry and the poetic aspire. *Chant*, then, represents for Leiris not a method but an objective, a rhetorical goal.

The difference in approach between "Musique en texte" and *A cor et à cri* is crucial and can be summed up in two words: music and *chant*. Leiris restricts the meaning of the term *music* to the prosodic features of language; the term *music* and its derivatives (musical, etc.) as well as related terms like *melody* always refer to the prosodic level of language, "les jeux phoniques tels qu'allitérations et autres rappels de sons en échos auxquels je m'adonne volontiers ici" [the phonic games such as alliterations and other repetitions and echoes of sounds to which I willingly devote myself here] ("Musique en texte" 115–16).

The music/prosody analogy is legitimate to the extent that the object of prosody is language considered as sound. Prosody governs the musical elements, strictly speaking, of spoken language (duration, intensity, pitch, timbre) as well as the organization of vocal output into properly linguistic and literary structures (rhyme, periodic structures, etc.). The latter are, in this sense, only special cases of the former. Like a sequence of musical notes, any spoken utterance can be evaluated as a series of sounds with all the characteristics of song. But in normal speech, most of the prosodic properties of language are considered secondary to semantic concerns. Moreover, among the written genres, any concern with prosody is necessarily limited to those rhythmic and phonological characteristics of words that can be transcribed. Poets who write down their words abdicate all control over tempo, pitch, and volume, with pitch, of course, being the most spectacularly neglected prosodic element of speech and, a fortiori, writing. All of the prosodic factors of music could, of course, be exploited and ultimately codified as a source of poetic effects, but this always implies a move away from writing and language and toward performance and actual music. Thus prosodic factors are most systematically exploited in the theater and in "theatrical" literary institutions like the poetry reading. But this is not Leiris's intention—his are eminently written texts.

Strictly speaking, then, Leiris's use of the term *music* depends on an overextension of the notion of prosody. This may seem like a quibbling remark, but it is important to understand Leiris's tendency to conflate the written and the spoken if we are to understand the importance of the distinction he makes between *chant* and music. Whenever Leiris speaks about the musicality or melody of a formulation, he means a certain kind of prosodic profile, namely, hammering rhythms and alliterative repetition. For evidence of the extent to which Leiris accepts the conflation of music and prosody, we need only refer to the frequency with which he takes the distinction for granted. In *Biffures*, for example, Leiris tells us that the expression "balancier de ma vie" is able to insinuate itself into his memory, even though it is only a "bout de phrase privé de tout attrait *mélodique*" (256) [a fragment of a phrase without any *melodic* attraction] (*Scratches* 218). Similarly, Leiris writes in "Musique en texte" of "ce procédé classique de la rime, qui joue sa musique" [this classical procedure of rhyme, which plays its music], describes end-stopped poetry as "point tant affaire de sens ou de mélodie que de structure matérielle du texte" [not so much a matter of sense or of melody as of the material (i.e., visual) structure of the text], and informs us that, although interested in the musical possibilities of poetry, "pas plus que je n'ai écrit de livrets d'opéra . . . je ne me suis exprimé dans la forme quasi musicale qu'est le vers régulier" [I haven't expressed myself in the quasi-musical form of regular verse . . . any more than I have written opera libretti] (90). In each case, music is used as a synonym of prosodic effect, as in the following untranslatable passage from "Musique en texte," one of the many whose task is to exemplify textually its meaning: "la mélodie malicieusement mystérieuse et mélancolieusement moutonneuse" (84). More generally, Leiris accepts the conflation of the written signifier with its sonorous counterpart, often making passing remarks like "mon ouïe intérieure—ou ma vision" [my inner ear—or my vision] (122), "à base phonétique et donc sonore" [phonetic and thus sonorous] (124), and so forth. For Leiris, the printed text is always actualized, always performed, always sonorous as well as visual, always *heard* as well as *understood*.

His definitions of *chant* work differently. Indeed, what is most curious about Leiris's use of the term *music* is that he completely isolates it from his definition of *chant*. If music and melody are synonyms of prosody, short-hand stand-ins for the small number of prosodic effects that can be integrated into the written text, then one might expect Leiris's notion of "song" to build directly on this identification, to use these definitions of melody and music as part of his definition of song. After all, in normal usage, song is defined by its superimposition of language and music. For Leiris's definition of the term *chant*, however, the opposite is the case. One of the primary characteristics of *chant*, as Leiris defines it, is precisely that it has nothing to do with music: "Pas de méprise: quand je dis 'chanter,' je ne veux nullement dire s'exprimer en se pliant à une musique comme dans le vers ou dans la phrase harmonieusement agencée" [Make no mistake about it: when I speak of "singing," I do not at all mean to speak of expressing oneself melodiously, as in verse or a harmoniously composed sentence] (*A cor et à cri* 104). *Chant* and "music" operate on different levels; the "vocality" of *chant* is "une affaire de ton plus que de musique au sens strict" [a matter of tone more than of music in the strict sense] (115–16). This is a constant of Leiris's descriptions of *chant*. Left implicit throughout *La règle du jeu*, this distinction is clearly articulated throughout *A cor et à cri*, giving rise to statements about sentences "*sans mélodie* particulière, mais que pourtant je garde en mémoire comme un *chant*" [with no particular *melody*, but which remain in my memory like a *song*] (139, emphasis added).

Chant, then, unlike music, has no direct relationship to the prosodic characteristics of language. It does originate in the same type of considerations that determine Leiris's use of "music" as a synonym for prosody, but they are transferred onto another level, that of thought. This transfer takes the form of a simple metaphor, banal in appearance, but crucial for his definition of *chant*. Leiris seeks a tone "pénétrant comme certaines musiques, mais musical seulement par métaphore puisqu'il échappe par nature aux notations précises de rythme et de mélodie et se fait entendre sur le plan de l'intellect plutôt que sur celui de l'ouïe" [penetrating like some musical refrains, but musical only metaphorically since it is by nature resistant to the precise notations of rhythm and melody and makes itself heard in the domain of the intellect rather than in that of hearing] ("Musique en texte" 95). This statement depends on a proportional relationship, with voice and hearing on one level and writing and intellect on another: *chant* is to the intellect what song is to voice. Just as song emphasizes elements of voice that are usually deemphasized in normal spoken discourse, as supplemental to the basic task of communicating a message, Leiris seeks a form of writing able to communicate elements of thought that are usually considered to be superfluous in normal discourse. In other words, *chant* is an attempt to create an art of the prosodic qualities of thought. Or, to reframe the initial proportion more clearly, if song is speech supplemented by music, then *chant* is to be a form of writing supplemented by a *prosody of thought*.

Throughout "Musique en texte" and *A cor et à cri* Leiris writes about *chant* as a way of introducing the marks of a mental equivalent of vocality into his writing.

> *Parler d'une voix qui*, sans appareil pesant, donne à entendre ce qu'elle veut qu'on entende et, par ses inflexions plutôt que par les arguments mis en avant, amène à croire aux vérités humaines—nécessairement personnelles—qu'elle énonce, comme si ma lignée littéraire . . . avait été . . . de *vivifier l'écrit en quelque sorte par son timbre*, autrement dit de rendre patent que *ces pages que nos yeux lisent sont sous-tendues par une voix*, en l'occurrence la mienne qui

non seulement conte volontiers ma vie mais est intrinsèquement comme ma vie même.

[*To speak with a voice that*, without any cumbersome apparatus, makes heard exactly what it wants heard and, by its inflections rather than by the arguments put forth, leads to a belief in the human truths—necessarily personal—that it enunciates, as if my literary lineage . . . had been . . . *to vivify the written word, so to speak, through its timbre*, that is, to make it clear that *the pages in front of our eyes are supported by a voice*, more specifically, my voice, which is not only willing to tell the story of my life but is intrinsically like my life itself.] ("Musique en texte" 115, emphasis added)

The shift from the spoken to the written to the cognitive in this passage is spectacular in its off-handedness; Leiris is working here in a metaphorical register that allows him to pass from one level to the next without hesitation, to simply *assume* the passage from speech to writing to thought.

A cor et à cri takes the form of an argument designed to justify this privileged mode of communication that Leiris calls *chant*. A series of short texts grouped thematically into three large sections ("Crier," "Parler," and "Chanter"), *A cor et à cri* uses the first two notions ("crying out" and "speaking") to clarify and exalt the third, which is that to which Leiris's writing aspires. The *cri* is quickly dispensed with, and most of the text focuses on a binary opposition between *chant* and speech (*parler*), where *chant* is defined by opposition to speech. (It should go without saying that despite the implied orality of the terms *chanter* and *parler*, Leiris remains squarely in the realm of the written.) The *parler/chanter* opposition gives a succession of equivalent antinomies: inert/animate, silent/perceptible, cold/hot, dead/alive.

Ecriture *morte* (qui traduit rétrospectivement la pensée) et écriture *vivante* (qui dans une grande mesure au moins la fabrique) seraient également des expressions adéquates pour faire saisir ce qu'ici je veux faire saisir et qui touche à l'essence même de ce métier par lequel, moins égoïstement centré sur ce qui se passe en moi, je ne me laisserais sans doute pas à tel point dévorer.

[*Dead* writing (which translates thought retrospectively) and *live* writing (which, to a great extent at least, produces it) would also be adequate expressions for getting across what I want to get across here and that touches upon the very essence of this vocation, which, had I been less selfishly centered on what is going on inside of myself, I would not have let devour me to such an extent.] (Leiris, *A cor et à cri* 107)

All of these oppositions have in common the radical thought and the devaluation of the representation of thought ("which translates thought retrospectively") in favor of the production of thought ("which, to a great extent at least, produces it"). The passage from speech to song is that from the inert to the animate, from the retrospective to the present: the goal of *chant* is the *enlivenement* of ideas.

> La plus grande part de l'effort d'un écrivain tant qu'il est animé par un souffle suffisant ne doit-elle pas, au contraire, tendre par des moyens obliques voire paradoxaux à vivifier l'idée—peu importe laquelle—qu'il veut faire partager ou qui lui est ce qu'au peintre est le motif?

> [The greatest part of the effort of a writer, as long as he is sufficiently inspired, shouldn't it be rather to tend by indirect or even paradoxical means to vivify the idea—no matter which one—that he wants to share or which is to him what the motif is to the painter?] (*A cor et à cri* 174)

The objective of "vivifying the idea" is linked to the active appropriation of the meaning of words by the poet. Words, in *chant*, generate ideas rather than merely translating them (*A cor et à cri* 112); they exceed the field of their dictionary definitions and make use of the relationships suggested by the form of words: "ce serait grâce à un élargissement de leur *champ* qu'il y aurait passage des mots au *chant*" [it would be due to an expansion of their *field* (*champ*) that there would be a passage from mere words to *chant*] (112). *Chant* works in the domain of connotation and intimate communication, not that of "la musique du vers." In this sense, it is closely related to the objectives of symbolism. It is clear, for example, what the ideal of an "échange de propos arachnéens au cours duquel presque rien n'est dit et presque tout discrètement suggéré" [arachnean exchange where almost nothing is said and almost everything is discretely suggested] ("Musique en texte" 174) owes to the Mallarméan ideal of suggestiveness, which is also linked to song by Mallarmé: "La contemplation des objets, l'image s'envolant des rêveries suscitées par eux, sont le

chant . . . Nommer un objet, c'est supprimer les trois quarts de la jouis-
sance du poème qui est faite du bonheur de deviner peu à peu; le *sug-
gérer,* voilà le rêve" [The contemplation of objects, the image taking off
from the reveries inspired by them, constitute *song . . .* To name an object,
that would be to eliminate three quarters of the ecstasy of the poem,
which comes from the pleasure of sensing little by little; *to suggest* it, that
is the dream] (*Oeuvres complètes* 869). But for Leiris, there can be no
question of adopting the dense, hermetic style of Mallarmé. Leiris, always
hesitating between Cratylus and Hermogenes, refuses to sacrifice the
rhetorical goal of communicability to those of personal vision and transcendent meaning.[8]

Thus *chant* is described as the least public form of writing. The goal of
chant is to move the reader, to communicate deeply rather than according
to the rules of reason. Metaphors of movement, depth, penetration, and
resonance appear repeatedly in Leiris's writing, along with a constant
disparagement of discursive logic:

> Si l'on chante, cela tend à toucher certaines fibres de certaines per-
> sonnes, à l'échelon le moins public . . . Lorsqu'on chante on vise à
> *émouvoir* (communiquer *en profondeur*) et ce n'est plus à la raison
> que revient la part du lion . . . je veux dire parler d'une voix plus
> *pénétrante* et meilleure *éveilleuse d'échos* que celle dont on use dans
> la conversation.
>
> [If one sings, it tends to touch certain people in certain ways, at the
> least public of levels . . . When one sings one seeks *to move* the
> audience (to communicate *deeply*), and it is no longer to reason that
> the lion's share goes . . . what I mean is to speak with a more
> *penetrating* voice and one that is better at *awakening echoes* than the
> one used in ordinary conversation.] (*A cor et à cri* 104, emphasis
> added)

Singing, then, means speaking (in writing), but speaking with a more
penetrating voice, a voice that can awaken echoes in the listener.

We still have no hint, of course, as to what this mode of writing might
have to do with actual music. Rather, Leiris borrows from the conventional set of commonplaces about music in order to explain the metaphorical usefulness of song within the autobiographical project: song,
understood by Leiris as *the* art of subjectivity and interiority, is linked to a

whole series of clichés and commonplaces of good, powerful communication like the acoustic metaphor of sympathetic vibrations and resonance: "chercher à être entendu de partenaires privilégiés qui vibreront à l'unisson ou plutôt de ce qui, chez ces partenaires, est susceptible de vibrer avec vous" [seeking to be understood by privileged partners who will vibrate in unison with you—or, rather, by that which in these partners is capable of vibrating with you] (*A cor et à cri* 103). In fact, Leiris doesn't restrict the meaning of *chant* to literature any more than to music. Leiris notes with satisfaction that the verb *chanter* also has a whole series of supplemental associations—"un peintre peut faire chanter ses couleurs" [a painter can make his colors sing] (103)—that have the sense of emphasizing, making things *stand out*, making them take on greater relief or vividness.

To reiterate: there is no attempt to link *chant* with actual song in *A cor et à cri*, and Leiris does not seek to link *chant* with the metaphorical music of rhyme, alliteration, assonance, and so forth. What, then, are the concrete characteristics of *chant,* and what differentiates it from other kinds of writing? Presumably, it should be possible to answer the question of what *chant,* as a form of writing, looks like and what makes it so powerful. Pressed to answer this question, Leiris admits that his definition of *chant* boils down to a question of style. But to the extent that he considers particular stylistic traits, it is only to refuse them. He accepts, as we saw, the conventional equation of poetic prosody and music, but he warns against confusing *chant* with the more general notion of "polished style":

> Observer des tabous de langage, procéder par périphrases ou euphémismes et, d'une manière générale, soigner son expression, lui donner toute l'efficience et l'élégance possibles (tendre vers le plus concis et le plus clair, varier le vocabulaire et les tournures, satisfaire à l'euphonie), *ce n'est pas encore chanter.*

> [Observing the rules and regulations of language, proceeding by periphrasis or euphemism, and, more generally, perfecting one's expression by giving it all the efficiency and elegance possible (tending toward the greatest concision and clarity, varying one's vocabulary and turns of phrase, showing a concern with euphony), *that is not yet singing.*] (*A cor et à cri* 106, emphasis added)

Good style is not enough. Neither, however, is the transgression of stylistic conventions. Leiris is not willing, as Joyce was, to tamper with the morphological structure of words or, like Faulkner, Simon, or Beckett, to violate the syntactic norms of sentence structure. And, unlike Céline or Queneau, Leiris does not look outside of the standard vocabulary for his words. Leiris's sentences, although their length and complexity often push his readers to their limits, never violate the requirements of French grammar. And his vocabulary, although vast, is quite conventional: even neologisms are quickly recuperated into the texture of the surrounding conventional French (see the discussion of words like *portel* and *para-nroizeuses*, below).

Once again, we see Leiris hesitating between the public and the private: neither hermeticism nor clarity, neither stylistic transgression nor elegance constitutes *chant*. So what's left? Leiris seems unwilling (or unable) to tell us. He does, however, give us hints in the form of examples. The series of self-contained texts that make up *A cor et à cri* continually reiterate the movement through the tripartite hierarchy from *cri* to *parole* to *chant*, as if to build up momentum and exemplify the movement they are trying to describe. Consider the following example, which recalls the pseudo-dictionary definitions of Leiris's *Glossaire: J'y serre mes gloses* in more than one way:

> Crier: trouer le calme plat.
> Parler: tresser un lien.
> Chanter: proférant, phrasant, psalmodiant, balbutiant, faire taire ce qui journellement vous fait mal et qui, sur le moment, sera tantôt écarté, tantôt creusé et mué en source d'enivrement.

> [To cry out: piercing the dead calm.
> To speak: weaving a link.
> To sing: proffering, phrasing, psalming, babbling, quieting that which troubles you from day to day and which, for the moment, will be either moved aside or explored and turned into a source of intoxication.] (104)

The distinction between *chanter* and *crier-parler* is clear here. After the terseness of the first two definitions, the length of the *chanter* definition is striking, as are its emphatic prosodic patterns. Made up of a series of short phrases separated by commas, marked by the presence of four gerunds in a row, and distinguished by the massive presence of assonance (no less than twelve *en* sounds and eight *é* sounds), this sentence creates a sense of strong rhythmic movement that supports the suspensive grammatical structure and helps to drive toward the end.

This example clearly links *chant* with the prosodic values of written elocution, that is, in Leiris's terminology, music. As I've already pointed out, however, Leiris insists on distinguishing the musical values of prosody from those of *chant*. *Chant* is to be a question of mental prosody. How, then, can the emphatic prosodic structure of sentences like this be considered to relate to the kind of mental prosody he refers to throughout *A cor et à cri*? Another example will help to answer this question. This time we'll focus on the relationship between the prosodico-grammatical construction of the sentence and the semantic structure of the utterance. It is the relationship between these two levels of meaning, syntactic and semantic, that reveals the specificity of Leirisian *chant*.

> Vouloir déterminer de quelle manière, l'inerte s'animant et les mots prenant apparemment leur libre essor, on passe, lorsqu'on écrit, du parler au chanter, quand ce n'est de la nullité du silence à quelque chose qui d'emblée se révèle sensible comme un chant, est—je gage—aussi follement naïf que le désir que, complices, nous eûmes jadis l'un de mes deux frères et moi de saisir l'instant précis où, couchés le soir dans nos lits, nous passions de la veille au sommeil, chute dans le noir dont au réveil on sait qu'elle a eu lieu mais sans jamais pouvoir connaître, tant la conscience était embuée, la façon dont le pas a été franchi.

> [To want to determine in what manner, the inert taking life and words clearly taking full flight, one passes, when one writes, from the spoken to the sung, when it isn't just from the nullity of silence to something that immediately reveals itself to be sensitive like a song, is—I wager—as insanely naive as the desire that, conspiratorially, we had ages ago one of my two brothers and I of seizing the precise instant at which, lying at night in our beds, we would pass from the waking state to sleep, a fall in the dark that upon waking one knows took place but without ever being able to determine, thanks to the clouding of consciousness, the manner in which the line had been traversed.] (*A cor et à cri* 111–12)

If we distinguish between the logically essential clauses and the restrictive or explanatory clauses of this sentence, a clear rhythm appears: a regular alternation between the elements of the main clause and the subordinate clauses that are distributed throughout the sentence. This alternation between elements of the main proposition and the grammatically inessential descriptive clauses manifests itself vocally. Whether reading silently or out loud, readers of this sentence will find themselves obligated to differentiate between the subordinate clauses and the main clauses through an actual (if reading out loud) or virtual (if reading silently) combination of pitch, volume, and tempo. In my reading, for example, pitch and volume are slightly lower for the subordinate clauses, and the tempo is a bit more rapid: there is a tendency to rush through the subordinate clauses in order to get back to the main proposition. This reading could be represented graphically like this:

Vouloir déterminer de quelle manière,
>   *l'inerte s'animant et les mots prenant apparemment*
>   *leur libre essor,*

on passe,
>   *lorsqu'on écrit,*

du parler au chanter,
>   *quand ce n'est de la nullité du silence à quelque*
>   *chose qui d'emblée se révèle sensible comme un chant,*

est
>   *—je gage—*

aussi follement naïf que le désir que,
>   *complices,*

nous eûmes
>   *jadis l'un de mes deux frères et moi*

de saisir l'instant précis où,
>   *couchés le soir dans nos lits,*

nous passions de la veille au sommeil,
>   *chute dans le noir dont*
>   au réveil
>   *on sait qu'elle a eu lieu mais sans jamais pouvoir*
>   *connaître,*
>   tant la conscience était embuée,
>   *la façon dont le pas a été franchi.*

This passage offers a clear example of *chant* as the superimposition of two logical orders. The forward-moving linearity of the main proposition is retarded by the insistence of the subordinate clauses, which are themselves structured by a complex network of internal rhymes and assonances. This intertwining of the strands of the main proposition and the subordinate clauses is further complicated by the clausula (beginning with "chute dans le noir"), which has its own set of subordinates, thereby creating a three-tiered semantic hierarchy. The logical back and forth movement between the main and subordinate clauses determines the rhythmic and vocalic patterns of the sentence, but the semantic import of this type of proposition is in turn conditioned by the syntactic relationships between the words that make up the utterance. It is this complex interplay between, on the one hand, the rhythmic, cyclical logic of prosodic and syntactical patterning, and, on the other, the forward-moving, semantically motivated logic of the proposition that Leiris calls *chant*: "Quand . . . cela chante, la source n'en est pas un mot . . . mais un groupe de mots qui s'appuient les uns sur les autres et, des plus élémentaires s'il se trouve, agissent par leur rapport et non comme si chacun d'entre eux faisait cavalier seul" [When . . . song emerges, the source is not a word . . . but a group of words that depend on each other and, be they of the most elementary sort, act through the relationship between them rather than as if each one of them rode solo] (*A cor et à cri* 112). The choice of words and their order on the page govern our access to the thoughts to be communicated. Leiris's goal is to use the former to accentuate the latter.

Although Leiris refuses to acknowledge using the devices of traditional rhetoric (tropes, etc.), his sentence structure seems close to that of the periodic structure recommended by Protagoras and Cicero. This is especially true of *A cor et à cri*, in which Leiris abandons the complex patterns of large-scale *tissage* that characterize *La règle du jeu* and the euphuistic excesses of texts like "Musique en texte." If, in fact, we can take the sentences studied here as examples of what Leiris means by *chant*, it would seem that this term is closely related to the very rhetoric Leiris refuses to accept. As Beaujour argues, Leiris's ignorance of (or unwillingness to acknowledge) the art of rhetoric does not keep him from using its principles. In this case, *chant* seems to designate the same kind of periodic structure Cicero recommends for the "high" style.

We must keep in mind, however, the special place that *A cor et à cri* and the other "late" autobiographical texts (*Frêle bruit, Le ruban au cou d'Olympia*) occupy with respect to Leiris's autobiographical project as it had originally been conceived in *La règle du jeu*. Beginning with *Fibrilles*, Leiris seems to be overwhelmed by the growing complexity of the material he has to work with; he finds himself unable to continue the *tissage* of his material and shifts to a simpler organizational procedure. This shift in strategy is described in the inaugural text of *Frêle bruit* in terms of pattern: *Frêle bruit* is to be thought of as an "archipelago or constellation" of independent texts. Once again, it is a musical principle that, in Leiris's eyes, distinguishes this strategy from those of "ordinary" writing or speech. This time, however, Leiris turns to a formal principle to justify himself: that of theme and variations. Instead of the "logical or chronological succession" that characterizes narrative literature, Leiris will "commencer par exposer le 'thème'—ie, narration pure et simple de l'anecdote—puis, en guise de 'variations' (cf. *L'art de la fugue* de Bach et les *Exercices de style* de Queneau), élaborer une suite de commentaires et digressions, tantôt documentaires ou spéculatifs, tantôt lyriques" [begin by stating the "theme"—i.e., a pure and simple telling of the anecdote—then, for the "variations" (cf. Bach's *Art of Fugue* and Queneau's *Exercises de style*), develop a series of commentaries and digressions, at times documentary or speculative, at others lyrical] (*Journal* 26 September 1966, 614). Beginning with *Frêle bruit* and continuing with *Le ruban au cou d'Olympia* and *A cor et à cri*, Leiris begins to explore this variational format, building his books out of a series of independent texts that go back and forth over the same territory, repeating a small number of propositions about their theme using variations in tone and formulation, varied imagery, and different autobiographical material. It is easy to imagine these texts as a kind of exploded essay from *Biffures* or *Fourbis*. And, in fact, Leiris tells us that *Frêle bruit* was composed using leftover *fiches* from the first three volumes of *La règle du jeu*, *fiches* that he didn't know how to integrate into the continuous texture of the earlier texts.[9] As for the later texts, like *Le ruban au cou d'Olympia* and *A cor et à cri*, they are composed using notations taken directly from his *Journal*. These last texts no longer use the system of *fiches* at all.

The relative simplicity of the "variation" format seems to be a relief for Leiris after the spiraling complexities of *Fibrilles* and the *tissage* technique. It is, at any rate, accompanied by a distinct lightening of tone and an emphasis on readability, which, after the arduous going of *Fibrilles*, is definitely a relief for the reader. This shift in strategy also implies an acknowledgment of the impossibility of continuing the *Règle* project according to Leiris's original plans. What's new in *Frêle bruit* is the toning down of the urge to totality. The quest for an overarching rule, which had spun out of control in *Fibrilles*, is replaced by a mood of resignation and a growing acceptance of the *need* to write, even in the absence of any metaphysical or ideological justification. Leiris is no longer trying to find the magic word (*maître mot*) that will unlock the secrets of his personality; his principal concern has become that of assuring the stylistic perfection of each of the small independent texts that make up the whole, without regard for the place of each text in that whole.

There is a sense, however, in which one might be suspicious of Leiris's use of the theme-and-variations metaphor. Perhaps Leiris is only using the ennobling connotations of the musical metaphor to justify publishing what, in a hostile interpretation, could be seen as scraps—leftovers that couldn't be used in his other volumes. Whatever the case may be, it is clear that Leiris's use of the theme-and-variations principle is less sophisticated than that used by Pinget. *Frêle bruit* is much more of a *recueil*, or collection, of loosely related texts than a unified work, making it hard to justify the specificity of the musical model. The primary distinguishing feature of this text and the other late autobiographical volumes is the semiotic independence of each successive piece. This had not been the case, however, in the first three volumes of *La règle du jeu*. There, invention is governed by a technique (*mise en présence*) derived from the relational wordplay of *Glossaire: J'y serre mes gloses*, and the primary mode of development involves the intricately orchestrated combination of thematic strands that Leiris calls *tissage*. We'll need to turn to *Biffures* and to the study of these more characteristically Leirisian techniques if we are to explore further the musical resonances of Leiris's theory of *chant*. It is in the early volumes of *La règle du jeu*, and especially *Biffures*, that the principle of *chant* as mental prosody is given its most complete and satisfying deployment.

MUSIC AND WORDPLAY

Throughout *Biffures* Leiris refers to his childhood obsession with phonographs and phonograph records, objects that have taken on for him a certain phantasmatic quality. This theme, which appears in the "Chansons," "Perséphone," and "Tambour-trompette" chapters of *Biffures*, can be taken to function as an allegorical emblem of Leiris's literary project, an ideal model for autobiographical memory. The exemplary value of the phonograph record for his project can best be understood by contrast with the musical score or literary text: unlike these written media, which can only capture those elements of a performance that can be notated, the sound recording also captures the elements of a performance that escape transcription. The durable, precise reproduction of musical events offered by the phonographic cylinder or disk symbolizes Leiris's utopic desire to bring to life the totality of subjective experience in his autobiography. Thus Leiris compares his pens to phonographic needles: "Je voudrais seulement qu'elles fassent chanter, comme un beau disque de phonographe les sillons à peine soupçonnables que je porte gravés dans mon coeur et dont leur transformation momentanée en un air de musique serait seule capable de momentanément me délivrer" (*Biffures* 23) [I would only ask that they draw music from the almost imperceptible grooves carved on my heart, grooves whose brief transformation into melody would be the only thing capable of briefly saving me] (*Scratches* 17).

Leiris's ideal book would be able to reproduce the minutest details of his affective life in the way that the phonograph is able to capture those elements of sound that resist notation. Leiris wants to pass from mere transcription to a more complete form of reproducing thought. Of course, thought being what it is (intangible), there is no way to simply record it; we lack the means to do more than transcribe it verbally. This ineluctable fact of life forces Leiris to fall back on a more moderate goal, that of supplementing the language of autobiography with techniques designed to render at least some of the particularities of affective experience. This is where song comes in: given the impossibility of simply recording thought, Leiris seeks a way to better render the specificity of his thought, to capture the qualitative aspects of thought in the way that song emphasizes the qualitative aspects of the human voice. For Leiris, these elements must be sought in the instrument itself—be it voice, as in the case of song, or the written word, as in the case of his autobiographical texts.

In a crucial passage of "Perséphone" (*Biffures* 89–90) Leiris analyzes the attraction song has always exercised over him, an attraction that he describes in terms of the mystery of the human voice. Singing, Leiris tells us, differs from speech not only by virtue of its melodious nature but also because it seems to come from somewhere else, like the subterranean world inhabited by Persephone. Music transforms speech into something that, no longer completely human, seems to come directly from nature itself.

> Le chant qui s'échappe de la bouche après avoir franchi la barrière blanche des dents, s'il prend naissance dans la gorge et suit le même chemin que la parole, diffère pourtant de cette dernière, non seulement à cause de sa nature mélodieuse mais parce qu'il nous apparaît comme venant de beaucoup plus loin . . . L'élocution musicale . . . [est] l'indice d'une connivence entre ce qui pouvait sembler n'être que voix humaine et les rythmes de la faune, de la flore, voire ceux du règne minéral où toute velléité de geste se transcrit en une forme figée. (*Biffures* 89)

> [The song that issues from the mouth after crossing the white barrier of the teeth, though it is born in the throat and follows the same path as speech, is nevertheless different from speech not only because of its melodious nature but because it seems to us to come from much farther away . . . Musical elocution . . . [is] the sign of a connivance between what could seem to be merely a human voice and rhythms of fauna and flora, even those of the mineral kingdom, where every impulsive motion is transcribed into a fixed form.] (*Scratches* 75)

Music links the humanity of the spoken word with rhythms—animal, vegetable, and mineral—that transcend the human; it envelops the voice in mystery.[10] Thus, "que ce soit la voix la plus vulgaire, issue de l'être le plus quelconque pour la romance la plus fade ou le refrain le plus trivial, mystérieuse est la voix qui chante, par rapport à la voix qui parle" (*Biffures* 89) [whether it is the most vulgar voice, issuing from the most ordinary sort of person in the most insipid love song or the most trivial ditty, the singing voice compared to the speaking voice is a mystery] (*Scratches* 75). Melody is the sign of this mystery. It marks the irruption of the realm of nature into human discourse by incorporating alien sound patterns into the otherwise familiar transparency of the spoken word. It is this crucial supplement, this mysterious "fairy cloak," that reveals meaning even as it seems to conceal the words. Melody *is* mystery.

Le mystère—si l'on veut à tout prix, pour les besoins du discours, donner une figure à ce qui, par définition, n'en a pas—peut être représenté comme une marge, une frange qui cerne l'objet, l'isolant en même temps qu'elle souligne sa présence, le masquant en même temps qu'il le qualifie, l'insérant dans un arlequin de faits sans lien ni cause repérables en même temps que la couleur particulière dont elle le teint l'extrait du fond marécageux où s'entremêle le commun des faits. *L'élocution musicale, comparée à l'élocution ordinaire, apparaît douée d'une semblable irisation, manteau de fée.* (*Biffures* 89, emphasis added)

[Mystery—if for the sake of the argument we wish at all costs to give features to what by definition has none—can be represented as a border, a fringe encircling the object, isolating it at the same time as it emphasizes its presence, masking it at the same time as it qualifies it, inserting it into a motley of things without identifiable connections or causes at the same time that the particular color with which it tints the object extracts it from the marshy bottom where most things are jumbled together. *Compared with ordinary elocution, musical elocution seems to be endowed with a similar iridescence, a fairy cloak.*] (*Scratches* 75, emphasis added)

The apparently gratuitous relationship between melody and words endows the object with added presence; melody is a fringe that focuses attention on its object, "extracting it from the marshy bottom where most things are jumbled together." It qualifies and masks, isolates and accentuates; it inserts language into a pattern of facts "without identifiable connections" with the object. This is the mystery that obsesses Leiris and that he tries to integrate into his work by finding ways to manipulate the printed word musically, to integrate the ineffable—"la traduction en un idiome purement sonore de ce qui ne pourrait être dit par le moyen des mots" [the translation into a purely sonorous idiom of that which could not be said through words alone]—into writing.

Understood in this fashion, the problem of *chant* becomes one of finding an equivalent for the mystery of musical elocution. Leiris finds a solution to this problem in the form of punning language games derived from the *Glossaire* and explicitly linked to song in the "Chansons" chapter of *Biffures*. This becomes clearer if we examine Leiris's discussion of song in *Chansons*. In a sense, the rather mystical explanation of music's affective power that we just analyzed is nothing more than an intellectualized version of the more down-to-earth description of song offered in "Chansons." There Leiris describes the mechanism responsible for the kind of mystery evoked in "Perséphone." Significantly, in "Chansons," Leiris describes the effect of melody on words in terms of punning, which is, as we recall, precisely the argument that "Musique en texte" uses to relate music to the poetic techniques of *Glossaire: J'y serre mes gloses.*

> L'emprise qu'ont toujours exercée sur moi les chansons . . . tient peut-être en partie . . . à un certain jeu, proche parent du calembour. Un jeu qui se produit entre l'air et les paroles . . . Ainsi, entre phrase proprement musicale et musique purement verbale de la phrase, s'opèrent des échanges . . . et, dans le texte lui-même, s'instaure un irréfutable découpage, qui ne coïncide que partiellement avec le sens. (*Biffures* 17–18)

> [The hold that songs have always had on me . . . may in part result . . . from something closely related to the pun. A play that occurs between tune and words . . . In this way, exchanges take place between the properly musical phrase and the purely verbal music of the phrase . . . and in the text itself an irrefutable fragmentation occurs that coincides only partially with the meaning.] (*Scratches* 11–12)

This "game" between the melody and the words, cause of the semantic ambiguities that often occur in song, is familiar to all music lovers. Song combines two competing modes of elocution, the linguistic and the musical, in a single object. The verbal rhythms and accents often conflict with the musical rhythms, creating the potential for confusion. It is this reciprocal interference between verbal and musical rhythms that makes song so fascinating for the young protagonist of "Chansons" and that brings the adult Leiris to use song as a sort of utopic paradigm for poetic creation. Because of this potential for conflict between musical and verbal syntax, the most banal statement, when enveloped in the "fairy cloak" or the "magnificent isolation" of music, becomes a potential enigma.

If Leiris has chosen song as his model, then, it is because music pulls words away from their conventional meanings, turning them into quasi-magic words. Song makes familiar words strange. For this reason, it reminds Leiris of his childhood tendency to misconstrue the meaning of overheard words and phrases. Song enables Leiris to slip back into that childlike frame of mind, where *all* language was cloaked in this kind of mystery. Leiris devotes long pages to analyzing this effect in a number of apparently nonsensical vocables such as "berçant la laisse," "petit tetable," "paranroizeuses," "reusement," and a variety of other oral oddities. Although they are now recognized to be simply childish misconstruals of utterly familiar words ("En guerre s'en allait," "petite table," "paroles oiseuses," "heureusement"), they still retain for Leiris the aura of *magic words*. Leiris remembers that because of their lack of any precise meaning, they enabled him to exercise his imagination by inserting them into vast networks of connotations that gave them deeper significance than a mere dictionary definition ever could. Such misconstruals are not signs in the Saussurian sense but interpretative vectors: there is no single definition to which they could be said to correspond but, rather, a whole range of feelings and objects. Take the word "tetable" for example, which the young Leiris invents after mishearing a verse from the opera *Manon Lescaut*. Having heard the line "Notre petite table" [our little table] and interpreting it as "Notre petit *tetable*," he frees the line from the original intent of the librettist and opens up an unexpectedly profound emotional space, defined not by a dictionary definition but by the intersection of a moment in a young boy's emotional history and a moment in a particularly intense drama about a fictional couple. The word has no precise function within its original dramatic situation, but it has, for Leiris, a complete mobility of meaning that is so powerful that he claims still to prefer his version of the line to that of the opera's libretto. Because it has no precise meaning of its own, such a word can take on as much meaning as the receptor cares to load into it, and in this way it can become a *révélateur*.

> Il est probable qu'il s'accroche toujours un peu de chose en soi aux basques de ces mots qui ont l'air de répondre à une réalité précise, mais sont en vérité dépourvus de toute espèce de sens. De là, vient leur allure de *révélateurs*, puisqu'ils sont par définition formules de ce qui est le plus informable, appellations d'êtres inouïs qui meubleraient un monde extérieur à nos lois. (*Biffures* 22)

> [Some element of thing-in-itself probably trails after these words, which seem to correspond to a precise reality but are actually without any kind of meaning. Hence their *revelatory* air, since they are by

definition formulas for what can least be formed, names for extraordinary entities that populate a world beyond our laws.] (*Scratches* 16)

The Kantian or, rather, Schopenhauerian ring of "thing-in-itself" and "world beyond our laws" is no doubt self-conscious here and at least partly ironic. But it fits right in with Leiris's autobiographical aims, because for Leiris words must do more than just represent objects and concepts (representation is described throughout Leiris's work as a "servile task"); they must tend toward the ineffable.

This desire to integrate the ineffable into his work is linked to music in Leiris's mind via the techniques of punning and wordplay. Leiris mentions in "Chansons" that the "jeu qui se produit entre l'air et les paroles [est un] proche parent du calembour" [play that occurs between tune and words (is) closely related to the pun], and the phenomena that Leiris describes in "Chansons" are indeed related to the paronomastic processes that Leiris had used as early as *Glossaire: J'y serre mes gloses*. Given the extreme complexity of the musical procedures used in *La règle du jeu*, it will be useful to turn first to the *Glossaire* for an introduction to the more complex techniques used in Leiris's autobiographical texts. This is a necessary detour if we are to show how wordplay relates to music in the looser discursive flow of *La règle du jeu*.

We can immediately draw at least one direct analogy between Leiris's description of song and the *Glossaire*. The phenomenon Leiris describes in "Chansons"—misunderstandings due to rhythmical conflicts between the verbal and musical components of a sung phrase ("un irréfutable découpage, qui ne coïncide que partiellement avec le sens" [an irrefutable segmentation that coincides only partially with the meaning])—corresponds precisely to what Gérard Genette, in his analysis of the *Glossaire*, calls "formal analysis." Essentially, it involves displacing the intended divisions between words in the sonorous flow of an utterance in order to create a new message (i.e., MORPHINE—*mort fine*). The general principle is that of an aural phenomenon analyzed in writing. The pun depends on a verbal performance (actual or virtual), but Leiris uses the analytic power of writing to transform the latent semantic ambiguities of the performance into a poetic, or at least pseudo-poetic, effect. The pun, like melody, imposes on words a logic that is foreign to their normal usage. Of course, the punning, paronomastic techniques of the *Glossaire* can in no way be said to have liberated words from their semantic meanings; on the contrary, the game depends on the play between signifier and signified: the effect of each entry results from the incongruity between the (implied) semantic equivalence between the key word and the definition. But these techniques do modify our access to meaning in a very real sense. The pleasure of Leiris's *Glossaire* stems in large part from the fact that the coherence of the glossary entry seems at first to be threatened by semantic incongruity but is then recuperated on the level of the signifier by the perception of sound patterns. To get the joke I have to hear the pattern, "me porter à l'écoute de ces éléments eux-mêmes, leur donner loisir de me parler" [force myself to listen directly to these elements, give them a chance to speak to me] ("Musique en texte" 99). The reader has to simultaneously follow the patterns on the page and the semantic transformations behind them in order to appreciate the convergences and divergences of sound and sense. The *Glossaire* uses "music"—phonological patterning—to recuperate semantic meaning, miraculously saving words from what Genette calls language's "horror of the semantic vacuum" (*Mimologiques* 371).

It quickly becomes clear, though, that the expressive possibilities of this type of writing remain quite limited. In song, "full" musical expression can make great art out of innocuous poetry, but the relatively limited number of expressive tools available for use in the *Glossaire* entries means that they tend to have at best a mildly humorous effect. The closest musical equivalents Leiris can come up with for this technique are scat singing and operatic vocalises. Other equivalents come to mind (humorous ditties à la Gilbert and Sullivan, nursery rhymes, etc.), but it is hard to put aside the feeling that the experience of the *Glossaire* is closer to "Hickory-Dickory-Dock" or "Am-Stram-Gram" than to the stirring poetic effects intended by Leiris's term *chant*. The *Glossaire* does, it should be noted, call to mind a respected musical institution, but one that is not normally associated with expressive power: the musical étude. Just as books of études have traditionally worked on problems of musical technique by systematically cycling through the twenty-four major and minor keys, Leiris works on technical problems of poetic expression by cycling through the twenty-six letters of the alphabet. The *Glossaire*, then, is perhaps best understood as a set of exercises, a preliminary exploration of a new technique, a kind of *Well-Tempered Alphabet*.[11] As it turns out, this is exactly the role Leiris will ascribe to the *Glossaire* in the history of his literary development given in "Musique en texte." There, with the aid of hindsight, he is able to see that although the *Glossaire* did have a kind of poetic purity, it lacked the expressive capacities that he has since sought to integrate into his writing. It is only with *La règle du jeu* that he will fully develop the expressive potential of the techniques developed in the *Glossaire*, using them as tools that are helpful in generating material and organizing it into large-scale, organically structured texts.

LANGUAGE FACTS, LANGUAGE FEATS

We are now ready to engage in a more comprehensive study of what Leiris in *La règle du jeu* calls *faits de langage*. This might be translated either as "language feats" (i.e., virtuosic displays) or "language facts" (the demonstration of little-known connections between words), and it is this mode of invention that most tellingly characterizes *La règle du jeu*. Leiris defines it by opposing it to other, more traditional modes of autobiographical invention. If, in traditional narrative, the event to be represented determines the words used in the text, the opposite is the case in *La règle du jeu*: there, it is the meditation on words that calls forth representation.

> Quels que puissent être les errements où risque d'entraîner l'emploi d'un subterfuge aussi peu rationnel . . . C'est en me répétant certains mots, certaines locutions, les combinant, les faisant jouer ensemble, que je parviens à ressusciter les scènes ou tableaux auxquels ces écriteaux, charbonnés grossièrement plus souvent que calligraphiés, se trouvent associés; c'est en disposant côte à côte (comme si je visais à les rajuster) ces signes épars ou épaves délavées, que je parviens à tirer de leur immatérialité de fantômes (auxquels c'est à peine si je croyais encore) ces souvenirs sans autre caractère commun que leur capacité d'être ainsi ressuscités . . . par le fouet magique de laquelle ils sont revigorés. (*Biffures* 119)

> [Whatever may be the mistaken ideas I risk espousing by the use of such an irrational subterfuge . . . Only by repeating certain words to myself, certain locutions, combining them, making them work together do I manage to resuscitate the scenes associated with these placards, crudely charcoaled more often than calligraphed; only by arranging these scattered signs, this faded jetsam, side by side in a row (as though I were trying to tidy them up) do I manage to derive

memories from their immateriality as phantoms (in which I scarcely believed anymore), memories without any shared characteristics except their capacity to be thus resuscitated . . . but by whose magical whip they are reinvigorated.] (*Scratches* 100–01)

The idiosyncratic definitions, alliterative developments, and illogical associations that Leiris uses to develop his text are designed to help him remember, to resuscitate the ghostly images of half-forgotten experiences. Playing with words, "les faisant jouer ensemble," is a manner of appropriating words for the autobiographical subject: "Cette façon de manipuler les mots—les remodeler, soit par une définition d'un type nouveau, soit par la notation des échos qu'à mon sens ils éveillent, soit par l'établissement d'un lien non logique entre tel mot et tel autre—est peut-être avant tout une manière pirate de me les approprier" [This way of manipulating words—remodeling them, whether by a definition of a new type or by noting the echoes they awaken in me or by establishing a nonlogical link between one word and another—is perhaps above all an underhanded way of appropriating them for myself] ("Musique en texte" 117). This goal helps to explain Leiris's fascination with the creative misunderstandings of his childhood that led him to invent words like "reusement," "tetable," "paranroizeuses," and "portel." They work especially well as *révélateurs* since they allow the speaker an unusual degree of freedom in using them, a freedom that, Leiris believes, allows unconscious or subconscious forces to come into play. Exotic or unfamiliar names and words serve a similar purpose (see Leiris's extended developments on such names and words as Perséphone, Khadidja, Esaü, and *verglas*). Their enigmatic quality gives them a semantic mobility that creates almost infinite combinatorial possibilities. But, as the *Glossaire* shows, it is not just these special words that work; any word can be separated from its normal connotations and reloaded with intratextual meaning.

Leiris wagers that the analogical and phonetic association of signifiers is just as important in generating insights into his submerged preoccupations as the narrative and argumentative referents of the text. Their effect on the reader, however, is somewhat different. For the reader, the key words of *La règle*, like the key words of the *Glossaire*, become strangely unfamiliar through a process of constant redefinition. In a sense, readers of *La règle* find themselves in the role of young Leiris: they don't know what words mean anymore and so must wait for Leiris to tell them. The meaning of any given word does not come from outside the semiotic network of the text (via the conventional dictionary definition); instead, it is progressively loaded into the word by the narrator. The key words take on more and more significance as autobiographical indicators even as they lose their conventional meaning. This last point is crucial: the process of verbal association is identified with the autobiographical subject, who alone can guarantee their integrity and coherence. The "subject"—in all senses of the word—of *La règle du jeu* is identified with the process of *mise en présence* itself.

Procedurally, the wordplay in *La règle* is of the same kind practiced in the *Glossaire*, with only the added element of discursive continuity necessary for its integration into the ongoing narrative. As Genette points out, many of the longer glossing developments of *Biffures* could be reduced to the compact syntax of the *Glossaire*: BLAISE—*blême falaise*, PERSÉPHONE—*perce aphone*, and so on (*Mimologiques* 367). But it would be a mistake to assume too quickly an identical function for the *Glossaire* glosses and the language feats displayed in *Biffures*. Whereas the *Glossaire* works "sans passer par aucune explication rationnelle" [without resorting to any rational explanation] ("Musique en texte" 121), *La règle* is completely committed to rational explanation. This difference is crucial: the narrative or thematic contextualization of the *faits de langage*—which recuperates the apparent irrationality of wordplay by placing it into narrative accounts of origins and causes—turns out to be precisely the space of autobiography. In *Biffures*, words are not only "poétiquement glosés" (poetically glossed) as they were in the *Glossaire*, they are also developed in what Leiris called in "Musique en texte" "the prosaic style of information" (122). In "Musique en texte" Leiris belittles this style, preferring the purity of abstract poetic play, but the trade-off is necessary for autobiography: the poetic shock or "spark" of the image, which was central to the surrealist aesthetic of Leiris's youth, is sacrificed to the autobiographical urge to explain and rationalize.

We can already see the effects of this "rationalizing" approach to wordplay in *L'âge d'homme*, where two images of a clearly surrealist nature— "elle est belle comme le mensonge" [she is as beautiful as deceit] and "beau comme un lever de rideau" [as beautiful as a curtain up]—are explained. The enigmatic "beau comme . . ." formula fits the pattern that

Breton borrowed from Lautréamont and tried to elevate into a paradigm of the entire metaphoric process. But Leiris decides to trade the potential aphoristic mystery of these expressions for the rationality of a narrative, contextualizing explanation. Thus, we find out that whatever poetic value the expression "elle est belle comme le mensonge" may have, it was originally intended as a straightforward comparison of a real woman and an iconographic picture titled *Le mensonge*. A strict surrealist analysis might have insisted on the metaphoric transfer involved in applying the predicate "beauty" to a concept to which it normally does not apply or on the moral provocation implied in what seems to be a paradoxically positive evaluation of lying. The introduction of the autobiographical explanation, however, obviates this approach. Similarly, the second metaphor—"beau comme un lever de rideau"—turns out to be a simple metonymic displacement of Leiris's childish anticipation before the start of a play. In both cases, what might have turned into an exercise in surrealist shock starts to take on the rationalizing tendency of ordinary-language philosophy or Wittgensteinian language games.

Some might object that by explaining these expressions in this way, Leiris explains them away, weakening their poetic appeal. Be that as it may, *La règle du jeu* generalizes this strategy without apology. There is a related problem, however, that Leiris feels obligated to address. Because *La règle du jeu* has none of the tight phonic economy that allowed him to analyze the *Glossaire* musically (i.e., in terms of the conflict between prosodic and semantic logic), he feels the need to account for this diffuseness and so devotes a page of "Musique en texte" to explaining why the writing of *La règle* should be considered musical, even though the musically inspired procedures of wordplay and punning intervene only intermittently. The "documentary" and narrative developments of *La règle* are, he tells us, to be understood as nothing more than an inconvenient but necessary support for the "winged song." In other words, they play the same role as the recitative in opera: "Sans doute, l'écriture poétique est-elle, par rapport à l'écriture ordinaire, un peu ce qu'était dans l'opéra traditionnel l'*aria* opposée au récitatif (d'une part le chant ailé, d'autre part celui qui ne s'élève pas au-dessus du documentaire)" [Undoubtedly, poetic writing is, when compared to ordinary writing, a bit like the traditional opera aria compared to the recitative (on the one hand, winged song, on the other hand, one that does not go beyond the documentary)]

("Musique en texte" 112). As in opera, the discursive text may predominate quantitatively, but it is the lyrical, paronomastic passages that are featured, since they, like opera arias, provide the moments of greatest intensity. This type of operatic analogy probably can't teach us much about opera or poetry, as it is really just a variant of the more familiar equation of poetry and song by opposition to prose, but Leiris is clearly pleased to find a musical equivalent for his literary practice, and with reason. The operatic analogy does much more than simply account for the necessary diffuseness of some parts of his text with respect to the sudden "poetic" incursions of *Glossaire*-style wordplay; it also serves to introduce a more important theme: that of temporality. Thanks to the musical metaphor, this apparently unwanted discursive or documentary element, Leiris's well-known prolixity, turns out to be much less of a liability than initially thought. Indeed, Leiris comes to see it as a necessary part of the poetic effect he is striving for. And once again, it is music that provides the most compelling argument for Leiris's literary praxis, explaining what he would later come to see as the poetic necessity of his turn to prose and long-winded autobiography.

MUSIC, TEMPORALITY, AND AUTOBIOGRAPHY

In one of his clearest statements on the relationship between poetry and music—his preface to Gilbert Rouget's ethnological text, *La musique et la transe* (Music and trance)—Leiris places the full weight of his demonstration on the temporal status of these two arts.

> Que la Musique se développe dans le temps, comme il en est de la poésie, qui n'est pas seulement un jeu d'idées et d'images mais a elle aussi ses valeurs rythmiques et mélodiques, voilà sans doute ce qui lui donne cette emprise: ne dirait-on pas que de tels états sont des paroxysmes auxquels on ne saurait atteindre sans une sorte d'imprégnation qui exige une certaine durée pour se produire et peut être regardée comme l'action plus ou moins insistante qu'exerce sur nous un déroulement extérieur auquel nous nous trouvons intimement associés?

> [That Music develops in time, just like poetry, which is not only a play of ideas and images but also has its rhythmic and melodic values, that, no doubt, is what gives it this grip on us: doesn't it seem

that such states are paroxysms that one could never attain without a
kind of impregnation that requires a certain duration in order to
make itself felt and that can be thought of as the more or less
insistent action that an external progression exercises on us when we
find ourselves intimately associated with it?] (9)

Only the temporal arts can affect "the whole person" in this way, "like a
possession." This is a power that the plastic arts do not have, because it
depends on extension in time.

> Pareil pouvoir, semble-t-il, ne peut être le fait d'une oeuvre plastique,
> aussi fortement qu'elle émeuve, car la contemplation visuelle . . . n'est
> pas fondamentalement liée à la coulée du temps comme l'est l'ap-
> préhension de quelque chose qui, par voie d'audition ou de lecture,
> entraîne l'esprit dans une manière d'aventure en laquelle on serait
> tenté de dire que c'est le temps lui-même qui s'exprime.

> [This kind of power, it seems to me, cannot belong to a work of the
> plastic arts, no matter how deeply it may move us, because visual
> contemplation . . . is not fundamentally linked to the flow of time in
> the way that the apprehension of something heard or read is, with its
> ability to lead the mind on a kind of adventure in which one might
> be tempted to say that it is time itself that speaks.] (Leiris in Rouget,
> *La musique et la transe* 9)

Not all poetic language fulfills the temporal requirements that give
music this power, however. Although Leiris uses the term *poetry* and
seems to be writing of poetic language in general in this passage, it is
more probable that he is thinking of texts of a certain length. In fact,
Leiris seems to have specifically narrative texts in mind, prose texts like
Proust's *A la recherche du temps perdu* (the last part of the passage just
quoted is lifted straight from Proust) and certainly at some level his own
Règle du jeu. In "Musique en texte," Leiris uses this same concern with
duration to justify his decision to work in prose. There he attributes the
Glossaire's lack of rhetorical power to the brevity of the entries: the
"brièveté d'éclair" (lightning brevity) of the *Glossaire* texts "laisse sur leur
soif auteur et lecteur, pour qui le concert est fini avant même que quoi
que ce soit de transportant ou de simplement attachant ait eu loisir de
faire se lover son chant" [leaves the thirst of both writer and reader
unquenched, since the concert is finished before anything spectacular or

even gripping has had a chance to unfurl its song] ("Musique en texte" 153-54). Brevity inhibits the rhetorical, invasive power of *chant*, which depends on duration. Thus, Leiris wonders about the *Glossaire*:

> Ce qui manque, n'est-ce pas l'envergure de conception qui permet non seulement à des mots de se combiner organiquement en une phrase où chacun aura sa juste place mais à une phrase d'attirer comme par aimantation une autre phrase qui la prolongera ou introduira à une nouvelle séquence, ainsi s'engendrant une mélodie susceptible de captiver par ses fluctuations? . . . Qu'il y a là une immense lacune, un peu de réflexion a suffi pour m'en convaincre et c'est un acquis sur lequel il n'y a pas à revenir.

> [Isn't it the creative scope that is missing that enables words not only to combine organically in a phrase where each one would have its rightful place but also allows one phrase to attract as if by magnetism another phrase able to prolong it or to introduce a new sequence, engendering in this way a melody able to captivate by its fluctuations? . . . A bit of reflection is enough to convince me that this constitutes an immense gap in my theory, and I will take it as a given in need of no further demonstration.] ("Musique en texte" 154)

What was missing from the *Glossaire*, in this view, the "immense gap" in his theory, was the kind of temporal dynamism that gives force to both music and narrative prose, the organic combination of words into sentences and the magnetic attraction between those sentences that invest prose with a "melodic," "captivating" force. It is, then, only in the main autobiographical texts that the pseudo-musical techniques of the *Glossaire* bear fruit by being integrated into large-scale prose structures that have the continuity and dynamism of musical communication. Far from being a liability, as Leiris had feared, the prolixity and narrative structure of *La règle* turns out to be one of its primary assets.

Musical temporality, as Leiris sees it, also possesses another crucial attribute, which Leiris invokes to justify his methods in *La règle du jeu*: unidirectionality. Leiris describes his method of composition for *La règle* as a kind of improvisation. He doesn't make sketches or outlines; he just lines up his *fiches* and goes, noting his thoughts as they come to him and making sense out of them as he advances in the text.[12] Interested in "ce temps toujours ouvert que l'on vit comme si chacun de ses instants ne prenait sens qu'à la lumière de l'instant suivant" [this ever evolving time in which one lives as if each instant only made sense in light of the following one] (Leiris in Rouget, *La musique et la transe* 9–10), Leiris tries to write in a way able to integrate the unidirectional temporality of musical performance into his work. The text is understood as the record of a performance.

This quasi-musical conception of writing as a kind of performance has important consequences not only for the structure and discursive feel of *La règle* but also for its definition of the autobiographical subject. In Leiris's language game an idea, once set down, is never taken back. This principle is important enough to provide the title for the first volume of *La règle. Biffures* takes its title from the performance principle, according to which words can never be taken back but only *biffé*, that is, crossed out but left visible, superceded but not occulted. Leiris wants his use of language to represent thought in time, complete with hesitations, bifurcations, and lapses. This principle of construction does indeed share the property of unidirectionality with music as heard in the concert hall or elsewhere (although the written score, of course, is no more unidirectional than the written literary text). More generally, though, it depends on what one might call the "conversational" fiction. According to this convention (adopted notably in stream-of-consciousness texts), the text is always understood as the transcription of thought sequences, and thought is, conversely, always considered to be coincident with enunciation, taking place in the present tense—in front of our eyes, so to speak. Just as a speaker can circle back to modify a statement but can never take back a formulation, the conversationalist text always amends rather than erasing, at least in principle.

In this way, one of the primary autobiographical referents of *La règle* is to be sought in the improvisational structure itself. Leiris's text takes the form of a mimesis of the *process* of remembrance rather than a series of representations of memories. It wants to be dynamic, not anecdotal. Leiris wants to imitate the temporal flow of thought, devaluing the starting and end points of thought in favor of the process of thinking: "J'entendais mettre plutôt l'accent sur l'acte même de bifurquer, de dévier, comme fait le train qui modifie sa direction selon ce que lui commande l'aiguille et comme fait la pensée, engagée quelquefois, par les rails du langage, dans on ne sait trop quoi de vertigineux ou d'aveuglant" (*Biffures* 279) [I intended, rather, to emphasize the very act of bifurcating, of deviating the way a train does when it obeys the switches and changes direction, and also the way thought does, sometimes taken by the rails of language toward something dizzying or blinding] (*Scratches* 239). The role of the "bifur(cation)" is to displace the emphasis from result to process:

> Tels furent bientôt les "bifurs," ma démarche tendant d'autre part à substituer aux exposés statiques, faits après coup, quelque chose de plus mouvant, de plus abandonné, qui serait en soi-même une suite de bifurcations ou de "bifurs" au lieu d'être seulement la description de ce à quoi, pour commencer, j'avais donné ce nom. (*Biffures* 281)

> [This was what these *bifurs* soon became, my procedure also tending to replace static accounts composed after the fact by something more unstable, something freer, that would itself be a series of bifurcations or *bifurs* instead of the mere description of what I had at first called by this name.] (*Scratches* 241)

This "something more unstable" acts as a palliative against the "life-lessness" of the *fiches* from which he works. Organized in advance, the information inscribed on the *fiches* quickly began to acquire for him "the funereal aspect of acquired knowledge." For this reason, he decides that the *fiches* can only work as signposts in an improvised structure. It is the transitions, the passage from one thought to the next, the creation of links between ideas that will henceforth be the focus of the text.

This insistence on the performative, improvisational, present tense of enunciation depends, as Beaujour reminds us, on a fiction. These are highly wrought texts written over a period of years. Any effect of actual thinking is just that, an effect: the mimesis of thought as process. It is important, nevertheless, as it will help us to understand some of the more far-reaching implications of Leiris's theory of autobiography, including the somewhat surprising fact that Leiris sees himself not so much as the performer of the autobiographical drama than as a member of the audience.

MUSIC, *MISE EN PRÉSENCE*, AND AUTOBIOGRAPHY

Punning and wordplay, the constant redefinition of words, and the search for unexpected relations between words: these are the techniques that have a musical lineage in Leiris's work. Their musicality is, at best, relative, and, in some cases, seems to be all but illusory, but if we accept my hypothesis that for Leiris *chant* and music are always thought of in terms of the superimposition of two logical schema, it is possible to agree on the meaning of the predicate "musical" when applied to these techniques. This fact in itself is of minor importance. But the impact of these musically defined techniques on the functioning of *La règle* as autobiography is profound. Language tends to replace events as the object of autobiographical discourse. Leiris directs our attention away from the documentary function of autobiographical anecdotes and onto the relationships between the words that give us access to those anecdotes.[13] This, in turn, implies a corollary displacement of the semiotic functioning of the representation. The general tendency of this new conception of autobiography is to replace the traditional emphasis on the events that make up the history of a life with the patterns of thought that reveal the specificity of the narrating consciousness. Leiris seeks to emphasize the definitive role of thought patterns in the determination of subjective identity. In order to demonstrate his individuality, that which makes him unique, he seeks to find a way to depict those elements of thought usually considered to be either incommunicable or inessential from the point of view of practical (argumentative, instructional, informational) discourse. These are the *qualitative* elements of thought, elements that fall into categories like the subjective, the ephemeral, and the affective: all those things that make up what I have been calling mental prosody and that Leiris calls *chant*. Leiris is not interested in telling his story in as streamlined a manner as possible or in arguing a point and getting on to the next one. He is concerned, rather, with rendering the qualitative aspects of subjective experience communicable.

Leiris's first attempt at autobiography, *L'âge d'homme*, involved the adoption of a documentary style that, although not exactly traditional, certainly owes much to texts like André Breton's *Nadja*. From our musical perspective, then, *L'âge d'homme* represents a kind of hiatus in Leiris's use of musical techniques. *L'âge d'homme* makes no attempt to use the kind of wordplay that had characterized the *Glossaire*: *faits de langage* are never the basis for invention in *L'âge d'homme*; the gravitational pull of confession is too great. To be sure, we see elements of prosodic invention toward the end of the "Lucrèce et Judith" chapter (*courtisane-courtine-*

pertuisane, Cléopâtre-*albâtre*), but these attempts are short-lived and cautiously contextualized. These and a few other minor examples aside (like the *bordel-portel* development, which has only an anecdotal value), Leiris does not yet use the musical manipulation of words as a tool for autobiographical invention.

There is a concomitant marginalization of theoretical speculation about music in *L'âge d'homme*. Music does figure prominently as a theme in *L'âge d'homme*, but it has not yet taken on the "theoretical" role (as it is called in *Operratiques*) that it will have in *La règle*, where it serves as a generative model for the composition of the text. Thus opera is featured in the "Tragiques" and "Judith" chapters but under the more general heading of *spectacles*. Opera has value primarily as a source of myths (i.e., Aunt Lise as the incarnation of various femmes fatales), not as a reflection on the status of song as a mode of expression. Similarly, jazz is mentioned primarily to evoke the ambiance of the twenties and to help set the scene. We do get the beginnings of a reflection on the way jazz works ("il agissait magiquement et son mode d'influence peut être comparé à une possession" [it functioned magically, and its means of influence can be compared to a kind of possession]), but in general Leiris's remarks about jazz treat it as background music, as a sign of the times (primitivism, frenzy, fraternal communion, sexual freedom, "la joie animale de subir l'influence du rythme moderne" [the animal joy of experiencing the influence of the modern rhythm]), rather than as a creative model (*L'âge d'homme* 161–62; *Manhood* 109). Thus, although the thematic presence of music is clearly important in *L'âge d'homme*, Leiris is more concerned with myths than with modes of signification; he does not yet see music as a model for literary production.

It is not until *La règle du jeu* that Leiris's work manifests his theoretical interest in music, and there it is accompanied by a profound transformation of the semiotic functioning of the text and the role of narrative in autobiography. It would be imprudent to simply assume a causal link between these two modifications, but it should be possible to show how they are linked through our definition of *chant* as the superimposition of two logics.

The radical turn that Leiris's autobiographical project took after *L'âge d'homme* proceeds from the idea that the autobiographical subject is not the sum of his experiences but a network of relationships. The job of autobiography is not to narrate a number of events in the life of an individual (the anecdotal is described as mere chance, contingency, inessential, *un coup de dès*, and so forth) nor to set forth an overarching interpretation of the individual's experiences (which implies a perspective inaccessible to the autobiographical subject) but to use experience as material to work with in order to explore the network of relationships that exist within consciousness. In *L'âge d'homme* Leiris tried to use mythical, allegorical paradigms to turn life into a theatrical spectacle; in *La règle du jeu*, it is thought, not events, that he wants to dramatize. Although this change in approach is motivated, at least in part, by the feeling that *L'âge d'homme* had already exhausted Leiris's stock of "adventures" (*Biffures* 271), this new approach amounts to nothing less than a complete redefinition of the function of autobiography.

Leiris analyzes this new method in a crucial passage of *Biffures* under the general heading of *mise en présence*, acknowledging the origins of this technique in the early poetic texts like *Simulacre*. In *Biffures* Leiris used a "puzzle of facts" as the basis for invention, much as he had used a "puzzle of words" in *Simulacre*. Both techniques respond to the same "diffuse need" to juxtapose and combine: "confronter, grouper, unir entre eux des éléments distincts, comme par un obscur appétit de juxtaposition ou de combinaison" (*Biffures* 277) [to confront different elements, group them, bring them together, as though moved by an obscure appetite for juxtaposition or combination] (*Scratches* 237). Leiris insists repeatedly on his desire to organize the anecdotal into nonnarrative, nonargumentative patterns: "Je constate qu'un seul dessein fut pour moi permanent: opérer une *mise en présence*, tracer des pistes joignant entre eux des éléments. Satisfaction prise à relier, cimenter, nouer, faire converger" (*Biffures* 285) [I note that one single purpose has remained consistent for me: the act of bringing things together, confronting them, creating paths that join different elements together. I take satisfaction in connecting, cementing, knotting, causing things to converge] (*Scratches* 244). This, as Beaujour has suggested, becomes in *La règle* an encyclopedic project, an attempt to give a totalizing view of a life. But unlike the encyclopedia, with its traditional organization of entries into alphabetical order, Leiris's new technique requires that each bit of information be related to the others in such a way that they have a kind of organic necessity, "comme si le tout ainsi solidement ligoté devenait inaliénable, tant de liens s'accumulant

qui sont autant de preuves qu'aucune pièce ne saurait lui être soustraite"
(*Biffures* 286) [as though the whole so solidly lashed together would
become inalienable, so many bonds accumulating, so many proofs, that
no part of it could be taken away] (*Scratches* 244). This is the role of
tissage, or the interweaving of themes.

In order to draw out what is musical about this combination of *mise en
présence* and *tissage*, we'll need to focus on their impact on the role of
"facts" in *La règle*. Using his *fiches* as a starting point for composition,
Leiris abandons the chronological and causal ordering of traditional autobiography. Facts, emptied of their purely anecdotal value, take on the
role of "nexuses of thought"—they are valued above all for the associations that allow them to be organized into patterns. Leiris's initial hypothesis is that his use of *mise en présence*, linked to the psychoanalytic
technique of free association, will enable him to discover a rule (i.e., "la
règle du jeu") able to extract poetic truth from the apparent randomness
of the events that make up a life. In this way Leiris reverses the normal
hierarchy of traditional autobiography, transforming a genre usually defined by its preoccupation with referential truth (the factual account of
the autobiographical subject's experiences) into a mode of exploration of
the psyche that works on a hypothetical level. The anecdotal has value
only as a "talisman" or a "catalyst," as a starting point, not an endpoint,
for autobiography. It is not the facts themselves that guarantee authenticity but the links between these facts that depend on the demiurgic
control of the autobiographical consciousness.

> Obéissant à mon désir de confronter, de rapprocher, d'établir des
> liaisons—je laissai de plus en plus s'aiguiller mon attention, non
> point tant sur ces expériences privilégiées que je me proposais d'ana-
> lyser, que sur les ramifications diverses qui pouvaient s'y brancher,
> voies de parcours dans lesquelles il ne tenait qu'à moi de me lancer et
> dont les recoupements multiples devaient finir par les tresser en une
> sorte de réseau semblable à ceux qui mettent en communication
> toutes les régions distinctes composant un pays. (*Biffures* 281)

> [Yielding to my desire to confront, to approach, to establish con-
> nections, I allowed my attention to go off track, not so much into
> the special experiences I intended to analyze as into the various
> ramifications that could branch out from them, routes down which
> I alone could set off and whose multiple resectionings had to

end when I wove them into a network like those which establish communications between all the different regions of a country.] (*Scratches* 240)

Narrative, although a necessary stage in this process since it provides the elements to be analyzed, is devalued. The urge to tell stories can become a "maladie anecdotière," a *trap* that threatens to distract from the primary task of clarifying the links that exist between the different "nexuses" (*nœuds*) of thought, organizing them into ever larger networks that show "le tout se dessinant progressivement, telle une forme jusque-là ignorée mais qu'on voit émerger d'un abondant lacis de traits, ici bifurcations, méandres, digressions diverses" (*Biffures* 283) [the whole gradually emerging as a form previously unknown but now looming up out of a complex network of lines] (*Scratches* 242). Thus invention for Leiris takes the form of concocting transitions. This is where Leiris locates the real work and the real value of *La règle*:

> Tout ce qui peut entrer de libre et de vivant dans mon travail devenant, en somme question de liaisons ou de transitions et celles-ci gagnant de l'épaisseur à mesure que j'avance, jusqu'à représenter les véritables *expériences* au détriment de celles qui garnissent mes fiches et ne sont plus que des jalons plantés de loin en loin pour diriger les ricochets de ma course. (*Biffures* 282)

> [Any free and vital quality in my work is really some sort of connection or transition, and the latter become thicker and thicker as I advance, until they themselves represent the true *experiences*, at the expense of those that fill my slips of paper and are no longer more than milestones set at long intervals to guide my ricocheting path.] (*Scratches* 241–42)

This technique of *mise en présence* fundamentally modifies the logical relations that order these texts. Leiris describes this process in terms of an alternative logic meant to lead the mind "hors des sentiers battus" [off the beaten track]. His use of logical "ruptures," "deviations," and "discontinuities" is set up against the tidiness of traditional argument and narrative: he groups facts "sans considération de date" [without consideration of their date], mixes in "événements survenus durant la période même où je rédige" [events occurring even as I write the text], replaces the "articulations du raisonnement" [articulations of logical reasoning] with the "engrenages d'écriture" [gear mechanisms of writing], "bifurcations," "meanders," and "various digressions," and so on (see *Biffures* 282–83; *Scratches* 242–45). This desire to link the innumerable "heteroclite objects" of memory (this is how they had been described in *L'âge d'homme*) into vast, multileveled networks of interlocking relationships determines Leiris's insistence on the process of *tissage*: events are no longer considered to have a single, stable meaning; they are understood as bundles of potential relationships, and Leiris's purpose in writing is to seek out these relationships and make them explicit.

The relationship between this compositional method and music—left latent throughout much of *Biffures*—is drawn out in two important passages toward the end of the "Tambour-trompette" chapter of *Biffures*. The first of these uses the musical principle of the leitmotiv to justify the global structure of *La règle*. The second links Leiris's technique of *tissage* to a form of musical development he associates with the opera overture. In both cases the operatic intertext serves not only to clarify an element of Leiris's style but to justify its role in the work, to validate Leiris's project through association with the accepted status these techniques have in musical composition.

Leiris first associates the goal of *La règle du jeu* with musical composition, cautiously using the concept of the leitmotiv.

> Si arbitraire et hasardeux qu'ait pu être mon point de départ, ce qui m'importe maintenant c'est de poursuivre la mise au jour et l'élucidation des thèmes qui transparaissent déjà dans mon fouillis de lignes . . . et en user finalement, avec les figures qui s'esquissent ainsi par degrés, comme d'espèces de *leitmotiv* de composition musicale, pour que de tout cela il jaillisse quelque chose . . . dont j'attends . . . qu'un peu de lumière s'en trouve apportée sur l'être que je suis en vérité et sur ce qu'il est en droit de retenir comme devant être le fondement de son activité. (*Biffures* 284)

> [However arbitrary and perilous my point of departure, what matters now is to continue illuminating and elucidating the themes already showing through my tangle of lines . . . to use them, with the figures thus gradually sketched out, as the leitmotivs of a musical composition, so that from all this something will issue . . . but which will, I expect, . . . when my task has come to an end, throw a little

light on the creature I really am and on what this creature has a right
to retain as the necessary basis for his activity.] (*Scratches* 242–43)

The meaning of the analogy with the leitmotiv in this context seems
transparent enough, but it is used in a way that could lead to some
confusion. Even though the "espèces de" seems to rule out any pretense
of precision here, it is worth pushing the analogy a bit further and
pointing out that Leiris has reversed the normal relationship of cause and
effect. The musical leitmotiv is normally used as a kind of signpost that
helps the audience to make connections between different elements of the
representation. From the composer's point of view, the leitmotiv helps to
unify the work structurally and thematically, but Leiris's literary leitmotivs play the exact opposite role: their meanings "s'esquissent . . . par
degrees" [reveal themselves . . . gradually] to the writer. In other words,
Leiris is hoping to *find* patterns in his work, rather than using his leitmotivs to consciously create large-scale patterns. Rather than assuming
the role of composer, he has put himself hypothetically into the role of
the operatic spectator, sifting through his material for clues to its meaning. Thus, although at first glance this use of the term *leitmotiv* seems
particularly weak (meriting its "espèces de"), it turns out to jibe perfectly
with Leiris's theory of *chant*, which characterizes autobiography as a
mode of discovery, not a mode of retrospection or rational construction.
From the very beginning of *La règle*, Leiris stakes the success of his
project on the expectation that by playing the role of spectator, by, for
example, letting language think for him, he will attain some kind of
privileged knowledge about himself.[14] This use of the leitmotiv as a metaphor of latent unity and a revealer of unconscious motivations (conditioned, no doubt, by Leiris's passage through surrealism and psychoanalysis) is typical of his use of the musical metaphor and suggests that if
Leiris consistently adopts the point of view of the audience in his use of
musical models, it is not due to some lack of understanding about what
composers do but because he thinks of himself as a spectator, or rather
auditor, at the concert of his own thoughts.

The leitmotiv metaphor shows Leiris willing to trust the value of *mise
en présence* over the long term, even though it has not yet offered any
verifiable results. Although Leiris does not yet know exactly what the
meaning of his various associations will turn out to be, he hopes that this
will appear in time. It is this same trust in unconscious determinations

that leads him to compare his method of *tissage* to the technique of musical development as it is practiced in orchestral music.

Tissage, the interweaving of different strands of thematic material, is the technique that, since Lejeune's *Pacte autobiographique*, has been most closely associated with Leiris. Lejeune, sensing that there might be something inherently musical about this way of organizing material, makes numerous allusions to music (e.g., "Prélude et fugue sur le nom d'Esaü") but without ever making explicit what that link might be. He seems to be drawing on a literary tradition that associates musicality with "loose" or "nonlinear" form, where musical logic is thought of as being supple or curved and opposed to discursive logic (usually equated with "la logique tout court"), which is thought of as being direct, straight, hierarchical.[15] Leiris also tends to makes this connection between looseness and music (as in his recurrent use of metaphors like *gauchissement* and curvature to describe the melodies of Verdi and Mozart), and so it comes as no surprise that he uses music to defend *tissage*, a procedure that, he fears, might be mistaken for sheer messiness or a lack of logical rigor. His musical defense of *tissage* also reveals the extent to which Leiris understands autobiography as an exploratory rather than descriptive or confessional genre.

Leiris closes *Biffures* with a particularly elaborate example of the *tissage* technique, which he prepares by linking it explicitly with musical composition. He equates this method of handling his material with a kind of thematic development borrowed from orchestral music.

> Jouets luxueux qu'il a pu m'arriver de tenir—ou de briser—entre mes mains, musiques exaltantes que, si souvent, j'ai pris un plaisir ambigu à entendre, c'est quelques-uns d'entre vous, plutôt, que j'exhumerai de mes fiches pour orchestrer ce final, tel un compositeur d'opéra qui, son ouverture à deux pas de la conclusion, reprend, en les entremêlant, les principaux des thèmes qu'il a exposés au début. (*Biffures* 295–96)

> [Those luxurious toys I held in my hands or broke, those uplifting pieces of music I so often listened to with ambiguous pleasure— it is one of them that I will exhume from my slips of paper to orchestrate this finale, like an opera composer who, his overture a step away from the conclusion, reintroduces and intermingles the main themes he introduced in the beginning.] (*Scratches* 252–53)

Here, as in his use of the term *leitmotiv*, Leiris seems to be guided by a sense of caution and a tacit acknowledgment of the need to avoid getting caught up in musical technicalities that are, at any rate, external to his project. His description of the technique is correct enough, as far as it goes, but primarily because at this level of generality, he can't go wrong. Leiris has made sure to refer to a form that, at least in the nineteenth-century Italian operatic tradition (Leiris's primary musical reference), is above all a *loose* form, a medley of themes with no strictly codified rules.[16] Nevertheless, pushing this metaphor a little further will allow us some important insights into Leiris's intentions. One might wonder, for example, why Leiris chooses to refer to the operatic overture here when he is approaching the end of his text. Is this a slipup or an oversight on Leiris's part? If so, one might forgive the oversight on the grounds that Leiris is not interested in the overall structural function of the overture in opera but, rather, in the compositional principle (condensed recapitulation) characteristic of the finale. But there is another level of explanation for this choice. The reference to the operatic overture serves as a sign that Leiris has decided to continue writing *La règle du jeu* in subsequent volumes. The first volume has come to an end, but it is to be understood as a prologue or prelude to the rest of the autobiography: the finale of *Biffures* is only the end of the beginning. This interpretation is supported by the clearly suspensive note on which the book ends—not with a sense of closure but with a clear promise of more to come. This impression that the real work is yet to come is supported by the final image of the book (a train halted in the countryside waiting for more track), an insistence on "putting things off till later" ("remise à tantôt"—the word *tantôt* is repeated three times), and the last sentence of the book, which trails off, grammatically incomplete, punctuated only by suspension points. If Leiris has decided to close the book with an overture, then, it is because all pretenses of ending have been put aside.[17] And it is significant in this regard that volume 2 of *La règle du jeu*, *Fourbis*, will carry through with the operatic fiction of this overture ending. *Fourbis* opens on the theme of the "lever de rideau" [raising of the curtain], introduced by an extended reference to Wagnerian mists and the dissipation of a "curtain of clouds." Perhaps nowhere in *La règle du jeu* do we see more clearly that Leiris would like to model the architectonic structure of his autobiography, as well as the more local concerns of composition, on the operatic, theatrical paradigm: autobiography as a mental drama, complete with arias, recitatives, and musical interludes.

MAKING SENSE MORE SENSORIAL ("RENDRE PLUS SENSIBLE LE SENS")

Leiris's turn to music as a model for his writing is probably best explained by the difficulty of explaining the alternative techniques used in his auto-biographical texts in more conventional literary or rhetorical terms and by the difficulty of justifying those techniques with respect to the triple imperative (personal, social, aesthetic) that governs his literary project. For lack of a better term, he turns repeatedly to music as the best available metaphor, the repository of a set of principles that help to explain what he sees as new and important about this mode of writing while at the same time justifying his disregard for "correct reasoning" and the logical demands of conventional linguistic discourse. Aware, though, that his autobiographical texts cannot be said to be musical, even by the standards of the kind of attenuated metaphorical definitions given in "Musique en texte," he is obliged to fall back on a more moderate metaphor, that of *chant*, which he defines as the superimposition of this alternative logic associated with music and the discursive logic that governs language. In its most characteristic form, then, the writing of *La règle du jeu* takes place at the intersection of two logical planes: the forward-moving, linear, referentially motivated logic of descriptive, narrative, and argumentative discourse and the cyclical, repetitive logic of asemantic patterning. This hybrid definition of *chant* corresponds to his desire to reconcile the private goals of self-expression with the more properly social objectives of communicating with and influencing a public. Leiris wants to forge a language "pénétrant comme certaines musiques" [as penetrating as some kinds of music] ("Musique en texte" 95) in order to transform the public language of everyday discourse into a private, penetrating, sensorial language, to promote the goal of intimate communication, and to distance language from merely utilitarian forms of communication. His goal is to make meaning perceptible, to make sense sensorial: "rendre plus sensible le sens" ("Musique en texte" 90).

To do this, Leiris concentrates on highlighting key words of his text, making them stand out in his readers' minds as the words from the refrain of Figaro's aria in the *Barber of Seville* stood out for him when he was a child: "comme un problématique archipel caillouteux surgissant d'un ruisseau au débit précipité en même temps qu'aux méandres inde scriptibles" (*Biffures* 26) [like a series of problematic pebbly islands jutting up out of a stream that rushed along but also meandered indescribably] (*Scratches* 19). As we've seen, if Leiris can be said to use language musically, it is in the sense that he subordinates the denotative function of language to the creation of patterns of relationships between words and the objects they denote. Denotation, on its own, corresponds to the centrifugal movement of public discourse but leaves Leiris dissatisfied because it tends to flatten the affective components of subjective experience.

The central problem of Leiris's aesthetic project could be formulated as follows: in modes of writing that are concerned primarily with the communication of content (concepts, stories, descriptions, opinions), the act of naming is the primary task. The extension of a discourse in time is considered to be incidental, an unavoidable consequence of the materiality of language.[18] But Leiris, who wants to transmit the particular qualities of phenomena ("rendre plus sensible le sens"), is dissatisfied with the generality of the linguistic sign, a dissatisfaction that can be ascribed to the limiting schematicism of language with respect to the density and multiplicity of subjectively experienced thought. William James, in "The Stream of Thought," describes this problem in terms of naming: "We name our thoughts simply, each after its thing, as if each knew its own thing and nothing else. What each really knows is clearly the thing it is named for, with dimly perhaps a thousand other things. It ought to be named after all of them, but it never is" (144). Leiris tries to solve this problem, the difficulty of communicating the multiplicity of thought, by making language itself the object of discourse, by doubling key moments of the representation with an exploration of the words that give us access to the representation, and by coupling the mimesis of memory, which takes place on the level of the signified, with a conspicuous mise-en-scène of the signifier. Leiris does not seek out the mot juste (he doesn't believe in it) but uses language in a way meant to show what happens to words once they enter into consciousness. He is interested in everything that underlies words, in the decisions that determine our choice of words as well as the factors that influence our understanding and misunderstandings of words. Thus if Gérard Genette is able to describe Leiris's work in terms of cratylism, it is not because Leiris believes that words really do (or should) reflect the essence of their object but because Leiris believes that words can and should be made to reflect the object *as he sees it*. The kind of precision Leiris seeks has little to do with factuality and everything to do with the movement of thought through consciousness: Leiris uses words to give solidity to the ephemeral movements of thought that normally escape formulation in the more pragmatic, results-oriented formulations of practical discourse. The act of naming is not the endpoint, the goal of this type of writing, but a starting point, because a name, always inadequate with respect to the totality of any given phenomenon, must always be explained. The analog density of subjectively experienced phenomena always escapes the descriptive powers of language, a digital medium that classifies objects by selecting one aspect of a thought at the expense of all the others. Musical logic, on the other hand, is concerned with the struggle toward meaning, the unfolding of meaning, in time, through pattern. It does not expose or demonstrate truth but works toward truth, treating the search for truth as a process of weaving relationships between terms. This is the type of truth that interests Leiris.

4

Samuel Beckett, Music, and the Heart of Things

For, to a certain extent, melodies are, like universal concepts, an abstraction from reality . . . These two universalities, however, are in a certain respect opposed to each other, since the concepts contain only the forms, first of all abstracted from perception, so to speak the stripped-off outer shell of things; hence they are quite properly *abstracta*. Music, on the other hand, gives the innermost kernel preceding all form, or the heart of things. This relation could very well be expressed in the language of the scholastics by saying that the concepts are the *universalia post rem,* but music gives the *universalia ante rem*, and reality the *universalia in re*.

Schopenhauer, *The World as Will and Representation*

THRENODY

Watt is the first of Beckett's heroes to complete the "process of steady interiorization" (Hugh Kenner) that makes Beckett's characters so unfit for life in the outer world and such dogged proponents of the attempt to "eff the ineffable." *Watt* also marks Beckett's first significant attempt to integrate music into a text, taking Huxley's slogan about the musicalization of the novel in a direction that Huxley most likely never imagined— by including two pieces of actual music, notated for performance. I'll begin my study of Beckett with a look at the first of these, the "threne" from chapter 1. This piece, at the locus of Beckett's formal and thematic concerns, has an emblematic status in his work and makes a useful introduction to and point of reference for most of the various experiments with music that we'll study in this chapter. The tune occurs early in chapter 1, soon after we meet Watt for the first time. Watt, en route to Mr. Knott's house, has rolled himself into a ditch to rest, and there, in that most Beckettian of postures, face down in the dust, he overhears what he takes to be a concert, a threne sung by a four-part mixed choir.

2. Four-Part Score for Threne from *Watt*

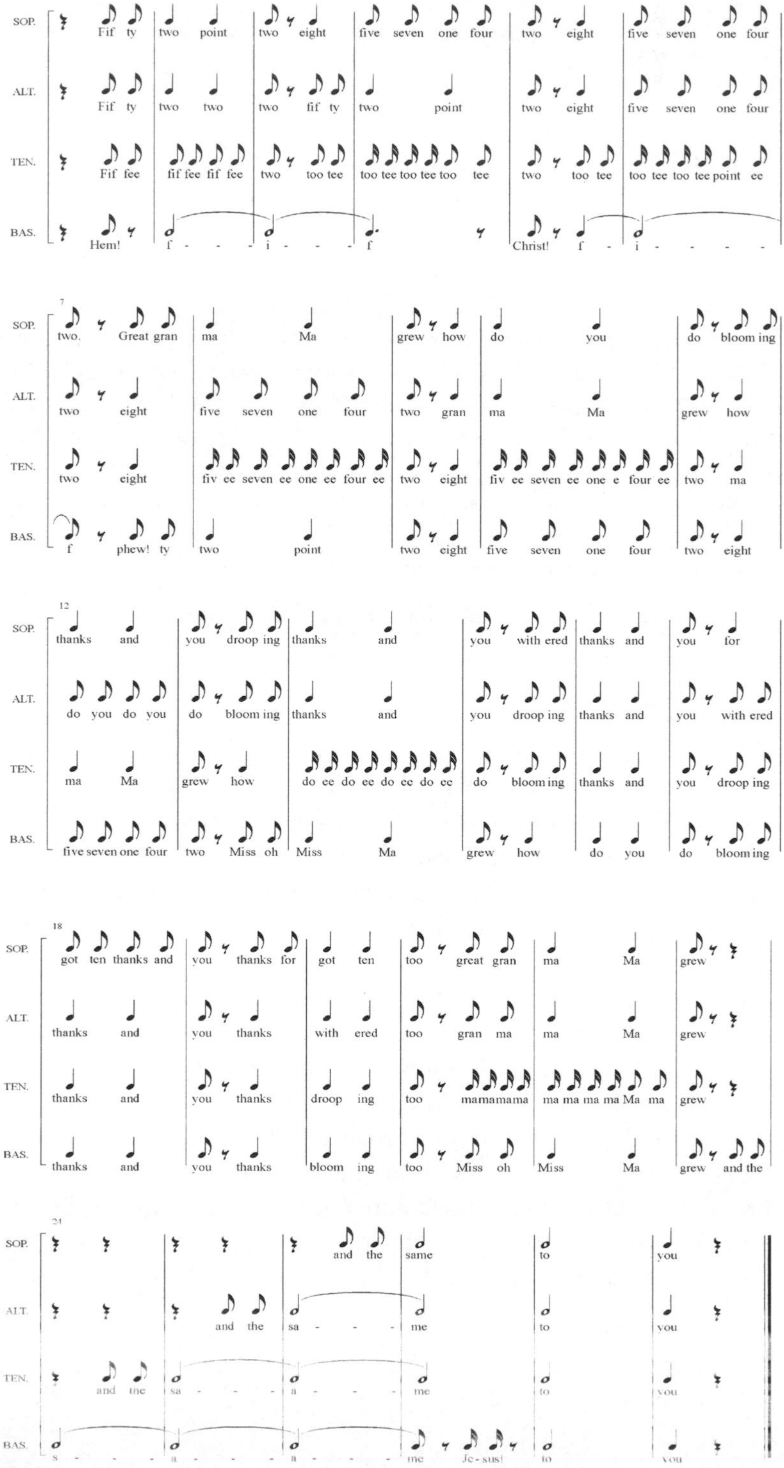

There are several important things to notice about the threne, first and foremost that it is pretty damn funny. The humor, though, isn't precisely verbal; it depends instead on the polyphonic play between the four voices and thus has a specifically musical dimension that deserves careful attention. To really appreciate the humor, the reader should try to imagine what a performance of the text might sound like. To this end, I'll follow Beckett's example and focus on the play between voices in the rhythmic score (figure 2), leaving aside, for the most part, tonal considerations. Although Beckett took the trouble to compose a melody for the piece (see figure 3), he has isolated it from the rhythmic score, relegating it to the closing "Addenda" section of the novel with all the other "precious and illuminating material" that "fatigue and disgust" have prevented from being incorporated into the body of the text.[1] My analysis focuses on features of the arrangement that relate the thematics of the lyrics to the specifically musical values of the piece.

The soprano, responsible for the melody, gives a straight reading of the text with no embellishments. Her job is not only melodic but semantic: she must make the text understood. Accordingly, her part is scored syllabically. The other voices echo the text sung by the soprano, but, as is usual in this kind of piece, they are free to modify the text, which they do by transforming the text in a series of successively sillier derivations. Thus

3. Melody for Threne

Threne heard by Watt on way for station. The soprano sang:

_ _ _

no symbols where none intended

_ _ _

the soprano's opening phrase ("fifty two point two eight five seven," etc.) becomes "fifty two two two fifty two" in the alto, "fiffee fiffee fiffee two tootee tootee tootee" in the tenor, and "Hem! fif Christ! fif phew!" in the bass. In a sense, the soprano plays the straight part against the bass's clowning antics while the inner voices move in between.

Musically speaking, the piece consists of three phrases. The first phrase (measures 1–7, lyrics: "fifty two point two," etc.) is sung homophonically. The bass, as one would expect in this type of texture, lays down a relatively static ground line over which the other voices sing note against note. The second phrase (measures 7–23) is sung in loose imitation. The soprano begins with "Greatgranma Magrew, how do you do?" and the other voices join in one by one—alto, tenor, bass—following the soprano's lead and creating an imitative effect that lasts for sixteen of the piece's twenty-nine measures. This pattern (soprano to bass) is then reversed in the last phrase. After a solid unison on the last "Magrew" of the second phrase, the bass begins the final phrase ("and the saame"), which the other voices pick up one by one (tenor, alto, soprano) before ending on another resounding unison: "to you." Since Beckett hasn't written out the melody for all four parts, we can't know exactly what he intended this passage to sound like, but his general intention is clear: it depends on the cumulative effect of the successive entries, with each voice building on the previous entries. I think of this last phrase as going something like the old Three Stooges greeting, sung in rising thirds:

CURLY:	Helloooooooo	— Hello!
MOE:	Helloooooooooooooo	— Hello!
LARRY:	Helloooooooooooooooooooo	— Hello!

Beckett's version of this gag adds one extra element, the final exclamation from the bass before the cadence:

SOPRANO:	And the saaaaaaame		to you.
ALTO:	And the saaaaaaaaaaaaame		to you.
TENOR:	And the saaaaaaaaaaaaaaaame		to you.
BASS:	And the saaaaaaaaaaaaaaaaaaaaame	Jesus!	to you.

It is important to notice how well the thematics of the lyrics fit the polyphonic texture of the music. The variations from part to part create a distinct personality for each voice. The bass, as we've seen, alternates between his purely musical role of harmonic support and the exclama-

tory antics that punctuate each phrase ("Hem! phew! oh! Jesus!"), while
the soprano gives a straight delivery of the text, and the inner voices add
more or less nonsensical embellishments. Here, for greater clarity, is the
complete text of the first verse as sung by the soprano:

> 52.2857142857142.
> Greatgranma Magrew, how do you do?
> Blooming thanks and you?
> Drooping thanks and you?
> Withered thanks and you?
> Forgotten thanks and you?
> Thanks forgotten too greatgranma Magrew
> and the same to you

After the initial "number" phrase, the second phrase takes the form of
a dialogue, followed by the third phrase, the cadential "and the same to
you." The dysphoric progression of the second phrase has the gloomy
comic effect typical of Beckettian vaudeville, metaphorically packing the
passage from youth to oblivion into the life span of a flower (from
blooming to drooping to withered to forgotten), a span that is itself contained in the space of a single conversation. But what happens to this
phrase in the other three parts? As the lyrics of this phrase pass from
voice to voice, the soprano's "greatgranma Magrew" becomes the alto's
"granma Magrew," then "mama Magrew" in the tenor, and finally "Miss
Magrew" in the bass. To this generational reduction corresponds a reduction in the number of predicates applied to the Magrews. The soprano
runs through all four terms of the series (blooming, drooping, withered,
forgotten), the alto only the first three, the tenor two, and the bass only
gets as far as blooming. Thematically speaking, this progression makes
perfect sense. Each successive generation of Magrews is in a slightly better
state than the preceding one. Greatgranma Magrew may be slipping off
into oblivion, but Miss Magrew is still in the bloom of health. There is
also, however, a purely musical, technical explanation for the reduction
in predicates. Since, according to the principle of fugal imitation, each
voice begins the phrase later than the preceding voice (they enter at two-
measure intervals), each successive voice has less time to complete its
delivery of the text in time for the final unison ("Magrew"). Syllables
must be cut out somewhere in order to prepare the unison, and Beckett
has designed his text so that the progression from greatgranma to Miss

Magrew, that is, from first entrance to last, allows a thematically motivated dropping of syllables, passing from four multisyllabic predicates (blooming, drooping, withered, forgotten) to one (blooming). Beckett has carefully thought out a way to fully integrate the music and text, using a properly musical technique (fugal imitation) to coincide with the thematics of the text. The musical format is not just an afterthought but an integral part of the meaning of the threne.

A brief analysis of the melody will help to reinforce this point. Musically speaking, the melody could not be simpler. It traces a simple scalar descent from the sixth to the tonic of the B-minor scale, repeating the pattern eleven times with only minor variations, and then ends with an inversion of the scalar figure that ends on the leading tone of the tonic key (i.e., A#). In other words, apart from the monotony of the first eleven repetitions of the pattern, the melody has one peculiarity, which is that it appears to end on a half cadence. This type of ending clearly reinforces the text's theme, which, as we've seen, is about circularity and cyclical temporality. By ending on the leading tone (the scale degree that cries out the most strongly for resolution), the melody seems to imply an infinite repeat. At least one repeat is explicitly called for (since there is a second verse of lyrics, which I will not analyze), but, unless we added a coda of some kind, the only way to resolve the tension of the half cadence would be to return to the beginning of the piece and start over—ad infinitum.

There is still one element of the lyrics I haven't touched on, which is the first phrase of the piece, the "number" phrase. What is this number—52.2857142857142—doing here in a piece that seems to want to present itself as either a comic street encounter or a gloomy meditation on the fate of the Magrew family? This question has sparked a fair amount of speculation.[2] Kenner, for example, points out that the number 52.2 and so on denotes the precise number of weeks in a leap year (366 divided by 7). This choice of a number relating to the annual cycle clearly reinforces the theme of cyclical temporality implied by the flowering and fading of the successive generations of the Magrew family. The number also happens to be an infinitely repeating irrational number: 52.285714 285714 285714 and so on, a fact that resonates with the implied infinite repeat called for by the lack of cadence in the melody. This number might also be correlated with the other irrational numbers that make up such an important part of the thematics of *Watt* (pi, cube roots, etc.) and Beckett's oeuvre in

general. All of these points are certainly valid, and they provide a necessary minimum of plausible evidence for explaining the number's presence in the threne. But are they sufficient? Do they justify the presence of
this apparently nonsensical line? I don't necessarily want to argue the
contrary, but I would like to use this question to suggest why any purely
thematic explanation of this type of piece will always leave us feeling
dissatisfied. First of all, it is essential to keep in mind that the threne
constitutes a comic interlude in the vaudeville tradition that Beckett
praised and imitated throughout his career. This piece belongs to a genre
of humorous ditties (à la Gilbert and Sullivan) in which unrecuperated
thematics and nonsense lyrics are not only allowed but welcomed as part
of the overall comic effect. The leap year number, then, may be just as
much an excuse for verbal acrobatics as anything else. More importantly,
however, we must keep in mind that any attempt to interpret the thematic
concerns of a piece like this without taking into account its material
presentation is tantamount to missing the whole point of the piece. Most
readings of the threne underplay the piece's most prominent feature,
which is precisely that it has been notated for performance. This is a grave
oversight. In order to go farther in the interpretation of this piece, then,
we'll need to focus on the specifics of its material presentation in relation
to Beckett's larger thematic concerns.

As I have already tried to suggest, this piece provides a magisterial
example of the adequation of form and content. And any reading of
Beckett that single-mindedly focuses on semantic content without careful regard for verbal construction, formal relationships on all levels, and
the constitutive role of the vehicle (be it the written medium of the novels
or the aural and visual elements of the theater) will miss crucial levels of
meaning. This is, of course, true of all literature in varying degrees, but it
is especially important for understanding Beckett, who, more than just
about anyone else, sought to replace the conventional "realist" use of
language (i.e., in which the emphasis is on denotation) with a more
comprehensive use of language that not only makes form an integral
component of the message but leaves content, in the traditional sense of
the word, behind altogether.[3] Beckett once described language as "a veil
that must be torn apart in order to get at the things (or the Nothingness)
behind it" (*Disjecta* 171). What then, it must be asked, is this "something
or nothing" to which he refers? What is behind this veil? And, to return to

the case in point, what is the particular brand of ineffable being effed in the threne?

As I mentioned earlier, Watt hears this piece while resting in a ditch on a country road in the middle of the night. This seems like an unlikely place and time to hear a concert by a four-part choir. And the narrator's curious insistence on the location of the voices—"from afar, from without, yes, really it seemed from without"—has an almost defensive ring that raises some questions. Should the threne really be understood as an overheard concert on a country road? Could it be an auditory hallucination? Or are we meant to suppose the presence of voices of an entirely different order? We cannot know for certain, but we do know enough about Watt to know that he has a difficult time distinguishing between what comes from within and what comes from the outside world. What, then, it might be asked, happens to our interpretation of this piece if we think of it in terms of imagined voices?

My hypothesis is that we should understand this piece as a representation of a disrupted subjectivity, that of a man who, unable to distinguish clearly between inside and outside, gives to all the voices he hears, including the voice(s) of consciousness, a hypostatic reality of the kind often associated with schizophrenia. Watt, it seems, has lost that fully internalized voice of consciousness, defined as a single unified entity, and begun to hear a multiplicity of voices, which he then projects into the outside world. Instead of the confident assumption of self-identity implied by the Cartesian cogito, we find consciousness depicted as a kind of echo chamber, where voices from the outside world enter into consciousness and echo off of each other, much in the manner of a fugue scored for a four-part choir.

At this early stage of analysis, I am not in a position to provide enough evidence to demonstrate convincingly that this was indeed Beckett's intention (that will be one of the primary tasks of the chapter to follow), but I think that it is possible to show that Beckett's text leaves this open as a possibility. It is not difficult to imagine Watt as a fairly unstable individual who just happens to overhear one day a simple exchange of pleasantries such as "How do you do, Great-grandma Magrew?" Of an obsessive nature, he is unable to get the words out of his head and discovers that they take on a life of their own, that they begin to proliferate, to repeat and modify themselves in various ways until they crowd out all other thoughts. If we accept this hypothesis, then it is possible to argue that the inscrutable, or ineffable, reality that Beckett is trying to eff in this piece is not so much some kind of wan truth about the eternal cycle of life or the futility of human striving (much less a genealogy of the Magrew family) but a representation of the way that such thoughts wend their way through the varied paths of consciousness. This piece is, in that sense, a kind of psychological study. One might even go so far as to say that it captures something essential about the way such obsessive thoughts work, that there is a certain sense in which this piece could be considered to attempt a realist account of a mental phenomenon that has proven to be all but impervious to traditional modes of representation. Beckett a realist? Beckett's work is rarely interpreted in terms of such familiar, down-to-earth phenomena as "tunes that get stuck in your head." But I would like to insist that Beckett's overarching goal is not limited, as some have supposed, to outsmarting or mystifying his audience or, as others have suggested, to translating into narrative terms the classic problems of metaphysics and epistemology. Whatever the merits of these two types of explanation may be, it should also be remembered that Beckett's works all participate in an attempt to represent as accurately as possible areas of subjective experience that have been particularly resistant to more established modes of representation. In this domain, Beckett's work suggests, musical models may have as much to offer as the more traditional models of literary representation.

1. Metaphors

Of all the writers considered in this study, it is Beckett who has carried out the most varied and far-reaching experiments with music. Most critics have recognized the importance of music for Beckett, and, indeed, it has become a cliché of Beckett criticism to use musical predicates when describing his work. Critics have generally understood that his interest in music has something to do with form, but there have been few attempts to deal seriously with the effect music has on the status of representation in his work. Most critics have been content to limit themselves to vague and/or clichéd comparisons, usually made in passing. A quick search through the bibliography yields titles like "'Sans': Cantate et fugue pour un refuge" by Edith Fournier, "Beckett's Dramatic Counter-point" by Paul Lawley, or Michael Robinson's book-length study, *The Long Sonata of the Dead*, which borrows its title from a passage in *Molloy*. Meanwhile, a sizable proportion of the articles and books on Beckett will make at least one allusion to music, some merely ornamental, others more or less serious, but few of them have been developed with much vigor.

Most attempts by literary critics to account for Beckett's work in musical terms have tended to focus on his extensive use of repetition and variation, which, it is true, he uses on a scale unprecedented in literary history. Beckett is perhaps the only author in memory to even attempt, much less pull off, a complete repeat of the entire text of a play (the da capo in *Play*), to build an entire novel around a small set of motivic cells (*How It Is*), or to devote long passages to exhaustively complete combinatorial enumerations (*Watt*). In short, no one has used exact and varied repetition so extensively and so expertly on all levels of composition, from the individual word to the totality. But repetition is not inherently musical, and no study of repetition in Beckett has successfully demonstrated the nature of the link between Beckettian repetition and music. And simply assuming that Beckett's frequent references to music guarantee the musical status of his repetition is to beg the question. This, I think, is why most pronouncements on the link between repetition and music in Beckett's work have been of the passing, unsubstantiated kind: "Like a *leitmotif*, the reiterated formula adds significance and intensity" (Rubin Rabinovitz); "verbal repetition serves Beckett as music, meaning, metaphor" (Ruby Cohn).[4] Most attempts to go farther tend to either implode from lack of evidence or end up emphasizing a few slippery metaphorical resemblances (as in Lawley's article on counterpoint, cited above, which tends to lose music in a haze of qualifications and as ifs).

As a playwright Beckett evolved away from his initial view of theater, in which the text predominates, and began to focus more and more on visual and aural images and effects, allowing the abstract patterning of sound and image to predominate as a source of dramatic interest, sometimes, as in *Quad*, to the complete exclusion of language. Beckett himself willingly generalizes from the aural to the visual, from sound to image, using music to reinforce his arguments for the importance of abstract movement and for repetition as a primary organizing force of the drama.

"Producers don't seem to have any sense of form in movement. The kind of form one finds in music, for instance, where themes keep recurring. When, in a text, actions are repeated, they ought to be made unusual the first time, so that when they happen again—in exactly the same way—an audience will recognize them from before."[5] This brings us to the other trend in Beckett's work that has tended to receive musical explanations: his overriding interest in prosodic values. Tempo, for example, is always a source of interest in his theater: Mouth, in *Not I*, delivers her text with breathless rapidity, while *Breath*, a play from the same period, makes a single inspiration and exhalation the subject of an entire (albeit short) play. One thinks also of Krapp's loving caress of the word "spooooooolll" or Winny, who can't always remember the words of her favorite poems ("one loses one's classics") but who can recall their rhythms ("Go forget me why should something o'er that something shadow fling").

Beckett's interest in prosody as a primary signifying element of performance also helps to account for his increasing interest in directing his own plays. Just about everyone who worked with Beckett in the theater and/or the media—from his preferred actress, Billie Whitelaw, to his preferred lighting technician, Jim Lewis, to the actor-director Pierre Chabert—has remembered Beckett's use of musical concepts to get across his ideas and remarked on the musicality of his approach to theater. Anecdotes on this theme abound: Beckett has used a metronome to regulate the rapidity of his actors' speech and a piano to fix pitch, and has even lent his own house slippers to actors in order to get just the right scraping sound, and so on.[6]

All of these issues—from formal issues involving repetition, variation, counterpoint, and so on to performance issues involving prosody and precision—are of the utmost importance in Beckett's work. But no attempt to trace their source to music can succeed without understanding why Beckett was so interested in this type of approach. Why does "the kind of form one finds in music" seem more valuable to him than traditional narrative and argumentative forms? What links this type of form to Beckett's subject matter? The first part of this chapter will try to address these questions. Starting from some of Beckett's early critical statements, I will try to show how his encounter with Schopenhauer's phenomenalist epistemology and musically oriented aesthetics made music an almost inevitable model for his early novels. I will then study his first attempts to put this model into practice and show where he ran into difficulties.

The second part of this chapter will be devoted to study of plays that use actual music. Curiously, few critics have devoted much thought to Beckett's use of actual music. This is surprising since, after the early attempts to integrate music into his novels metaphorically, Beckett quickly saw the limitations of this approach and abandoned it entirely. Beginning with the threnody in *Watt*, Beckett's first experiment with a musical score, the profusion of musical metaphors that characterized early novels like *Dream of Fair to Middling Women* and *Murphy* will all but disappear from his work. The first trilogy (*Molloy*, *Malone Dies*, *The Unnamable*), notably, makes almost no mention of music. Then, in the period immediately following the trilogy, music suddenly reappears: not in the prose, and not metaphorically, but in person, on stage. After the trilogy Beckett turns to music only when it can be performed. This happens tentatively at first—in places like the doggy ditty of *Waiting for Godot*, the "Death and the Maiden" theme in *All That Fall*, and Winnie's song (from *The Merry Widow*) in *Happy Days*—then with increasing confidence and originality in what has been called Beckett's media period. It is the later radio and television plays of this period that I will focus on in part 2, especially the two radio plays that specifically address the question of the relationship between music and language: *Words and Music* and *Cascando*.

Beckett eschews the traditional theatrical uses of music—as accompaniment or as background, mood, or incidental music—and integrates it wholly into the dramatic fabric of these plays. Thematically speaking, *Cascando* is most closely related to the inwardly focused novels that preceded it, particularly the trilogy and *How It Is*, and will help us to understand how music is related to the use of language in those novels. *Words and Music*, on the other hand, will lead us into a look at Beckett's late television works, primarily ". . . but the clouds . . . ," *Nacht und Träume*, and *Ghost Trio*. Starting with *Words and Music*, I will try to show how music can be used as a key to unlock the meanings that these plays, which are among the most enigmatic of Beckett's entire (and always highly enigmatic) oeuvre, hold out, tantalizingly, just beyond our grasp.

BECKETT, SCHOPENHAUER, AND MUSIC

Any study of music in Beckett must begin where Beckett does, with Schopenhauer. In his first published prose work, the essay *Proust* (1932),

Beckett uses an explicitly Schopenhauerian analysis of Proust's poetics to distinguish Proust's manner from previous styles like nineteenth-century realism and Baudelairean symbolism. Significantly, the essay closes with a climactic development on music in Proust that borrows heavily from Schopenhauer's defense of music. Beckett uses Schopenhauer's dictum about music as "an art that is perfectly intelligible and perfectly inexplicable" (*Proust* 92),[7] refers explicitly to the philosopher on several occasions, and borrows all of his non-Proustian examples straight from *The World as Will and Representation*. His ostensible purpose in this passage is to argue for the centrality of music in Proust's project ("A book could be written on the significance of music in the work of Proust"; "Music is the catalytic element in Proust" [*Proust* 92]), but Proust seems to serve mainly as a screen on which he can project Schopenhauer's description of music as an art of ideal semiotic purity. The climactic tone and strategic location of this passage seem to suggest personal conviction on Beckett's part, and, indeed, although he is certainly right to insist on Schopenhauer's influence on Proust, Beckett focuses so strongly on Schopenhauer that he seems almost to lose sight of the novelist.

The influence of Schopenhauer is apparent throughout the *Proust* essay. Beckett shares Schopenhauer's phenomenalist view of human knowledge as well as his conviction that art can provide at least fleeting access to the ideal plane of the Kantian thing-in-itself. He devotes a fair amount of space to Schopenhauer's epistemology, going so far as to borrow his equation of the thing-in-itself with the Platonic Idea, but he distances himself from Schopenhauer's metaphysics of will. The extent of Beckett's adherence to Schopenhauer's thought becomes apparent in passing statements like the following, in which he refers to the philosopher to clarify his meaning but without adopting his terminology wholesale: "the world being a projection of the individual's consciousness (an objectivation of the individual's will, Schopenhauer would say)" (*Proust* 19). Here, Beckett has adopted a less romantic, more clearly phenomenological vocabulary that contrasts with some of the Platonizing, Schopenhauerian formulations of the essay but without abandoning Schopenhauer altogether. This hesitation is entirely characteristic of Beckett, and much of his subsequent work will manifest a similar struggle with the temptation of idealism. If I lay so much stress on Schopenhauer's thought in what follows, it is because his formulations offer the most useful way to frame the questions that Beckett's various uses of music seem to pose. What I would like to stress is that Beckett shares Schopenhauer's preoccupation with the Kantian problematic of the relationship between perceived and perceiver (which Beckett will later refer to as the "crise sujet-objet" [subject-object crisis]) and that, like Schopenhauer, Beckett situates music at a strategic point in the artistic quest for truth, defining it in such a way that it can be used as a model for literary creation.

For Schopenhauer, the Will (*die Wille*), that life principle of the universe, is objectified in the Ideas, which are in turn objectified in phenomenal reality. Music is considered by Schopenhauer to be a mimetic art, much like painting and literature, but whereas the other arts can only imitate phenomenal reality (i.e., objects as they are perceived), music imitates the will itself. This, for Schopenhauer, places music on the same level of being as the Ideas, guaranteeing it an essential quality that the other arts lack. Schopenhauer considers that the other arts (especially poetry) are able to use their representations of phenomenal reality to give us fleeting glimpses of the ideal plane of the thing-in-itself but that musical representations, able to bypass the plane of phenomenal reality altogether, are one degree closer to the absolute reality of the Will than any of the other arts. Beckett, in his brief summary of Schopenhauer's theory, suggests that "music *is* the Idea itself":

> The influence of Schopenhauer on this aspect of the Proustian demonstration is unquestionable. Schopenhauer rejects the Leibnitzian view of music as "occult arithmetic," and in his aesthetics separates it from the other arts, which can only produce the Idea with its concomitant phenomena, whereas *music is the Idea itself*, unaware of the world of phenomena, existing ideally outside the universe, apprehended not in Space but in Time only, and consequently untouched by the teleological hypothesis. (*Proust* 92, emphasis added)

Context shows that Beckett intends this passage as a simple description of Schopenhauer's view of music, but he has in fact already parted ways with Schopenhauer, who makes a point of distinguishing between the Ideas and Music ("it is the same will that objectifies itself both in the Ideas and in music, though in quite a different way in each"; "there must be, not indeed an absolutely direct likeness, but yet a parallel, an analogy, between music and the Ideas" [*The World as Will* 257–58]). It is unclear whether we should read Beckett's formulation as an intentional divergence from Schopenhauer or a slip, but whatever the case, the point to retain is that it is this essential quality of music (i.e., that it "is," or is a "parallel" of, the Ideas) that interests Beckett and that will make it useful for him as a model of essentiality for literature.

These considerations lead Beckett directly into one of his many characterizations of music as an art of semiotic purity. To sharpen this characterization, he defines music with respect to the listener, who, "impure," is incapable of truly understanding music because he tries to interpret it semantically, by "incarnating" the Idea in a conceptual "paradigm": "This essential quality of music is distorted by the listener who, being an impure subject, insists on giving a figure to that which is ideal and invisible, on incarnating the Idea in what he conceives to be an appropriate paradigm." Thus Swann, as Beckett puts it, "identifies the 'little phrase' of the Sonata with Odette, spatialises what is extraspatial" (*Proust* 92). Of course, all listeners, to the extent that they are human, are impure. We live in a phenomenal world, a world that is a composite of subject and object, form and content, and the temptation to identify music with one's own particular preoccupations is all but unavoidable. But Beckett, in what follows, strenuously condemns the tendency to "particularize" music semantically. The meaning of a musical phrase must never be reduced to a verbal expression, since music, in Schopenhauer's formulation, "never expresses the phenomenon, but only the inner nature, the in-itself, of every phenomenon, the will itself" (*The World as Will* 261). This demand for purity (a crucial term that returns over and over in the *Proust* essay) in the interpretation of music leads Beckett to enunciate, in embryonic form, the critique of language that will later constitute the backbone of his poetics. It comes here as an attack on opera lyrics:

> Thus, by definition, opera is a hideous corruption of this most immaterial of all the arts: the words of a libretto are to the musical phrase that they particularize what the Vendôme Column, for example, is to the ideal perpendicular. From this point of view opera is less complete than vaudeville, which at least inaugurates the comedy of an exhaustive enumeration. These considerations explain the beautiful convention of the "da capo" as a testimony to the intimate and ineffable nature of an art that is perfectly intelligible and perfectly inexplicable. (*Proust* 92)

Here, although using only examples taken from Schopenhauer, Beckett reveals his personal stake in this ideal value of music.[8] For one thing, the condemnation of opera as a "hideous corruption" goes well beyond Schopenhauer.[9] Moreover, the force with which he insists on the ideality of music, its "essential" quality, and its immaterial and intimate nature suggests personal conviction, while the references to vaudeville's "comedy of an exhaustive enumeration" and to the profundity of the da capo convention prefigure important themes in Beckett's later work.[10] Although the intent of this passage is to comment specifically on the relationship between words and music in opera, it is grounded in a much broader critique of language that is central to Beckett's poetics. Not incidentally, this critique of language is often linked to music in his writing. But in order to understand the basis for this critique as well as its links to music, we'll need to understand the distinction that founds it, which, once again, comes from Schopenhauer.

One of the central themes of *The World as Will and Representation* is the distinction between perceptual and conceptual modes of consciousness. Schopenhauer, in his critique of Kant, claims that all the difficulties of Kant's philosophy stem from his failure to distinguish between *perception* (or, more accurately, the "representation of perception in space and time") and *concepts*, which are "thought merely *in abstracto*" (*The World as Will* 437). Schopenhauer makes this distinction the basis for the exalted role he ascribes to the arts in his system. The value of philosophy is in its ability to explain the world conceptually, but it is up to the arts to offer us sensual, perceptual knowledge. This is not merely a distinction between knowledge and pleasure, science and play but between types of knowledge. Schopenhauer asserts that the mission of art is as serious as that of philosophy but that art is concerned with knowledge of a perceptual variety, the only kind that can lead us to the noumenal knowledge he identifies with the Platonic Ideas: "For the Idea can be known only through perception, but knowledge of the Idea is the aim of all art" (*The World as Will* 242). Art, in this scheme, can only be valid to the extent that it avoids the concept. The fault of all inauthentic art, which includes for Schopenhauer allegorical painting and imitative music (Schopenhauer claims to prefer any Rossini overture to Haydn's *Creation*), is their dependence on the concept at the expense of the perceptual immediacy of impressions. This theory of art puts literature in an ambiguous position since literature, by definition, uses language, which Schopenhauer identifies entirely with the concept. And yet he places literature just below music in his hierarchy of the arts. This apparent contradiction calls forth an explanation of how concepts are used in language. Using Venn diagrams to demonstrate the way concepts overlap and modify each other in discourse, Schopenhauer argues that the difference between poetry and "drier" forms of writing is in the fact that it uses concepts that overlap in such a way as to call forth precise images, offering "perceptive representatives" to the imagination.

> The abstract concepts that are the direct material of poetry, as of the driest prose, must be so arranged that their spheres intersect one another, so that none can continue in its abstract universality, but instead of it a perceptive representative appears before the imagination . . . Just as the chemist obtains solid precipitates by combining perfectly clear and transparent fluids, so does the poet know how to precipitate, as it were, the concrete, the individual, the representation of perception, out of the abstract, transparent universality of the concepts by the way in which he combines them. For the Idea can be known only through perception, but knowledge of the Idea is the aim of all art. (*The World as Will* 242)

Beckett follows Schopenhauer's distinction between perception and conception quite closely in the *Proust* essay. Proust's theory of involuntary memory is given special attention in this regard, as is his impressionism. Both are explained as using "inspired perception" to glimpse the ideal plane of the noumenon. Thanks to the reduplication of present and past in involuntary memory, "the experience is at once imaginative and empirical, at once an evocation and a direct perception, real without being merely actual, ideal without being merely abstract, the ideal real, the essential, the extra-temporal" (*Proust* 74). Likewise, Beckett defines Proust's impressionism as the "non-logical statement of phenomena, in the order and exactitude of their perception, before they have been distorted into intelligibility in order to be forced into a chain of cause and effect" and adds that "we are reminded of Schopenhauer's definition of the artistic procedure as 'the contemplation of the world independently of the principle of reason' " (6).

The "distorting" effect of the intellect is, according to Beckett, the primary culprit in the inaccessibility of the Kantian thing-in-itself to human consciousness. For this reason, "the conclusions of the intelligence are merely of arbitrary value, potentially valid." "An impression," on the other hand, "is for the writer what an experiment is for the scientist—with this difference, that in the case of the scientist the action of the intelligence precedes the event and in the case of the writer follows it" (*Proust* 84). Beckett asserts that it is only by removing objects from abstract conceptual categories and the causal schemata they imply that art can attain its goals. At times he goes farther than Schopenhauer, hinting at the course his future work will take by suggesting the value of ignorance and even insanity, any tool that can help to achieve the complete subordination of intellect to perception: "When the object is perceived as particular and unique and not merely the member of a family, when it appears independent of any general notion and detached from the sanity of a cause, isolated and inexplicable in the light of ignorance, then and then only may it be a source of enchantment" (23). Conceptually oriented modes of thought, abstract, discursive, and obsessed with causality, will always be limited by their derivative, *post rem* nature. This, for example, is the mistake of realist narratives, which operate along conceptual, not perceptual, lines. Baudelaire too falls down in Beckett's eyes as being too allegorically, conceptually oriented. Even Dante, the single most important figure of Beckett's formative period, is criticized for his allegorical bent. Proust, on the other hand, is always praised for his adherence to the concrete modes of perceptual consciousness: "Proust does not deal in concepts, he pursues the idea, the concrete" (79). And Proust's (ap)perceptive attitude toward music is one of the signs that in his writing he approaches the status of the "pure subject, almost exempt from the impurity of will" (90). Beckett praises Proust's narrator for his ability to see that Vinteuil's music must be understood as "the ideal and immaterial statement of the essence of a unique beauty, a unique world, the invariable world and beauty of Vinteuil," rather than in the impure terms of specific human situations.

It is crucial for our understanding of the role of music in Beckett's work to emphasize that the concept—aligned with representation and the mediating, distorting influence of the intellect—is superficial, that is, limited to a surface understanding of phenomena. Beckett defines phenomenal reality as a surface: "*Reality*, whether approached imaginatively or empirically, remains a *surface*, hermetic" (*Proust* 74). Representational art, therefore, can be no more than the mere statement of surface, "the grotesque fallacy of a realistic art—'the miserable statement of line and *surface*,' and the penny-a-line vulgarity of a literature of notations" (76). What counts is what is behind this phenomenal surface, and Proust, in Beckett's view, was not only capable of getting behind surfaces but "was incapable of recording surface": "The copiable he does not see. He searches for a relation, a common factor, substrata. Thus he is less interested in what is said than in the way in which it is said" (83).

Having aligned the concept with the surface of phenomenal reality, Beckett turns to music as an art aligned with perception, the thing-in-itself, and the *beyond* of noumenal ideality. Because it does not use concepts, music can, when interpreted correctly, remove the intellectual barriers that keep human understanding on the phenomenal surface of things and communicate an experience approaching the status of the contemplation of the thing-in-itself. The concept is superficial; music has ontological depth. Because it does not refer the attention of the listener to phenomena, music may become transparent with respect to the realm of essences. In his letter to Axel Kaun, Beckett takes this opposition between musical depth and conceptual superficiality as the basis of his argument for a "literature of the unword":

> Is literature alone to remain behind in the old lazy ways that have been so long ago abandoned by music and painting? Is there something paralysingly holy in the vicious nature of the word that is not found in the elements of the other arts? Is there any reason why that terrible materiality of the word *surface* should not be capable of being dissolved like for example the sound surface, torn by enormous pauses, of Beethoven's *Seventh Symphony* so that through whole pages we can perceive nothing but a path of sounds suspended in giddy heights, linking unfathomable abysses of silence? (*Disjecta* 172, emphasis added)

Music provides a model for the possibility of a new relationship with language.[11] Here again, language is seen as a *surface*, a veil or barrier that needs to be "dissolved" because the "vicious nature" of the word-cum-concept blocks access to the plane of the ideal. Three times in this letter Beckett describes this movement through the linguistic surface toward the beyond that lies behind it. The third time music is equated with this other side:

And more and more my own language appears to me like a veil that must be torn apart *in order to get at the things (or the Nothingness) behind it.*

As we cannot eliminate language all at once, we should at least leave nothing undone that might contribute to its falling into disrepute. To bore one hole after another in it, *until what lurks behind it—be it something or nothing—begins to seep through;* I cannot imagine a higher goal for a writer today.

At first it can only be a matter of somehow finding a method by which we can represent this mocking attitude towards the word, through words. In this dissonance between the means and their use it will perhaps become possible *to feel a whisper of that final music or that silence that underlies all.* (*Disjecta* 171–72, emphasis added)

Here music figures not only as a means to the realm of the absolute but as a cognate of the thing-in-itself. This order of reality clearly resembles the plane of the Platonic Ideas, an identification that Beckett hedges by allowing the possibility that there might in fact be nothing behind. The task of the modern artist, then, must be to find ways of boring holes in, rending the veil of, and adopting a mocking attitude toward language in order to explore whatever, be it something or nothing, lies behind it. In a sense, Beckett is staking out territory here, trying to find a niche for himself and his future work. He insists that Joyce is not headed in this direction, that Gertrude Stein may be, but for the wrong reasons, and that he himself is not sure exactly how to go about achieving this goal except that it might involve a stage of what he calls "nominalist irony." He makes it clear that he is not recommending that poets abandon language and become musicians but that they work to modify our relation to language. The question then becomes what exactly the new relationship should be.

At this stage of analysis, the best way to explain what Beckett is driving at is by returning to his description of the "impure" listener who tries to listen to music conceptually. Whereas impure listeners try, like Swann, to spatialize music (that is, to attach semantic meanings to it, reduce the musical statement to a set of conceptual equivalents), poets try to purify their discourse of conceptual meaning, try to use language musically in order to go beyond the superficiality of the plane of the feasible and to get at the thing-in-itself. The concept, of course, is an inherent element of the encoding and decoding of linguistic messages, but concepts, in their normal usage, are at the same time too general, since a concept can only be a category, a label with a potentially infinite number of denotata, and too precise, since any concept is only an instance, a particularization of some in-itself. The "nominalist irony" Beckett mentions as a technique for achieving this nonconceptual literature might be expressed as a radicalized variant of the Schopenhauerian description of poetic language in terms of intersecting conceptual spheres: by relating words to one another in such a way that individual concepts compete and interfere with each other, the poet might be able to force the reader to adopt a mode of interpretation able to participate in this other, higher mode of knowledge identified with the realm of Ideas and the Kantian noumenon. We find examples of this kind of nominalist irony throughout Beckett's work, especially in the *Texts for Nothing*, which, especially concerned with language problems, often play with the inadequacy of the concept, sometimes (as in the second and third examples below) for comic effect.

> How many hours to go, before the next silence, they are not hours, it will not be silence, how many hours still, before the next silence? (*Texts for Nothing* VI, *Collected Shorter Prose* 91)

> It will be another evening, all happens at evening, but it will be the same night, it too has its evenings, its mornings and its evenings, there's a pretty conception, it's to make me think day is at hand, disperser of phantoms. (*Texts for Nothing* V, *Collected Shorter Prose* 88)

> This unnamable thing that I name and name and never wear out, and I call that words. It's because I haven't hit on the right ones, the killers, haven't yet heaved them up from that heart-burning glut of words, with what words shall I name my unnamable words? And yet I have high hopes, I give you my word. (*Texts for Nothing* VI, *Collected Shorter Prose* 91)

If the aim of the poet is perceptual knowledge, Beckett argues, this kind of irony is a necessary part of the poetic process, since words have access only to other words: "For every time one attempts to force words to carry out a true transfer [*transbordement*], every time that one attempts to make them express something other than words, they align themselves in such a way as to cancel each other out mutually. This, no doubt, is what gives life all its charm" ("Le monde et le pantalon," *Disjecta* 125, my translation). The goal of the poet, then, is to use language in such a way that conceptual thought empties out of discourse, is transformed into the kind of *perceptual* thought that Beckett, following Schopenhauer, identifies with music. Beckett seeks the "ideal real," that is, an experience that is "at once imaginative and empirical, at once an evocation and a direct perception, real without being merely actual, ideal without being merely abstract, the ideal real, the essential, the extra-temporal" (*Proust* 74).[12] His gambit is that words might be combined in such a way that, logically irreconcilable, they would lose their normal conceptual meanings, creating a message where none of the discrete concepts used nor any combination of global predicates could be taken as the message's meaning. This meaning would remain unspoken, present only in the relations between terms, in the movement from one to the next.

This program for literary creation will be developed in the section of *Dream of Fair to Middling Women* where the hero Belacqua announces his "aesthetic of inaudibilities." Belacqua, "tired of the harlots of earth and air," has decided that he wants to write a book "where the phrase is self-consciously smart and slick, but of a smartness and slickness other than that of its neighbours." The terms of each sentence, in other words, will be designed to be incompatible with those around it: "The blown roses of a phrase shall catapult the reader into the tulips of the phrase that follows." "The experience of my reader will take place between the phrases, in the silence, communicated by the intervals, not the terms, of the statement, between the flowers that coexist, the antithetical (nothing so simple as antithetical) seasons of words, his experience shall be the menace, the miracle, the memory, of an unspeakable trajectory" (*Dream* 138). It is the "between," the "intervals," the "unspeakable trajectory" that count, not the terms of the statement. This reminds Belacqua of Rembrandt, in whose art it is neither the explicit subject of a given painting nor the technique but "the implication lurking behind the pictorial pretext threatening to invade pigment and oscuro" that interests him. Here again, Beckett's thought is governed by the same opposition between surface and beyond that we found in the Axel Kaun letter, with the material surface of the canvas threatened by the pseudo-Platonic implication that lurks behind it, threatening to overcome the material constituents of the piece (138). And this brings Belacqua, inevitably, to music and specifically to Beethoven's late work, in which, once again, the meaning remains unspoken, merely implied in the "dire stroms of silence, in which has been engulfed the hysteria that he used to let speak up, pipe up, for itself" (139).

MUSICAL METAPHORS AND THE EARLY FICTION

Belacqua's aesthetic of inaudibilities is clearly in line with the Schopenhauerian theories we've examined, but how will Beckett put it into practice? This turns out to be more difficult than expected. In fact, in the first stages of his career as a novelist, this musical theory of language has very little impact on the semiotic functioning of his novels. Instead, Beckett alternates between more or less standard narrative passages, on the one hand, and complaints about the futility of standard narrative, on the other. Language *about* music, it seems, takes the place of the kind of direct musicalization of language he envisages. This is certainly the case in *Dream of Fair to Middling Women*, Beckett's first attempt at a novel. In it, Beckett uses music as a way to think about the ordering of narrative material that, although somewhat unconventional, leaves the semiotic functioning of that material within the text fundamentally unchanged. At this early stage, it's not at all clear what differentiates his thought on the musicalization of the novel from the kind of loose metaphor we looked at in novelists like Huxley. Beckett links music to a critique of the Balzacian novel but doesn't yet seem able to draw out of the metaphor any useful alternative to the kind of narrative he criticizes. Instead, he uses music to complain about the difficulty of telling stories.

It is worthwhile to review how Beckett handles the musical metaphor in this *roman de jeunesse* in order to make clear the magnitude of the advance in his subsequent texts, both in the use of music and in the type of representation involved. In a certain sense, many of Beckett's later experiments with music are already implied in *Dream*, but he hasn't yet hit on the crucial semiotic element that makes music such a necessary point of reference in his later work. Neither his subsequent use of music nor the single-minded attempt to get at the essence of self that reached its most powerful expression in the trilogy is visible in *Dream*. What appears in *Dream* is primarily dissatisfaction—with the modes of representation, the approximative brand of psychological analysis, and the outmoded forms and techniques of the traditional novel. Beckett uses the musical analogy to voice this dissatisfaction, but he still thinks of music from a strictly literary standpoint rather than attempting to look at literature from a musical perspective.

Musical metaphors are everywhere in *Dream*. The novel's narrator freely uses musical terms interchangeably with rhetorical and grammatical terms. Thus a digression is a "cadenza" (*Dream* 179), repeated passages are "da capo" (4, 236), meanings are "orchestrated" rather than clarified (10), ending remarks are codettas (125), whispers are pianissimo, and so forth. *Dream* tends also to use music as a source of metaphors for different types of mental activity. A spate of directionless musing is a "cantilena" (201), going out for a think requires "winding up the cerebro-musical-box" (202), a drunk is "more Seventh Symphony and contrapanic-stuck, than usual" (188), and when Belacqua goes "womb-tomb," his hidden mental world is described in terms of "white music" (182). This loose use of the musical metaphor dominates Beckett's considerations of novelistic form as well. Characters emit "lius" (i.e., notes), which are organized into "tunes." Scenes with more than one character are described in terms of "harmonic composition," replete with "chords," "duos," and "tuttis" (68, 117–18). In one passage, he describes the interaction between characters in terms of the multithematic development of the sonata: "We could chain [the Syra-Cusa] up with the Smeraldina-Rima and the little Alba, our capital divas, and make it look like a sonata, with recurrence of themes, key signatures, plagal finale and all" (49).

There is one formal analogy of this kind that is particularly important. It runs through the entire novel, simultaneously commenting on the latest developments and carrying out a critique of the traditional novel in general. This metanarrative parable, about a musical instrument called a liu-liu, is introduced for the first time by the narrator in order to explain why one of the characters, Nemo, "cannot be made, at least not by us, to stand for anything." The narrator decides to tell "a little story about China in order to orchestrate what we mean." In the ironic mocking tone that characterizes the entire novel, he tells us about Lîng-Liûn, a philosopher's apprentice who makes a liu-liu, a musical instrument composed of twelve reeds that, when blown into, give twelve different notes. He then suggests that, ideally, each of the characters of his novel would correspond to one note on the liu-liu: "If all our characters were like that—liu-liu minded—we could write a little book that would be purely melodic, think how nice that would be, linear, a lovely Pythagorean chain-chant solo of cause and effect, one-figured teleophony that would be a pleasure to hear. (Which is more or less, if we may say so, what one gets from one's favourite novelist.)" The monophonic music of the liu-liu, then, corresponds to a condescendingly simplistic conception of the traditional novel: simple, linear, monophonic, and, although pleasant enough, unchallenging. Beckett's character Nemo, however, is more complex; he refuses to fit into the structures of simple-minded realism: "But what can you do with a person like Nemo who will not for any consideration be condensed into a liu, who is not a note at all but the most regrettable simultaneity of notes . . . a symphonic, not a melodic, unit. Our line bulges every time he appears" (*Dream* 10–11). The feigned regret is not meant to fool anyone. The implication is that if Beckett's novel appears to be a structural mess (and it does), this is because Beckett refuses to bow to the reductive, schematic tendency of more conventional novels. His character is too complex to fit the normal patterns, and Beckett refuses to simplify. In fact, moans Beckett's melodically minded alter ego, *none* of his characters fits the traditional pattern: "The lius do just what they please, they just please themselves. They flower out and around into every kind of illicit ultra and infra and supra. Which is bad, because as long as they do that they can never meet. We are afraid to call for the simplest chord. Belacqua drifts about, it is true, doing his best to thicken the tune, but harmonic composition properly speaking, music in depth on the considerable scale is, and this is a terrible thing to have to say, ausgeschlossen" (117). The link established here between complexity of character ("the lius do just what they please") and complexity of form ("harmonic composition properly speaking, music in depth on the considerable scale") prepares a long development on the nineteenth-century novel, incarnated here by Balzac and "the divine Jane" Austen. This critique revolves around the opposition between traditional novelistic form, identified with monody, and the harmonic, symphonic complexity of real people.

This opposition between symphonic and monodic texture is one of the many variants of the polyphonic metaphor we considered in chapter 2 and seems to have been a fairly common trope of the experimental avant-garde of the time.(See, for example, Edmund Wilson's *Axel's Castle*, which was published in 1931, the same year as Beckett's *Proust* essay and one year before *Dream*. Wilson opposes "symphonic" and narrative structure in the novels of Joyce and Proust.) Beckett had no doubt seen such metaphors around, not only in Proust but also in Gide (*Les faux-monnayeurs*, with its *Kunst der Fuge* intertext, appeared in 1925), Huxley (*Point Counter Point* came out in 1928), Thomas Mann (*Tonio Kröger*, 1903), and, most importantly, in the work of Beckett's friend, mentor, and employer, James Joyce. But if the polyphonic liu-liu metaphor could be attributed to mere literary fashion, it also points in the direction of Beckett's future work. In a sense, this metaphor poses the questions that all the rest of his work will try to answer but does so in such a way that Beckett does not yet see the solutions that will make his mature work so distinctive.

The primary target of the polyphony/monody opposition is the psychological schematicism of conventional novels. Beckett points out that real individuals cannot be defined by a few simple traits in the way that they usually are in the novels of Balzac, Austen, and the like. This type of novelist, having turned his creatures into "clockwork cabbages," misses precisely what is most interesting about people and personality. Beckett then uses the musical metaphor to lead into another metaphorical register, a kind of cosmic or interplanetary metaphor. To the "clockwork cabbages" of Balzac and Austen, he opposes his own characters, which he describes as subject to a centrifugal force that precludes manipulation: "They are no good from the builder's point of view, firstly because they will not suffer their systems to be absorbed in the cluster of a greater system, and then, and chiefly, because they themselves tend to disappear as systems. Their centres are wasting, the strain away from the centre is not to be gainsaid, a little more and they explode" (*Dream* 119). In another passage he explains that the movement of his characters is "based on a principle of repulsion." They do not combine but "like heavenly bodies . . . scatter and stampede, astral straws on a time-strom, grit in the mistral" (119). This lack of coherence, described here in the cosmic terms of heavenly bodies, exploding systems, gravitational clusters, and astral straws, will determine in large part the course his subsequent work will take. How, it asks, can one write about interpersonal relationships when the personalities themselves tend to explode into incoherence when scrutinized? This is perhaps the central lesson of *Dream*: there can be no exploration of relationships between subjects until the nature of the subject itself is clarified. After *Dream*, Beckett's novels will tend to focus increasingly on a single narrator/character, and introspective exploration will replace social interaction as the focus of his work. Henceforth, social interaction will either disappear or be reduced to parody, and psychology, in the conventional sense of the word, will increasingly be replaced by the exploration of the psyche, conceived on a cosmic scale in terms of exploding systems and clusters in the void.

Significantly, the cosmic, Pythagorean metaphor is as typical of Beckett's descriptions of music from this period as of his descriptions of mental functioning. We find, for example, both the musical and the mental in the cosmic image of the following passage.

> The night firmament is abstract density of music, symphony without end, illumination without end, yet emptier, more sparsely lit, than the most succinct constellations of genius. Now seen merely, a depthless lining of hemisphere, its crazy stippling of stars, it is the passional movements of the mind charted in light and darkness. The tense passional intelligence, when arithmetic abates, tunnels, skymole, surely and blindly (if we only thought so!) through the interstellar coalsacks of its firmament in genesis, it twists through the stars of its creation in a network of loci that shall never be coordinate. The inviolable criterion of poetry and music, the nonprinciple of their punctuation, is figured in the demented perforation of the night colander. (*Dream* 16)

This is an extremely dense passage, made up of at least three interwoven metaphorical strands. I will give a more complete analysis of this passage later in this chapter, but for now it will suffice to point out the metaphorical link that Beckett makes between music, interstellar space, and what he calls here "the passional movements of the mind." This type of Pythagorean link—where music mediates between the microcosm of human thought and the macrocosm of planetary, stellar movement—is crucial for understanding Beckett's attempts to describe objects that, like thought, would normally resist description. Belacqua makes a similar move in the aesthetic of inaudibilities passage. His attempt to formulate his project leads him into a comparison with Beethoven's music. But his description of Beethoven's music quickly abandons the musical vocabu-

lary and turns not this time to the macrocosmic terms of celestial movement but to a related metaphor, also borrowed from the physical sciences: subatomic movement.

> I think of [Beethoven's] earlier compositions where into the body of
> the musical statement he incorporates a punctuation of dehiscence,
> flottements, the coherence gone to pieces, the continuity bitched to
> hell because the units of continuity have abdicated their unity, they
> have gone multiple, they fall apart, the notes fly about, a blizzard of
> electrons . . . And I think of the ultimately unprevisible atom threat-
> ening to come asunder, the left wing of the atom plotting without
> ceasing to spit in the eye of the physical statistician and commit a
> most copious offence of nuisance on his cenotaphs of indivisibility.
> (*Dream* 139)

Beckett, at this point in his artistic development, has a tendency to turn
to physics—and extremes of scale, whether of the astronomic or microscopic variety—to suggest the abstract quality of temporal, nonspatial
phenomena like thought and music. This tendency will remain evident in
his second (first published) novel, *Murphy*.

Murphy continues in much the same vein as *Dream*. Beckett studies the
interactions between a large band of characters and peppers his discourse
with a variety of loose musical metaphors. There is one chapter, however,
that distinguishes *Murphy*: the crucial chapter 6, subtitled "Amor intel-
lectualis quo Murphy se ipsum amat." This chapter (107–13) is presented
as a "justification of the expression 'Murphy's mind' " and has a special
status within the novel. (It is the only subtitled chapter and is referred to
by several notes sprinkled throughout the rest of the novel.) In fact, as the
first passage of any length in Beckett's work to claim to describe the
workings of a mind, it has a special status in all of Beckett's work up to
this point. Significantly, both music and astrophysics turn up in this
description.

Murphy thinks of his mind as divided into three zones: light, half light,
and dark. Each zone corresponds to a different mode of thought, a different type of imaginative act. The movement is from the concrete representation of external reality (first zone), to passive contemplation (second zone), and finally to a third zone of complete interiority. The first
zone involves a mode of thought that is primarily narrative in intent,
where imagination is applied to "the elements of physical experience,"

arranging them as it pleases. This is a kind of Balzacian imagination, concerned with the outside world and using actual physical experience but able to manipulate it at will. The second zone of "unparalleled beatitudes" corresponds to the Schopenhauerian mode of aesthetic contemplation, disinterested in and purified of the imperatives of Will. The third zone is of an entirely different order.

Here, as in the previous description of Beethoven's music and the one before that on the "passional intelligence," Beckett turns to a cosmic metaphor borrowed from the physical sciences: "non-Newtonian motion." The third zone, the narrator tells us, is Murphy's preferred zone: "as his body set[s] him free more and more in his mind," he takes to spending more and more time "in the dark, in the will-lessness," like "a mote in its absolute freedom," experiencing "the sensation of being a missile without provenance or target, caught up in a tumult of non-Newtonian motion." This third zone, "the dark," is "a flux of forms, a perpetual coming together and falling asunder of forms." It contains "neither elements nor states, nothing but forms becoming and crumbling into the fragments of a new becoming, without love or hate or any intelligible principle of change." "Here there was nothing but commotion and the pure forms of commotion. Here he was not free, but a mote in the dark of absolute freedom. He did not move, he was a point in the ceaseless unconditioned generation and passing away of line."

We should note the emphasis on relations between nonspatial entities and the dynamic, purely temporal nature of the processes described. Although music is not explicitly mentioned anywhere in the passage, all of the various predicates used—"flux of forms," "forms becoming and crumbling," "the ceaseless unconditioned generation and passing away of line," "the fragments of a new becoming," "pure forms of commotion"— could apply just as well to music as they do to thought, at least at this level of abstraction. And although music is never mentioned, the Schopenhauerian intertext—the absence of "love or hate or any intelligible principle of change," "will-lessness," "absolute freedom"—seems to increase the probability that Beckett had music in mind at some level. But what makes this passage truly significant, especially in light of Beckett's later development, is that it marks the first full-blown attempt to describe a completely abstract realm of thought. Like music, this inner mental life resists attempts to describe it and forces recourse to metaphors. And if Beckett turns to the cosmic metaphor rather than to the traditional social and psychological metaphors that have nourished realist descriptions of both mental life and music, it is because he wants to emphasize precisely those aspects of cognition that have no expression in the outside world. The realm of thought described here prefigures the realm he will explore in *The Unnamable*, but here Beckett is still trying to describe it from an exterior vantage point rather than trying to work it from within. He describes Murphy, from the outside, as "a mote in the dark of absolute freedom," "a point in the ceaseless unconditioned generation and passing away of line," rather than adopting the point of view of that mote. Beckett's next novel, *Watt*, will carry him one step farther on the path to adopting the inside perspective of *The Unnamable*.

So far we've seen the contrast between this second, more properly "Beckettian" realm of thought that he would like to explore and his attempts to describe it that make use of rather conventional narrative techniques. Even his descriptions of music and Murphy's hidden mental world remain subject to the same rules of description that govern any fiction. The only real innovation is that his terms tend to be a little farther out, able only to allude to the indescribable qualities of thought and music by using metaphors of extremes of scale. *Watt* marks a clean break with this approach. There Beckett tries a new way to implement the semiotic lessons of music. We've already seen one aspect of this attempt in the threne; now we'll turn to another aspect of the same project, the attempt to represent a purely perceptual, nonconceptual approach to interpreting phenomena. Although it is in many ways an unsuccessful novel, *Watt* has moments of brilliance and marks Beckett's first complete departure from the conventions of the traditional novel. The central theme of *Watt*—the hero's sudden loss of the ability to adequately name objects and events and his subsequent search for "semantic succor" in shapes and movement—prepares the way for the type of searching we find in the trilogy.

WATT'S LOSS OF MEANING

This theme is introduced in chapter 2 with the arrival of the Galls, father and son, who have come "to choon the piano." The scene itself (67–70) is simple enough: Watt escorts the Galls to the music room, and they set about tuning the piano, discover that it is beyond repair, and, after a gloomy comic flourish, leave. That's it. But for Watt the scene has great importance: it is "perhaps the principal incident of Watt's early days in Mr. Knott's house" and marks an important turning point in his life. Beginning with the visit of the Galls, "all the incidents of note" observed by Watt take on a life of their own, a life resistant to the modes of interpretation Watt had used up till that point. The narrator, Sam (who, having met Watt some time after his stay at Mr. Knott's house, acts as Watt's spokesman throughout the novel), explains how this event prefigures and resembles these other "incidents of note" during Watt's stay at Mr. Knott's house. It resembled them

> in the sense that it was not ended, when it was past, but continued to unfold, in Watt's head, from beginning to end, over and over again, the complex connexions of its lights and shadows, the passing from silence to sound and from sound to silence, the stillness before the movement and the stillness after, the quickenings and retardings, the approaches and the separations, all the shifting detail of its march and ordinance, according to the irrevocable caprice of its taking place. It resembled them in the vigour with which it developed a purely plastic content, and gradually lost, in the nice processes of its light, its sound, its impacts and its rhythm, all meaning, even the most literal.
>
> Thus the scene in the music-room, with the two Galls, ceased very soon to signify for Watt a piano tuned, an obscure family and professional relation, an exchange of judgments more or less intelligible, and so on, if indeed it had ever signified such things, and became a mere example of light commenting bodies, and stillness motion, and silence sound, and comment comment. This fragility of the outer meaning had a bad effect on Watt, for it caused him to seek for another, for some meaning of what had passed, in the image of how it had passed. The most meager, the least plausible, would have satisfied Watt, who had not seen a symbol, nor executed an interpretation, since the age of fourteen, or fifteen, and who had lived, miserably it is true, among face values all his adult life, face values at least for him. (*Watt* 70)

The scene with the Galls had initially been described in the standard language of realist narrative, using terms able to inscribe it in a network of human ends and means. These have been replaced here with terms that act as simple markers, enabling Sam to describe events in terms of space, time, and mode without naming objects or assuming any chain of cause and effect. This event, initially understood, as Sam reminds us at the beginning of the second paragraph quoted above, in terms of "a piano tuned, an obscure family and professional relation, an exchange of judgments more or less intelligible, and so on," has now lost this "outer meaning." The new terms have no discernible link to the anthropomorphic, goal-oriented activity of the incident as described initially. Coordinated only by sequential modifiers ("ended," "continued," "past," "from beginning to end," "over and over again," "before," "gradually") and with no causal indicators, this event becomes, in Watt's mind, a series of formal occurrences: "it developed a purely plastic content, and gradually lost, in the nice processes of its light, its sound, its impacts and its rhythm, all meaning, even the most literal." Watt can now only understand it at a preconceptual level. The terms used here are not meant as *abstractions* (i.e., from specific objects like "piano" to more general terms like "instrument") but as references to *perception*; Sam names only concretely perceptible entities like "lights"/"shadows," "silence"/ "sound," "stillness"/"movement," "approaches"/"separations," and so on. And we should note that, as in the *Proust* essay, conceptual thought is aligned here with surface ("This fragility of the *outer meaning* had a bad effect on Watt") and opposed to perception ("for it caused him to seek for another, for some meaning of what had passed, in the *image* of how it had passed"). This marks a complete reversal from the usual realist hierarchy, in which perception is aligned with surface (i.e., "mere appearances"), and conceptual interpretation is aligned with the depth of "true" understanding.

Watt functions here as a purely perceiving subject. Unable to situate his perceptions conceptually, his mind registers them with the neutral indifference of a video camera or tape recorder. Disoriented by the sudden "fragility of the outer meaning," seeking meaning in indistinct images, he finds himself forced to attempt to understand not by viewing phenomena as effects of causes or by classifying them conceptually but by analyzing them exemplificationally, much like someone listening to an unfamiliar piece of music or watching a nonrepresentational film.[13] The conceptual terms that normally allow perception to be transformed into elements of a teleologically oriented narrative (terms like "the Galls" "tuning" "the piano," etc.) have dropped out; all that Watt has left to work with are these unclassifiable perceptions and the formal relationships between them, the various processes, connections, movements, and impacts that make up an event.[14]

Watt has lost what Husserl called the natural attitude. Like the phenomenologist, Watt studies phenomena, making no assumptions about their causes or status outside consciousness. But Watt's condition is more extreme: he does not simply "bracket" or suspend judgment, he is unable to do otherwise, he has lost the ability to judge or otherwise project meaning onto phenomena. He hasn't lost all of the Kantian categories, however. He is still able to situate objects spatially, temporally, and modally into "approaches," "separations," "rhythms," "shadows," and so on. What he has lost only becomes apparent in light of the Schopenhauerian distinction between perception and conceptual thought that we looked at earlier. Brute perception remains, but the ability of the intellect to name objects and events has been seriously compromised. Watt has discovered the incommensurability of things and consciousness, has discovered himself unable to impose meaning on the objects perceived in consciousness, and experiences this discovery as a loss, the loss of meaning.

Stated in these terms, a comparison with Sartrian *nausée* seems to impose itself. Like Watt, Roquentin discovers the fundamental otherness of things with respect to consciousness. He is constrained to acknowledge that objects have an independent existence that precludes the simple attribution of human categories to them. Just as Roquentin finds himself sickened and threatened by the opposition between things and consciousness, Watt finds his ability to interpret events undermined by their otherness, by the fragility of their semantic surface. The crisis in both *La nausée* (published just before World War Two, in 1938) and *Watt* (written during the war) follows from the intuition that consciousness and things are incommensurable, that things, although they can only be known in consciousness, must be assumed to have an existence outside of consciousness, an existence that cannot be explained or justified by consciousness.

There is an important difference, however. Sartrian nausea is primarily an affective response to this ontological intuition. Roquentin discovers with horror that he must now modify his understanding of his place in the world, and this crisis manifests itself as a change in the affective

coefficient attributed to objects in his relations with them. He feels re-
pelled and frightened by their "absurd," "unjustifiable," "unknowing,"
"solid" existence (*La nausée* 183–92), but—and this is crucial for the point
I am trying to make here—this does not modify in any fundamental way
the manner in which his relations with objects take place. Roquentin
continues to function much as he always had, only with the troubled
conscience of someone no longer comfortable with his place in the scheme
of things.

Watt's crisis originates in the same kind of ontological intuition but
has an added, more debilitating dimension. Watt's crisis not only modifies his affective experience of the world but brings about a severe epistemological crisis, radically impairing his ability to function rationally.
Suddenly unable to attribute semantic meaning to events, he must develop a whole new set of strategies for dealing with even the simplest of
occurrences. In Sartre's formulation of the problem, the intellect continued to function as it always had; only the affective value of the relation
had changed. In Beckett's formulation, the very ability of the intellect to
process information and make use of it has been seriously impaired.

This difference expresses itself in the destiny of the two heroes. Roquentin, inspired by the song "Some of These Days," decides that he can
overcome the crisis by becoming a novelist, by asserting his transcendence as a subject. Watt, on the other hand, slips into solipsism and, it is
suggested, finishes in an insane asylum. Significantly, music plays a central role in both of these crises, and the way music is used in these novels
provides an important insight into the crucial difference between Sartrian and Beckettian aesthetics.

In *La nausée*, a piece of music offers a symbol of salvation. *La nausée*
concludes with the famous "Some of These Days" sequence (243–50),
during which Roquentin hears a piece of music and decides that he must
become a novelist rather than a historian. He takes the song "Some of
These Days" as a symbol of the Beaux Arts, as a way of asserting freedom
and dignity in the face of the absurdity of "existents." But Roquentin pays
little attention to the semiotic specificity of the song as a piece of music.
Rather, he looks *through* the song, using it as a catalyst for narrative. He
imagines a figure of the plight of the noble artist: this Jew who, despite his
sordid existence in some high-rise overlooking New York, composed the
tune; this Negress who sang it. The song, from his point of view, serves as

a monument to their struggle in the face of existence. The value of the song, Sartre tells us, is that it is, in a certain sense, eternal: "It is." Roquentin does not seek the meaning of the song in the notes, the existents, but "behind them," on the level of Being. In other words, Sartre, like Beckett, situates the value of music on a transcendental plane (which, in passing, he takes care to distinguish from the Platonic plane of essences), but in order to make his ethical point, he has reduced the piece to the sheer fact of its creation. He shows no interest whatsoever in the semiotic specificity of the tune or in music as a particular mode of signification.[15]

For Beckett, on the other hand, the semiotic functioning of music is at the heart of the problem. In *Watt* music is linked to the onset, not the resolution, of the crisis. The fact that Watt's great transformation takes place in the music room of Mr. Knott's house and coincides with the Galls' inability to tune the piano seems meant to suggest the way that music is connected with his transformation. In fact, all the signs leading up to Watt's epistemological metamorphosis point to a kind of failure of music. There is a disused ravanastron hung on the wall "from a nail, like a plover" (*Watt* 68), that seems to comment implicitly on the broken piano, just as the bust of Buxtehude (an early proponent of the tempered tuning system) watching over the scene comments on the Galls' failure to tune it. The Galls, in their turn, comment on the impossibility of escaping the transitory nature of existents, the very problem that, for Sartre, seemed to be resolved by music.

> The piano is doomed, in my opinion, said the younger.
> The piano-tuner also, said the elder.
> The pianist also, said the younger.

Watt's loss of meaning, framed by a collection of dead and dying instruments and instrumentalists, coincides precisely with this gloomy reflection on mortality, as if Watt's transformation was in fact a reaction to past, present, and future losses of music, a form of mourning. The piano, the piano-tuner, and the pianist are all doomed. All that has permanence is the fact of their passing.

This last remark calls for a reexamination of the first paragraph of the passage cited at the beginning of this section. If we look closely at the nature of the description, we see that it stands out as an attempt to describe shifting relationships, abstracted from the objects that constitute the terms of those relationships. The incident described is conceived above all as an *event*, and objects have value in this description only to the extent that they are in motion. Thus, the majority of nouns in this passage are derived from verbs, often in gerund form ("the passing," "the quickenings and retardings," "shifting," "its taking place") or other nominalized verb forms ("connexions," "movement," "approaches," "separations," "march and ordinance," "processes," "impacts"). Watt no longer sees in terms of conceptually defined units that relate in various ways, he sees only the temporal aspect of those relationships. Objects and individuals tend to "break up into an arrangement of appearances" and "vanish in the farce of their properties" (*Watt* 70–71). Roquentin too had begun to see objects as being made up of "soft, monstrous masses, in disorder" (*La nausée* 182), but Watt, having discovered the resistance of outside reality to human categories, suddenly finds himself unable to affix concepts to these shapeless collections of disorganized properties. All he perceives clearly is movement, the shifting relationships between nameless elements.

This corresponds to a shift in the primary mode of interpretation used by Watt. Watt's understanding of the scene is not primarily denotative in orientation (where the terms refer to established concepts like "piano," "tuning," etc.) but, as Goodman would say, exemplificational. Watt interprets the scene by thinking of it as a "mere *example* of light commenting bodies, and stillness motion, and silence sound, and comment comment." For him, events can only be understood as "incidents . . . of great formal brilliance and indeterminable purport," "simple games that time plays with space," things that happen "with the utmost formal distinctness" but that are "nothing" in themselves (like the "something or nothing" that is supposed to lie behind language in the Axel Kaun letter).

It is clear that this insistence on the "purely plastic content" of events, on their exclusive manifestation in "nice processes," sensory "impacts," and "rhythm," their conspicuous lack of semantic meaning, and the temporal emphasis of the description all point toward music. It would be incorrect simply to identify this new mode of interpretation with music (if only for the reason that Watt operates on primarily visual, rather than auditory, input), but the musical context for this passage suggests that Beckett had music in mind, and it is clear that this exemplificational, temporal, nondenotational mode of making meaning is as characteristic of musical interpretation as of Watt's new mode of interpretation. (Cinematic images also satisfy these criteria.) The relation between Watt's experience of events and musical experience, then, is not one of identity but of inclusion: both music and Watt's world share this emphasis on asemantic relationality and temporal flow, on a mode of signification that is opposed to denotation in that it completely subordinates the semantic content to formal relationships shifting in time.

In a very real sense, Watt is not so much a character as the embodiment of a mode of consciousness; he is an experimental subject. Beckett has imagined Watt as a consciousness suddenly cut off from the intellectual capacity that allows events to be interpreted in conceptual terms in order to explore what a purely perceptual existence might look like. "In search of semantic succour," he must try to understand events in terms of formal relationships taking place in time. The loss of semantic meaning has created the need for a metaphorical musicalization of the world. But Watt's perceptual faculties are in no better shape than the broken-down piano the Galls finally give up on. Watt, to follow the metaphor, must find a way to retune his perceptive faculties (on this point, see Lees). The rest of the novel will deal with his attempts to come to terms with this new mode of relating to the world. Watt finds himself completely unable to generalize, whence the numerous complete (or, more often, only nearly complete) combinatorial enumerations that make up a large chunk of the novel: unable to determine the rules that govern various transformations, his only way of describing a series of events is to report them, one by one, in the order of their occurrence. This will also affect his comportment in the outside world. Indeed, by the time Sam meets him, Watt has begun to permute his sentences in various ways (inverting the order of the words, the order of the letters in the words, the order of sentences, etc.) and begins to mirror Sam's every move, imitating him but in reverse, going so far as to walk backward, crablike, and so on.

These experiments with permutation, inversion, and music mark Beckett's first attempt to truly break with traditional, descriptive litera-ture. Motivated by the desire to achieve his ends by perceptual, noncon-ceptual means, Beckett attempts to explore here the assumptions that govern description in the traditional sense. Watt also marks the mo-ment when Beckett abandons the metaphorical use of music. Henceforth, Beckett will only use music in performance situations in the theater. In order to understand why music disappears from the novels at this point in Beckett's development, we'll need first to turn to the theater and to the new role that Beckett finds for music in his work.

2. Music

VOICES AND IMAGES

Une histoire et une phénoménologie de l'intériorité (qui peut-être nous manque) devraient rejoindre ici une histoire et une phénoménologie de l'écoute . . . Ce que les premiers chrétiens écoutent, ce sont encore des voix extérieures, celles des démons ou des anges; ce n'est que peu à peu que l'objet de l'écoute s'intériorise au point de devenir pure conscience.

[A history and a phenomenology of interiority (which we seem to lack) should meet up here with a history and a phenomenology of listening . . . What the first Christians listened to was still external voices, the voices of demons or angels; it's only bit by bit that the object of listening is internalized to the point of becoming pure consciousness.]

Roland Barthes, "Ecoute," L'obvie et l'obtus, my translation

It is useful at this juncture to recall the point of departure of this chapter, the threne heard by Watt in a ditch on his way to Mr. Knott's house. As I had suggested, the threne raises an important question: where do these voices that Watt hears come from? The narrator tells us, in almost biblical tones, "And it was to him lying thus that there came, with great distinctness, from afar, from without, yes, really it seemed from without, the voices indifferent in quality, of a mixed choir" (*Watt* 32). This almost defensive insistence on the exteriority of the voices—"from afar, from without, yes, really it seemed from without"—seems to suggest the possibility that Watt's impression is false and that these voices may actually emanate from the "within" of his mind. Or perhaps they reach him from a different kind of "without" that still needs to be defined. We cannot know for certain here whether the threne should be understood as an auditory hallucination, as an overheard concert on a country road, or as a manifestation of voices of an entirely different order. But any attempt to understand Beckett's work must seriously entertain all three of these possibilities if it is to come to terms with the nature of the voices that, beginning with Watt, all Beckett's heroes hear and wonder about. This is a defining feature of their predicament. As their interest in the outer world wanes, it is progressively replaced by an obsession with voices. The attempt to determine the provenance and nature of the voices becomes a metaphor of the search for self that doubles and in some cases replaces the more traditional voyage or quest motif that also figures the search for self in Beckett's work.

Beginning with *Watt*, Beckett's characters speak of only two things, voices and images. Or, more precisely, they are obligated to speak because they hear voices and because they need to see images. If they could make the image, or if the voices would stop, then they could be silent and rest.[16] In order to make the voices stop, they need to exorcise them, to say them, to exhaust them by explaining them, "for to explain had always been to exorcize, for Watt" (*Watt* 75). The exhaustion of the voices and the creation of the image—these are the goals of all Beckett's narrators, even though they can also be a source of fear (ending means rest but also cessation, death). These two imperatives make up the givens of the Beckettian universe, and, beginning with the trilogy, all Beckett's texts fit into this pattern in one way or another.

The voices make a logical place to continue our investigation of music in Beckett's work not only because of the conventional link between voice and song but because Beckett himself often links questions about the nature of the voices to music:

But Watt heard nothing of this, because of other voices, singing, crying, stating, murmuring, things unintelligible, in his ear. With these, if he was not familiar, he was not unfamiliar either. So he was not alarmed, unduly. (*Watt* 27)

Was it a song in my head or did it merely come from without? ("The End," *Collected Shorter Prose* 57)

One day I shall stop listening, without having to fear the worst, namely, I don't know, what can be worse than this, a woman's voice perhaps, I hadn't thought of that, they might engage a soprano. (*Three Novels* 364)

"I do of course hear cries. [*Pause.*] But they are in my head surely. [*Pause.*] Is it possible that . . . [*Pause. With finality.*] No no, my head was always full of cries. [*Pause.*] Faint confused cries. [*Pause.*] They come. [*Pause.*] Then go. [*Pause.*] As on a wind. [*Pause.*] That is what I find so wonderful. [*Pause.*] They cease. [*Pause.*] Ah yes, great mercies, great mercies. [*Pause.*] The day is now well advanced. [*Smile. Smile off.*] And yet it is perhaps a little too early for my song." (*Happy Days, The Complete Dramatic Works* 163–64)

As a general rule, the only voices that matter in Beckett are personal voices, the voices that seem to come from within: all Beckett's characters must, like Moran, deal with "what I heard, in my soul I suppose, where the acoustics are so bad" (*Three Novels* 112). This is an important point, since images, associated with vision, are always situated by Beckett's narrators on the outside. The visual image, it seems, has a necessary spatial component that links it with the outside world. Thus Watt speaks of his memory of the incident with the Galls in these terms: "it continued to happen, in his mind, he supposed, though he did not know exactly what that meant, and though *it seemed to be outside him*, before him, about him, and so on" (*Watt* 73, emphasis added). This distinction between inside and outside, then, needs to be handled carefully. Inside cannot be strictly identified with a corporeal space or even an imaginary mental space. Beckett's characters don't know where the voices come from (although they seem to be inside), and they don't know where to locate the images (although they seem to be outside).

The relationship between inside and outside is further complicated by the nature of the Beckettian quest, the search of Beckett's narrators for this "I" that is somehow related to the voices that they hear. The narrative voice—the voice that we the audience have access to in Beckett's texts—can only be understood as an intermediate voice, equally estranged from the founding voice of the ego and from the outside world of social relationships and interpersonal communication. The voice that speaks (or writes) in the Beckettian text is nothing but an intermediary between an inside/ego that (we suppose) must exist (but that the narrative voice cannot locate) and an outside/world that remains equally inaccessible to knowledge. The narrative voice is in between: his inside is still the I's outside.

Perhaps that's what I feel, an outside and an inside and me in the middle, perhaps that's what I am, the thing that divides the world in two, on the one side the outside, on the other the inside, that can be as thin as foil, I'm neither one side nor the other, I'm in the middle, I'm the partition, I've two surfaces and no thickness, perhaps that's what I feel, myself vibrating, I'm the tympanum, on the one hand the mind, on the other the world, I don't belong to either. (*Three Novels* 383)

This I as tympanum, as in between, as that which separates the founding ego from the outside world, without being *of* either, becomes one of the major themes of Beckett's work.[17] When consciousness turns inward in the self-reflexive, introspective movement typical of Beckett's writing and of philosophy, the "natural" identity between consciousness (usually figured as a voice) and self (usually figured as a place) begins to falter. The quest to say I, in this sense, is the search for a founding voice, the voice of what could be called, following Wittgenstein, "the philosophical I," an ontologically grounded ego. This is why the related questions of provenance ("where do the voices come from?") and ownership ("are they mine?") have such importance in Beckett's work. Beckett's characters have lost what Husserl called the natural attitude, they have lost their faith in the identity between consciousness and self that is necessary for efficient action in the outside world of social and practical concerns. The primary symptom of this loss is that, like some schizophrenics or the early Christians in the Barthes epigraph cited above, the voice of consciousness gets lost or becomes confused with an other's voice or even with a plurality of other voices.[18] In Beckett, these voices always have a hypostatic reality (i.e., they are actually heard) and often become so intrusive that they make it all but impossible for the character who hears them to comport himself or herself successfully in the "outer world" (*Watt* 43).

This is a problem that grows gradually in importance throughout Beckett's career. In *Molloy* the narrating protagonists (Molloy in the first part, Moran in the second) still seem to have a certain degree of autonomy with respect to the voices they hear: the "masters" and "messengers" that force them to speak, write, and search are understood as coming from outside, from a real, if not realist(ic), outside world. But by the time we get to *The Unnamable*, it becomes clear that things are more complicated than that: "Unfortunately it's a question of words, of voices, one must not forget that, one must try and not forget that completely, of a statement to be made, by them, by me, some slight obscurity here" (*Three Novels* 384). Narrative discourse in the novels becomes increasingly a form of mimicry: the narrator's job is to imitate the voices he hears in his head. This notion appears in Beckett's work as early as *Watt*, when we find out that "Watt spoke as one speaking to dictation, or reciting, parrot-like, a text, by long repetition become familiar" (154), but does not become a major theme until *The Unnamable* and, especially, *How It Is*, which opens with the words "how it was *I quote* before Pim with Pim after Pim how it is three parts *I say it as I hear it*" (7).

The hypostatization of voices, then, is a theme that has its origins in the early fiction. But it only comes to the forefront in the sixties, at the time that Beckett started to experiment with the broadcast media. Moreover, it is in the media plays that Beckett has given the most striking and original incarnations of these hypostatized voices. Some of them, to be sure, conform to familiar psychological conventions and would not be out of place in a realist work. Into this category falls the television play *Eh Joe*, where we find Joe haunted by the latest incarnation of the accusing voice of his guilty conscience. Similarly, some of the radio plays depict voices of lost loved ones (as in *Embers*) or other memory voices that force their way into consciousness, bidden or unbidden (as in *That Time*). In *Krapp's Last Tape* the voice of memory is hypostatized in the succession of tape recordings from previous years. But in other plays, like *Not I*, and in the works that concern us here, there is no attempt to lend any kind of realist verisimilitude to the voices. They are simply presented as a given of the mental universes depicted.

An understanding of these voices is a necessary precondition for the study of music in Beckett's media plays, because the role of the music is determined by its interactions with the speaking voices. So far we've considered Beckett's use of music almost exclusively from the point of view of his fiction, but it is in the media plays that Beckett's lifelong meditation on the relationship between music and text begins to bear fruit. Rather than simply positing a formal or rhetorical analogy between music and text (as we saw Pinget and Leiris do), Beckett uses the radio medium to stage literal confrontations between language and music. This interest in the use of actual music had manifested itself timidly in earlier plays like *Waiting for Godot* (which uses a ditty at the opening of act 2 to make a point about circularity) and *All That Fall* (which uses excerpts from Schubert's *Death and the Maiden* to emphasize the thematics of the piece). But beginning in the media plays of the sixties, Beckett begins to make a much more daring use of music, having it interact with language in ways that would be all but impossible in the less controlled environment of the stage or in the written medium of the novels. For this reason, it would be difficult to overestimate the importance of Beckett's shift to the radio and television media for his use of music. This shift marks one of the main turning points in his use of music.

CASCANDO AND WORDS AND MUSIC

Beckett's most important statement on the relationship between music and language comes in a series of three radio plays from the early sixties, *Rough for Radio I*, *Words and Music*, and *Cascando*. They present the clearest picture of what music means for Beckett and suggest why music is a necessary reference in this work and not simply a metaphorical embellishment as it mostly still was in *Dream*. These pieces explicitly pose the central question that concerns us here: What can music teach us about language, literature, and the way the mind works? Beckett once said, speaking of *Cascando*, "It does I suppose show in a way what passes for my mind and what passes for its work" (Brater 45), and this statement applies equally well to the whole series. But rather than depending on statements about music to make his point (as all the authors we've studied up till now have done), Beckett takes advantage of the aural possibilities of the radio medium and presents actual samples of music and spoken text. And unlike traditional radio plays, which, when they use music, tend to give it a subordinate role as background, incidental, or mood music, these plays present both Music and Words as primary forces in the dramatic texture.

I'll focus primarily on *Cascando* and *Words and Music*, treating *Rough for Radio I* as an early draft for *Cascando*. Although *Rough for Radio I* was never completed (both the parts for Music and for Words were left blank, with only dashes to indicate where they were to enter), never performed during Beckett's lifetime, and of clearly inferior quality, it makes a useful point of reference for the study of *Cascando*.[19] It deals with the same set of themes and uses the same triangular dramatic setup but inscribes it in a more or less realist framing device—an interview between "He" and a certain "She" who appears to be a journalist, critic, or other interested member of He's audience. I'll be referring to *Rough for Radio I* occasionally for confirmation of my readings of *Cascando*, because the greater explicitness called for by the framing device makes the piece useful for

deciphering some of the highly cryptic, coded statements that characterize *Cascando*.

Words and Music and *Cascando,* then, can be considered as a kind of
diptych. Both plays were composed at about the same time (in 1961 and
1962, respectively) and have an evident identity of intention, using the
triangular relationship between three characters to explore the creative
process. Both plays have three characters, a voice (named Words in *Words
and Music* and Voice in *Cascando*), a character named Music who, as his
name suggests, manifests himself only through instrumental music, and a
controlling figure (named Croak in *Words and Music* and Opener in
Cascando) who is responsible for regulating and evaluating the performances of the other two.

In *Words and Music*, Music and Words, goaded by Croak, must work
together to create an image. The piece, as a pseudo-allegory of the artistic
process, works by personification. Words and Music act like a couple of
wayward servants governed by a doddering old man. The performance
we overhear is a command performance in the strictest sense: Croak, as
master, chooses the themes to perform, tells the two performers when to
start and stop, and makes up their audience of one. Words, who addresses
Croak as Milord, and Music, who salutes him with a "humble muted
adsum," demonstrate great respect for and complete subservience to
Croak. Croak, in turn, appears to be equally dependent on their services.
Music and Words are his "balms" and his "joys," and the level of satisfaction he gets from their performances depends on the extent to which he
can make them work together.

Cascando is built around a similar triangular relationship between
three characters, but the similarities between the two plays end there.
Whereas Croak and his servants appear to know each other intimately,
the three characters that make up *Cascando* seem to inhabit entirely
different universes. Music and Voice represent modes of discourse that
are completely incommensurable. Throughout the play they remain un-
aware of each other and of the Opener. Only the Opener can hear all parts
at once. He can control the other two, turning them on and off by
"opening" and "closing," but this is the only control he has. Unlike Croak,
he can neither coerce them nor determine the content of their discourses.

Beckett, it should be noted, had very little to do with the music for
these pieces. Beckett's younger cousin John composed the music for

Words and Music, and Marcel Mihalovici composed the original score for *Cascando.*[20] Moreover, Beckett wrote the texts without any specific music in mind. In both cases he completed the scripts before work on the music had even begun and made no effort to control the musical composition. He only approved what had already been composed and, in the case of *Words and Music,* gave some advice for revision to his budding-composer cousin. This brings up another important difference between these plays. In *Words and Music,* Beckett gives careful indications for the music and makes it clear that Words and Music are meant to coordinate their efforts. The end product of their collaboration is a song. Moreover, the script gives musical indications like "burst of tuning," "great expression," "brief rude retort," and so on that show that Beckett had a clear, if general, idea of the kind of music he wanted. *Cascando,* on the other hand, contains no indications whatsoever as to the type of music that is to be used or the qualities it is meant to express. As befits the premise of the play, in which Music, Voice, and the Opener inhabit three separate universes, the script makes no attempt to link the music thematically or stylistically with the text or to ensure that the music will correspond to any general or specific features of Voice's discourse. As for Voice, his text could have been lifted directly from one of Beckett's trilogy or post-trilogy narratives; it is essentially a reworking of familiar Beckettian themes, strongly reminiscent of *How It Is,* not an attempt to cover new ground. The status of the spoken text, then, like that of the music, is that of a borrowed discourse. It is taken as a given, *tel quel*; it comes from elsewhere. If we remember that in *Rough for Radio I* Beckett did not even bother to compose a text for Voice, it begins to seem probable that Voice's text functions not as a vehicle for thought in the play but as an object of thought. Voice and Music are not meant to signify on their own; they are to be taken, rather, as samples of music and text, representatives of differing modes of thought.

I've been calling Music, Voice, and Words characters up to this point, and although they do in a very real sense have this status, there is an important distinction that needs to be made. Music, Voice, and Words are not characters in any traditional sense of the word but, rather, disembodied discourses that, presumably, could not exist on their own. Like Mercier and Camier, Didi and Gogo, and Hamm and Clov before them, Music and Voice (or Music and Words) are unimaginable except as a couple: each has his specialty and could not survive without the other.

Moreover, as a couple, they are completely dependent on their masters, Opener and Croak. The nature of the interaction between the three figures makes it clear that they are inseparable, not so much independent characters as the constitutive elements of a single consciousness. This is a common feature of Beckett's dramatic and narrative situations. From *Molloy* and *Endgame* to *Company* and *What Where*, wherever there are multiple characters they interact in ways that suggest they should not be taken as individuals but as projections or hypostatizations of functions within a consciousness. Can we really assert, for example, that the narrator of *The Unnamable*, who has no body, is a character? Or that the three disembodied voices of *Company* are characters? Certainly not in the classic, Aristotelian sense of the word. Beginning with the trilogy, all of Beckett's fictions take place within the framework of an imagining consciousness. There is no objective reality in Beckett and hence no individuals, only images and words in a consciousness that is itself multiple. In this sense, then, it is the trio as a whole that constitutes a character in *Cascando* and *Words and Music*. This pseudo-allegorical use of personification means that these pieces could be thought of as descendants of the medieval psychomachia because they play out an internal struggle that is also a cosmic battle between opposing forces.

CASCANDO

Cascando depicts a simple situation presented in the most enigmatic of terms. The difficulty of the piece is not in the complexity of the relationship between Opener, Voice, and Music but in determining the values we are supposed to assign to these figures. As is often the case with Beckett, he works metaphorically but refuses to name any single extratextual situation, idea, or problem that would be the ultimate referent of the metaphor. He leaves it up to us to ground his metaphors in stable conceptual terms, if we can. In this case, he uses an oblique reference to a familiar everyday activity—listening to the radio—to set up the dramatic context, but he refuses to invest that setting with any realist specificity. This type of oblique metanarrative reference—to radio in a radio play—is typical of the self-referential element of many of Beckett's conceits (like the many sly references to the stage in *Godot* and *Endgame*). This technique also has the advantage of creating a concrete image that can be quickly grasped by the audience while ensuring that the play operates on a level that resists all attempts to reduce it to a univocal, allegorical meaning. It also makes the play extremely difficult to analyze cogently. Before turning to the respective roles of Music and Voice in the play, therefore, we'll need to clarify the dramatic situation, examine the status of the metaphors that govern the fiction, and determine a strategy for unlocking the meaning that the play dangles before us while making sure not to sacrifice the polysemy that Beckett always makes sure to preserve. I'll examine the role of the Opener first.

Opener, like Voice and Music, is defined by his function. His job is to control the discourses of Voice and Music, which he does by "opening" and "closing." Throughout the play, the performative verb "I open" (or its counterpart, "I close") has the effect of turning on (or off) the music and words heard by the audience. The choice of the verbs "open" and "close" may seem puzzling at first but seems meant to imply that the discourses of Voice and Music function like radio broadcasts, following the French expression "ouvrir/fermer la radio," which has the idiomatic sense of turning on/off the radio.[21] Several prominent features of the drama lend credibility to this "broadcast" hypothesis. For one, Opener can turn Music and Voice on and off at will, but his control ends there. He can give us access to Words and Music but cannot determine what comes out. Conversely, Voice and Music function with complete independence and in total ignorance of each other and Opener.[22] Like radio broadcasts, their voices come from an indeterminate elsewhere and exist for Opener as a pure availability of discourse. Thus, their performances appear to continue even when Opener, having closed, has cut off his (and our) access to them. He opens, we hear a bit of narrative/music, he closes, and the next time he opens, the narrative/music has progressed to a new point. This continuity, only implied in *Cascando*, is made quite explicit in *Rough for Radio I*:

SHE: Is it true the music goes on all the time?
HE: Yes.
SHE: Without cease?
HE: Without cease.
SHE: It's unthinkable! [*Pause.*] And the words too? All the time too?
HE: All the time.
SHE: Without cease?

HE: Yes.
SHE: It's unimaginable. [*Pause.*] So you're here all the time?
HE: Without cease. (*Complete Dramatic Works* 237)

The performance continues whether we are tuned in or not. Thus, if one wanted to adapt the piece for the stage, one could imagine a setting for the play with a single actor, Opener, flanked by two radios that he turns on and off.[23] Opener, then, is, in a certain sense, as much a part of the audience as we are. He can evaluate ("Good. Good"), encourage ("Come on!"), and express his distress ("God, God") but without it having the slightest effect on Voice or Music. Like the inquisitorial light of *Play*, all he can do is give the command to perform without being able to otherwise influence the course of the performance. This is in effect another of Beckett's many metaphors for the obligation to speak. Like the light in *Play* and torture in *What Where*, the radio reference in *Cascando* makes it clear that Music and Voice perform because they cannot do otherwise.

Ultimately, though, Beckett refuses to fully endorse the broadcast metaphor. As is often the case in his work, he suggests the metaphor without giving enough clues to base a complete interpretation of the play on it. There is no mention in *Cascando* of anything that might be opened and closed or turned on and off, be it a radio, window, door (as Martin Esslin suggests), or anything else. This suggests that we need to consider other possible referents for the open/close formulation. Another promising candidate comes from the field of hydraulics. In both French and English, the verbs "open" and "close" could apply to a tap or faucet or even (borrowing a well-worn figure of speech) metaphorical floodgates. Of course, *Cascando* doesn't mention any of these things either, but if we look for a way to reconcile the broadcast metaphor with the hydraulic metaphor, keeping in mind the kind of discourse we actually hear in *Cascando*, it seems likely that Beckett uses the open/close formulation to suggest the more general notion of *flow*. This is a concept that applies equally well to electrical currents, liquids, discourse, and that material that most concerns us here: thought. Indeed, if we take the play as a mentalist metaphor, as I do, then Opener's use of the verbs "open" and "close" inevitably calls to mind the notion of the stream of consciousness. This hypothesis is supported by a passage from *Mercier and Camier*: "Even side by side, said Mercier . . . we are fraught with more events than could fit in a fat tome, two fat tomes, your fat tome and my fat tome. Whence no doubt our blessed sense of nothing, nothing to be done, nothing to be said. For man wearies in the end of trying to slake his drought at the fireman's hose and seeing his few remaining tapers, one after another, blasted by the oxy-hydrogen blowpipe" (*Mercier and Camier* 87). Music and Words, then, should be understood as two manifestations of a mental stream that flows without interruption. What we the audience hear is but a small sample of what is being voiced at every moment in the private sphere of a conscious-ness that may or may not be that of the Opener. In *The Unnamable* (the closest thing to a stream-of-consciousness novel Beckett ever wrote), he also associates the broadcast metaphor with an ongoing stream of thought: "I wonder what the current broadcast is about. Worm probably" (*L'innommable* 147, my translation).[24]

Of course, the flow metaphor applies to both Voice and Music, and the goal, from our musical perspective, must be to determine the particulari-ties of Music within the context of this metaphor. How can we draw out what is specific to the music in this play? It is extremely difficult in a piece like this to assert that music, or anything else for that matter, *is* this or *represents* that. For one thing, we'll need to guard against relying on commonplace views of music of the type that Martin Esslin uses when, in his BBC presentation of the play, he asserts that Voice is responsible for the narrative and the "emotions [are] expressed by Music."[25] As it turns out, the play is perfectly explicit on the question of emotion, and what is emphasized is not Music's expressive power but, on the contrary, its complete otherness with respect to Opener's affective life. Opener judges, can be scared, does not know why he must open, and so on, but he shows no concern for the emotive content of either the narrative or the music. His only concern is that music and words seem to be coming together. The kind of identification we see in Esslin's statement, then, which de-pends on various a priori assumptions about the nature of music, risks confusing the issue. Part of the problem of *Cascando* is determining what it is that music is and does. To assume that we already know this would be tantamount to giving up on the piece, much like those who insist that Godot stands unequivocally for God or that *Endgame* is simply a nuclear holocaust play. In this regard, it is significant that at no point in the play are the names Voice or Music used. The characters are identified as such in the dramatis personae, but we cannot rule out the possibility that this designation has only a technical value, more for the use of the actors and engineers involved in the play than for the purposes of interpretation. Beckett has offered no guarantee that the musical tones we hear are meant to play the role of or represent music per se within the dramatic, metaphorical structure. The first step of analysis, therefore, is to wipe our interpretive slates clean, to open ourselves up to the observation of the relationships at work in *Cascando*, putting aside our normal assumptions about what music may be or do.

What, then, can we say about Music? At this initial phase of analysis, the first, most obvious, and most important remark is that Music is one of the two modes of discourse available to Opener. It is the relationship between Music and Voice, as mediated by Opener, that signifies in the play, not the content or characteristics of either of the two discourses in isolation. Moreover, what is compelling about this relationship from Opener's point of view is the possibility that Music and Voice might "come together." Like the narrators of *The Unnamable* and *How It Is*, Opener's goal is to end, and the prerequisite for this result is the coming together of Music and Voice.[26] Opener sees signs that this end is imminent and expresses his satisfaction at that prospect.

> OPENER: From one world to another,
>   it's as though they drew together.
>   We have not much further to go.
>   Good.

Even at this early stage of analysis we can understand why Opener is pleased about the prospect of rest and the end of his task, but this state-ment poses other kinds of questions. What, for example, is this vast distance—"from one world to another"—that separates the two? (The French version goes even farther: "d'un *astre* à l'autre" [from one *star* to another].) What, that is to say, do Voice and Music stand for that they can "come together" (or, as the French version has it, "tombent d'accord" [fall into agreement]) despite being separated by an interplanetary or interstellar distance? Opener too has considered this question. Opening and closing seem to have deadened his curiosity, but, he tells us, "there was a time" when he did try to answer this type of question, and his answer always took the form of a humble parable, "an image like any other," which he agrees to share with us. This image provides crucial clues for interpretation, especially in conjunction with his previous assertion that "from one world to another" Music and Voice seem finally to be coming together.

OPENER: —There was a time I asked myself, What is it?
There were times I answered, It's the outing.
Two outings.
Then the return.
Where?
To the village.
To the inn.
Two outings, then at last the return, to the village, to the inn, by the only road that leads there. An image like any other.
But I don't answer any more
I open
[*With Voice and Music*:]
As though they had linked their arms.
Good.
Good!

Opener traces here a structural metaphor. All the terms of this little fable can be recuperated for interpretation, but only by taking them as a metaphor for a relation, not as a metaphor directly applicable to music and language. That type of identification can only come after the nature of the relation has been clarified. For this it will be necessary to take the terms of the metaphor one by one.

"It's the outing" ("promenade" in the French version). Beckett's heroes have always been peripateticians, for whom walking, thinking, and self-knowledge go hand in hand. In many of the early fictions, walking had figured a means of escape from the kind of intense introspection to which all of Beckett's heroes are subject.[27] In his later work, Beckett makes much more of this figure, beginning with the trilogy, in which walking serves as one of the primary metaphors of the search for self. Thus Molloy heads through the forest to his mother's house with Moran on his trail, and Mahood's character in *The Unnamable* follows a concentric spiraling path toward home. In the trilogy, *How It Is*, and much of the prose fiction right up through *Company* and *Worstward Ho*, walking plays much the same role, although, following the downward logic of Beckett's imagination, it often becomes falling, crawling, and, eventually, total prostration. In *Cascando*, walking (and falling) plays a central thematic role in the story Voice has to tell, which is about a typically Beckettian derelict shambling through the countryside.

Opener's version of the peripatetic metaphor has the dignified allure of an outing or promenade. The promenade is characterized as a round-trip journey. The outward journey is to the village, the return to the inn: "Two outings, then at last the return, to the village, to the inn, by the only road that leads there." This back and forth movement between the inn and the village recalls the travels of Don Quixote and Sancho Panza. But whether or not Beckett had Cervantes's novel in mind, it is clear that Beckett intends to inscribe the relationship between Music and Voice into the kind of polarized structure that characterizes the relationship between Quixote and Panza. Beckett exploits this type of pairing throughout his career, not only in the Music-Words relationship of *Cascando* and *Words and Music* but also in *Godot, Endgame, Mercier and Camier*, and elsewhere. Moreover, this type of relationship is entirely in keeping with the critical statements on the opposition between language and music seen in the *Proust* essay and can usually be understood in terms of the opposition between realism and idealism. This last point is of particular significance, since the opposition between language and music is intimately related, for Beckett, to the opposition between realism and idealism in philosophy.

Although Music and Words were said earlier to be separated by an astral distance, their trajectories are identical. They start at the same place, have the same destination, follow the same path, and return to the same place. The fact that Opener can describe them in one passage as being separated by an astral distance and then assert that they follow the same path together makes clear the high level of metaphorical abstraction at work. The effect of this tension is compounded when Opener adds to the image the intimacy of linked arms: "As though they had linked their arms."

Understanding the nature of the relationship between Voice and Music, then, requires solving a kind of riddle. What kind of "road" (*chemin*) is in question here? On one level of metaphoricity, we know that there is only one road between the village and the inn and that Music and Voice travel it together, perhaps arm in arm. On another level of metaphoricity, we know that Voice and Music can tend toward agreement ("draw together") but only from one world (or star) to another. This is the enigma that is at the heart of the piece: *what kind of road can be traveled by Music and Voice and yet allow for the kind of cosmic distance between them that seems to be implied by the words* astre *and "world"?*

Having determined the thematic centrality of the Schopenhauerian, phenomenological problematic that traverses Beckett's work (the "subject-object crisis"), we have the key necessary to the solution of the riddle. We might almost say that for Beckett there is only one question and only one response. The question always involves the relationship between subject and object, and the answer must always be sought in consciousness. In fact, it is possible to identify the metaphorical road in question here with consciousness itself, especially if we remember that we have already seen an unambiguous example of this equation in a passage from *Dream of Fair to Middling Women*, discussed earlier, that linked the "night firmament" with both music and the "constellations of genius" of the mind.

> The night firmament is abstract density of music, symphony without end, illumination without end, yet emptier, more sparsely lit, than the most succinct constellations of genius. Now seen merely, a depthless lining of hemisphere, its crazy stippling of stars, it is the passional movements of the mind charted in light and darkness. The tense passional intelligence, when arithmetic abates, tunnels, sky-mole, surely and blindly (if we only thought so!) through the interstellar coalsacks of its firmament in genesis, it twists through the stars of its creation in a network of loci that shall never be co-ordinate. The inviolable criterion of poetry and music, the non-principle of their punctuation, is figured in the demented perforation of the night colander. The mind suddenly entombed, then active in an anger and a rhapsody of energy, in a scurrying and plunging towards exitus, such is the ultimate mode and factor of the creative integrity, its proton, incommunicable; but there, insistent, invisible rat, fidgeting behind the astral incoherence of the art surface. (*Dream* 16)

This passage moves from a general metaphor comparing the night sky and "the passional movements of the mind" to a figure of artistic creation as a cosmic effort toward "exitus." The "road" in *Cascando* corresponds well to this "inviolable criterion of poetry and music," which involves "perforating" the night sky, finding a path out. Remarkably, this passage shares almost the entire metaphorical structure of *Cascando*: the simulta-

neous presence of music and words ("poetry and music"), of trans-
ference and transit ("tunnels," "twists through," "perforation," "exitus"),
the cosmic vocabulary that equates thought with interplanetary movement ("interstellar," "astral"), and the search for a way out, for a way to
open. Ending, as it does, with a kind of manifesto on the incommunica-
bility of the "proton" of thought and on the necessity of the "astral
incoherence of the art *surface*," this passage helps to link the metaphorical
tissue of *Cascando* with the theoretical preoccupations of the *Proust* essay
and the letter to Axel Kaun—depth and surface, subject and object, music
and language.

This passage clearly offers support for a phenomenological reading of
Opener's fable as a metaphor of consciousness and artistic creation. And
yet we need to be very careful when talking about "mental functioning,"
"consciousness," and "thought" in *Cascando*. More precisely, we'll need
to reconcile these themes with the fact that Opener flatly refuses to take
responsibility for Music and Voice as something he would have thought.
He states expressly that the music and words are *not* in his head, that they
are not his voices, that they do not belong to him. This, in fact, is one of
his primary themes.

> What do I open?
> They say, He opens nothing, he has nothing to open, it's in his
> head.
> They don't see me, they don't see what I do, they don't see what
> I have, and they say, He opens nothing, he has nothing to open,
> it's in his head.
> I don't protest any more, I don't say any more,
> There is nothing in my head.
> I don't answer any more.
> I open and close.

If Opener insists that neither the music nor the voice comes from his
head ("They say . . . it's in his head . . . There is nothing in my head"),
then how can we make a case for Music as a form of thought? Here again,
we'll need to insist on the precise terms of the argument, which are crucial to understanding Beckett's meaning. If we focus on the terms of the
initial accusation—"It's in his head" ("c'est dans sa tête" in the French)—
we see that it can have at least three meanings.

First, a strictly literal interpretation of this proposition would insist on location: it's *in* his head. The implication is that the voices are literally located in his head, that they originate in his mind. His negative response, then, would imply something like "No, I did not find all this in my head; it comes from *elsewhere*." This is a question of location, and Beckett seems very close here to enunciating a twentieth-century myth of inspiration. All Opener can do is open these discourses that have been channeled through him for some obscure reason but that he cannot control. Beckett's "I open," in this sense, seems to be very close to Rimbaud's "On me pense/Je est un autre" [One thinks me/I is an other] or the Lacanian "Ça pense," which could be translated, variously, as "It thinks," "Id thinks," or even with the formulation William James once proposed: "There is thinking." Following this line of reasoning, we might say that *Cascando* is about creation as something that is fundamentally impersonal.

Second, a less literal, "ordinary-language," or Wittgensteinian approach to this passage would insist that the statement "It's in his head" is supposed to mean something like "He's making it up" or "He's deluded," as in the figure of speech, "It's all in your head." If we follow this line of reasoning, Opener's negative response would mean something like, "No, I'm not making this up" or "I'm not crazy, this really is what I hear." This approach, of a more or less realist bent, might initially stress common-sensical questions of interpretation like, is Opener hallucinating or lying? And if not, then what is the status of these voices? Eventually, we would have to decide whether or not to believe Opener's reiterated negative responses to these questions and imagine what actual sources there could be for such voices.

Finally, the "No, I'm not just making it up" interpretation is also reconcilable with an idealist or solipsistic approach to the question of the truth value of phenomena. According to this view, perceived and imagined stimuli are considered to have, at least potentially, precisely the same status within consciousness.[28] Thus Opener's negative response to the accusation "It's in his head" could be taken to mean either "No, I'm not making it up" (realist approach) or, more subtly, something like "Even if this is not an objectively verifiable reality, it has the same force within consciousness; my imaginings are as true (to me) as my perceptions" (idealist approach).

In other words, the question here becomes, Do we read this as a statement about fictional discourse as a message from beyond, funneled through the speaker by some unspecified agent (as in number 1 above), or as a statement about the truth value of fictional discourse (as in both the realist and idealist approaches of numbers 2 and 3)? I think Beckett intended for this statement to have both meanings. I also think that it is possible, and crucial for our understanding of *Cascando*, to reconcile them. One way to do this is through Wittgenstein's famous gloss on the "philosophical I" as an unanalyzable horizon of being, which sheds valuable light on this play and on much of Beckett's work in general.

According to Wittgenstein, the relation of subject to world is like that between an eye and the field of sight: like an eye, "I" can never enter its own field of sight. The I, in this special, philosophical (i.e., nonpsychological) sense, can only be posited as a limit, a horizon of consciousness, and not something that individuals can be said to experience empirically. "You do not really see the eye," Wittgenstein tells us, "and from nothing in the field of sight can it be concluded that it is seen from an eye." Any attempt to "see" the eye would require positing another that would in turn remain invisible, outside of its own field of sight. Wittgenstein concludes from this that

> there is therefore really a sense in which in philosophy we can talk of a non-psychological I.
> The I occurs in philosophy through the fact that the "world is my world."
> The philosophical I is not the man, not the human body or the human soul of which psychology treats, but the metaphysical subject, the limit—not a part of the world. (*Tractatus* 5.641, 151–53)

In this view, "solipsism strictly carried out coincides with pure realism," because "the I in solipsism shrinks to an extensionless point and there remains the reality co-ordinated with it." The relevance of this eye metaphor to Beckett's work is striking. Beckett's work is full of observing eyes that cannot themselves be observed, from the thematized camera eye in *Film* and the eye that is opposed to the burned-out "eyes of flesh" in *The Lost Ones*, to the witnessing eyes of the twelfth *Text for Nothing* that make it clear that in order to finally answer the question "Who's speaking?" "all the peoples of the earth would not suffice, at the end of the billions you'd need a god, unwitnessed witness of witnesses" (*Collected Shorter Prose* 112).

These considerations help to resolve the double meaning of the "It's not in my head" statement as a spatial metaphor (i.e., "It's not *in* my head") and as a truth metaphor ("I'm not making it up"). Opener is meant to have the status of an intermediary voice for this Wittgensteinian "philosophical I"; he is the representative of this entity that can only be understood as a horizon or limit of being. The voice and music turned on and off by Opener cannot be situated in a head (i.e., a real or imaginary mental space) because they come from elsewhere—not, to be sure, the Muses or the gods (as in theories of inspiration from antiquity) but from this nonpsychological, ontologically stable subject that must be posited by the speaking subject but that can only be said to exist outside of the empirical plane. Thus, like the narrator of *The Unnamable*, Opener is merely a spokesman for this "I" whom he knows only through the transmissions he receives. Indeed, it might be said that Opener *has* no inside, that if "there is nothing in [his] head," it is because he is himself nothing but a disembodied voice, exactly like the musical and verbal voices he opens and closes.

We are finally to the point where we can begin to suggest the values assigned to Music and Voice in *Cascando*. But once again, the semantic muteness of Music, the fact that Music cannot denote or define but only exemplify and connote, makes determining its exact role quite difficult. This fact raises an important question for interpretation: Would a detailed analysis of the music written for *Cascando* help us understand the play better? Certainly, such an analysis would be interesting and worthwhile in its own right, but I don't think this type of analysis is crucial to our understanding of the play as a whole. Such an analysis would probably wind up telling us more about how different composers have understood the work than about the hidden meaning of Music's dramatic role in *Cascando*. A brief consideration of the genesis and performance history of the piece will help to buttress this claim.

We have already seen that Beckett had no hand in writing the music and that he gave no clues in the script as to what the music should sound like. Moreover, Beckett has approved the composition of several different scores for the piece. And despite significant differences between the versions I have heard, the overall effect of the piece remains constant.[29] In this sense, the different scores written for the piece are, from a dramatic point of view, interchangeable. How can this be? Doesn't this imply a scandalous devaluation of the music's role in the piece? Not if we recall that neither the music nor the spoken text can carry the semiotic burden of the piece alone. It is the relationship *between* Music and Voice, mediated by Opener's commentary, that signifies in *Cascando*. Neither Music nor Voice can be understood in isolation.

Music, in this sense, is presented in negative relief in the play, as a mode of expression that makes meaning primarily by virtue of its opposition to Voice. The oppositional value of Music becomes clear in a passage in which Opener rejects once more the idea that Voice and Music come from him, insisting that they are not in his head.

> OPENER: They said, It's his own, it's his voice, it's in his head.
> VOICE: [...]
> OPENER: No resemblance.
> I answered, And that ...
> MUSIC: [*Brief*] ....
> OPENER: ... is that mine too?
> But I don't answer any more.
> (*Complete Dramatic Works* 302)

The aggressive irony of the "is that mine too?" shows that Opener uses music here as an obvious example of alterity, whereas with Voice there might still have been confusion. Music seems to Opener to prove his point unequivocally: How could *that* come from me? Initially, then, Music must be taken to function as a radicalized example of the complete alterity of discourse. The questions now become, On what grounds are Music and Voice opposed, and in what sense are they "coming together"? The answer comes from Voice.

Voice's discourse alternates between two primary modes: a narrative mode, which Beckett in his notes calls the "élément histoire" (story element), and an "élément soi" (self element), which has a distinct metanarrative emphasis. The story element comprises a narrative about a derelict named Woburn who stumbles through a barren, wintry, and vaguely Irish coastal landscape. The self element is a metanarrative discourse about the necessity of finishing: ". . . if you could finish it you could rest . . . not before . . ." We have already seen that from Opener's perspective the end will come when Voice and Music "come together," when they "agree" or metaphorically link arms ("se donnent le bras"). To this we must now add that from Voice's point of view (remember that he has no awareness of Opener or Music), ending and rest can only come when he has finished his story, when he finally gets it right, when he *sees* this character he calls Woburn (Maunu in the French version).

> VOICE: [*low, panting*] —story . . . if you could finish it . . . you could
> rest . . . sleep . . . not before . . . oh I know . . . the ones I've
> finished . . . thousands and one . . . all I ever did . . . in my life . . .
> with my life . . . saying to myself . . . finish this one . . . it's the
> right one . . . then rest . . . sleep . . . no more stories . . . no more
> words . . . and finished it . . . and not the right one . . . couldn't
> rest . . . straight away another . . . to begin . . . to finish . . . saying
> to myself . . . finish this one . . . then rest . . . this time . . . it's the
> right one . . . this time . . . you have it . . . and finished it . . . and
> not the right one . . . couldn't rest . . . straight away another . . .
> but this one . . . it's different . . . I'll finish it . . . I've got it . . .[30]

We should notice the alternation between first and second person in this passage as well as the breathless syntax and diction of Voice's discourse, which is highly reminiscent of *How It Is*. As befits a story about the search for self, Voice addresses himself in the second person as often as in the first. He has grammatically divided himself into two parts: the first person, who accomplishes things ("the ones I've finished . . . thousands and one . . ."), and the second person, who is obligated to accomplish more ("if you could finish it . . . you could rest . . ."). This type of pronominal play recalls *The Unnamable* ("I'll never say I again") and, especially, *Company*, in which the protagonist is divided into three parts, distinguished by the use of the first, second, and third persons.[31] If Voice could finish his story, he would have no more to accomplish and would be able to identify himself fully with the first person.

Of course, it is already perfectly clear—to us, if not to Voice—that the present story is not the right one and that, in fact, there can be no right story, only an infinite series of incorrect or incomplete ones. This is a standard feature of the Beckettian predicament, well known to his readers. But, having said that, we still haven't answered the central question raised by Voice's desperate attempt to get his stories right. How, after all, does Voice judge his stories? How does he *know* whether he has got it right or not? This question turns out to be crucial for understanding the relationship between Voice and Music. Voice's general meaning, of course, is that every story he tells turns out to be an insufficient expression of whatever truth it is that he is supposed to express. But there is a hidden temporal element in this passage that must be emphasized. A subtle but persistent feature of Voice's discourse is that he doesn't know until *after* he has completed a story that it is incorrect: "and finished it . . . and not the right one . . ." This holds true throughout *Cascando*. Voice tells stories based on some model, example, or standard of truth. He then compares the finished product to the model, and only then does he find out that the story was not the right one. He then goes on to revise his account ("he's changed . . ."), test it again, and register his new failure: "not enough . . ." This process, which repeats itself over and over in Voice's narrative, makes it clear that there is some model or criterion to which his stories are supposed to conform. His stories are not invented ex nihilo. However bizarre they might appear, they are being judged against some point of reference. The truth, or lack thereof, of Voice's stories is *verifiable*.

Opener follows precisely the same pattern, first speaking and then checking his words against some criterion of truth. This pattern is established in the opening line of the piece: "It is the month of May . . . For me. [*Pause.*] Correct." First comes the statement (wholly unverifiable for the audience, since we have no access to his point of reference), then a pause while he consults his model, and then the conclusion that he is correct (at least in this assertion). The personal nature of the statement and the verification stage are made explicit in the second and third clauses, " . . . For me. [*Pause.*] Correct," which seem to imply that the first clause, not yet correct, was in need of a slight modification before the statement could be judged adequate.

This statement about the month of May has provoked a great deal of critical consternation. Why on earth does Opener evoke the month of May here? There is, no doubt, more than one legitimate way to explain this statement, but all the attempts I have seen seem somehow unsatisfactory. Some, for example, point out that Opener will later link May with springtime and the theme of annual renewal ("you know, the reawakening"). Others point out that there is a character in *Footfalls* named May and that, as Deirdre Bair reminds us, Beckett's mother was named May. Should we then read some kind of biographical significance into this line or emphasize the theme of seasonal rebirth? Both of these points of reference are helpful up to a point, but no matter how many intertexts or thematic correspondences we find for it, this kind of reference to a spe-

cific extratextual reality in an otherwise abstract piece will remain perplexing. Given that it serves no descriptive or atmospheric purpose (this
is not a pastoral; there is no attempt to create a springlike mood), we
must ask if it serves any other purpose. The key to answering this question, I think, is to understand that this statement must not be treated
from a purely thematic perspective but examined in terms of its function.
The point of this declaration is not to engage the play in a network of
seasonal or filial or reproductive thematics (or, at least, this is not the *only*
goal) but to make a statement about the status of statements. This is a
sentence that comments upon itself, and one of its primary goals is to
establish the temporal sequence that it exemplifies (statement, verification, refusal/acceptance) as a theme of the play.

The significance of this determination becomes apparent if we look
more closely at how the process of verification is deployed in Voice's
discourse. We can see this process of speaking, comparing, and rejecting
in action throughout Voice's narrative, as in the following passage, which
presents it in miniature: ". . . I've got him . . . I've seen him . . . I've said
him . . . we're there . . . nearly . . . no more stories . . . all false . . ." In the
first four cells of this passage, Voice thinks he may have finally succeeded
in his quest. We can sense the growing excitement of each successive
affirmation, culminating in the triumphant "we're there," followed by
what I imagine as a pause while Voice compares his story to the model
and finds that it is not quite up to par ("nearly . . ."), and then a movement of perhaps bitter disappointment as the implications of the
"nearly" sink in: "no more stories . . . all false . . ." This increase and
decrease in excitement could be depicted by a crescendo and decrescendo
(and would almost certainly have to be performed that way by the actor
playing Voice), or it could be represented graphically in the following
manner:

we're there . . . nearly . . .

I've said him . . .   no more stories . . .

I've seen him . . .

I've got him . . .   all false . . .

This three-stage process of assertion, comparison, and evaluation is
perfectly compatible with the standard theories of mimesis as the *re*-
presentation or imitation of a preexisting phenomenon. It also matches

up with the theory of expression as the pressing out or *ex*-pression of some preexisting thought. First there is the phenomenon (which, existing only in consciousness, cannot be communicated); then there is the attempt to describe it, which can only come after the fact; and then there is the comparison of the two. With this in mind, we are at last in a position to give a clearer characterization of Music's function in this relationship.

Beckett, by insisting on the posteriority of language with respect to phenomena, follows here the Schopenhauerian assertion that language, which operates through the concept, can have only a *post rem* relationship to absolute reality. Schopenhauer asserts that both music and language lack the particularness of phenomena but in different ways: music, taken as a direct imitation of the will, precedes phenomena, expressing their essence, while the concept is an a posteriori abstraction from perception.

> For, to a certain extent, melodies are, like universal concepts, an abstraction from reality . . . These two universalities, however, are in a certain respect opposed to each other, since the concepts contain only the forms, first of all abstracted from perception, so to speak the stripped-off outer shell of things; hence they are quite properly *abstracta*. Music, on the other hand, gives the innermost kernel preceding all form, or the heart of things. This relation could very well be expressed in the language of the scholastics by saying that the concepts are the *universalia post rem*, but music gives the *universalia ante rem*, and reality the *universalia in re*. (*The World as Will* 263)

This is the crux of the opposition between Voice and Music. It determines both the necessity and the impossibility of their coming together. Voice uses language, which, having a *post rem* relationship to phenomena, can never fully express them. Voice's stories are "never the right one." Music, on the other hand, may be able to express the "innermost kernel preceding all form" (if we are to believe Schopenhauer), but, and this is precisely the point, *we can't tell*. What Music cannot do is name that which it expresses. Music can be present as a stream of pure thought, but it can't share with us what that thought is about because it does not denote. Music's discourse, if it does in fact have the *ante rem* relation to phenomenal reality that Schopenhauer attributes to it, is *full* in the sense that it not only corresponds adequately to phenomenal reality but has an essentiality that phenomena lack. Language, on the other hand, can never adequately express phenomena, because it is always only the imitation of an imitation, an abstraction from perception. Beckett uses music in *Cascando* to point to the vast, unnamable tracts of being that remain outside language's domain; music serves as an example of that to which his words aspire. But the music is itself subject to its inability to tell us what it means. If Music and Voice could come together, if Opener could combine Voice's ability to name with Music's ability to communicate the innermost kernel preceding all form, only then would he have an adequate representation of (his) reality.

I am not trying to argue that *Cascando* should be understood simply as a dramatization of a point of Schopenhauerian aesthetics but that Beckett, like Schopenhauer, is acutely attuned to the lack that is at the heart of language. For Beckett, every expressive or descriptive statement must always lead to a new attempt to express, since language is inherently inadequate to its object: "And finished it . . . and not the right one." Music appears to Beckett, as it did to Schopenhauer, as promising the possibility of a more complete form of communication.

We've already, I think, sufficiently established the *post rem* quality of the verbal discourse of Voice and Opener. But how can we show that Beckett intends for Music to represent the corollary *ante rem* status that Schopenhauer ascribes to music? Is it possible to prove that Beckett also intended to ascribe this role to music? Schopenhauer's assertion, of course, was that all music (or at least all *authentic* music) has an *ante rem* relation to phenomenal reality. But relying on Schopenhauer to establish Beckett's intention won't do, since we can't be sure that Beckett means to follow Schopenhauer. Given the semantic muteness of Music (and the fact that we don't have direct access to the phenomena in question in *Cascando*), there is no way that I can see to demonstrate conclusively, from the evidence available within the play, that Beckett intended to use music in just this way. We can, however, prove this point indirectly, because there is a large body of evidence distributed throughout Beckett's work that does support this claim. For one thing, Beckett has used the term *ante rem* on several occasions, notably, in some of the Schopenhauerian passages of *Proust* and in the "aesthetic of inaudibilities" section of *Dream*, where Belacqua describes Beethoven's music in Schopenhauerian terms: "He listens to the Ferne, the unsterbliche Geliebte, he unbuttons himself to Teresa ante rem" (139). Beethoven's music is not taken to describe the here and now or the actual women Beethoven has loved but the ideal beyond ("Ferne"), their inner essence.

The most important source of evidence, however, for the claim that Beckett does follow Schopenhauer in using Music as the *ante rem* corollary of language's *post rem* relation to phenomena comes from Beckett's other media plays. Of these, the most important is *Words and Music*. There, Music acts as a guide for Words, leading him in the quest to make the image. Music, it turns out, has a role to play in creating images, the leading role.

WORDS, MUSIC, IMAGES

In *Words and Music*, Beckett uses the same triangular setup as *Cascando* to make his point. Like his homologue Opener, Croak's job is to induce Words and Music to perform. And as in *Cascando*, it seems clear that what takes place is understood to occur within the confines of a consciousness. Croak, however, has a much more intimate relationship with his voices than Opener: the three interact as would the master and servants of a comedy. The play depicts the expressive progress of Words and Music, who, goaded by Croak, proceed, in a five-stage process, from a total lack of success in rendering the themes proposed by their master to what appears to be a resounding success at the end of the play. This progress results from their increased cooperation: together Music and Words are able to improve upon the clichéd rhetoric of Words's first speeches and the equally clichéd sentimentality of Music's early interventions. Their collaboration results in first a song on old "Age" and then a final song on the theme of the "Wellhead," both sung by Words, with Music teaching, encouraging, and accompanying Words. Because the meaning of the play depends so much on this narrative progression from worst to best, it's worth following Words and Music step by step through the successive stages of their development. Once again, the semantic muteness of Music will require that we focus analysis on Croak and Words. It is only through the relationship between the three that we can determine the specificity of Music's role.

The play opens to the sounds of Words and Music warming up. We hear a "small orchestra softly tuning up," then Words practicing a hackneyed discourse on the theme of "Sloth."

WORDS: Sloth is of all the passions the most powerful passion and indeed no passion is more powerful than the passion of sloth, this is the mode in which the mind is most affected and indeed—[*Burst of tuning. Loud, imploring.*] Please! [*Tuning dies away. As before.*] The mode in which the mind is most affected and indeed in no mode is the mind more affected than in this, by passion we are to understand a movement of the soul pursuing or fleeing real or imagined pleasure or pain pleasure or pain real or imagined pleasure or pain.

Notice that Words is rehearsing here the oratorical device of the *definitio*. Beckett has chosen a rhetorical topic that emphasizes language's alignment with concepts. Here, however, he also links conceptual thought to the deformation of rhetorical pragmatism, present in Words's speech as hyperbole. Beckett also takes care to make clear the inadequacy of this approach. Words, to develop his theme, chooses to explore it conceptually, using the indefinite present tense of the dictionary definition and classifying Sloth first as a "passion," then as a "mode," then returning to refine his definition by defining the term "passion," and so on in what looks likely to be an infinite series of ever finer distinctions and qualifications, each as conventional (medieval, scholastic) as the previous. The timely arrival of Croak, however, puts an end to Words's warm-up.

With the arrival of Croak, the petty enmity between Words and Music (expressed above in Music's interruption) is momentarily swept under the carpet, as Croak, greeting the two as Joe (Words) and Bob (Music), entreats them to "Be friends!" (Croak, we should note, never refers to either Words or Music as such, preferring to call them Joe and Bob. As in *Cascando*, Beckett resists endorsing the use of the names Music and Words within the metaphorical structure of the text.) After excusing himself for being late, Croak proposes the first theme: love. Words, although still not quite warmed up, picks up the theme first, trying to use his sloth speech verbatim, altering it only enough to replace the word "sloth" with "love."

WORDS: [*Orotund.*] Love is of all the passions the most powerful passion and indeed no passion is more powerful than the passion of love. [*Clears throat.*] This is the mode in which the mind is most strongly affected and indeed in no mode is the mind more strongly affected than in this. [*Pause.*]

CROAK: *Rending sigh. Thump of club.*

WORDS: [*As before.*] By passion we are to understand a movement of the mind pursuing or fleeing real or imagined pleasure or pain. [*Clears throat.*] Of all—

CROAK: [*Anguished.*] Oh!

WORDS: [*As before.*] Of all these movements then and who can number them and they are legion sloth is the LOVE is the most urgent and indeed by no manner of movement is the soul more urged than by this, to and—
[*Violent thump of club.*]

On automatic pilot, Words can't even keep his terms straight and momentarily slips, in the last line, from love to sloth. Croak's initial "rending sigh" and anguished "Oh!" suggest that, although perhaps frustrated by Words's hesitation, he may be susceptible to even this glib disquisition. Whatever the case, he cuts Words off immediately when it finally becomes apparent that he is simply recycling a canned speech. Croak then turns to Music, commanding him to give it a try ("Bob!"). Music's version, however, is only "worthy of foregoing," that is, clichéd and alternating between exaggerated expressiveness and expressionless bombast. Croak cuts him off in turn.

The first round ends in failure, and Croak decides now to introduce another theme: age. Croak summons Words to begin, and Words, who seems to be caught off-guard, can only come up with a "faltering," confused attempt to render the theme: "Age is . . . age is when . . . old age I mean . . . if that is what my Lord means . . . is when . . . if you're a man . . . were a man . . . huddled . . . nodding . . . the ingle . . . waiting—" Croak cuts him off quickly and turns to Music, who does little better. At this point, Croak, no doubt frustrated by their ineptitude, decides to link Words and Music together for the first time. In a rage, he thumps his club, subjects them to a bit of verbal abuse ("Dogs!"), and demands that they perform together, which, despite the initial protestations of Words, they do—badly at first and then with increased success. A new pattern begins here. Words proposes a line of text, which he tries to sing; Music suggests improvements on the singing; and Words adopts the improvements. This results in the following song, which, after a belabored line-by-line rehearsal, is performed in toto with Words "trying to sing" to Music's accompaniment.

Age is when to a man
Huddled o'er the ingle
Shivering for the hag
To put the pan in the bed
And bring the toddy
She comes in the ashes
Who loved could not be won
Or won not loved
Or some other trouble
Comes in the ashes
Like in that old light
The face in the ashes
That old starlight
On the earth again.

Their song transforms the age theme into a nostalgic evocation of lost love and the unpredictability of memory. Although the emotional potential of this song seems to be undercut by throwaway lines like "Or some other trouble" and words like "hag" and "toddy," it nevertheless has a powerful effect on Croak, who can manage at first only a "long pause" and then, in a choked "murmur," the words "the face," repeated five times. The reasons for this reaction, and the intensity of the song's effect on Croak, seem obscure initially but become apparent in what follows. We quickly understand that Croak's murmur is in fact a command: having latched on to the mention of "the *face* in the ashes" from line 12 of the age song, he is telling Words and Music to develop this theme for their next bit. This is a significant development: the attentive auditor of *Words and Music* will have remembered that the face theme has been present from the beginning of the piece: Croak, upon his arrival, excused himself for being late. The stated reason for this tardiness, which could only seem obscure at the time, was an encounter with the face: "I am late, forgive. [*Pause.*] The face. [*Pause.*] On the stairs. [*Pause.*] Forgive." The meaning of this explanation becomes apparent in light of this new emphasis on the face. Both "the face . . . on the stairs" and "the face in the ashes" belong, presumably, to this same "She," later named Lily, "who loved could not be won/Or won not loved/Or some other trouble." At this point, the play's thematics coalesce, and Croak's goal becomes clear: to have Words and Music evoke the image of this beloved face. The introduction of the face theme marks the turning point of the play.

At first, Music tries to lead Words into the face theme, as he had with the age theme, but Words refuses to follow. After one minute of "warmly sentimental" music, Words, ignoring Music's "warm" suggestions and finally silencing him with a sharp "Enough!" delivers a prolonged description of the face in "cold" tones. There are two striking features to this description. One is the cold tone (the word "cold" is repeated four times). The other is the relative lengthiness of the description. At the thematic heart of the play, a proper understanding of this passage will require a wide-ranging intertextual analysis, which I will save for later (the next section), as it would distract from the specifically narrative point I am trying to make here. Suffice it to say for now that Words's description of the beloved face culminates in a "reverent" evocation of—we might as well call her by her name—Lily opening her eyes. After the long, "cold" prose description of Lily's face, Words makes a clear and sudden "change to poetic tone." It is the reverently evoked opening of the eyes that brings about the transition into the wellhead theme.

> . . . a little colour comes back into the cheeks and the eyes . . .
> [*Reverently.*] . . . open. [*Pause.*] Then down a little way . . .
> [*Pause. Change to poetic tone. Low.*]
> Then down a little way
> Through the trash.

Music takes this as a cue and immediately comes to assist. Together they move on to a new theme, the fifth and final theme of the play, called the wellhead theme in the script. They develop it in the same way they did the age poem, with Music giving first "discreet" and then "more confident" suggestions. After one rehearsal, with Music leading Words as before, they attempt a complete run-through, with Words's cracked voice and Music's accompaniment.

> Then down a little way
> Through the trash
> Towards where
> All dark no begging
> No giving no words
> No sense no need
> Through the scum
> Down a little way

To whence one glimpse
Of that wellhead.

At this point, Croak lets his club fall and leaves without a word. But Words, who had been so uncooperative in the early stages of the play, has had a complete change of heart. Despite the sudden departure of Croak, he begs Music to continue. At first he gets only a "brief rude retort" for his troubles, but finally Music consents to play through the wellhead theme twice more, after which the play ends on a "deep sigh" from Words.

One might wonder why Croak departs as he does. Does he leave in disgust or, conversely, because he is overwhelmed by emotion? The two possibilities are not mutually exclusive: Beckett's overriding preoccupation with the expressive limitations of art (compare what he writes in *Three Dialogues*) precludes any possibility of total satisfaction. It is quite possible that Croak's sudden departure is meant to suggest a kind of postperformance letdown of the type experienced by voice in *Cascando*: almost there . . . almost there . . . no . . . not good enough. Unlike *Cascando*'s Opener, however, Croak's response to the performances of Words and Music is primarily emotional. This affective emphasis is reflected by Words, who is obsessed with the "passions," as well as in the expressive bent of Music's performances. There is no attempt on Croak's part to explain, metaphorically or conceptually, the function of Words and Music. Croak's modus operandi is affective, not cognitive, and his relationship with Words and Music is of a much more intimate nature.[32] Beckett seems to be at great pains to show, first, that the music and words have a powerful and apparently painful effect on Croak and, second, that he nevertheless refuses to go without them. Croak's typical response to the performances of his servants is "anguished." The predicate "anguished" is applied to Croak six times in the script, always to indicate his reaction to one of Words's or Music's performances. The script also calls for further signs of Croak's suffering in the form of six "groans," one "rending sigh," one "alas," and two (loaded) silences. Even Words's most hackneyed speeches are able to get this kind of "anguished" reaction from Croak. Nevertheless, whenever there is, for whatever reason, a gap in the performance, Croak either thumps his club impatiently or cajoles and bullies his servants into picking up their performance where they left off, moving in the blink of an eye from positive ("My comforts! Be friends!") to negative ("Together dogs!") reinforcement.

At the end of the play we are left to puzzle out what it is about these words and this music—which seem, to us, to be such woefully inadequate attempts to articulate the themes proposed by Croak—that makes them able to move Croak in this way. The most likely reason for this anguish becomes apparent in the succession of themes chosen and in the kinds of development they are given by Words and Music. The themes proposed, we must assume, are taken from Croak's personal preoccupations. Moreover, Words and Music treat each theme in increasingly intimate detail. They make a gradual approach to the most secret areas of Croak's affective life. We know, for example, from Croak's reactions and allusions that the face image has special importance for him ("Lily!"), and I think it is this personal stake of Croak in the proceedings that explains his reactions. Croak, who has seen the face, who has access to this phenomenon that we as spectators can only guess at, knows what Music and Words are referring to and is able to use even these inadequate performances as a springboard to the image he wants to recall. If we look more closely at the way Words develops each successive theme, the exact nature of the progression, from most abstract to most intimate, becomes clear.

Words is torn at the outset between his subservience to Croak and his initial dislike for Music. If Croak's primary mode is "anguished," Words's primary mode is "imploring." Music seems to provoke the same kind of pained reactions in Words as in Croak. But whereas Croak seems to relish this emotion, Words fears it and tries to avoid it by pleading with both Words and Croak for release. Words's initial dislike for Music is already quite apparent at the opening of the piece when Words asks, "How much longer cooped up here in the dark? [*With loathing.*] With you!" The first three times Music plays we hear "audible groans and protestations" ("No!" "Please!" "Mercy!" etc.) from Words. Later, when Croak commands the two to perform together, Words tries to resist with an "[*Imploring.*] No!" repeated twice. But, overruled, he is forced to perform with Music. By the end of the play, in what turns out to be the most notable transformation of the piece, we find Words twice "imploring" Music to play some more. Words, in other words, has effected a complete reversal over the course of the play: his initial "imploring" entreaties to silence Music have given way to his equally imploring demands for Music to play.

This change in his attitude toward Music seems to be linked with the evident evolution in his elocutionary style over the course of the piece. This progress can be charted in his treatment of the five themes: sloth, love, age, the face, and the final wellhead theme. Words's first speech on sloth is, as we've seen, delivered in rehearsal tones before Croak's arrival; the stage directions specify that his speech is to be "rattled off, low," and it is clear that Words is simply warming up. Upon the arrival of Croak, Words shifts into performance mode and delivers his speech in "oro-tund" and "very rhetorical" tones, with an unintentionally humorous "prosaic" digression on love of the flesh and a moment of referential uncertainty delivered with "sudden," although perhaps artificial, "grav-ity." As in the sloth warm-up, his style is outlandishly clichéd through-out. It is not until the third theme (age), delivered with the help of Music, that Words breaks out of the formulaic thoughtlessness of his first two speeches. After one last "faltering" attempt to salvage his worn-out sloth speech, his style improves remarkably. With the help of Music, he begins "trying to sing." This improvement involves a notable rhetorical shift, from the universal intemporality of the dictionary definition ("Sloth/ Love *is* of all the passions the most powerful passion . . .") to the narrative mode of the exemplum ("Age is *when* to a man/Huddled o'er the ingle"). Words has abandoned the attempt to manipulate pure concepts and adopts a second rhetoric of poetic diction and allegorical narrative. This rhetorical shift is doubled in the written text by a typographical shift from the prose appropriate to argumentative discourse to the vertical *mise en page* of poetry and song. Beckett seems to be making use here of the traditional identification of poetry with song, and this identification may help us to interpret the fact that Words tries to sing but sings poorly. Just as Words can only imitate, without fully integrating, the lessons of Music, poetic elocution can only partially incorporate musical values. Music has now adopted a leading role, teaching Words his lines one by one, proposing suggestions for improvement, and providing encourage-ment. Words can only do his best to keep up.

Words, however, still has enough self-confidence to strike out on his own for the fourth theme. This is the face theme, which, apart from two brief interventions from music, is developed exclusively by Words, who refuses all the warm suggestions that Music offers. Words takes advantage of the opportunity to explore an even more intimate side of Croak's personal preoccupations. In total contrast to the rather impersonal allegorical narrative on age ("Age is when," etc.) that preceded it, the face narrative explores the domain of the singular: a memory. Words has been through this theme before, knows that it has great importance for Croak, and, despite the coldness of his delivery, is able to tear an anguished cry from Croak ("Lily!"), which is the only mention in the play of an individual's name (apart from Bob and Joe, of course). Words's description culminates in the "reverently" expressed moment of truth, and this moment of truth (the opening of Lily's cherished eyes) brings about the need for more music. This time it is Words himself who cues Music's entrance, which he does by shifting to a "poetic tone."

This leads Words and Music into the final theme of the session, the wellhead theme, which, significantly, is *not* requested by Croak but seems, rather, to follow naturally from the face theme. Here again, Words follows Music's lead, "trying to sing." After the conceptual generality of the first two themes, the allegorical generality of the third, and the personal specificity of the face theme, the wellhead theme moves into an entirely new realm. The reality of this place can only be suggested in negative terms: there is "*no* begging/ *No* giving *no* words/ *No* sense *no* need." The qualification "*no* words" is especially remarkable in a text pronounced by a character named Words: all he can do is point to his lack of access to this region, this wellhead that can only be fleetingly "glimpsed." Words and Music have reached the threshold of what Beckett, in the *Proust* essay, called "transcendental apperception," that mode of perception "that can capture the Model, the Idea, the Thing in itself" (90).

The overall trend in Words's discourse, then, is clear: from the generality of the concept (the sloth and love themes), through the hybrid (i.e., half-conceptual, half-narrative) status of the allegorical fable (the age theme), then on to the perceptual singularity of memory (the face theme), and culminating in the approach to the quasi-mystical realm of apperception evoked in the wellhead theme. It seems likely that it is this climactic evocation of the wellhead that converts Words, allowing him to overcome his initial distaste for and rivalry with Music. Unable to do more than evoke the wellhead negatively, he is now ready and willing to hear Music play the wellhead theme through twice, with no groans of protest and without trying to intervene himself. Music, with its *ante rem* access to unmediated reality, is able to lead Words to the threshold of the wellhead. But Words, forever subject to the *post rem* condition of language, can go no farther.

As for Croak, we're not sure what has happened to him. We hear only the sound of his club falling, the "shocked" cry of "Master" from Words, and the tread of Croak's feet as he leaves. It seems likely that Croak's abrupt departure is meant as a sign that he is overcome with emotion and/or disappointment. But what is the significance of the wellhead theme, which seems to provoke his departure? Words's mimesis of the passage from conceptual abstraction through perceptual specificity and into apperceptual transcendence seems to be meant as a kind of ritual designed to afford Croak access to this privileged realm of being known as the wellhead. As for the wellhead, it provides a clear metaphor for the same kind of stoic blanking of conceptual thought advocated by Schopenhauer and described so eloquently throughout Beckett's work in terms of an ideal state of aesthetic contemplation. Described as "all dark," the wellhead recalls the dark tunnels, spheres, refuges, and abstract mental places evoked in texts like *Murphy*, *The Unnamable*, *How It Is*, and *Company*.

All of Beckett's characters seek out this privileged state of inner communion; some of them desire it with great vehemence. We find this theme developed discursively as early as the *Proust* essay and evoked in narrative terms in texts like *Murphy*, in which Belacqua seeks a way to achieve this state at will, to "systematize what was in fact a dispensation." Murphy too devotes himself to the search for a mechanism that will enable him to achieve this state of grace with regularity. (His excessive affection for rocking in his rocking-chair is due to his belief that rocking helps him to achieve the desired mental state.) This, I believe, is how the performance of Words and Music should be understood, as a kind of ritual, a formalized set of actions performed at regular intervals and designed to help Croak achieve this state of mystical communion. Like Murphy, Croak seeks to "systematize what was in fact a dispensation"; he believes, somewhat superstitiously, that the performances of Music and Words will enable him to reach the wellhead. In *Words and Music*, however, the ritual seems to fail. The fact that at the end of the play we hear Croak's painfully slow departure and the sound of his "shuffling slippers, with halts" seems to imply that the rite has not brought about the desired transformation. In order to understand the full import of this last remark, we will need to take a more general look at the use of ritualized performance in Beckett's media plays.

Presented as a regular occurrence, Croak's command performance should be understood as a ritual designed to enable him to pass into the mystical mental domain of the wellhead. The performance of Words and Music is a focusing device of the kind found in all rituals. This ceremonial collaboration between music and language also informs Beckett's use of music in two important, enigmatic television pieces: *Ghost Trio* and *Nacht und Träume*. In both of these plays, a piece of music is invoked as a means for achieving a privileged state of aesthetic contemplation of the type evoked in *Words and Music*. Also at the heart of this thematic network—music, ritual, a female face, and "transcendental apperception"—is another television piece from the same period: *". . . but the clouds . . . ,"* in which the same obsession with a face is the theme. *". . . but the clouds . . ."* is named after and built around not a piece of music but a line from Yeats's "The Tower," which it uses in the same way *Ghost Trio* and *Nacht und Träume* use the Beethoven and Schubert music after which they are named. Although *". . . but the clouds . . ."* uses a poem and not a piece of music, the function of the interpolated text is the same: it serves as a focal lens, which, it is hoped, will enable the protagonist to achieve the desired state of quasi-religious exaltation. In each of these plays, the music and/or text is the means, and the object of devotion is neither a wellhead nor a godhead but a female presence. My analysis of these pieces will focus on the ceremonial role of music and text.

DEVOTIONAL MUSIC: FROM *WORDS AND MUSIC* TO *GHOST TRIO*

Words and Music, as we just saw, portrays in a self-deprecatory, partly parodic manner the art of bringing an image alive to consciousness. The goal is to revive the image of the beloved face whose eyes seem able to provide a kind of mental passageway to a realm of apperceptive beatitude. The longest phase of Words's progress from the merely conceptual to the apperceptual involves his description of Lily's beloved face. But what is the significance of this face? What is its symbolic function? To answer these questions we'll need to go back and consider Words's description of the face, omitted earlier. This description takes place within the context of, as Claus Zilliacus delicately puts it, a moment of postcoital recuperation.

Seen from above at such close quarters in that radiance so cold and faint with eyes so dimmed by . . . what had passed, its quite . . . piercing beauty is a little . . . [. . .] blunted. Some moments later however, such are the powers of recuperation at this age, the head is drawn back to a distance of two or three feet, the eyes widen to a stare and begin to feast again. [. . .] Now and then the rye, swayed by a light wind, casts and withdraws its shadow. [. . .] the whole so blanched and still that were it not for the great white rise and fall of the breasts, spreading as they mount and then subsiding to their natural . . . aperture—[MUSIC: Irrepressible burst of spreading and subsiding music with vain protestations from WORDS.] [. . .] I resume, so wan and still and so ravished away that it seems no more of the earth than Mira in the Whale, at her tenth and greatest magnitude on this particular night shining coldly down—as we say, looking up. [*Pause.*] Some moments later however, such are the powers . . . the brows uncloud, the lips part and the eyes . . . [*Pause.*] . . . the brows uncloud, the nostrils dilate, the lips part and the eyes . . . [*Pause.*] . . . a little colour comes back into the cheeks and the eyes . . . [*Reverently.*] . . . open.

This face image has great importance in Beckett's work. It occurs, for example, in *Krapp's Last Tape*, in which Krapp's recorded voice gives a strikingly similar close-up evocation of a face, described from above, against a background of swaying vegetation, after making love, with a brief mention of breasts and a reverent evocation of opening eyes.

I asked her to look at me and after a few moments—[*Pause.*]—after a few moments she did, but the eyes just slits, because of the glare. I bent over her to get them in the shadow and they opened. [*Pause. Low.*] Let me in. [*Pause.*] We drifted in among the flags and stuck. The way they went down sighing, before the stem! [*Pause.*] I lay down across her with my face in her breasts and my hand on her. We lay there without moving. But under us all moved, and moved us, gently, up and down, and from side to side.[33]

The correspondence between these two descriptions is obvious, almost term for term, although with varying emphasis in each. We find variations on this image throughout Beckett's work, from the extended descriptions of the face in early texts like *Dream of Fair to Middling Women* and *More Pricks than Kicks*, to more enigmatic, allusive references to it in late pieces like *Ohio Impromptu* ("I saw the dear face and heard the unspoken words . . .") and *Company* ("Above the upturned face [. . .] Eyes in each other's eyes you listen to the leaves," etc.). Moreover, there are clear analogies between Krapp's mention of the way the eyes "open" and "let me in" and the metaphorical passage through Lily's open eyes in *Words and Music*. In the narrativized descriptions of his early texts, Beckett presented the image with such a wealth of detail and so much stress on its place in a romantic crisis that it is difficult to speak of it in other than biographical terms. It seems probable that the memory of this image had great personal significance for Beckett. In the later media plays, however, Beckett treats the image in a way that discourages biographical speculation. Instead, he uses the face as an almost anonymous figure of the necessity and difficulty of evoking images.

"*. . . but the clouds . . .*" is a play about the invocation of the face. It depicts the efforts of a male figure, M, to recall the face of a woman, W, in imagination. The central visual image is a "closeup of woman's face, reduced as far as possible to eyes and mouth," and this visual image is accompanied by a verbal description of the speaker's attempts to invoke the image, to call forth "those unseeing eyes I so begged when alive to look at me." The voiced-over narrative describes in clearly ritualistic terms M's nightly attempts to see W. The ceremony, as presented by the narrating V (V is defined in the script as "M's voice"), begins in much the same way that Opener began *Cascando*, with a verification of terms: "When I thought of her it was always night. I came in [. . .] No— [. . .] No, that is not right. When she appeared it was always night. I came in [. . .] Right."[34] V begins with the narrative of his nightly ritual, but, as in *Cascando* (and as is appropriate for any *post rem* linguistic description of a psychic reality), he must check his formulations against the phenomenon to be depicted. Here, the verb "to think" is rejected as implying too much willful action on M's part, and it is replaced with the more passive act of *registering* W's appearance. V goes on to describe, from a neutral, camera-like perspective, his preparation for the ritual, and this description will be faithfully reproduced on-screen by the camera. This preparation involves first taking off his street clothes, then donning a "light grey robe and skullcap," entering his "little sanctum," and adopting a ceremonial crouching posture.

> Right. Came in, having walked the roads since break of day,
> brought night home, stood listening [. . .], finally went to
> closet— [. . .] Shed my hat and greatcoat, assumed robe and
> skull, reappeared— [. . .] Reappeared and stood as before, only
> facing the other way, exhibiting the other outline [. . .], finally
> turned and vanished— [. . .] Vanished within my little sanctum
> and crouched, where none could see me, in the dark. [. . .]

As usual with Beckett, all the terms of this description are essential, in
particular the skullcap, which suggests the ceremonial garb of prayer but
also suggests mental activity, what goes on in the skull. And in this regard
it is significant that, although described as a skull*cap* in the stage notes, V
refers to it as a "skull." The dual nature of the "skull"—as a symbol
of mental activity and as a reference to the ceremonial nature of the
occasion—is confirmed by the subsequent reference to the "little sanctum" where "none could see me, in the dark." This sanctum suggests both
a holy place for prayer (*sanctus*) and the abstract mental place (i.e., *inner* sanctum) where so many of Beckett's characters and narrators have
crouched, lain, crawled, wondered, and pleaded. V then goes on to introduce the ritual itself: "Then crouching there, in my little sanctum, in the
dark, where none could see me, I began to beg, of her, to appear, to me.
Such had long been my use and wont. No sound, a begging of the mind,
to her, to appear, to me. Deep down into the dead of night, until I
wearied, and ceased. Or of course until—" At this point, the camera
switches to a shot of W ("closeup of woman's face, reduced as far as
possible to eyes and mouth"), which we see here for the first time. Later,
V begins an account of the various possible outcomes of his ritual. There
are only four:

> One: she appeared and [. . .] In the same breath was gone. [. . .]
> Two: she appeared and [. . .] Lingered. [. . .] With those un-
> seeing eyes I so begged when alive to look at me. [. . .] Three:
> she appeared and [. . .] After a moment [she pronounced the
> words:] . . . clouds . . . but the clouds . . . of the sky . . . [. . .]
> Right. There was of course a fourth case, or case nought, as I
> pleased to call it, by far the commonest, in the proportion say
> of nine hundred and ninety-nine to one, or nine hundred and
> ninety-eight to two, when I begged in vain [. . .]

The subject of this play—M's attempts to invoke the beloved feminine image—becomes clear here. M specifically states that he is unable to make the image appear at will and that to do so he has adopted this ritualistic strategy for invoking the image. Having no direct, rational means for invoking the image, M takes a *superstitious* approach: he doesn't know exactly what can induce the image to appear, so he obsessively repeats the ritual gesture of purification (donning of ceremonial garb), the ceremonial crouching posture, and the fetishistic begging process, night after night. This "begging of the mind" clearly resembles prayer, and the goal of the prayer is to invoke the apparition of W, who seems to represent a combination of the ideal feminine and love lost, much as we find them represented by the feminine face in *Krapp* and *Words and Music*.

Although "*. . . but the clouds . . .*" is built around a poetic rather than musical intertext, it does point us in the direction of music. The "begging" theme of "*. . . but the clouds . . .*" refers us to another of Beckett's television plays, *Nacht und Träume*, where begging is explicitly associated with music. The piece is named after and built around Schubert's lied of the same name (op. 43, no. 2; on a text by Matthäus von Collin), which is about man's *soif de l'idéal*: men eavesdropping on night's dreams and, at daybreak, calling out for night and dreams to return.

> Heil'ge Nacht, du sinkest nieder,
> Nieder wallen auch die Träume,
> Wie dein Mondlicht durch die Räume,
> Durch der Menschen stille Brust.
> Die belauschen sie mit Lust;
> Rufen, wenn der Tag erwacht:
> Kehre wieder, holde Nacht!
> Holde Träume, kehret wieder!

> [Sacred night, you sink down upon us;
> dreams too drift down
> (as your moonlight drifts through space)
> into the stilled hearts of men.
> Men joyfully listen to these dreams,
> calling out, when day awakes:
> "Return, sweet night!
> Return, sweet dreams!"]

The song resembles "*. . . but the clouds . . .*" thematically in its linking of night and visions, opposed to the lack that characterizes day. Moreover, Beckett, in the script for his piece, specifies that only the last line of the song—"Holde Träume, kehret wieder!" [Return, sweet dreams!]   is to be sung and that the last seven measures of the song (text: "Kehre wieder, holde Nacht! Holde Träume, kehret wieder! Holde Träume, kehret wieder!") are to be hummed. Beckett, in other words, has chosen from this song the two lines that, with their pleading imperative verbs ("kehre, kehret"), tender epithet ("holde"), and familiar (*du* and *ihr*) forms of address, invoke the same type of familiar pleading, the same submission to the comings and goings of images that we find in "*. . . but the clouds. . . .*"

The piece opens, in silence, on a shot of A, who is "a man seated at a table, right profile, head bowed, grey hair, hands resting on table." We then hear the last seven measures of Schubert's lied, first hummed and then sung by a voiced-over tenor. The male voice, presumably, is that of the figure we see on stage, although A gives no sign of singing or humming: this seems to be a *singing of the mind,* much like M's "begging of the mind" in "*. . . but the clouds. . . .*" After the music ends, the lights fade down on A as he "bows his head" and adopts a dreaming posture, head on his hands. We then watch A dreaming and, in superimposition, his dream. In the dream we see A's "dreamt self"—named B in the script— seated at a table, also dreaming, while a pair of disembodied hands go through a ritual of Christian comfort giving: laying on of hands, cup conveyed gently to lips, brow wiped. B then raises his head "to gaze up at invisible face" (Beckett has not forgotten the face), after which he goes back to sleep, head cradled in the comforting hands. With the end of the dream, A wakes, and we immediately hear the lied, first hummed, then sung as before, followed by an exact repetition of the dream sequence. The form of this piece could be expressed as AA, or, as the younger Beckett would have said, da capo.[35] And, as in *Waiting for Godot,* the single repetition is enough to suggest an infinite series. Just as in the lyrics of the lied, awakening brings with it the immediate desire for more dreams. And, as Deleuze points out in "L'épuisé," both A and B dream at their desks, not in bed; their dreams should not be taken as dreams of sleep and rest but as the desired outcome of their nightly ritual.

It remains to be seen what exactly music has to do with the invocations enacted in these plays. In what sense is music a necessary part of the ritual? In a preliminary way, we can say that music acts as a figure of the mental concentration required to successfully invoke the image. Music can serve as an aid in the begging of the mind necessary to call forth the image. Croak, we'll recall, used a combination of commands, pleas, endearments, and insults to get Words and Music to perform. But this pleading was only a preliminary stage of the invocation. The real act of supplication was carried out, by Words and Music, for Croak. Only the ceremonial coming together of Words and Music in song offered hope of acceding to the nether region of the wellhead. Similarly, it is the song itself that constitutes the begging ritual in *Nacht und Träume*. In *Words and Music* the musical performance acted as a stimulant; in *Nacht und Träume* it acts as a calmative; but in both cases it facilitates access to the object of adoration.

The unique feature of the musical ceremony in *Nacht und Träume* is that, as far as we can tell, it always works. Both times the "Holde Träume" line is pronounced, A sleeps and dreams of comfort. Unlike *Words and Music*, in which the combination of music and words appears to fail to bring about the desired transcendence, and unlike "*... but the clouds...,*" in which we are told that the begging ritual fails 998 times out of a thousand, the dreamer in *Nacht und Träume* is two for two. And yet, if the *appearance* of the face is the goal, the *Nacht und Träume* ritual must also be considered a failure. We do not see the face, nor does A. We watch A dreaming of B, who gets "to gaze up at invisible face," but the face does not actually appear in the field of vision. We see only the soothing effects of this presence. This is a dream about comfort, but the dream does not provide that comfort itself. These qualifications have their importance. The fact that Beckett specifies the "invisibility" of the desired face (both to us and to A) serves as a reminder of the ultimate failure of all art that Beckett described in places like the *Three Dialogues*. Just as A's dream is about a kind of comfort it cannot dispense, *Nacht und Träume* is about the quest for a kind of truth it cannot achieve. Beckett follows Schopenhauer in positing the noumenal value of aesthetic contemplation (the only activity that, according to Schopenhauer, can allow us to transcend momentarily the restrictions of phenomenal reality), but he refuses to suggest, as Schopenhauer does, that aesthetic contemplation can offer more than the promise of such transcendence.

The common theme of all these plays is a man's inability to make the beloved image appear at will and the various strategies he adopts to invoke it. These strategies may be deemed ritualistic to the extent that they involve a repetitive, formalized performance of fetishistic gestures designed to invoke a higher power. As Beckett put it in *The Unnamable*, "It's easier to build the temple than to make the deity appear in it," and these pieces are about building and maintaining temples, keeping alive the cherished image in order to revisit it (or, rather, in the hopes of being revisited *by* it) again and again. Having no direct, rational means for compelling the image to appear, all of these characters take a super-stitious approach to image making: they don't know exactly what can induce the image to come back, so they obsessively repeat the actions that have been linked to success in the past. Like Freud's child playing *fort-da*, their ritual is a game that they have mastered and that guarantees them, therefore, a limited sort of success. They feel obscurely that the ritual is linked to the apparition of the beloved figure but remain unable to ex-plain the link rationally or guarantee its success.[36]

If we take these begging rituals as metaphors for artistic creation, it becomes possible to relate them to the same preoccupation with expres-sion (or, rather, its impossibility) that has always characterized Beckett's work, only transposed from the fiery intransigence of the early work into a register of old age and failing imagination, nostalgia, and regret. In what is no doubt his most famous critical statement, Beckett had described the dilemma of the modern artist in terms of a devotion to failure. For the modern artist there is only one valid subject: "The expression that there is nothing to express, nothing with which to express, nothing from which to express, no power to express, no desire to express, together with the obligation to express" (*Disjecta* 139). This obligation to express in the absence of any sufficient means of fulfilling the obligation has always been at the center of Beckett's thematics and has always been figured within his texts. In the major works from the "siege in the room" period (during which Beckett wrote the first trilogy and *Godot*), the object or initiator of the quest is thought of as a male figure, always inaccessible and most often presented as a kind of god. Knott already plays this role in *Watt*. So do Godot, Youdi (*Molloy*, second part), the various agents and caretakers in *Malone Dies* and *Molloy*, and the voices of *The Unnamable*. These figures represent the imperative to express by requiring that the characters we see provide reports to them, wait for them, or, more generally, "witness" them in some way. In the later work, this inaccessible, godlike father figure tends increasingly to be replaced by an equally inaccessible, and equally imperious, feminine object of desire, no longer understood as the godhead but as the fading memory of a beloved face. In narrative terms, then, the face in "... *but the clouds* ...," *Words and Music*, and *Nacht und Träume* must be considered as yet another incarnation of the obligation to express. The face is *that which must be seen*, and the need of these characters to see the face is so great that they literally consecrate their lives to it.

There is one more television play that explores the same confluence of themes: *Ghost Trio*, which was written in 1975 (one year before "... *but the clouds* ..."). *Ghost Trio* is perhaps the most enigmatic of all of Beckett's works, but it also, perhaps, is the one that benefits most from an understanding of Beckett's mentalist, phenomenologically oriented understanding of music. It is in *Ghost Trio* that all the elements of Beckett's discourse on music—music as an *ante rem* antidote to the *post rem* lack of language, as the focal element of a ritual, and as an expressive object worthy of the most intensely absorbing attention—come together. Music, understood in this way, provides an important key for unlocking the meaning of this television play, which has continued to stymie critics, even Beckett's most alert and devoted critics, ever since its first broadcast.

In *Ghost Trio* we observe a man, named F in the script, hunched over his cassette player listening intently to the Beethoven trio named in the title. His intense concentration on the music suggests a form of "begging of the mind" of the same sort described in "... *but the clouds*. ..." The action takes place in a room, which, like all of Beckett's enclosed spaces, acts as a metaphor for consciousness, situated somewhere between the unknowable ego and the equally unknowable outside world. In fact, Beckett's depiction of the room seems intended to suggest the kind of impoverished phenomenal reality described by Plato and Kant and opposed to the unmediated essences of the plane of Platonic ideas and the Kantian noumena. This, at least, would explain why *Ghost Trio* makes so little use of the graphic powers of the television medium. Shot in black and white, the action takes place in a set depicting a space that is so studiously nondescript it suggests not so much a room as the abstract concept of a room. Carefully stripped of all individualizing characteristics, the room contains, apart from F, only six props: a door, a stool, a

cassette player, a window, a mirror, and a pallet. The props are so sche-
matically represented that a voice-over is needed to confirm their identity, and the script even specifies that the cassette player is "not [at first]
identifiable as such." In the German production, supervised by Beckett,
the cassette player was represented by a featureless box, which can be
seen, gripped by F, in figures 4 and 5. The entire play is dominated by this
image of a man performing that most Beckettian of activities: waiting
anxiously. In this case, we are told, he is waiting for an unnamed female
entity referred to only as "her."

The play is divided into three acts of about five minutes each: a "pre-
action," an "action," and a "re-action." The first two are narrated by a
female voice. She provides some basic exposition in act 1 (leading the
audience through a kind of guided tour of the room that involves identifying each object, including F) and then leads F through a series of
formalized, almost ritualistic activities in act 2. The third act is a "reaction" in two senses: first, F performs an exact repetition or reenactment
of his activities from act 2 (with no voice-over this time); second, and
perhaps more importantly, the camera begins to follow F around the
room, as if it was "reacting" to the knowledge acquired in act 2.

The unidentified "her" that F is said to be awaiting never does come
(although it seems likely that she bears some relation to the female narrating voice), but whenever F "think[s] he hears her," he snaps to attention, gets up out of his seat, sets down the cassette, opens the door, and
looks outside, presumably to check for signs of "her." This "checking"
gesture involves a ritualistic pattern—much like that in ". . . *but the
clouds . . .*"—that is repeated four times over the course of the play: the
first and third times F goes to the door, he then continues on to explore
the room's other aperture (the window) and sparse furnishings (mirror
and pallet); the second and fourth times, he returns directly to his seat,
picks up the cassette player, and resumes listening to the music.

Although the actions carried out by F in act 2 are repeated exactly in act
3, what the audience sees changes drastically. This is because the camera
begins to alternate between a long view of the entire room and views that
are taken from the first-person perspective of F, as if we were looking
through his eyes. These views include a shot out the window (a night view
of "rain falling in dim light"), F's face reflected in the mirror (the first
time we have been shown F's face), and, perhaps most significantly, the

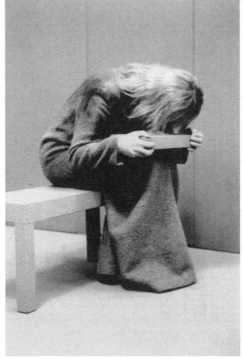

4. *Ghost Trio*, General View. Photograph by Hugo Jehle.

5. *Ghost Trio*, Close-up with Cassette Player. Photograph by Hugo Jehle.

view through the open door, which shows a small boy who stands at the threshold just long enough to shake his head negatively twice before turning and leaving.

This is the plot of the piece, to the extent that one can call it a plot. Beckett has clearly taken care to suggest, without naming it explicitly, the anguish of a man waiting to meet his long-overdue lover. There is, then, a clearly implied melodramatic subtext for the play. (The original title for the piece, as Sydney Homan reminds us in *Filming Beckett's Television Plays*, was *Tryst*.) But Beckett refuses to follow this narrative option any further. Rather than attempting to load this image with meaning and significance by showing us the events leading up to and away from it (its causes and/or consequences), Beckett chooses instead to remain within the chamber. It is there that meaning is to be sought. Thus we are shown several lingering close-ups of the various objects in the room, and the voice repeatedly emphasizes the importance of paying close attention to their physical features ("Look," "Look closer" [two times], "Look again"). Moreover, the cryptic, repetitive actions of F seem to reinforce by their very ambiguity the importance of basing interpretation on the precise way in which things happen.

Throughout all of this, F does not speak. His role, it seems, is to listen and look. Like the Opener in *Cascando*, who could turn his voices on and off but not control them, F does not seem able to actively alter his environment. In contrast to *Cascando*, however, the choice of music and its thematic associations play a significant role in the unfolding of the piece. What F listens to, apart for signs of "her" arrival, is this tape recorder emitting excerpts from Beethoven's *Ghost Trio* (Pianoforte Trio in D, op. 70, no. 1, "Geistertrio"). Beckett uses only the largo from the trio, and within this movement, he isolates statements of the "Ghost" theme, the theme that, with its "proliferating chromatics" and "scurrying tremolo" motif, suggested the "Ghost" nickname to E. T. A. Hoffmann, who saw in it a "magic circle of strange forebodings."[37] The title already suggests the two primary thematic zones of Beckett's play: "ghost" thematics and "trio" thematics. The trio in question could be defined any number of ways in the play. The primary trio consists of the piece's three characters: F, the messenger boy who comes to the door in the third part, and the "her" whom F awaits. There are also a number of peripheral trios: the play is in three parts, there are three possible emplacements for the camera, the room has three visible sides (east, north, west), and, stretching things a bit, we could consider the three constitutive media of the fiction—words, music, and images—as a trio.

Equally important is Beckett's use of the "ghost" thematics implied by the title. Each member of the trio has a certain phantomatic quality, especially this absent female presence that hovers over the play like a spirit, incarnated only by the voice (*logos*) of the narrator. This etymological dimension of the title is crucial. The German word *Geist*, like the Latin *spiritus* and its derivations, also means "soul" or "spirit." All of these terms, moreover, are synonyms of "thought" and are exploited in the play by Beckett in the role he attributes to music, which functions in large part as a symbol of thought. As I will try to show, by accepting music as a figure of thought, we can make sense of many clues given in the piece that would otherwise remain all but uninterpretable.

F does not speak; he cannot tell us what concerns him, and so the question arises: What is he thinking? The voiced-over narrative gives us only one hint: "He will now think he hears her," which, in act 2, is the signal for F to stop listening to the music and make his rounds of the room. During these "checking" interludes, F's attention is directed outside, toward this woman he seeks, first at the door, peering out into the corridor onto which it opens, and then at the window. Apart from these interludes, however, F's attention is always focused on the cassette recorder and the music. F, we might say, uses the ghost music in much the same way that Swann used the "petite phrase" of Vinteuil, "spatializing" it (as Beckett put it in his *Proust* essay), turning it into a reflection of his sole preoccupation, which is his long wait for "her."

Beckett gives us a variety of visual clues that help to reinforce this interpretation by carefully associating the music with two key elements of the décor. Music is linked most obviously with F, since he is the one listening to it, but Beckett also takes care to identify the music with the door. In fact, the first two times we hear the music (in act 1, before F is introduced into the décor), the camera shifts to a close-up of the door. The script specifies that the music and the shot of the door are to coincide and be held for five seconds. Before the music is associated with F, then, it is clearly and emphatically associated with this mysterious door. Later, in act 3, the music will also be associated with the mirror in an equally emphatic, although more oblique, way. The script specifies that the mirror and cassette player resemble each other by their dimensions and calls for identical close-up shots of the two items in order to make this point visually.[38] The meaning of these two associations—first with the door, then with the mirror—is not initially clear but can be understood because the door and mirror have, in turn, their own set of associations. The door, of course, is where F goes first to look for "her." This is where she will have to come, if she comes. The door is also associated with the boy, who, like the messenger in *Godot*, comes twice—once in act 2, although we do not see him, and once in act 3, where we see him give a negative shake of the head. Assuming that things work here as in *Godot*, the boy acts as a messenger for "her," and his negative shake of the head means that she will not be coming. In this way the music is associated with "her" but also with the outside, *in general*. The association between the mirror and the music, on the other hand, is an *inward* association: the mirror is where F twice examines his reflection. By associating the music with the mirror, the script implies an identification of the music and specular thought, thought turned back onto itself.

To sum up: on the one hand, music is associated with "her" and the outside (or, more precisely, with F's thoughts turned outward); on the other hand, the music is linked to the self-reflexive, specular mode of thought associated with the mirror. The script also couples the music to one other element of the piece, and this is the association that turns out to be decisive for our understanding of the narrative progression depicted in the play. This element is the camera.

The music, at first glance, appears to play a strictly situational role, as an element of the representation rather than as a vehicle for representation. If we were to judge by the reverent posture and apparent anxiety of F, the music would appear to function either as a distraction from the anguish of waiting for this woman who never does arrive or as a reminder of her longed-for presence. But just as it would be improper to base an interpretation of *Ghost Trio* exclusively on the melodramatic subtext, it would be improper to consider the role of the music exclusively in these psychological terms. The function of the music must be sought on another level. Just as the voice encourages us to "look closer," we must also listen closer.

The attentive spectator of *Ghost Trio* comes to realize that the audibility of the music depends on the location of the camera and that this relationship itself evolves over the course of the play. The closer the camera moves to F, the more clearly the music is heard. Curiously, though, this relationship between the camera and the music appears to change over the course of the play. A glance at the script confirms this impression. The camera has three possible emplacements, A, B, and C, with A being farthest away and C closest (see figure 6). In act 1, the music is always inaudible when the camera is set at A and becomes gradually louder as the camera moves to B and C. But suddenly, at the end of act 2, there is a subtle but remarkable event: the music becomes, as the script specifies, "audible for first time from A."

How can we explain this modification? Why do the conventions of camera placement and audibility change over the course of the play? Our answer to this question will require that we first consider Beckett's general approach to the filmed media. Beckett's use of the camera remained remarkably consistent over the course of his entire career, although somewhat eccentric with respect to the mainstream vocabulary of the film canon, and will enable us to interpret the meaning of the shift in the camera/audibility relationship in *Ghost Trio*.

In retrospect, it seems almost inevitable that Beckett would eventually come to experiment with the filmed media. As early as *Watt*, Beckett had tried to depict the kind of observation usually associated with the camera and the objective recording capabilities of film. Indeed, the primary effect of Watt's loss of meaning was that he turned into a kind of hybrid consciousness, part perceiving device and part intellect. Like a camera, Watt has the ability to register data mechanically, and although he can still use language and concepts, his problem is that he has difficulty coordinating the two functions. For Watt, the immediateness of the relationship between the intellect and the perceptive faculties has been lost. He views the objects that come into his field of vision with the same kind of detachment with which the television audience views the images projected onto the screen. Indeed, he seems unable to do otherwise. The difference between viewing an object directly and viewing a filmed image of that object is that the latter activity requires a supplementary step, a specifically intellectual act of decoding the symbols on the screen. But for Watt, even directly perceived objects require this supplementary intellectual effort. Normally, the process of decoding a viewed image is carried out by the observer at an automatic, subconscious level, but Watt must

6. Camera Emplacements for *Ghost Trio*. Diagram by Jack Mohr.

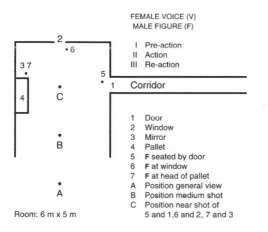

FEMALE VOICE (V)
MALE FIGURE (F)

I   Pre-action
II Action
III Re-action

Corridor

1   Door
2   Window
3   Mirror
4   Pallet
5   F seated by door
6   F at window
7   F at head of pallet
A   Position general view
B   Position medium shot
C   Position near shot of

Room: 6 m x 5 m   5 and 1,6 and 2, 7 and 3

make a conscious effort to decode. He has lost the direct, innate link between direct perception and intellect, and even the simplest images require his full attention.

Beckett, in all his work with film, brings this decoding process, usually taken for granted, to the fore as part of his strategy to thematize perception. He makes the moment of visual reception part of the signifying structure of the play. This emphasis on the decoding process appears clearly in *Ghost Trio*, in which the almost complete dearth of narrative contextualization means that before viewers can begin the process of interpretation, they must consciously scan the screen, searching intently for clues. Beckett makes it clear that nothing in the scene before us is irrelevant, but he refuses to tell us what anything means. The "familiar room" of *Ghost Trio* is a gray box of precisely specified dimensions that contains only a few props, carefully organized into quadrants: door on the east, window to the north, bed and mirror to the west. We are not told what these elements might mean, but it becomes clear that they can have no realist functionality. No one crosses the threshold of the door, no one lies on the bed, and the first time the camera shows the mirror it reflects nothing. These objects can only be read metaphorically, as the embodiment of functions. The entire first part of the piece is devoted to emphasizing this fact. Twice the Voice invites us to "look again," and we are encouraged, in a series of shots that alternate between a global view of the room and close-ups of the various element of the décor, to scan the images carefully: it is up to us to decide how to look, how to use what is there. Beckett ensures that, like Watt, we need to relearn how to look, to "look again."

This brings us back to the role of the camera. The camera has always acted as a metaphor for observing consciousness in Beckett's films. The camera is that which pursues. This convention is established in his first film, *Film*, in which "the protagonist is sundered into object (O) and eye (E) [equals the camera], the former in flight the latter in pursuit," and in his first television piece, *Eh Joe*, where the camera "pursues" Joe around his room before settling into a long, slow zoom that ends in an extreme close-up of Joe's face. The camera plays an equally active role in *Ghost Trio*, that of the self, posited as an observing eye (like Wittgenstein's philosophical I/eye), watching over another incarnation of the self, as object. This is where the relationship between the camera, the music, and F comes into play. Each of these figures acts as a symbol of self in one of its several modalities: the camera plays the role of observer, F plays the role of observed, and music, one might say, plays the role of observ*ing* consciousness.

Beckett, in other words, appears to be using the ambiguously suggested melodramatic setup as a kind of shorthand framing device designed to guide us in the direction of a more general reflection on the relationship between subject and object in the phenomenal world. The only thing we know for certain about "her" is that she is outside. (Every time F thinks he hears her, he runs to the door.) By the end of the play, after four false alarms, we come to suspect that, like Godot in *Waiting for Godot*, she will never come. We also suspect that none of the stereotypical plot devices of melodrama—running off with another man, dying of consumption, tragic miscommunication, and so on—will suffice to explain this absence. If she does not come, it is because the outside, in general, is excluded from this chamber. Beckett takes the image of a man thinking about and waiting for a woman who will never come and turns it into a kind of epistemological parable about the inside of consciousness and the inaccessible outside of unmediated reality. The chamber, as is so often the case in Beckett, can be thought of as a metaphor for the skull, with its apertures (door, window) that allow information to come in but not reality itself. Or, as Schopenhauer might have said, the *in-itself* is radically excluded from consciousness; humans have access only to the mediated realm of phenomena.

If this analogy is accepted, the nature of the relationship between camera, music, and meaning in *Ghost Trio* can be addressed more fully. At the very end of the play, as the music swells and we listen to the entire close of the Beethoven largo, the camera slowly closes in on F as he raises his head and his eyes stare directly back into the camera. This is only, as the script reminds us, the second time we have seen F's face. The first time we saw F's face (at the beginning of act 3), he was gazing at himself in the mirror. This act of gazing into the mirror was itself a repetition of the gesture that marks the dramatic crux of act 2, the moment that might, in Aristotelian terms, be termed the drama's crisis, turning point, or moment of recognition. F, while making his first round of the room in act 2, had looked at himself in the mirror. This apparently insignificant gesture caused the narrator to gasp ("Ah!") with surprise. This reflexive gaze into the mirror, then, seems to mark an important event, a rare and perhaps transformative moment of self-awareness that helps to bring about the change in perspective of act 3. As such, it provides the last clue necessary for unlocking the meaning of the relationship between the music and the camera.

The observing eye, as Wittgenstein noted, cannot observe itself. Thus, like the image of one's face in the mirror, knowledge of self can only be specular, indirect, mediated. If the chamber in *Ghost Trio* is taken as a metaphor for the skull-like space of consciousness, then the camera seems to embody the inwardly turned gaze of self-observation, while F stands for the subject observed. But this observed self, Beckett seems to be saying, is only knowable through the objects of its attention. The only clues to knowledge of the observed self provided in *Ghost Trio* are the furnishings of the chamber and, above all, the music, which, as one critic has put it, acts as "an index of subjectivity" (Russel 23). This is why, as our knowledge of F increases, we hear more of the music. But this kind of knowledge, based on indirect evidence, can only progress to a certain point. We have already seen that the music refers to the outside world (through its association with "her"); we must now also link it with the inwardly directed mode of attention suggested by F's dysphoric gaze into the mirror. Combining these two associations, we might be able to sum up the overall message of the play something like this: the inner self is as unknowable as Plato's realm of essences; F's reflected visage represents a threshold every bit as impermeable to direct knowledge of self as the outer threshold represented by the door.

The task Beckett has set for himself in *Ghost Trio* is to make this point using nothing but the materials implied by the image of a man in his room, listening and waiting. Because he refuses to develop the narrative implications of the image, Beckett must find other ways to get his idea across, and the solution he hits upon is to mobilize the recording technology itself as a signifying element of the work. He uses the camera work and audio track, which are usually kept discreetly in the background, subordinated to the dramatic concerns of the story told, and makes them play active roles in the piece, entering into the diegesis and interacting with F. Even the décor, by its very lack of realist specificity, plays an important role in getting across the idea of the impoverished phenomenal reality inside the chamber, contrasted with this feminine presence awaited by F and hinted at by the music. This enables Beckett to invoke implicitly the love-triangle melodrama but to do so in a way that cancels out the temptation to settle for an unequivocally psychological interpretation. Not even an unsympathetic or inattentive spectator could mistake this piece for an uninspired vignette about a man waiting interminably for his beloved to arrive, because Beckett's use of camera, music, and décor overrides the melodramatic reference, relegating it to a secondary role and directing the attention of viewers toward his larger message.

I would say instead that this play is about a subject getting to know itself. "Her," the invisible focus of attention, may not have appeared, but this subject, divided in three (camera, F, and music), has progressed one step farther in its self-knowledge, has come one step closer to uniting this three into one. If, in *Ghost Trio*, the camera represents the observer and F the observed, then music represents the membrane or tympanum that links the two, mediating between the self as ego and the self as other, inside and outside, voice and image.

Conventional wisdom tells us that in narrative words act as windows onto a world, while music provides a kind of mirror of the soul. A word, according to this optical metaphor, directs the attention of the reader or listener through the word onto the denoted object; it acts as an intermediary lens, allowing the reader to peer into the fictional world of the representation. Music, on the other hand, lacks this semantic transparency. It is not a transitive substance: listeners must search for musical meaning in themselves. It is in this sense that music is understood to be reflective. Rather than acting as an intermediary between consciousness and a third entity, it sends the viewer/listener's gaze back to its point of origin, back to consciousness. Beckett's fascination with music, I believe, was motivated by his ambition to realize the reflective potential of music in literature, to use literary language as a tool for directing attention inside. It is in this sense that his work can be said to approach, or to attempt to approach, the status of music. All Beckett's characters are mirrors for their narrators, deforming mirrors.[39] And narrative itself is understood by Beckett as the medium for a specular relationship with self, a detour to self through the exterior world of language and representation. Beckett takes care to situate all his work on the razor edge of phenomenal reality, to identify it with this membrane, or tympanum, that is consciousness. From that vantage point he attempts to report on the two types of perception available to consciousness: the "inside" of specular thought, which, having no real spatial dimension, is identified with voices and music; and the "outside" world of external stimuli, which is associated with spatiality and visual images.

MUSIC, INSIDE, OUTSIDE, AND FEASIBILITY

We've looked at attempts to express the inside in texts like *Murphy* (the "Murphy's mind" chapter) and *Cascando*, but it is no doubt the trilogy—with its voyage from the outside (the forests, towns, and strands where Molloy and Moran roam) to the almost pure inside of *The Unnamable*—that constitutes Beckett's most complete statement on the nature of the inside. This gives rise to what is, from the musical perspective of the present study, a nagging question: Why is the trilogy so silent on the question of music? This is indeed somewhat of an enigma. Why, after writing three novels absolutely loaded with musical references and even examples of music, does Beckett suddenly fall silent on this topic in his masterpiece, only to pick it up again immediately afterward in pieces like *Godot*, *All That Fall*, and the various media plays we've examined? Perhaps the most obvious explanation involves the fact that the trilogy marks Beckett's big breakthrough: having finally demarcated the territory he wants to explore (the attempt to "say I") and having wholly devoted himself to the task of bringing his discoveries to light, he forgets about everything else, including one of his favorite metaphors. This answer seems plausible, as far as it goes. But there is, I think, a more complete answer that involves a change in the way Beckett understands music. I would argue that in fact it is only with the trilogy that Beckett finally understood what, so to speak, music had been trying to tell him all along. In the early novels, those we studied in part 1 of this chapter, Beckett had used music as a way to describe metaphorically those elements of consciousness that, having no perceptible physical manifestation, are normally considered indescribable. In this, the musical metaphor had essentially the same status as the cosmic, interstellar metaphor with which it was often associated. But this metaphorical use of music meant that Beckett was still working in the descriptive mode of the traditional psychological novel. The musical metaphor enabled him to work with the themes that interested him, that is, thought and the workings of the mind, but limited him to the denotational superficiality of description. He was still describing thought from the outside, able only to talk *about* it. It is only with the trilogy that Beckett stops describing, breaks completely with the descriptive modes of realism, and adopts an exemplificational mode of creation that, although it has no clearly perceptible links to music, comes closer to it semiotically.

The lesson of music for the trilogy is to stop describing and start exemplifying. The question there is never "What shall I describe now?" but (as one of Beckett's narrators says somewhere) "What shall I have him think now?" Thus, although it may not be apparent on a first reading, the opening of Molloy's story—"I am in my mother's room"—has only an incidental descriptive value; the primary referential vector of the statement runs not to its denotata but to the execution of the thought "I am in my mother's room," to the type of thought it exemplifies. This statement does, it is true, provide the first element in the description of a décor, but, more importantly, it provides the first step in the process of a mind trying to understand itself. Merely implied at this early stage, Beckett's exemplificational intent becomes clearer as the trilogy progresses. The famous closing sentences of *Molloy*, for example, which have perplexed so many critics, give a perfect example of a statement that, because it refers from one level of reality to another, must be understood in terms of the type of thought it exemplifies: "Then I went back into the house and wrote, It is midnight. The rain is beating on the windows. It was not midnight. It was not raining" (*Three Novels* 176). The contradictory content of the statement removes all possibility of interpreting it as a simply descriptive gesture. The truth value of the first part appears only in its contradictory relation to the second part. This relationship then refers us to the emitting consciousness. The reader trying to reconcile the two contradictory parts of the statement must ask, What type of thought does this kind of contradiction exemplify? The possible answers are numerous in this case, ranging from the trivial (i.e., "a narrative gesture of good riddance"), to the technical ("shift from one diegetic level to another"), to the abstruse ("effing the ineffable," "the indicible," "the unnamable"). Once we have collected enough statements of this kind (and they are plentiful, especially in *The Unnamable*, in which we find numerous statements like "Dire Je. Sans le penser" [Say I. Without thinking it]), paying attention to what they tell us about the emitting consciousness, we begin to discern the patterns that are the real subject of the trilogy and that cannot be reduced to the semantic value of individual statements taken in isolation. Beginning with *The Unnamable*, all of the various narrative and dramatic devices that Beckett adopts have the goal of making it clear that Beckett is not only giving us information about a world but showing us a mind in action. And as the trilogy progresses, the exemplificational function of the language takes on increasing importance, while the descriptive function approaches zero, giving the texts an increasingly "abstract," "nonrepresentational" feel.

These are still, to be sure, fundamentally mimetic texts. What differentiates them from more traditional forms of mimesis is that the object of representation is located neither in the outside world of objects and events nor in the inner world of subjective experience but in the intermediate realm of consciousness. This intermediate zone is understood to function like the tympanum, by vibrating in sympathy with the impulses transmitted to it. It is a purely relational medium, with no content of its own.

Beckett's art, then, is musical to the extent that it aspires to be a relational, exemplificational art rather than a denotative, descriptive art. Any attempt to account for Beckett's achievement must focus on the relations between terms, not on the terms themselves, for, as Moran reminds us, "The falsity of the terms does not necessarily imply that of the relation, so far as I know" (*Three Novels* 111). Names falsify, necessarily. They always limit and circumscribe fields in a way that is at once too precise (since names deal, necessarily, with the plane of the feasible) and too vague (since a name can only determine an abstract category). Beckett, beginning with *Watt*, abandons the traditional goal of establishing cold truths in the form of statements. He attempts to replace the emphasis on description and other forms of predication with an emphasis on stories that signify primarily through the movement they trace and the types of thought they exemplify.

This concern with relations at the expense of the terms of the relation also helps to explain the status of the visual image in Beckett's later media work. The value of any of the various terms of a narrative (such and such a woman that I loved, a place that I knew) is incommunicable. As a reader, I can never fully understand the meaning of this anonymous woman's face on a punt in the reeds or of the sound of gravel crunching underfoot on a stretch of beach. The usual ("realist" or "traditional") procedure is to supplement this lack by adding specificity in the form of narrative contextualization or using other rhetorical devices (figures of pathos and bathos, etc.) designed to convey the significance of a given narrative element. The Beckett of *Dream of Fair to Middling Women* still works this way at times. But the founding moment of Beckett's career, the insight that transformed the Joycean author of *Dream of Fair to Middling Women* and *More Pricks than Kicks* into the author of *The Unnamable*, is the realization that all the biographical detail and rhetorical heightening in the world will only allow the reader a limited, relative glimpse of the importance and meaning of any such element.

This is the insight that is the subject of *Three Dialogues*. Consider the mysterious smile of the Mona Lisa, the "petit pan de mur jaune" of Vermeer/Proust/Bergotte, or the "ruban au cou d'Olympia" of Manet/Leiris (or, more generally, the crashing waves, peaceful or ominous landscapes, celestial or hellish visions, portraits of heroes and harlots, and all those other triumphs of representation that are cherished in our culture). Beckett tells us in *Three Dialogues* to forget all these successes, which, in this perspective, can only be considered relative successes. Since, in Beckett's absolutist aesthetic, such relative successes are tantamount to failure, Beckett urges us instead to make the inevitable failure of art art's only subject. Thus, the job of the artist, as Beckett sees it, is "to admit that to be an artist is to fail, as no other dare fail, that failure is his world and the shrink from it desertion, art and craft, good housekeeping, living . . . I know that all that is required now, in order to bring even this horrible matter to an acceptable conclusion, is to make of this submission, this admission, this fidelity to failure, a new occasion, a new term of relation" (*Disjecta* 145). The radicality of this view is apparent; Beckett is proposing nothing short of reframing the entire history of Western art as a wrong turn down a blind alley. So that although Beckett's musical, "relational," view of language and images bears a strong resemblance to Leiris's theory of words and events as "nexuses of thought," it also seems to pose a direct threat to Leiris's autobiographical project. Indeed, Leiris's autobiography, with its search for "complete communication," seems to be exactly the type of expressive project that Beckett critiques in *Three Dialogues*: whereas Leiris devotes his entire autobiography to an increasingly desperate quest for full expression and complete communication, Beckett begins by denouncing these as unattainable goals that should be abandoned immediately. On the other hand, just as Leiris is aware of the inevitable failure of his project (and of the necessity of continuing anyway), Beckett must know that his "failures" do, paradoxically, succeed.

This approach to representation, because of the *post rem* nature of language, can only be asymptotic. The attempt to *see* this Wittgensteinian "I" always calls for another eye to witness the first; the attempt to *say* "I" always calls for yet another narrative voice; the attempt to arrive home always implies another loop of the spiral; every term always calls for another term to define it. In this sense, the infinite regression of narrators (telling stories about narrators telling stories about narrators), the unending, concentric spiral of his voyagers toward their destination, the dogged struggle to say "I" and end can all be understood as figures of Peirce's infinite regression of referential meaning. Beckett's use of language submits to the logic of Zeno's arrow, always traveling toward but never reaching its target. Every relation becomes a term in a new relation, which becomes in its turn a term in another relation, and so on.

As an element of the author's consciousness, Beckett's work repeatedly reminds us, any term taken on its own remains fundamentally incommunicable. Words can only be cold labels for the warm reality of phenomena. From the point of view of the narrating subject, the content of a thought may be the only thing that matters, but this content, this "incommunicable proton of thought" (*Dream*), will always remain just that, incommunicable. This is part of the point of *Words and Music*: the songs that so move Croak can only leave the audience feeling rather cold.

Croak, to explain his emotion, would have to resort to the refrain that Beckett favored in his critical writing of a certain period: "Je me comprends." Whatever emotion the audience feels at Croak's displays of emotion comes from the sense of loss that this apparently disproportionate response implies. There are, to be sure, moments in Beckett's work when the affective significance of an image shines through in a momentary burst of strong emotion (as in the punt scene in *Krapp's Last Tape*), but they are always undercut by the knowledge of the futility of striving for "full" expression. And for this reason, the many isolated references to the "outside" or the world "up there" are always brief and suffused with a sense of loss: "And I have no doubts, I'd get there somehow, to the way out, sooner or later, if I could say There's a way out there, there's a way out somewhere, the rest would come, the other words, sooner or later, and the power to get there, and the way to get there, and pass out, and see the beauties of the skies, and see the stars again" (*Texts for Nothing* IX, *Collected Shorter Prose* 103). In Beckett's work, the terms of the relation are used as markers, as the pretexts or motives the author needs in order to be able to perform. But the only communicable aspects of the work are impersonal semiotic operations carried out in the abstract. Beckett, therefore, works his images by taking them out of whatever narrative context—whether historical, biographical, or other—they might have had and placing them instead into the signifying structures of the work, which treat them without regard for their affective content.[40] The relations between terms may remain the only communicable part of a work, but they are all too often ignored in our habitual obsession with what Beckett calls the "surface" meanings of words, that is, their denotative value. Words must be used and events must be represented (whence Beckett's famous quip on why he continues to use language: "What else would you have me do, Monsieur, it's all that we have"). But Beckett uses them to get at what is behind words—"to batter at the fundamental invisibility of things on the outside until invisibility itself becomes a thing" (*Disjecta* 130). Thus the images evoked, as well as the words used to evoke them, must be understood as stand-ins for entities that have no precise relation to words. They seem to have something to do with the Kantian noumenon and the Platonic Idea, but these terms too, I'm sure Beckett would agree, remain entirely inadequate.

5

Music, Metaphysics, and Moral Purpose in Literature

Only music
can take the place of thought . . .
and only thought
can, in its turn, take the place of music.

Roberto Juarroz

SAYING I

The structure of this book reflects the distinction made in chapter 1 between the three primary approaches to the literary use of musical models favored by modernist writers: formalist, expressivist, and essentialist. This tripartite distinction is helpful for isolating the specific techniques most characteristic of these writers, but it is not my intention to suggest that these three uses of music are mutually exclusive or that they cover the entire field of possible musical models. It would be more accurate to say that in any work in which a musical model is used, each of these three functions will be present to some degree, although one of them will tend to predominate. Pinget, for example, is primarily interested in using music as a formal model; yet he also insists on the importance of achieving the more properly expressive goals of "innateness, spontaneity, [and] inspiration" ("Robert Pinget" 144). Conversely, Leiris's goals are primarily expressive, but the permutational techniques he practices in the *Glossaire* have a clearly formalist dimension. Moreover, both Pinget and Leiris explain their musical techniques in terms of the essentialist imperatives of a powerful, perhaps transcendental Other, which Pinget calls the "murmur" and Leiris calls "a world outside our laws" and which appears in both cases to be related to the psychoanalytic domain of the unconscious. As for Beckett, he followed Schopenhauer into musical essentialism but

253

also used music as a formal model in his novels and remained pre-occupied throughout his career with the expressive power of music.

Whether approached as a formal, expressive, or philosophical problem, the common goal of these writers is, as Beckett put it, to say I, "dire je." For each of them, the use of musical models is determined by this self-contemplative project. They are aware that their quest is a metaphysical one, but they agree on the necessity of adhering exclusively to rational means in the pursuit of their goal. Indeed, this is part of the originality of their mode of literary production. The interdependence of subject and object, complicated by the inadequacy of the denotative function of language and the potentially infinite meanders of literary reference, makes the project of even locating, much less describing, a subject in isolation from its environment a doubly anomalous one. And yet, having embarked on what is soon recognized as a hopeless quest for descriptive, affective, and ontological plenitude, they resolve to carry on without abandoning the rational tools of analytic discourse, even when the inadequacy of these tools has become apparent. They refuse to succumb to mysticism.

Given the inherent contradiction between the transcendental goal and the rational means of execution, the task in which they find themselves engaged is an infinite one. This helps to explain why closure is anathema to their aesthetic. Pinget turns to the model of theme and variations because his narrators can never decide on a final version of events; Pinget's narrators discover that the attempt to tell the simplest story gives rise to an apparently infinite number of potential alternatives that can never be resolved into a single sequence. Leiris too struggles with the problem of the truth value of literary statement, a problem that becomes all the more acute in autobiography, with its ideal of a complete coincidence of the represented subject and the existential subject. Leiris's awareness of the impossibility of this coincidence explains the almost infinitely questioning, self-reflective strategies that characterize the latter volumes of *La règle du jeu*. Finally, Beckett's narrators work in the domain of the ill seen and the ill said: they know that even if they were able to accurately observe a given phenomenon, they would be unable to find the words needed to communicate it, but they must nevertheless continue to try. Pinget, in the obsessive rehashing of trivial anecdotes, Leiris, in the minuteness of his self-analyses, and Beckett, in the anguished attempt to have said and be done, are all engaged in the same pursuit of presence to self. And all maintain the same dogged refusal to declare victory prematurely, to settle for approximations of the truth, or to bow down before the inadequate solutions offered by conventional wisdom. Although engaged in an apparently infinite task (the description of subjective experience in the objectifying medium of language), they refuse short cuts. They insist on the importance of working toward the description of a pure subject and of doing so in full knowledge of the inherent impurity of the phenomenal context within which they must work.

In these conditions, the search for self becomes an attempt to explain the uncertain data of subjective impressions in terms of generalizable laws. They seek the point where metaphysics meets mental *physis*. Thus Pinget speaks of "reconciling innateness with calculation," which for him involves the artful channeling of irrational impulses. He identifies these, in Jungian fashion, with the collective unconscious: "We are all, indeed, more or less dependent on the collective unconscious, whose nature we can only glimpse by examining as best we can those manifestations of it which we perceive in ourselves" ("Robert Pinget" 146). Pinget borrows from Jung an *alchemical* ideal for literature: "The transformation of matter. The work on words is on the same order of concerns. The philosopher's stone of the great alchemists was the gold of a liberated consciousness" ("Entretien" 178, my translation). Leiris also writes of his search for truth in alchemical terms, describing it in his article on John Dee, "La monade hiéroglyphique" (in *Brisées*), in terms of the "absolu palpable" (absolute palpable), which he defines as "a concrete substance hiding yet promising [*recelant*] all secrets" (18, my translation). Beckett too seeks this kind of alchemical reconciliation of contraries. To Leiris's notion of the absolute palpable, Beckett responds with the more properly phenomenological notion of the "ideal real," which he defines as "an experience that is at once imaginative and empirical, at once an evocation and a direct perception, real without being merely actual, ideal without being merely abstract . . . the essential, the extra-temporal" (*Proust* 74). Each of these objects figures the reconciliation of the material world (stone, palpable, real) with the spiritual world (philosopher's, absolute, ideal), promising a union of self and other, mind and matter. In this way, Pinget, Beckett, and Leiris attempt to situate their work at that point where the individual consciousness encounters the supra-individual forces that govern human thought.

This type of project might even be considered to govern, however subtly, *all* attempts to use music as a model for discursive thought. This conjunction of self and other, the semantic and the semiotic, subjective experience and objective laws, has been identified with music from time immemorial. To cite an obvious example: the traditional association of verse and music via "la musique du vers" depends on the extrahuman category of *number*, the introduction of the semantically driven structures of human thought into the universally valid, exemplificational structures of verse. As we saw in chapter 1, the category of number has as much importance for Mallarmé and Valéry as it did for the neo-Platonist poets of the Renaissance and appeals to them for much the same reason that it appealed to Pythagoras: it provides a way to link up the different elements of existence into a great chain of being, to reconcile the vagaries of individual experience with the immutable laws that govern the harmony of the spheres. But whether or not this is true of all musical models for literature, there can be no doubt that this Pythagorean ideal determines the ways Pinget, Leiris, and Beckett use music. Leiris's descriptions of music invoke Pythagorean and Schopenhauerian paradigms to suggest the same kind of reconciliation: music is "the sign of a connivance between what could seem to be merely a human voice and the rhythms of fauna and flora, even those of the mineral kingdom where every impulsive motion is transcribed into a fixed form" (*Scratches* 75). Beckett too uses Pythagorean and Schopenhauerian conceptions of music to mediate between the microcosm and the macrocosm, mind and matter: "The night firmament is abstract density of music, symphony without end . . . the passional movements of the mind charted in light and darkness" (*Dream* 16). And Pinget admires Bach's music for its ability to channel irrational impulses into elegant structures: "The irrational, controlled and measured in masterly fashion, is the very wellspring of [Bach's] creative power" ("Robert Pinget" 148).

Music, then, symbolizes a form of individual expression justifiable in supra-individual terms, whether those of the collective unconscious, nature, noumena, or number. Why is music used so consistently in this way? Perhaps because the acoustical laws that govern musical expression offer a ready-made model of the kind of grounding principle these writers seek for literary expression. Musical creation, because it has a physical basis in the harmonic series and the physiological mechanism of sound perception, promises the possibility of justifying all artistic expression in terms of ontological necessity rather than in terms of the (trivial) desire to entertain, inform, or confess. Truth itself is redefined as the intersection of the subjective categories of consciousness and the objective categories of the natural sciences. This suggests that the implicit metaphysical question raised by any literary use of a musical model is whether it is possible to found literary statement on laws that can be shown to be as universal as those of the harmonic series in music. Music seems to offer the promise of a resolution to many of the traditional antinomies between objective fact and subjective experience (the perceptible and the intelligible, nature and culture, mind and matter, subject and object, and so forth). Musically inspired literary techniques tend, then, to be linked to the search for a kind of truth defined in quasi-scientific terms, rather than in the more familiar discursive terms of factuality and verisimilitude. Thus Pinget places full confidence in the improvisatory structure of his novels because he believes that the mechanisms of the unconscious will guarantee the meaningfulness of whatever comes out; Leiris defines *chant*, in expressive terms, as a mode of literature that will allow him to reveal that which differentiates his voice from all others "by its *inflections* rather than by the arguments set forth" ("Musique en texte"); and Beckett seeks to use language in a way that will forgo the superficiality of the concept and penetrate to the ontological depth of things and what Schopenhauer called their "perceptive representatives."

Seen from this perspective, the search for truth requires subjecting discourse to tests that go well beyond the usual semantic and referential criteria of truth in normal linguistic discourse. Instead of using tests of veracity, factuality, and verisimilitude to defend the value of their work, Pinget, Leiris, and Beckett turn to the exemplificational realm of syntactical relationships and to the ontological realm of substance. They are engaged in a contemplative project that has a scientific dimension: self-observation with the goal of discovering a *mechanism*, the mechanism that governs human thought. As Beckett once put it: "Being *has* a form. Someone will find it someday. Perhaps I won't but someone will. It is a form that has been abandoned, left behind, a proxy in its place."[1] This scientific, experimental dimension of the music/literature problem must not be ignored. Indeed, it is not only writers and artists who have been interested in the relationship between music, mind, and substance but also those engaged in research in the physical and social sciences. One particularly interesting example of the appeal to music as a paradigm for scientific research is provided by Claude Lévi-Strauss. His work, moreover, has particular relevance for the authors discussed here as it helped to shape the worldview of their generation.

LÉVI-STRAUSS: MUSIC AND THE ONTOLOGY OF STRUCTURE

It might seem almost inevitable that music would appeal to a structuralist like Lévi-Strauss, since music provides a clear example of a purely relational art, and Lévi-Strauss had insisted from the very beginning of his career on the all-encompassing importance of relational meaning over functional or semantic meaning: "The error of traditional anthropology, like that of traditional linguistics, was to consider the terms, and not the relations between the terms" ("Structural Analysis in Linguistics and in Anthropology," *Structural Anthropology* 46). But taking music as a model of relationality only partially explains music's importance for Lévi-Strauss. After all, the primary model for structural relationality has always been the phonetic model borrowed from linguistics. Taken as a simple model of relationality, music offers no distinct advantage over the phonetic model. And yet Lévi-Strauss returns over and over to music in his work to explain key concepts and justify the validity of the structuralist approach to myth. Another element of musical discourse that helps to explain its appeal for Lévi-Strauss is the notion of polyphony. Lévi-Strauss admired the ease with which the orchestral score conveys the "vertical" relationships between independent but interrelated parts. In "The Structural Study of Myth" (*Structural Anthropology* 212), Lévi-Strauss uses the musical score as an analogy for the "vertical" or "paradigmatic" reading of myths that he practices, in which interpretation requires superimposing different versions of a myth and sorting through the paradigmatic substitutions that have taken place, a procedure designed to reveal the Ur-myth hidden behind them.[2] This analogy between the paradigmatic reading of myths and the vertical superimposition of staves in the orchestral score helps us to understand another important aspect of Lévi-Strauss's interest in music, but here again, other analogies might have served just as well. It is not until later in his career, with the publication of the four-volume series *Mythologiques*, that the full significance of Lévi-Strauss's interest in music as a model for the structural interpretation of myths appears with any clarity. It is in the "Overture" to volume 1, *The Raw and the Cooked*, and in the "Finale" to the last volume, *The Naked Man*, that Lévi-Strauss offers his most complete accounting of the relationship between music, myth, and mind.

Lévi-Strauss's remarks on the relationship between music and myth, it should be noted, enter into the same kind of confusing slippages between loose analogies and literal description that we have had several occasions to remark upon over the course of this book. Both in the "Overture" to *The Raw and the Cooked* and in the "Finale" of *The Naked Man*, Lévi-Strauss offers descriptions of the relationship between music and myth that are less than convincing when taken literally. Nevertheless, these slippages provide highly illuminating insights into Lévi-Strauss's thought that can help lead us to an understanding of the ontological underpinnings of structuralism as Lévi-Strauss defined it. This understanding will, in turn, help to show what is at stake in the relational game practiced by Pinget, Leiris, Beckett, and many of their contemporaries.

In *The Raw and the Cooked*, Lévi-Strauss not only uses music as a methodological analogy for the type of structural analysis carried out in *Mythologiques* but also invokes it as a formal model for the published study itself. He does so, however, in a somewhat perplexing manner. After arguing briefly in the "Overture" for the existence of a fundamental link between musical forms and mythic forms, he gives each chapter of *The Raw and the Cooked* a musical heading (symphony, sonata, cantata, fugue, etc.), without, however, making any attempt to exploit or even justify the implied analogies between his text and the musical forms he invokes. As is so often the case, the musical metaphor seems to serve as no more than an ennobling oppositional marker. In this case its primary function is to act as justification for the somewhat loose structure of his study. Music is taken to provide a defense against those who might object to the lack of the strictly hierarchical organization characteristic of most treatises in the social sciences.[3]

There is nothing especially reprehensible about this loose use of the musical metaphor, but Lévi-Strauss couples it with a more far-reaching argument, one that goes to the heart of his project. Music and mythology, Lévi-Strauss tells us, go together, because "music and mythology both appeal to mental structures that the different listeners have in common"

(*The Raw and the Cooked* 26). If this is true, then it makes perfect sense for a study of myth to shed the usual structures of scientific discourse in favor of quasi-musical structures. But one would have expected, in that case, to find a more rigorous use of the musical metaphor, combined with a more vigorous explanation of its validity. Neither of these is forthcoming. Other uses of music in *Mythologiques* are similarly shallow. After offering a useful formal analogy between the baroque fugue and mythical thought in the "Finale" to *The Naked Man*, Lévi-Strauss seeks to link the advent of polyphonic music causally to the demise of mythical thought in the Occident, arguing that the first took over the functions of the latter (652–53). This is a provocative but highly questionable historical thesis, and Lévi-Strauss does not even try to marshal any evidence for it.

Why, then, this insistence by Lévi-Strauss on using music to describe both his own book and the functioning of myth? What does music enable Lévi-Strauss to do that makes it such a compelling reference for him? A crucial clue comes late in the "Finale" to *The Naked Man*, when Lévi-Strauss analyzes Ravel's *Bolero* as a "horizontal fugue" (660–67). This is an apparently self-contradictory label, one that could only be accepted at the price of confusing polyphonic simultaneity with the successivity of permutational transformation. Lévi-Strauss intentionally blurs the fundamental distinction between polyphony and variation, suggesting that the successive variations that make up *Bolero* could just as easily have been superimposed fugally. In his opinion, therefore, Ravel's *Bolero* is, for all intents and purposes, a fugue, only developed "horizontally" rather than "vertically." Conventional musicologists and composers would make little sense of this conflation of variation and polyphonic superimposition, but it nonetheless offers a decisive clue about Lévi-Strauss's intentions. This tendency to conflate the *simultaneous* (polyphony) and the *similar* (variation) by reference to the verticality of paradigmatic substitution is a canonical move of the strict structuralist approach practiced by Lévi-Strauss, Jakobson, and others. The structuralist preference for the synchronic over the diachronic comes out clearly in this kind of identification. However farfetched this comparison might appear from a musical point of view, it reveals Lévi-Strauss's vested interested in abolishing the distinction between synchronic and diachronic structures. One need only refer back to *The Raw and the Cooked* for confirmation of this fact. There Lévi-Strauss had asserted that the primary characteristic of music is not, as it was for Bergson and Husserl, its singularly temporal mode of being but its *atemporal* nature: music and myth are both, for Lévi-Strauss, "instruments for the obliteration of time" (16).[4]

The real interest of Lévi-Strauss's passages on music and myth, then, is not to be sought in the comparisons themselves, which are often inexact or questionable, but in the reasons he offers for turning to music as a model for mythical analysis. Indeed, it is precisely those points at which the uncertain logical status of these analogies becomes most apparent that reveal Lévi-Strauss's true stake in the musical model. All of the distortions in his music-myth comparisons can be attributed to the larger objectives of his anthropological project. Music interests Lévi-Strauss as a model for myth not only because it is a relational art but because he sees in it a clear justification for the ontological premises of structuralism as a whole: music, as Lévi-Strauss understands it, constitutes a clear example of an art that can transcend the level of "articulate expression" (i.e., language) (*The Raw and the Cooked* 15) and link the sensory to the intelligible—the very characteristic that he seeks to attribute to myth.

Music's grounding in physical reality thus becomes the basis for an argument designed to establish an equally objective grounding for the patterns of mythical thought. As we saw in the previous section, Pinget, Leiris, and Beckett invoke music for similar reasons, but whereas these writers allow the relationship to remain on the metaphorical level appropriate to literary expression, Lévi-Strauss's argument calls for a more than metaphorical link. If it is to have scientific validity, he must find a firm ontological foundation for the mental structures under consideration. Thus he uses the various analogies between musical form and myth described above to suggest the existence of an actual functional identity: both music and myth, he argues, owe their efficacy to the properties of a "natural system," to their "rootedness in nature" (*The Raw and the Cooked* 24–25). Music operates directly on the individual's senses, whereas myth operates on the level of social consciousness, yet both are grounded in mental structures taken to be a universal component of human consciousness. "Just as music makes the individual conscious of his physiological rootedness, mythology makes him aware of his roots in society. The former hits us in the guts; the latter, we might say, appeals to our group instinct. And to do this, they make use of those extraordinarily subtle cultural mechanisms: musical instruments and mythic patterns"

(28). Comparing musical instruments to mythic patterns is a bit like comparing apples and appraisals, but it helps Lévi-Strauss to argue his main point, which is that mythic schemata are grounded in cognitive and social structures that, despite their apparent immateriality, are as real as the acoustic and physiological laws that govern musical communication. Lévi-Strauss uses the analogy with music to ontologize structure, but not metaphorically, as Pinget, Leiris, and Beckett do; his claim is a literal one: "In other words, music and mythology appeal to mental structures that the different listeners have in common . . . these structures can only be termed general if one is prepared to grant them an objective foundation on the hither side of consciousness and thought" (26). The goal of ontologizing mental structures, of attributing to them the absolute reality of ultimate substance, makes manifest an essentialist streak in Lévi-Strauss's thought: any such attribution can only be metaphysical in nature. As a scientist, though, he feels it necessary to argue that the goals of structuralism are neither idealist nor formalist but materialist, deterministic, and realist (27). To argue this point, he uses the classic expressivist argument for the use of musical models, that of a direct appeal to the senses ("the joy of music is, then, the soul's delight in being invited, for once, to recognize itself in the body" [*The Naked Man* 657]) and then applies it to myth. Although, he argues, myth works on the plane of the social and music on that of the sensorial, both operate in the same manner (relationally) and for the same (ontological) reasons. Thus both can ensure "the fusion of the two categories of the sensory and the intelligible" (657). Lévi-Strauss, in other words, presents an *essentialist* theory of myth, supported by an *expressivist* argument about music and a *formalist* analysis of mythical narratives.

There is a fundamental difficulty in this argument: Lévi-Strauss is obliged to concede that myth, as a linguistically transmitted form of knowledge, is, semiotically speaking, closer to language than to music. But since he *wants* to show that myth is on the same plane as music, he must find some way to equate the two. He does this by arguing that myth and music are alike in their mutual opposition to language. He formulates the problem this way. On the one hand, "mythology occupies an intermediary position between two diametrically opposed types of sign systems—musical language on the one hand and articulate speech on the other" (*The Raw and the Cooked* 27). This proposition follows necessarily from the observation that myths, as linguistically transmitted phenomena, must display at least some of the characteristics of linguistic structures. On the other hand, and more importantly for Lévi-Strauss, both music and myth "in their different ways, transcend articulate expression" (15). From this second proposition, it follows that, since both music and myth are ontologically rooted universals, then myth can be grouped with music and opposed to language on the grounds that the mythic schemata are not themselves linguistic (and hence merely arbitrary) in nature: they "transcend" language. Lévi-Strauss returns to this argument in the "Finale" of *The Naked Man* (647–48), insisting that music and myth should be grouped together by opposition to language because "music and mythology are each to be defined as language from which something has been subtracted." Music is language without semantic meaning ("sound without sense"), while myth is meaning without language: "a pure semantic reality . . . detached from its linguistic base, with which the story it tells is less intimately connected than ordinary messages would be." This last proposition is especially difficult to accept. Lévi-Strauss finds himself in the awkward position of arguing that although individual myths share both the same medium (language) and the general structural properties of literary forms of narrative (*muthos*), the global properties of myth must nevertheless be radically distinguished from other forms of narrative, on the grounds that they somehow provide more direct access to the deep structures that constitute social thought.

Lévi-Strauss, seeking a scientific foundation for anthropology and the social sciences in general, is in search of a scientific object, that is, one that can be shown to obey generalizable rules. This object, Lévi-Strauss argues, can be found in the structures of social thought. But where are these structures to be sought? There can be no question of locating this object of scientific inquiry in the individual consciousness, if only for the reason that the thought of individuals, impossible to quantify, has remained impervious to scientific investigation. This is why, in the polemical finale to *The Naked Man*, Lévi-Strauss refuses to accept the standard humanistic categories of the social sciences, according to which the individual constitutes the basic unit of study. Lévi-Strauss posits instead the existence of impersonal, universal structures that supersede individual thought as the true object of anthropology: "The social sciences, following the example of the physical sciences, must grasp the fact that the reality of the object

they are studying is not wholly limited to the level of the subject apprehending it" (*The Naked Man* 638). According to Lévi-Strauss, the individual "subject" is nothing more than "the insubstantial place or space where
anonymous thought can develop, stand back from itself, find and fulfill its
true tendencies and achieve organization, while coming to terms with the
constraints inherent in its very nature" (625). Of course, anthropologists
studying myths must rely on stories told to them by individual infor-
mants. There is no other way to collect the necessary data. But if anthropology is to achieve its scientific aims, Lévi-Strauss argues, it must learn to
look beyond the stories told by individuals and seek out their relation to
the implicit sociological and biological mechanisms that mythic thought
reveals. The key to the understanding of myths is not in what they denote
but in the social and mental patterns they embody.

> We have to resign ourselves to the fact that the myths tell us nothing
> instructive about the order of the world, the nature of reality or the
> origin and destiny of mankind . . . On the other hand, they teach us a
> great deal about the societies from which they originate, they help to
> lay bare their inner workings and clarify the *raison d'être* of beliefs,
> customs and institutions, the organization of which was at first sight
> incomprehensible; lastly, and most importantly, they make it pos-
> sible to discover certain operational modes of the human mind,
> which have remained so constant over the centuries, and are so
> widespread over immense geographical distances, that we can as-
> sume them to be fundamental and can seek to find them in other
> societies and in other areas of mental life, where their presence was
> not suspected, and whose nature is thereby illuminated. (639)

This is the goal of all authentic forms of structuralism as Lévi-Strauss
understands it: to seek out the intrinsic properties of universal structures
grounded in societal patterns that are in turn overdetermined by the
basic organization of the human brain. This "cerebral organization" is
taken to be the ultimate referent of all forms of thought, mythic or
otherwise.

> Genuine structuralism . . . seeks first and foremost to grasp the
> intrinsic properties of certain types of categories. These properties
> do not express anything external to themselves. Or, if it is felt that
> they really must refer to something external, that point of reference

has to be the organization of the brain envisaged as a network whose various properties are expressed by the most divergent ideological systems in terms of some particular structure, with each system revealing, in its own way, modes of interconnection of the network. (627)

For Lévi-Strauss, the goal of scientific objectivity requires a radical relativization of the level of perception of the individual subject; Lévi-Strauss sees this level of thought as epiphenomenal, a perhaps inessential by-product of the deeper, biologically determined mental structures shared by all humans. In *The Naked Man* this subordination of individual thought to universal structures takes on an aggressive, polemical tone and helps to situate the type of search for self carried out by Pinget, Leiris, and Beckett with respect to one of the major intellectual debates of the post–World War Two period: that between structuralism and phenomenology over the status of the subject.

WRITING THE SELF BETWEEN STRUCTURALISM AND PHENOMENOLOGY

Lévi-Strauss professes a deterministic, materialistic worldview, one borne out by his willingness to treat human thought as an epiphenomenon overdetermined by universal biological and social structures. One of the consequences of this aspect of Lévi-Strauss's thought is its antihumanism, that is, its tendency to attribute ontological primacy to impersonal structures rather than human individuals. By contrast, phenomenological thought, in its Husserlian mode, tends toward idealism in its attribution of ontological preeminence to the individual consciousness. The incompatibility of these two doctrines is clear: as mutually exclusive as quanta and waves, digital and analog, they provided the two competing models that were to dominate research in the arts, humanities, and social sciences during the postwar years.

The work of Pinget, Leiris, and Beckett can be profitably examined as an attempt to mediate between the contrary tugs of structuralist antihumanism and phenomenological idealism. It comes as no surprise, of course, that the literature of this period should reflect the influence of the two major schools of thought that dominated the intellectual landscape of postwar France. Nevertheless, it is crucial for the present study to note the manifestations of this philosophical debate in their work, since it helps to account not only for the particular type of literary experiments carried out by these writers but also for their interest in using musical models for their work.[5]

Pinget, Leiris, and Beckett each define the self in terms compatible with those of phenomenological thought: not as a body or as a set of accumulated experiences (empirical definition) or as the freedom to choose among the courses of action available (existentialist) but as a consciousness, as the substance through which the world appears. In tacit or explicit agreement with the primary tenet of Husserlian phenomenology (the transcendental status of the individual consciousness), they each seek, in their own way, to refine our understanding of consciousness and its mechanisms, whether it be by highlighting the temporal structures of consciousness (Pinget), by tracing the circuitous routes that words follow as they wend their way through consciousness (Leiris), or by depicting the submergence of the traditional Cartesian subject in the flood of voices and images that impinge upon the consciousness of Beckett's narrators. Conversely, each of these writers acknowledges that the consciousness under scrutiny, despite its apparently transcendental status, seems to be controlled by an outside force, be it the "murmur," as for Pinget, the "world outside our laws" of Leiris, or the "je, toute dernière personne" that subtends the voices heard by Beckett's narrators. Their attempt to account for the supra-individual forces that impinge on consciousness leads them to use techniques that have been associated with structuralism. The emphasis is placed not on the terms of their narratives (the events, objects, and people named) but on the relationships *between* those terms. Thus Pinget's technique for elaborating variations based on a single story functions according to the same principle that Lévi-Strauss considers to be at work in the cultural functioning of myths. Similarly, Leiris's techniques of *mise en présence* (bringing together) and *tissage* (interweaving) are related to the structural techniques of juxtaposition and classification: "to confront different elements, group them, bring them together, as though moved by an obscure appetite for juxtaposition or combination" (*Scratches* 237). And Beckett's search for the shape of being is founded on the principle enunciated in Belacqua's aesthetic of inaudibilities: the experience of the reader is to take place "between the phrases, in the silence, communicated by the intervals, not the terms, of the statement" (*Dream* 138). (This position is confirmed in *Molloy* by Moran's offhand assertion that "the falsity of the terms does not necessarily imply that of the relation" [*Three Novels* 111] and is illustrated by the pronounced permutational character of so much of Beckett's work from *Watt* to *Quad*.) In each case, the search for self is conceived as the search for a structure. Or, as Beckett put it in *Proust*: "The copiable he [Proust] does not see. He searches for a relation, a common factor, substrata. Thus he is less interested in what is said than in the way in which it is said" (83).

If music serves so consistently as a model for this search, it is because music is understood as an art in which the semantic determinations of conscious intention meet the ineluctable laws that govern matter. Each of these writers turns to music as part of the attempt to reconcile empirical observation with conceptual thought, to account for the deeply rooted, albeit naive, intuition that the subject's consciousness constitutes the entire universe but without relinquishing the pragmatic knowledge that consciousness exists in a world that is fundamentally alien to it. Thus the writers studied in this book use music as both a figure of consciousness in its constitutive temporal dimension (à la Bergson and Husserl) and as a model of relational meaning (as for Lévi-Strauss). In both cases the denotational function of language is devalued. Having recognized that a full accounting of subjective experience in the objectifying realm of concepts is beyond reach, these writers seek answers in the movement from one word to the next and in the patterns created by those words; they seek to compensate for the inability of language to penetrate to the source by using language to build structures that are complete in their own way. The initial impulse to say all is regretfully abandoned with the realization that the denotative function of language is inadequate for the purpose of communicating the qualitative aspects of subjective experience. Language, as they see it, only begins to communicate this kind of knowledge when shaped into self-sufficient constructs that grow according to their own internal logic. Thus, their work provides an ideal testing ground for Theodor Adorno's assertion that "subjective modes of reaction . . . mediate the laws of form rather than reflecting reality" ("Trying to Understand *Endgame*" 17). All the words in the world will not suffice to adequately name the simplest of subjective experiences, but, as one of Beckett's narrators suggests, with typical humor, twenty good ones, used correctly (that is, relationally), might be enough to exemplify the laws that govern that experience: "blank words, but I use them, they keep coming back, all those they showed me, all those I remember, I need them all, to be able to go on, it's a lie, a score would be plenty, tried and trusty, unforgettable, nicely varied, that would be palette enough, I'd mix them, I'd vary them, that would be gamut enough" (*Three Novels* 408). If these words could be proven to act according to rules that have the universal validity of the harmonic series and the acoustic laws that govern musical communication, then the code of the self might at last be broken. But apparently they can't, and so the search continues.

MUSIC, REPRESENTATION, AND RESPONSIBILITY

By focusing so exclusively on subjective experience, on the one hand, and the search for universal structures, on the other, these writers tended to concede the middle ground of social and interpersonal relations that had traditionally provided the main themes of literary narrative. This withdrawal from the middle left these writers vulnerable to criticism by the proponents of traditional modes of realism in literature. Criticism of this perceived failing in their work took several different forms but tended to identify it with a morally suspect understanding of literature's social function. The intellectual effort required to appreciate modernist works was clearly too great to expend on mere entertainment literature. So what, some were asking, was the point of all this effort? What message were these writers trying to communicate to their audience, and how did that message relate to the successful conduct of life in the modern world? These questions appeared all the more pressing in the intellectual climate of postwar France, which was marked by the moral and physical catastrophe of World War Two, the economic and ideological turmoil of reconstruction, the end of empire and the beginning of the cold war, social conflict between the Communist Left and the Gaullist Right, and so forth. Moreover, Sartrian existentialism, with its ethic of personal responsibility, had taken up a dominant position in mainstream discourse. In this context, the postwar avant-gardes appeared to show a troubling lack of concern for the issues facing contemporary society. Indeed, their interest in using models borrowed from music, the non-referential art par excellence, might have been adduced as a sign of their purported disregard for the social concerns of the day. Perhaps surprisingly, then, it was lines of reasoning associated with musical aesthetics that would provide some of the principal arguments used to defend this mode of literature against accusations of irresponsibility. But in order to trace the relationship between music and the ethical defense of modernist literature, it will be necessary first to review the arguments invoked for and against the postwar avant-gardes.

Some, like Georg Lukàcs, rejected the modernist aesthetic entirely. In such essays as "Art and Objective Truth" and *The Meaning of Contemporary Realism*, Lukàcs takes a dim view of modernist writers, characterizing them in the first essay as "contemporary virtuosos of form without content" (60) and complaining in the second about the "dogmas of 'modernist' anti-realism" (17). Lukàcs regrets their "rejection of narrative objectivity" and emphasis on subjective experience, singling out Beckett for particularly harsh treatment. Lukàcs argues that only a return to the realist values of traditional narrative can fulfill the ethical obligation of literature, which he associates with the political goals of Socialism, filtered through the Aristotelian poetic ideal of "investing observed detail with typical significance" (*Meaning* 45). Lukàcs seems to have been singularly unsympathetic to the concerns that motivated this shift in perspective. And yet, if, as I argued above, these writers sought to depict reality in a way that would reveal the general laws governing the interaction of consciousness and its objects, then it seems possible to argue that the modernists were in fact interested in achieving the Aristotelian objective promoted by Lukàcs: investing the particulars of (subjectively) observed detail with the "typical significance" of general laws. There were, at any rate, legitimate reasons to believe that only a willingness to confront the problems raised by subjectivism could achieve the goals promoted by Lukàcs. Adorno makes this point forcefully in his essay on Beckett, "Trying to Understand *Endgame*":

> Realism is not—as some claim—beyond subjectivism but rather lags behind it . . . In art, unreconciled reality tolerates no reconciliation with the object; realism, which does not reach the level of subjective experience, to say nothing of reaching further, merely mimics reconciliation. The dignity of art today is not measured by asking whether it slips out of this antinomy by luck or cleverness, but whether art confronts and develops it. In that regard, [Beckett's] *Endgame* is exemplary. (17)

Sartre, writing in 1939, makes a similar point. In "M. François Mauriac et la liberté," he uses the metaphor of Einsteinian relativity to outline a phenomenologically oriented conception of the novel. Thus he criticizes Mauriac for not realizing that "the theory of relativity applies in its entirety to the fictional universe, that in a true novel, just as in the world of Einstein, there is no place for a privileged observer." And lest there be any doubt as to what Sartre thinks about omniscient narrators, he concludes by equating the pretense of omniscience with the forfeit of art: "God is not an artist; neither is M. Mauriac" (quoted in Nadeau 192–93, my translation).

Sartre's role in the debate between modernism and realism is somewhat ambivalent, however. Although his insistence on phenomenological perspectivism accords nicely with Adorno and with modernist aesthetics in general, and although Sartre was supportive of some of the experiments of the *nouveau roman* (he wrote a preface for Nathalie Sarraute's *Portrait d'un inconnu*), his theory of literary commitment, or *engagement*, seems to lead back in the other direction, toward what Lukàcs, in "Art and Objective Truth," calls the "propagandistic" function of literature. This becomes apparent in Sartre's well-known "Présentation" of *Les temps modernes*, which prefigures the arguments of *Qu'est-ce que la littérature?*

> Indeed, for us, the writer . . . is "in the mix," no matter what . . . Since the writer has no way to escape his historical situation, we demand that he willingly embrace it; that situation constitutes his only chance: it is made for him and he for it. One regrets the indifference of Balzac during the events of 1848, the frightened incomprehension of Flaubert during the Commune; one feels regret *for them* . . . Since we act upon our historical moment by our very existence, we have decided that this action must be voluntary. (Quoted in Nadeau, 196–98, my translation)

For Sartre, as for Lukàcs, the social responsibility of the artist entails an attention to contemporary social and historical problems and must be addressed directly on the thematic level of the text. This conception of artistic responsibility is present in all of Sartre's theater and fiction but makes its presence felt most strongly in the three completed volumes of *Les chemins de la liberté*, which adhere to the traditional techniques of realist narrative and suffer from the thinly disguised authorial manipulations typical of the *roman à thèse*.

Not surprisingly, neither Sartre's stance on political commitment nor his conception of the novel won many adherents among the postwar avant-garde writers. Sartre's position drew a memorably sharp response from Robbe-Grillet in *Pour un nouveau roman*. Since Pinget, Beckett, and Leiris have said so little about the social function of their work, and since Robbe-Grillet's arguments speak to many of the more general ethical issues raised by the work of the postwar avant-gardes as a whole, I will examine his formulation of these issues, presenting them as a characteristic attempt to defend the artistic practice of the postwar modernists.[6] Significantly, although Robbe-Grillet's argument is formulated in large part as a dissenting response to the Sartrian theory of politically committed writing (and to the Soviet doctrine of Socialist realism), Robbe-Grillet maintains one of the primary assumptions of Sartre, which is that all art must be evaluated in terms of its social utility.[7] In his essays in *Pour un nouveau roman*, he attempts to provide a defense of his own literary practice in terms that also apply to postwar modernism generally speaking and to do so in a way that addresses the political and ethical concerns of Sartre.

Robbe-Grillet's defense of the *nouveau roman* has two components. He first responds to the objections of readers and critics who, sharing the realist orientation of the mainstream novel, criticize these works for having no identifiable thematic content (in the traditional sense of a paraphrasable story and/or message opposable to the work's form). The second component of his argument builds on the first in order to address the question of literature's social function.

The objection that Robbe-Grillet's novels suffer from an apparent lack of content is related to the problem of meaning in music, albeit indirectly. The early novels of Robbe-Grillet appeared contentless to their first readers because it was not clear how his unusual narrative syntax was to be resolved into a story. It took some time for readers to understand that a novel like *Le voyeur* or *La Jalousie* did in fact have a story to tell and that the difficulties readers had in locating it were due to problems in deciphering the novel's unfamiliar narrative syntax. Specifically, it was necessary to understand that Robbe-Grillet, following in the wake of the stream-of-consciousness novel, was practicing a form of what has been called phenomenological realism.[8] The story is presented from the point of view of a perceiving subject, before the succession of discrete perceptions have been sorted and organized into causally linked events. This is why Robbe-Grillet so often invokes the active participation of the reader in the creation of the novel: the reader is called upon to carry out a task (sorting and ordering into causal chains) that had traditionally been performed by the narrator.[9] The difficulty of Robbe-Grillet's novels—and the same is true for Pinget, Beckett, and Leiris—is not due to a lack of content but, rather, to a new way of organizing that content: an unfamiliar syntax.

Robbe-Grillet concludes from this that his novels provide exemplary demonstrations of the interrelation of form and content. By changing the way narrative information is presented, they change the meaning of that information. In so doing, his novels highlight in a particularly vivid manner the preponderant role of syntactical conventions in creating the mimetic illusion. This is an issue of great importance for the representational arts in general. Realism, according to Robbe-Grillet, is simply a matter of habit. If it is possible for a casual reader to read a Balzac novel exclusively "for the plot," this is because the conventions that govern Balzac's representations are so familiar to us that they are all but transparent. But as soon as the representational conventions in vigor are modified, the status of the mimetic illusion becomes increasingly unstable, and narrative syntax plays an increasingly important role, forcing the reader to ask "why this thing had to be said in just this way and no other." It becomes clear that content, defined in semantic terms as a story, argument, or message, is inseparable from the syntactic rules that govern form. Just as someone learning a new language must pay close attention to sounds and symbols that would be transparent to a native speaker, someone learning a new narrative syntax must pay close attention to the materiality of the text, and this is what Robbe-Grillet asked his readers to do. But to those early readers who were unwilling to take on the new reading habits required of them, his novels seemed simply to pass from one image to the next without providing anything that could be construed as a story, much less a message relevant to the concerns of ordinary people.

Robbe-Grillet's redefinition of content lends a distinctly musical resonance to his argument. One consequence of his approach to the novel is that the specific subject matter of a novel is considered to be an almost indifferent set of materials with which the writer works in order to create meanings that are nondenotational in nature. (In Robbe-Grillet's work, the narrative energy of his subject matter varies widely, including lurid images of murder, mayhem, and sexual violence but also the notoriously detailed descriptions of unremarkable household objects for which he was often mocked.) What must be emphasized is that the meaning of the work derives not from the subject matter itself but from the procedures used to manipulate it. This conception of the novelist's subject matter as raw material approximates the way the term *material* is used in the Western classical tradition in music. The melodic, harmonic, and rhythmic material of a symphony or string quartet is not the end result of composition but the *basis* for composition. Dvořák and Janáček did not compose folk tunes, they composed *with* them. Robbe-Grillet was fully aware of this similarity and often referred to music to explain why he put so much emphasis on the syntactical construction of his novels and films.[10]

Having redefined the relationship between form and content in this way, Robbe-Grillet attempts to justify his work in terms of ethical responsibility. He agrees with Sartre that literature has an important social function to fulfill, but he identifies that function not with the propagandistic function of literature but with the search for solutions to problems of representation.

> Let's give back to committed writing, then, the only sense it can have for us. Instead of being political in nature, commitment is, for the writer, the full consciousness of the current problems of his own language, the conviction of their extreme importance, the will to resolve them from the inside. That is, for him, the only chance of remaining an artist and also, no doubt, by an obscure and distant causal path, to be good for something—perhaps even for the revolution. (*Pour un nouveau roman* 39, my translation)

Robbe-Grillet invokes here the same principle emphasized by Ricoeur in *The Rule of Metaphor* and *Time and Narrative*: the cognitive advantages afforded by indirect, deferred reference.[11] All of the arts work through this "obscure and distant causal path" of indirect reference, which is why its social function cannot be judged solely as a function of its subject matter: to the extent that a work of art instructs, informs, or preaches, it performs a function that it shares with other, directly political modes of discourse. A novelist who defined utility in terms of an exclusive attention to the transmission of ideological messages would do better to write political pamphlets (and would, in a sense, already be doing that). Instead, Robbe-Grillet defines the novel's political efficacy in cognitive terms. By striving conscientiously to represent reality with ever-greater accuracy, the writer helps to identify epistemological problems that might not have been apparent otherwise. The novelist is, therefore, politically justified in focusing exclusively on "the current problems of his own language," because the resolution of representational problems will lead to a more accurate understanding of the world around us, which, it is hoped, will lead in turn to more effective political action.

Like Adorno (and the pre-*engagement* Sartre), Robbe-Grillet argues that traditional realism is obsolete. The conventions that govern realist narrative reached maturity in the nineteenth century in response to a set of social and historical circumstances that no longer exist. If these conventions appear natural or "realistic" to modern readers, it is only by virtue of their familiarity. There is, in other words, nothing inherently realistic about realism. On the contrary, the conventions of traditional realism can impede our access to reality, since they tend to perpetuate a nineteenth-century worldview, blinding readers to those aspects of reality that can't be accommodated within the epistemology that gave rise to realism. For Robbe-Grillet, then, the task of the modern writer has less to do with describing conditions in the modern world than with working to develop new forms of representation, "forms capable of expressing (or of creating) new relations between man and the world" (*For a New Novel* 9). In contradistinction to Lukàcs's emphasis on the *propagandistic* function of literature, Robbe-Grillet emphasizes the *exploratory* function of literature. "For the function of art is never to illustrate a truth—or even an interrogation—known in advance, but to bring into the world certain interrogations (and also, perhaps, in time, certain answers) not yet known as such to themselves" (13–14).

For Robbe-Grillet, this function of "bringing into the world" is inherently political. Any major modification in the epistemological presuppositions of a given community will necessitate a corresponding shift in the social comportment of that community. Thus Robbe-Grillet emphasizes the importance of contesting the conventions that govern the traditional realist novel. Those "notions périmées," as he calls them (character, story, political commitment, the distinction between form and content), have been rendered obsolete by our increasing awareness of the complexity of the relationship between mind and matter. If the conventions of realism serve to uphold the interests of a waning bourgeoisie by perpetuating its worldview, then the artist who seeks substantive social change must work to replace that worldview with one that corresponds more closely to the actual material and economic conditions that govern society. In Robbe-Grillet's opinion, this makes the "new novelists"— along with their counterparts in the many postwar avant-garde movements in philosophy and the arts—the agitators most likely to bring about a truly meaningful revolution. Despite the relative absence of social themes in their choice of subject matter, their role in demolishing outworn epistemological attitudes will help to bring about "new relations between man and the world," a necessary precondition of any true revolution. Significantly, then, Robbe-Grillet defends the autonomy of artistic practice with an instrumental view of art's function. Indeed, apart from situating art's social function on the level of form rather than content, this view is not so far from that of Sartre and could even be reconciled with the more stringently ideological formulations of Lukàcs.[12]

It is important to remember at this point that this debate over ethical responsibility is not peculiar to Robbe-Grillet's novels nor even modernism as a whole. Modernism simply provides a particularly vivid example of a problem that has dogged the arts since at least Plato: how to defend the social utility of a practice that derives part of its very reason for being from its lack of (immediate, pragmatic) utility. This is one of the eternal ethical problems of aesthetics. And if the problem surfaces in a particularly acute way in the work of the postwar avant-gardes, it should be remembered that music is even more vulnerable to this kind of doubt.

Music provides a particularly pressing problem for aesthetic theory because in the absence of denotation, music must be evaluated in terms that are extremely difficult to draw out of the abstract realm of sounds and syntax and relate to the problems faced by individuals once they leave the concert hall.[13] In a very real sense, then, Robbe-Grillet, by writing novels that minimize the importance of the objects represented and emphasizing the formal processes that govern textual production, shifts the debate over literary meaning onto semiotic terrain that is usually occupied by musicologists. In fact, Robbe-Grillet's emphasis on convention busting bears a striking resemblance to the arguments advanced by Theodor Adorno in defense of twelve-tone music. The overlap between their aesthetic theories will provide an opportunity to consider one of the most significant lessons of music for this generation of writers: how to reconcile the centripetal search for formal and technical mastery with the requirement that art be something more than a pleasant diversion from the problems of daily life.

It comes as no surprise that Adorno was well equipped to contribute to the defense of modernist literature in articles like "Trying to Understand *Endgame*" if we consider that he had long been a proponent of the twelve-tone music of the second Viennese school. Their abandonment of diatonic tonality was every bit as radical as the abandonment of traditional realism offered by the *nouveau roman*. Just as the *nouveau roman* rejected the Aristotelian emphasis on plot and character, the twelve-tone composers rejected diatonic tonality's traditional role as the basis for musical composition. Moreover, as a representative of the Frankfurt school of social theorists, Adorno had sought to defend the new music in terms of its social function.

Adorno, like Robbe-Grillet, focuses his analysis on demonstrating the conventionality of what had, up to that point, been considered natural: "the new music rises up in rebellion against the illusion implicit in such a second nature [diatonic tonality]. It dismisses as mechanical these congealed formulae and their function" ("Music and Language," *Quasi una fantasia* 2). There is, however, an element of added difficulty in providing a utilitarian defense of music, whether experimental or traditional, which is the problem of representation. Robbe-Grillet was still defending a manifestly representational art that could be shown to have an immediate impact on the ways in which we view the world around us. His argument, although following a more roundabout path than most previous theories of representation, had the effect of confirming the centrality of representation in the literary production of meaning. Music, however, as a semantically diffuse art, has been notoriously difficult to defend in ethical terms for precisely this reason: outside of representation, it seems, lies only irresponsibility.

The semantic indeterminacy of music would seem to preclude a defense of music's utility in social or ethical terms.[14] Nevertheless, this is precisely the argument Adorno sets out to make. Significantly, his defense of twelve-tone music incorporates elements of a theory of musical representation. It might seem surprising that such a demanding musical purist as Adorno, with his uncompromising insistence on the principle of "structural listening," would appeal to a representational model for meaning in music, but this is in fact a constant of his formulations of musical meaning. It appears most clearly in his *Introduction to the Sociology of Music* but is present, at least implicitly, in all his studies of music and musicians, from Bach to Berg and Mahler to *musique concrète*.[15] For Adorno, as for Robbe-Grillet, the meaning of the work of art derives from its relation to historical and social structures: "Musical forms," Adorno tells us, "even constitutive modes of musical reaction, are internalizations of social forms" (*Introduction* 221). Musical value, in other words, is conceived in Marxist, Hegelian terms, as fully embedded in history, and Adorno's solution to the problem of musical meaning is to treat it in terms of the Marxist doctrine of historical materialism. Since, as Marx said, the "mode of production of material life conditions the social, political, and intellectual life process in general" (Marx and Engels 4), it follows, concludes Adorno, that "music can do nothing else but *represent*, in its own structure, the social antinomies which also bear the guilt of its isolation" (*Introduction* 70, emphasis added). Musical structures are, like all forms of human activity, shaped by sociohistorical forces, and so they necessarily provide reflections of the society and epoch from which they emanate. They "can do nothing else." We might say, then, that Adorno understands music as a representation of history in the same sense that Schopenhauer understood music as a representation of will: music provides a secondary manifestation of an ontological prior. Like will for Schopenhauer, structure for Lévi-Strauss, number for Pythagoras, and the Ideas for Plato, history is "that which exists," and all else is but a representation of that existence.

History is, in this sense, a deterministic force for Adorno. Nonetheless, within the set of material constraints provided by history, the individual has a certain amount of freedom, however limited, that can make itself felt in unpredictable ways. Thus, some artists will display a reactionary tendency to struggle against or refuse to recognize the forces of history, while others will carry on in blind submission to those forces, pandering to the laziness of their audience. Only a small minority of composers will have sufficient insight to perceive the direction in which history is moving and the courage necessary to implement their discoveries. In order, therefore, to determine the stature of a musical composition, it is necessary to consider the work in relation to its historical context: the aesthetic value of a work corresponds to its ability to incite audiences to recognize their place in history. Adorno's fierce dedication to the second Viennese school and his equally vigorous condemnations of jazz and Stravinsky derive from his belief that only twelve-tone music had adequately faced up to the historical obligations of the age.[16]

The parallel between this position and Robbe-Grillet's is clear. Both defend the autonomy of art, the artist's right (or rather obligation) to focus exclusively on "the current problems of his own language," in terms of social responsibility. They agree with Lukàcs that art must comment on the material conditions of its society, but for them this commentary takes place through advances in technique. Those advances, it is hoped, will play some part in transforming society for the better. This effect depends not on changing the subject matter about which that society thinks (i.e., the content of art) but by transforming the ways in which that society thinks. If music bears a mimetic relation to the forces of history, it can be a progressive art only to the extent that it incites its audience to develop new interpretative strategies. Thus "true musicality," Adorno asserts, "rests on the ability to have experiences. Its concretion is a readiness to deal with things that have not yet been classified, approved, subsumed under fixed categories" (*Introduction* 179).[17]

The mimetic, representational aspect of Adorno's theory of aesthetic value has another important consequence for our understanding of modernist literature. For Adorno, language and music are not opposites but complements; they are related dialectically, not antithetically: "the demarcation line between [music] and the language of intention is not absolute; we are not confronted by two wholly separate realms. There is a dialectic at work. Music is permeated through and through with intentionality. To be musical means to energize incipient intentions: to harness, not indulge them. This is how music becomes structure" (*Quasi una fantasia* 2–3). Drawing the consequences of Adorno's argument suggests that the interpretation of music is an inherently metaphorical process. We know, of course, that even the most neutrally technical descriptions of music are metaphorical in nature. (As Adorno has said, the only "true" interpretation of a piece of music is a performance.) But this is not the point. Adorno seems to be suggesting that the primary task of the musical listener is to construct an appropriate verbal representation of the work. Rather than simply abandoning oneself to the sensual pleasures and momentary effects that are the prime sources of gratification for the casual or distracted listener, it is necessary, first, to follow the logic of a piece in order to be able to isolate and analyze its salient features and then to organize those determinations into a representation that applies to the extramusical world. In this way, Adorno preserves the autonomy of musical meaning (i.e., the fact that "music speaks of nothing other than itself") while at the same time ensuring that musical meaning can be shown to address those "issues of immediate human concern" evoked by Thomas Pavel.[18]

Like literature, music engages in a representational exchange with its audience. But whereas literary works provide representations to their readers, representation in music is the responsibility of the audience. This argument resonates with Jean-Jacques Nattiez's suggestion that "music is not a narrative, but an incitement to make a narrative, to comment, to analyze" (*Music and Discourse* 128). The audience uses the musical work as a stimulus to create its own representations. On this level of interpretation, the primary difference between the literary work (as Robbe-Grillet describes it) and the musical work (as Adorno describes it) is a difference in the vector of representation. Musical works provide the audience with abstract symbols that the audience interprets by applying semantic labels to them; modernist literary works provide the audience with representational symbols that must be interpreted by determining what kinds of abstract thought they exemplify.

In the case of music, however, this task is complicated by the fact that the listener must never presume to have fully resolved the meaning of the piece into language. The key for any such interpretation is that it help to explain the maximum number of specific facts about the work, both on the local level and on the level of large-scale structures, while respecting the semantic indeterminacy of the music. It is in this sense that Adorno's definition of the relationship between music and language is dialectical. An interpretative representation that is only able to explain a piece in general terms is incomplete, but a representation that is contradicted by even the most minor detail needs revision. A single anomaly demolishes the validity of the interpretation, as does a single unexplained feature. One implication of this dialectical approach to interpretation is that all such schemes fail sooner or later. It is also true, on the other hand, that it is precisely these anomalies and aporias that provide the most telling information about the intention of the work, since they act as incitements to revise, refine, and understand better. The only real danger is in taking one's reading as something more than just a provisional metaphor, a heuristic device.

Adorno, as we have seen, tends to fall back on historical referents when describing the meaning of a work. Although he emphasizes the need to maintain the proper degree of metaphorical distance between the interpretation and the target work, his readings do at times make untenably literal claims about the ideological intentions of the works studied. Some of Adorno's followers in the "new musicology" push this type of reading to abusive extremes, using musical compositions primarily as an excuse to advocate whatever social cause preoccupies them at the moment.[19] As a heuristic tool, this kind of reading may have its uses, but the moment such a reading is taken as "the" meaning of the piece, it starts to tell us more about the ideology of the interpreter than it does about the meaning of the work. Music too can be used as a form of propaganda. In the final analysis, then, the interpreter must assume full responsibility for any representations derived from a musical work. Music provides the incitement to make meaning but provides no guarantees of success.

Robbe-Grillet, as we have seen, makes a similar argument, insisting on the importance of using a dialectical process of inference and confirmation in the interpretation of literary works. If form and content are interdependent, then the reader of a novel must check every hypothesis about the object of representation against the formal presentation of that object, and vice versa. Here again, it should be emphasized that this process is by no means limited to modernist literature or music. All interpretation, whether aesthetic or otherwise, depends on this give and take between hypothesis and verification. But the works of postwar modernism enforce this dialectical attitude by undermining the foundations upon which the traditional definition of content was built. Those readers accustomed to thinking of reading as a simple process of collecting information about a world suddenly found themselves asked to interpret novels as one would interpret a piece of music—by identifying structures, procedures, and relationships and then speculating about the intention governing their deployment. Or, to put the same idea in Goodmanian terms, these works forced their readers to read exemplificationally rather than denotationally.

The major ethical problem posed by the postwar literary avant-gardes, in this sense, was not so much that they avoided addressing contemporary social problems in their work but that they destabilized the traditional relationship between form and content (where content determines form). In so doing, they upset the traditional epistemological hierarchy between author and audience. Pinget, Leiris, Beckett, Robbe-Grillet, and like-minded modernists speak from a position of epistemological weakness, offering no authoritative explanations of what things mean. Instead, they devote all their energies to exploring *how* things mean. Forced to acknowledge that their access to ultimate truth is as limited as ours, they make no claim to have better insight or to have more of a right to speak. What they do have to offer is a scientific interest in studying the subjective experience of the individual, combined with the artisan's interest in perfecting the technical means available for the accurate representation of that experience. As in music, this approach to literature depends on the progressive accumulation of meaning within a closed system. The ultimate goal of these writers was to refine the means of representation at their disposal to such an extent that meaning would have no need to be asserted by an authoritative spokesman but would surface on its own, like solids coming out of solution in a centrifuge.

Notes

1. MUSIC, MIMESIS, AND METAPHOR

1. For an ambitious attempt to tell the entirety of this history in detail, see Winn, *Unsuspected Eloquence* and *The Pale of Words*.
2. See Ong for a basic introduction to the mnemonic role of music, rhyme, and repetition in oral narratives. Paul Zumthor's *Oral Poetry: An Introduction* also makes a handy reference.
3. In the *Phaedrus*, Socrates' argument for the superiority of philosophy over rhetoric and poetry is linked to a condemnation of writing. Socrates identifies poetry—whether sung, spoken, or written—with writing, arguing that poets, like scribes and copyists, are too exclusively concerned with transmitting the outer shell of knowledge (words) and not that knowledge itself (ideas). The philosopher, on the other hand, deals in ideas, and for Socrates only ideas count; the actual mode of inscription of those ideas into the real world is considered to be of little importance. If the spoken word is considered superior to writing, this is because the philosopher, Socrates believes, should be there, in person, to defend his ideas against objections and to provide further clarification where necessary. There are, however, some interesting inconsistencies in this argument. One of these results from the Platonic tendency to attribute a transcendent status to ideas. For Plato's Socrates, the spoken word is superior to writing, but, paradoxically, he relegates the act of speaking to a secondary, marginal status, as if it were possible to have speech without speaking. Socrates' argument seems to imply that the speaker should be able to make his ideas known directly, that the presence of the speaker guarantees the meaning of his words but that the act of actually pronouncing those words is of no consequence. If, however, one allows that the speaker's presentation might have an impact on the meaning and reception of the ideas communicated, then one must also allow poets and rhetors (and, presumably, musicians too) a role in the production of meaning and the discovery of truth. The distinc-

tion between performance/inscription and ideas is not as clear-cut as Plato's Socrates would have us believe. (For a more far-reaching critique of the *Phaedrus*, see Derrida, *De la grammatologie*. See also Walker's critique of Derrida's reading in "The Deconstruction of Musicology.")

4. See Yates on Baïf's ongoing preoccupation with this ideal. See also Ronsard's *dédicace* for his *Livre des mélanges* of 1560 (reprinted in Strunk, *Strunk's Source Readings*), which runs through a range of classical examples in its argument for a renewed union of music and poetry.

5. Monteverdi, in the preface to his *Scherzi musicali* of 1607. See Strunk, *Source Readings in Music History*, vol. 2, *The Renaissance*.

6. This point is made at length in the *Politics* (see Strunk, *Source Readings* vol. 2, *The Renaissance* 23–34) and again in the *Poetics* (see note 7).

7. This is what the *Poetics* has to say about music: "Epic poetry and Tragedy, Comedy also and Dithyrambic poetry, and the music of the flute and of the lyre in most of their forms, are all in their general conception modes of imitation. . . . For as there are persons who, by conscious art or mere habit, imitate and represent various objects through the medium of color and form, or again by the voice, so in the arts above mentioned, taken as a whole, the imitation is produced by rhythm, language, or 'harmony,' either singly or combined. Thus in the music of the flute and of the lyre, 'harmony' and rhythm alone are employed; also in other arts, such as that of the shepherd's pipe, which are essentially similar to these. In dancing, rhythm alone is used without 'harmony,' for even dancing imitates character, emotion, and action, by rhythmical movement" (I.2–5). Presumably, music, like dance, is meant to imitate "character, emotion, and action," but Aristotle neglects to mention how it does this and passes immediately to the main subject of the *Poetics*, imitation "by language alone."

8. Rousseau would no doubt have been displeased to see his theory of expression linked to musical romanticism in this way. His intention had been, following the pattern we have already had several occasions to observe, to argue for a return to an originary melding of music and words analogous to the Greek idea of *mousike*. Rousseau promoted a theory of music that emphasized not instrumental music and harmonic complexity (which he saw as aberrations) but a return to a simpler melodic style built around the natural resources of the human voice, which he saw as the ultimate source of expressive power. In keeping with his belief in the superiority of nature over culture and the nobility of primitive man (his *bon sauvage*), Rousseau wanted to revive a simpler, more natural style of vocal music, exemplified by his opera *Le devin du village*.

9. See Guichard; Sieburth.

10. For an excellent analysis of Mallarmé's somewhat paradoxical use of these terms, see Johnson (178–80).

11. Although this notion runs counter to one of the central tenets of structuralist linguistics (which stresses the arbitrary relationship between signifier and signified), it should not be taken to imply that Eliot has lapsed into naive cratylism. What this statement reveals, rather, is the psychological or mentalist orientation of Eliot's poetics. From a psychological point of view, Eliot is perfectly correct in asserting that competent language users do not dissociate sound and sense. Emile Benvéniste, who was no stranger to the structuralist approach, makes a similar point: "Between the signifier and the signified, the connection is not arbitrary; on the contrary, it is *necessary*. The concept (the 'signified') *boeuf* is perforce identical in my consciousness with the sound sequence (the 'signifier') *böf*. How could it be otherwise? Together the two are imprinted on my mind, together they evoke each other under any circumstance. There is such a close symbiosis between them that the concept of *boeuf* is like the soul of the sound image *böf*. The mind does not contain empty forms, concepts without names" (45). The structuralist distinction between sound and sense, in other words, runs contrary to the subjective experience of competent language users.

12. I find incidental support for this assertion in the modern use of the term *voice*, which has undergone a similar widening of meaning. No longer exclusively associated with the spoken word and performance, voice takes on the more general meaning of "personal style," that is, those elements of written elocution that give us access to the specific personality and "thought patterns" of a writer.

13. Consider the following testimony of André Breton: "I do not admire Flaubert, yet when I am told that by his own admission all he hoped to accomplish in *Salammbô* was to 'give the impression of the color yellow,' and in *Madame Bovary* 'to do something that would have the color of those mouldy cornices that harbor wood lice,' and that he cared for nothing else, such generally *extra-literary* preoccupations leave me anything but indifferent" (*Nadja* 14, emphasis added). Breton refers here to a form of representation that is, to be sure, highly refined and somewhat paradoxical, but it is still representation: Flaubert intends for his words to send the reader away from the verbal performance and into the extraliterary world of colors and odors.

14. It is illuminating, in this regard, to consider the difficulty these writers had in their attempts to depict musical performances. Such passages often strike the reader by the way they mix great discursive confusion with the rhetorical register of the sublime. There was, it seems, interest in rendering musical

effects in prose (especially the great expressive power of romantic music) but few tools available for doing so. Certain passages of Balzac's *Gambara*, an extreme but representative example of this tendency, offer all but unreadable hodge-podges of musical terms and ecstatic exclamations, strung together only by indicators of consecutivity: "and then, and then, and then." This is not, of course, to impugn Balzac's literary skill or his knowledge of music (although that knowledge was, by his own admission, not great) but, rather, to highlight the immense difficulty of rendering the logic of musical performance in the syntax of the realist novel. Even Hoffmann's musical narratives show a tendency to veer back and forth between flat description and metaphysics, as if to emphasize the unbridgeable gap between the merely discursive realm of narrative and the transcendent realm of music.

15. It was James Joyce who first brought Dujardin's novel out of obscurity by crediting it with stimulating his interest in the interior monologue/stream-of-consciousness technique. See Edel for a good discussion of this attribution and the origins of the term *monologue intérieur* (30–32).

16. This is a common feature of the literary use of musical models. Writers tend to use their experience as musical consumers to reason about the production of literature. They show little regard for the intentions of composers and the specific concerns of musical composition. Instead, they focus on the effect that a work (or body of work) has had on them and try to use that experience as the model for their literary praxis. The convoluted logical status of this type of model is one of the principal sources of difficulties facing the critic who tries to decode them.

17. See chapter 5 for a more detailed look at Lévi-Strauss's interest in music as a model for structural anthropology.

18. This history will be taken up again, briefly, in chapter 2.

19. This is one point on which philosophers have been able to agree. See, for example, Aristotle; Ricoeur, *The Rule of Metaphor*; and the closing chapter of Goodman.

20. A more complete description of musical meaning would have to take into account the other aspects of musical composition—timbre, volume, tempo, orchestration, and so on. I have left consideration of these elements aside in order to simplify the discussion. This choice is perhaps justified since these aspects of music are not governed by musical notation. They require the insertion of verbal scripts into the score and can vary noticeably from performance to performance without hurting the integrity of the piece. I should also point out that my remarks here are only applicable to those works governed by what has come to be called standard musical notation, that is, the notational system in effect in the Occident since Bach and that is still

the dominant, if contested, notational system used today. Although this definition excludes many types of music (non-Western, avant-garde, etc.), it offers the most precise description of the music considered by the authors studied here.

21. Note that Beardsley's three theories—Expression, Signification, and "Formalist"—correspond to the three approaches to the literary use of musical models considered in this study. All musically oriented writers bring to their work a certain understanding of what music is and does, and this understanding necessarily affects the kind of musical models they use for their writing. I would not go so far as to assert that my tripartite division of the field is able to account for every literary use of music, but it does provide a convenient way to organize this study around the broad trends in the field, one that, if we are to believe Beardsley, is built on a strong consensus as to what the salient features of musical signification are.

22. Beardsley himself suggests as much in the fifty-page postface to the 1981 edition of *Aesthetics*, which is devoted to developments in the field since the 1958 edition. Beardsley dwells at length on Goodman's work, and, although skeptical of many aspects of Goodman's theory, he acknowledges the important contribution the concept of exemplification has made to aesthetic inquiry and uses it to patch up some of the lacunae of the first edition.

23. Only natural objects lack reference entirely. A work of art is always designed with some symbolic intention, even when that intention involves a large proportion of "lack of intention," as in Cage's theories involving chance methods of composition. This is one of the things Duchamp's ready-mades show: the act of framing a urinal or a bottle rack makes it refer in new ways. Duchamp's ready-mades provoke thought to the extent that they force us to ask what it is that they refer to, what makes a "framed" bottle rack worthy of different kinds of attention than a bottle rack in its "natural" state.

24. Goodman, a self-proclaimed nominalist, would have written "label" instead of "quality." As a general rule, I sacrifice Goodman's technical vocabulary to conventional usage in the hope that what I lose in precision and concessions to what he calls "shameless Platonism" will be compensated by ease of comprehension.

25. Again, I have simplified somewhat. In strict Goodmanese and for purely technical reasons, it is more accurate to say that this poem exemplifies "all labels *coextensive with* the term sonnet," and so on.

26. Thus some qualities of a work are easy to rule out of consideration because they are not normally (conventionally) included as signifying elements of the work. For example, a musical score written on yellowed parchment does not

exemplify the quality of being written on a yellowed parchment. But if it were presented as an example of a historical document, as in a museum, it might.

27. Pavel gives an excellent description of the ways that convention—defined as a set of constantly evolving tacit agreements between the concerned parties in the literary transaction—determines which aspects of a work will be considered salient and which will not (114–35).

28. The quotations by Gardner, McIver Lopes, Cometti, and Robinson are taken from a symposium on "The Legacy of Nelson Goodman," published in the *Journal of Aesthetics and Art Criticism* 58.3 (summer 2000).

29. Another, more recent, and equally provocative exploration of the semantic dimension of fictional discourse is Walton, *Mimesis as Make-Believe*. Walton proposes to understand fictional discourse as an outgrowth of childhood games of make-believe: the audience of a work of fiction is understood in Walton's theory as using that work as a prop in one or more games of make-believe, relating it to his or her own situation within the limits prescribed by the fictional work. Walton's work provides an interesting counterpoint to the theories described here, especially to Goodman's theory of representation as denotation, to which Walton provides a robust rebuttal. If I have chosen not to pursue Walton's work further here, it is because he is relatively uninterested in the question of narrative syntax, and, as we shall see, it is around questions of syntax that the exploration of musical meaning and its relations to literature must converge.

30. See "On the Apprehension of Qualities of Tone" in Helmholtz (119–51), especially the section relating to the cochlea (137–51).

31. This description of the place theory, which requires an understanding of the harmonic series and the role of overtones in determining the perception of consonance and dissonance, is incomplete. For a less schematic description of the theory and of its relevance to musical signification, see Pierce (102–11) or any good manual on the physics and physiology of music.

32. From an acoustic point of view, differences between vowels correspond to differences in musical timbre. The shape of the throat and mouth, the position of the tongue, and so on modify the harmonics of the base pitch of a spoken vowel. Consonants are, from an acoustic point of view, noise: they have no clear pitch center.

2. ROBERT PINGET AND THE MUSICALIZATION OF FICTION

1. See, for example, the introduction to Sollers et al., *Tel Quel: Théorie d'ensemble*, published collectively by the Tel Quel group, which asserts that "writing [*écriture*] in its productive function is not representation" (9) and argues for

the need "to articulate a politics linked logically to a non-representative dynamic of writing" (10). For Deleuze's critique of representation, see page xix of the preface to *Difference and Repetition*, where it is most succinctly formulated. See also Dällenbach's and Ricardou's various texts on the theory of the *nouveau roman*. Both Dällenbach and Ricardou elevate nonreferentiality to an exalted status, making it the ideal of all literature.

2. From Aristotle's "è tôn pragmatôn sustasis." In their influential French translation of the *Poetics*, Dupont-Roc and Lallot render this as "l'agencement des faits en système" [the organization of the facts into a system] (55). For an important critique of this translation, see Ricoeur, *Time and Narrative* (32–33). Ricoeur stresses the act of organizing over the organization into a system, making the *muthos* more of a process than a form. This does not affect the point I am trying to make here, which is that the *muthos* (whether system or process) is defined by its content: the organization of the events/*faits*.

3. For a more complete discussion of Joyce's interest in music as a model for narrative, see Aronson (37–64) and the relevant documentation in Richard Ellmann's biography of Joyce, *James Joyce*. See also Stuart Gilbert's discussion of "Sirens" in *James Joyce's* Ulysses and the many references to musical models for narrative in Joyce's correspondence. (Aronson lists a number of these.)

4. The *moment privilégie*: "And thinking again of the extra-temporal joy which I had been made to feel by the sound of the spoon or the taste of the madeleine, I said to myself: 'Was this perhaps that happiness which the little phrase of the sonata promised to Swann . . . was this the happiness of which long ago I was given a presentiment . . . by the mysterious, rubescent call of that septet?'" (*Remembrance of Things Past* 3:911). The *impression*: the "little phrase" of Vinteuil's sonata "was what might have seemed most eloquently to characterise . . . those impressions which at remote intervals I experienced in my life as starting-points, foundation-stones for the construction of a true life; the impression I had felt at the sight of the steeples of Martinville, or of a line of trees near Balbec" (Proust, *Remembrance of Things Past* 2:262). In another example, the analogical operation involved in metaphor, which resides in neither of the objects compared but in the "resonance" between them, is compared to the resonance between musical intervals. What all of these phenomena have in common, apart from the intense pleasure they cause in the one who experiences them, is their dependence on the mind's ability to forge an extratemporal ideality by establishing an analogical link between what is there at the present moment (the physical stimulus, be it a madeleine, bell tower, or melody) and what is absent (the childhood reminiscence, aesthetic impression, or undiscovered truth).

5. There have been numerous attempts to study Proust's interest in music in relation to the structure of the *Recherche*. Of these, I would cite three. In *Musique et structure romanesque dans* La recherche du temps perdu, Matoré and Mecz use the notion of the leitmotiv to explain the large-scale structure of the novel. Milly's *La phrase de Proust: Des phrases de Bergotte aux phrases de Vinteuil* works, as its title suggests, on the scale of the individual sentence/phrase. Nattiez's more sophisticated *Proust musicien* provides a cogent critique of the desire to account for Proust's interest in music in formal terms.

6. Said's remarks on *Doctor Faustus* in *Musical Elaborations* (46–50) pursue this line of reasoning. In Mann's introduction to *Stories of Three Decades*, he offers a kind of minihistory of his use of music: "[In *Tonio Kröger*] I first learned to employ music as a shaping influence in my art. The conception of epic prose composition as an interweaving of themes, as a musical complex of associations, I employed later, in *The Magic Mountain*. There the verbal *leitmotiv* is no longer employed, as in *Buddenbrooks*, for the sole purposes of form, but has taken on a less mechanical, more musical character, endeavoring to mirror the emotion and the idea" (cited in Aronson 31–32).

7. Butor has written several essays on the subject, including "La musique, art réaliste" and his excellent essay on Beethoven's *Diabelli Variations* (*Dialogue avec 33 variations de Ludwig van Beethoven sur une valse de Diabelli*), which takes itself the form of variations on a theme. See also chapter 15 of his *Improvisations on Butor* (172–89). Duras used the musical metaphor as early as *Moderato Cantabile*, but her interest in the relationship between music and narrative repetition comes to the fore in her theater, especially in plays like *Savannah Bay*, *India Song*, and *La música*. Robbe-Grillet used music as a *mise en abyme* metaphor for narrative repetition in *La Jalousie* and makes music (especially serial music) the primary formal metaphor for his films, beginning with *L'année dernière à Marienbad*. See the *Édition vidéographique critique* of his films and "Entretien" for Robbe-Grillet's views on the importance of music in his work.

8. "*La question de la coexistence ou de la co-naissance de la forme et du contenu a fait récemment l'objet d'études très intéressantes. Mais elle ne m'est d'aucun secours dans mon travail étant une vue théorique. Elle ne peut que me prouver, une fois mon livre terminé, que* cette coexistence est la seule réalité poétique*" ("Une interview" 551–52, my translation, emphasis added).

9. See *Robert Pinget à la lettre*: "Bach—My favorite musician. . . . I listened to the Great Passacaglia every day while writing my novel *Passacaille*" (31). Other well-known passacaglias, easily recognizable as such, include the Crucifixus from Bach's *Mass in B minor*, Dido's Lament from Purcell's *Dido and Aeneas*, and, more recently, Webern's Opus 1 (*Passacaglia for Orchestra*).

10. See Bukofzer.

11. The title of *Le Libera* also implies a musical intertext, the *Libera me domine*, which, as part of the Catholic liturgy (the burial service), is often set to music, as in Verdi's *Requiem*.

12. In *Contrepoints,* Escal rules out consideration of the musicality of texts like *Passacaille* for much the same reason.

13. I should add here that this is the critic's problem, not Pinget's. The title of the novel makes no promises about musicality; it offers no guarantees but merely suggests a metaphorical framework for interpretation. It is only when the reader starts to make inferences about the relationship between the two arts based on the metaphor proffered by the novelist that the metaphor becomes a problem. It is perfectly legitimate to read *Passacaille*—or *Point Counter Point*, or Joyce's "Sirens" chapter—without stressing the musical intertext.

14. In order to preserve their literary quality, extended quotations from *Passacaille* are given in the original French and then as they appear in English in Barbara Wright's translation, *Passacaglia*, with page references to both editions. As for the short motivic quotations, which are so numerous that dual referencing would have been obtrusive, I have provided only the translated text, using my own translations, and I give page references to the original French edition.

15. See Vidal (101, passim). For more examples of this approach to Pinget's work, see Baetens, "Passacaille"; Baetens, *Aux frontières*; and Duvert. The basic text for this approach is Starobinski's edition of and commentary on Saussure's study of anagrams in *Les mots sous les mots*.

16. The first of these motifs appears on pages 7 (two times, once reversed), 10, 18, 22, 34, 36, 74, 87, 130; the second on pages 7, 12, 14, 30, 69, 74, 87, 125, 122, 130; and the third on pages 7, 8, 9, 24, 34 (varied), 49 (varied), 38, 44, 88, 97.

17. To bring home this point it might be helpful to ask what, for example, an inversion would look like in literature. Perhaps a negation (I do/I do not), or a question and answer ("Muß es sein?—Es muß sein!"), or a pronominal shift (I/you) or some other kind of logical shift (go/come), or a combination of all of the above (May I come now? No, you must stay away always!). On the other hand, perhaps inversion should involve a more literal prosodic transformation (Hello?/Hello!) or, *tout bêtement*, an anagrammatical reversal (now/won). Arguments can, and have, been made for all of these possibilities, but none can approximate the functions of musical inversion in more than a superficial or parodistic way.

18. Both Beckett and Robbe-Grillet will evolve in the same direction as Pinget and at roughly the same time. The narrative avant-garde of the fifties, it seems, devoted itself primarily to the exploration of what has been called

"phenomenological realism" (Renato Barilli), that is, the depiction of what the ("real") world might look like from the perspective of a purely perceiving subject. In the sixties, these writers take yet another step away from traditional (i.e., "Balzacian") realism. A good number of Beckett's short prose texts from the sixties, as well as Robbe-Grillet's *La maison de rendez-vous* (1965) and *Projet pour une révolution à New York* (1970), share many of the "musical" characteristics of Pinget's *Le Libera* (1968) and *Passacaille* (1969). This new development sparked some interest (at least in the academic criticism of the seventies) in making a distinction between the *nouveau roman* and the *nouveau nouveau roman*. For my part, I subscribe to the equation of these earlier texts with "phenomenological realism" and will try, in the remainder of this chapter, to sort out some of the philosophical links that the new developments of the sixties seem to suggest.

19. The word "murmur" is omnipresent in *Passacaille*. A few examples: "how to believe this murmur, the ear is faulty" (8), "this almost inaudible murmur interrupted by silences and hiccups" (9, 99), "the weakening murmur" (12), "noting in the margins of a murmured phrase" (19, 74), "so much so that a phrase murmured ages ago at harvesttime was just spoken this evening" (82), "to quiet the murmur" (125), and so on.

20. This concept is a fundamental one not just for Pinget but for all the writers considered in this book. Both Leiris and Beckett will describe similar phenomena and use the word "murmur" in much the same way that Pinget and Blanchot do here. This is also a term that appears in the writings of philosophers as diverse as Bergson and Derrida to describe much the same concept: that of a dimly perceived, ill-understood voice that speaks constantly in consciousness and is linked in some unclear way to the very definition of what it means to be conscious.

21. See the first part of Ricoeur's *Time and Narrative*, "The Circle of Narrative and Temporality." This idea is also linked to the Bergsonian theme of language as an inherently "spatializing" medium.

3. MUSIC AND AUTOBIOGRAPHY (LEIRIS *LYRIQUE*)

1. All unmarked translations are my own and are generally of texts that have not yet been translated into English. Most others are from Lydia Davis's translation of *Biffures*, published as *Scratches*. I have modified several of Davis's translations when they did not seem to me to capture some essential aspect of the text.

2. *Le ruban au cou d'Olympia*, which takes its title from Manet's *Olympia*, is one of the few exceptions to this rule.

3. See the interview with Louis-René des Forêts, "La passion de l'opéra," in the Leiris issue of *Magazine Littéraire*, no. 302 (September 1992): 56–58. Des Forêts remarks several times on the shallowness of Leiris's understanding of instrumental music.

4. See also the development on "authenticity" and "communication" at the end of *Fibrilles*. Other formulations of this triple project abound in Leiris's work: "J'éprouve un désir impérieux de justifier *objectivement* ce système *subjectif*, de lui trouver des fondements qui dépassent ma personne" [I feel an imperious desire to justify *objectively* this *subjective* system, to found it on principles that transcend my person] (*Frêle bruit* 310); "demander à la poésie, pour moi comble de la beauté, de tout englober—*le Beau, le Vrai, le Bien*—et de jouer un rôle efficace de révélatrice et de guide" [to ask of poetry, for me the pinnacle of beauty, to englobe all—Beauty, Truth, Goodness—and to play a useful role as initiator and guide] (*A cor et à cri* 150); "mon style dont je tiens moins à ce qu'il soit *beau style* que *style exact* doublement *et sensible*: véridique quant à ce qui est dit, ressemblant quant à moi qui dis" [my style, about which I care less that it be *pleasing* than that it be doubly *precise and sensitive*: truthful about what is said and faithful to the image of the speaker] ("Musique en texte" 174).

5. See Genette's "Signe: singe," *Mimologiques*; Beaujour.

6. Henceforth, in order to minimize possible confusion between the two, I will use the French term *chant* to designate Leiris's purely literary usage of the term; the English term "song" will be reserved for the musical mode of expression sensu stricto.

7. Denis Hollier, following Octave Manoni, speaks of Leiris's "je sais bien mais quand même" [yes I know but still] syndrome. See the discussion between Hollier and Jean Jamin in the Leiris issue of *Magazine Littéraire*, no. 302 (September 1992).

8. We might notice, in this regard, the Mallarméan ring of the fragment quoted earlier, "vivifier l'idée," which is immediately tempered by the "peu importe laquelle" and incorporated into the flow of the sentence. Leiris admires Mallarmé and shares his totalizing dream (as shown in *Fibrilles*, in which Mallarmé's *Livre*—Leiris's reading material in the hospital after his suicide attempt—is his major reference), but his desire to please and to move others requires an adherence, however tenuous it may at times become, to the overriding principle of ease of communication.

9. A note on Leiris's *fiches*: Leiris wrote his autobiographical texts using notes jotted on index cards (*fiches*). These index cards, which he kept in files organized thematically, served as the basis for composition. Leiris sometimes described the early stages of the composition of *La règle du jeu* as a simple matter

of stringing the *fiches* together and providing suitable transitions. As we shall see, however, this process quickly became considerably more complicated.

10. We should note that Leiris is following here Schopenhauer's analogy between voice and the orders of life in the natural world. Schopenhauer saw the natural world as organized hierarchically into increasingly complex forms of being, expressed in the progression from the mineral to the vegetal, animal, and human. This hierarchy was mirrored, as he saw it, in the superposition of voices typical of the four-part chorale: from bass to tenor to alto to soprano. (I give a somewhat more complete discussion of Schopenhauer's musical theory in chapter 4.)

11. It is interesting to note in this regard how amenable music is to the use of technical problems as a stimulus for invention. Bach's *Well-Tempered Clavier*, of course, largely transcends its function as a pedagogical or technical work. There is nothing "preliminary" about it. The same must be said for many well-known musical works that have a strong pedagogical quotient, such as Bartók's *Microcosmos* or the études of Debussy, Chopin, and others. One could profitably question the relationship between music and literature from this perspective. Take Bach's use of the BACH motif in *The Art of Fugue*. Does this kind of playful artifice make him a *leirisien avant la lettre*? Or is there something in music that makes this kind of purely technical feat more appropriate than in literature, where the use of paraliterary devices is almost automatically relegated to the aesthetic limbo of Oulipean experimentation? Technique, in the absence of expressive intention, seems to have a validity in music that it does not have in literature.

12. Maubon, in *Michel Leiris au travail*, confirms this impression of improvisation. The study of Leiris's manuscripts suggests that for *La règle du jeu* he composed directly from his *fiches*, without the help of any intermediate outlines or sketches.

13. This tendency to turn the medium of expression into the object of attention is a recurrent theme in Leiris's work. In "Perséphone," for example, Leiris describes an occasion where he was able to observe a solar eclipse through a piece of smoked glass. For Leiris, the real show was not the eclipse itself but "this business of the smoked glass." "It hardly mattered what there was to see; all that counted was the way one went about looking at it" (*Scratches* 104). The phonograph also gets this kind of attention. Leiris devotes several pages of *Biffures* to the mechanical operation of the phonograph, which, as a child, interested him as much as the music. For Leiris, as for Marshall McLuhan, the medium has a tendency to become the message.

14. "The most accurate of all the portraits I will have made of myself will perhaps be . . . the one I draw, unwittingly, when I try to formulate an idea, any idea at

all, no matter how far removed from my stock of habitual preoccupations" (*Scratches* 248). See also, among many other similar formulations, the various prefaces to the *Glossaire* and *Frêle bruit* (20).

15. This tendency dates back to at least Aristotle, who equates "looseness" with musicality in the *Rhetoric*, comparing the relative lack of structure of the oratorical exordium to that of the musical prologue.

16. The entry for "overture" in the *Oxford Encyclopedia of Music* makes a point of stressing this tendency toward looseness.

17. The decision to treat this ending of *Biffures* as a prelude to the rest of the autoportrait takes on even greater significance when we examine it in context. In the pages that precede this passage, Leiris had flirted briefly with the idea of abandoning *La règle du jeu* for good, citing his apparent inability to avoid the pitfalls of confession, his diminishing pleasure in writing the text, and his growing feeling of *dessèchement*. Here we see that he has definitively rejected that option and instead decided to continue, even if it means going on "à tort et à travers" [without rhyme or reason].

18. Perelman makes this point in his characterization of the "demonstration" in logic and mathematics, which is opposed to the paralogical modes of argumentation taught by rhetoricians (448).

4. SAMUEL BECKETT, MUSIC, AND THE HEART OF THINGS

1. Page 247 in the Olympia edition. The later Calder edition is even less complete. It omits the melodic transcription entirely, a fact that creates a strange anomaly in the "Addenda" section, where the melodic notation is announced but not included. Why has the melody been isolated from the rhythmic score in this way? "Fatigue and disgust" may well have been the deciding factors. Certainly, harmonizing such an odd melody in four voices would have been quite a bit of work, and Beckett's voice-leading skills might not have been up to it.

2. See Kenner (*Samuel Beckett* 104–05) on this line, as well as Senneff; Lees; and Park.

3. Beckett liked to paraphrase Hanslick's famous thesis on musical beauty, in which "form *is* content, content *is* form," using it, for example, to praise Joyce's *Work in Progress* (*Disjecta* 27). Similarly, he explained that he admired Proust because "Proust does not deal in concepts" but "pursues the idea, the concrete" (*Proust* 79). Beckett also insisted on the importance of "the shape of ideas" over the content of those ideas (*Beckett at 60* 34) and claimed to be "less interested in what is said than in the way in which it is said" (*Proust* 83). Examples like these could be multiplied almost at will.

4. From, respectively, Rabinovitz, *The Development of Samuel Beckett's Fiction* (74), and Cohn, *Just Play* (139).

5. To Charles Marowitz (*Encore* [March–April 1962]: 44). This often quoted statement can be found in Knowlson and Pilling (283) and elsewhere.

6. See the interviews with Whitelaw, Lewis, and Chabert in the *Samuel Beckett* issue of *Revue d'esthétique* (Chabert). See also Chabert's "Rehearsing Pinget's *Hypothesis* with Beckett" in Knowlson.

7. Beckett also uses this idea to close his mock lecture on "Le concentrisme."

8. See Schopenhauer's comments on opera, vaudeville, and the da capo in *The World as Will* (263–64).

9. Compare, especially, the altogether milder formulation of Schopenhauer, who, while asserting the superiority of music, allows that the words and drama of opera do have an important function: "Music can . . . enter into a relationship with poetry. But it must never make this the main thing . . . With regard to this superiority of music, and insofar as it stands to the text and the action in the relation of universal to particular, of rule to example, it might perhaps appear more suitable for the text to be written for the music than for the music to be composed for the text. With the usual method, however, the words and actions of the text lead the composer to the affections of the will that underlie them, and call up in him the feelings to be expressed; consequently they act as a means for exciting his musical imagination. Moreover, that the addition of poetry to music is so welcome, and a song with intelligible words gives such profound joy, is due to the fact that our most direct and most indirect methods of knowledge are here stimulated simultaneously and in union" (*Philosophical Writings* 115). Schopenhauer did, apparently, launch vitriolic attacks against "Grand Opera" elsewhere, but these do not apply to opera in general (see Magee 185).

10. Exhaustive enumeration—from the enumerations, as exhausting as they are exhaustive, of *Watt* to the series of missed rendezvous in *Mercier and Camier*, the search for the *bon pensum* of *The Unnamable*, and the permutation of paths in *Quad*—maintain a central place in Beckett's poetics. So does vaudeville—the gags and sung ditties in *Watt*, *Godot*, and *Endgame* and the pratfalls in *Krapp's Last Tape* and the *Acts without Words*—and the "beautiful convention of the 'da capo,'" a term that occurs frequently in his writing and that provides the only adequate description of the full textual repeat specified in plays like *Play* and *Nacht und Träume*. As for his feelings about the opera, his nephew Edward Beckett (executor of the author's literary estate and a professional flautist), confirmed to me that Beckett genuinely detested opera. It is important to note, however, that his dislike of opera did not extend to other forms of song, notably, the German lied. Beckett's admiration for Schu-

bert, for example, led him to use his lieder in more than one piece. As we'll see, it was not the simple fact of setting texts to music that bothered Beckett in opera but the "penny-farthing" plots and purely "local" view of causality, situations, and emotions.

11. Painting does too, but only to the extent that it is an allographic art, that is, to be contemplated in its own right for its own sake and not just as a representational and therefore conceptual medium.

12. Compare this "ideal real" with Leiris's alchemical goal: the "absolu palpable," formulated in his article on John Dee ("La monade hiéroglyphique," *Brisées* 18).

13. Actually, I know of no films that have the degree of abstraction suggested by this passage, where there are no recognizable objects or events. It might be possible to imagine someone so unfamiliar with the conventions of cinema as to be unable to recognize the figures filmed or, more simply, to think of an abstract animated cartoon. It's interesting to note in this perspective, though, that animated films have held, for the most part, to the representational values of live subject cinema and that that most exotic of all rare birds—the commercially successful abstract film—is perhaps best exemplified by the abstract sequences of *Allegro non troppo* and *Fantasia*, two films designed as visual accompaniments to music. The predominance of the music, it seems, is able to justify the incorporation of abstract sequences, even to an audience that would otherwise demand strict representational values.

14. Molloy will later have a similar problem in the auditory domain, namely, making sense out of the words he hears: "the words I heard, and heard distinctly, having quite a sensitive ear, were heard a first time, then a second, and often even a third, as pure sounds, free of all meaning, and this is probably one of the reasons why conversation was unspeakably painful to me" (*Three Novels* 50).

15. This view of the transcendent value of music is confirmed in Sartre: "To the extent that I get it, the symphony *is not there*, between these walls, at the tip of these bows ... It is entirely outside of the real ... The *Seventh Symphony* is not in time at all. It escapes, therefore, completely from the real. It presents itself in person, but as if absent, as if outside of my reach ... I don't really hear it, I listen to it in the imagination" (*L'imaginaire* 243–45, my translation; cited by Schloezer, 58–63).

16. For more on the notions of exhaustion and making the image ("faire l'image"), see Deleuze, "L'épuisé," in Beckett, *Quad et autres pièces*.

17. And, more generally, of much contemporary thought. This is a place where much of the thought considered in this book converges. Beckett's use of the word "tympan" recalls the use Leiris makes of it in "Perséphone." See also

Derrida's "Tympan" in *Marges de la philosophie*, a text written in response to Leiris. Derrida follows some of the history of the relationship between voice and thought there and in places like *De la grammatologie*.

18. For an interesting if highly speculative account of the relationship between consciousness and the interiorization of voices that may or may not correspond to what Barthes had in mind with a "phénoménologie de l'écoute," see Jaynes, *Origin of Consciousness in the Breakdown of the Bicameral Mind*.

19. See Zilliacus, who follows *Cascando* through all stages of composition.

20. Mihalovici has written an article on the project. See Zilliacus for more background information and a list of bibliographical references. Mihalovici's article, unfortunately, contains little information about Beckett's input into the plays. Bair suggests, in her biography of Beckett, that this input was all but nonexistent.

21. The play, it should be noted, was originally written in French and performed on Radio France. Beckett later translated it into English for a BBC production. Unfortunately, to my knowledge, no recording of the French production survives. There are, however, two fine recordings of the play in English: the BBC production, with music by Marcel Mihalovici, and the American NPR production, with music by William Kraft. I have spent many hours studying these recordings and have also had the good fortune to speak with William Kraft about his role in the NPR production. For these reasons, I have chosen to use the English version as my primary text (as printed in the *Complete Dramatic Works*), with only occasional references to the original French (as printed in *Comédie et actes divers*).

22. This is a point that can be inferred from context. *Rough for Radio I* provides further confirmation. There it is explicitly stated that Music and Words have no awareness of each other: "—They are not together?—No.—They cannot see each other?—No.—Hear each other?—No.—It's inconceivable!"

23. This assertion is also confirmed in *Rough for Radio I*, when the visiting woman is invited to turn the voices on and off herself, which she can do by "turning [a knob, presumably] to the right." Beckett, it should be noted, would not have approved of the idea of mounting a stage adaptation of *Cascando*. This is a piece about disembodied voices in which the theme is perfectly matched to its medium. On top of this, Beckett was well known for his fierce resistance to any mise-en-scène that would lend a sense of realist specificity to the carefully constructed ambiguities of his work.

24. Beckett's English translation is slightly less explicit on this point: "I wonder what the chat is about at the moment. Worm presumably" (*Three Novels* 375).

25. Esslin: "It is the Opener who opens and shuts the doors that give us access to the voice and the emotions expressed by music which emerge out of the

depths of the mind." (From the first English-language production of *Cascando*, broadcast on the BBC Third Programme, 6 October 1964. Recording available at the British National Sound Archive.)

26. Opener's desire for ending contrasts with "He's" attitude in *Rough for Radio I*, where the thought of ending is a source of terror. HE: ". . . what the trouble is? . . . they're ending . . . ENDING . . . this morning . . . what? . . . no! . . . no question! . . . ENDING I tell you . . . nothing what? . . . to be done? . . . I know there's nothing to be done . . . What? . . . no! . . . it's me . . . what? I tell you they're ending . . . ENDING . . . I can't stay like that after . . ."

27. See, especially, "Ding-Dong," from *More Pricks than Kicks*, in which walking eases the torment of introspection by recalling "the faint inscriptions of the outside world" (39). The walking image also provides a metaphor for the importance of the relations between terms, which are always understood by Beckett to be more important than the terms themselves. Thus, in "Ding-Dong," Belacqua finds "torment in the terms and in the intervals a measure of ease."

28. For support for this equation of internal and external stimuli, we could turn to various thinkers of an idealist bent, beginning with Schopenhauer: "For the *object* as such exists always only for and in *perception*; now perception may be brought about through the senses, or, in the absence of the object, through the power of imagination" (*The World as Will* 443). Or, alternatively, Descartes: "Matter of experience consists of what we perceive by sense, what we hear from the lips of others, and generally whatever reaches our understanding either from external sources or from that contemplation which our mind directs backwards on itself" (82).

29. I have heard both the Mihalovici and the Kraft productions of *Cascando*, and, assuming that the most important features of both pieces are audible to an inexpert but interested listener like myself, I would venture to make the following remarks: both pieces feature noticeable changes in mood between an agitated sound surface and a calm, otherworldly mood; these changes in mood seem meant to match the alternations in Voice's part between the "story element" and the "self element" (which will be discussed shortly). Both composers, in other words, seem to have understood and respected the dramatic intentions of Beckett's script. They have also, it seems, approached the music in the same general way (with the polyphonic instrumentation, lack of a clear tonal center, and abstract sound surface typical of "serious music" in the postwar years). A more detailed analysis of the music would require close study of the scores, but these are, to my knowledge, unobtainable. It might be interesting to ask what kind of musical gesture would be able both to respect

the spirit of the piece *and* to make a significant difference in its overall meaning. It is hard to imagine that this would be possible. Surely, we would have to disqualify such disruptive gestures as inserting show tunes or silence or incongruous sounds into the musical slots of *Cascando*. To be eligible for inclusion in *Cascando*, the music need only work within the constraints provided by Beckett.

30. In every quotation from *Cascando*, all ellipses are Beckett's, as are the dashes that appear in other passages. These are important conventions for the performance of this piece since the actor must differentiate prosodically between the self-imposed pauses that follow each burst of speech and the abrupt endings that indicate that he has been cut off by Opener.

31. "Use of the second person marks the voice. That of the third that cantankerous other. Could he speak to and of whom the voice speaks there would be a first. But he cannot. He shall not. You cannot. You shall not" (Beckett, *Company* 8).

32. Interestingly, the relationship between these two plays is much like that between Leiris's *A cor et à cri* and "Musique en texte," where music is understood, respectively, as a complementary counterpart to and incommensurable other of words. As in *A cor et à cri*, *Words and Music* deals with song (words supplemented by music), and the central problematic of the play is affective. *Cascando*, on the other hand, like "Musique en texte," treats words and music as incommensurable, inhabiting entirely different spheres of consciousness.

33. This passage appears twice in the play.

34. The bracketed ellipses, here and in the following quotations, replace stage directions that might distract from the thematic point at issue.

35. Actually, there is one significant difference: in the first sequence, A is still in the field of vision; in the repeat, the camera moves in slowly to a "close-up of B, losing A." The actions remain exactly the same, but the point of view has changed.

36. See Freud's *Beyond the Pleasure Principle* for his account of repetition as it relates to the unconscious and the death instincts.

37. From liner notes to the Teldec D 125207 recording of the piece. The liner notes also inform us that Romain Rolland speculated that Beethoven may have intended the piece as a reflection of the Countess Erdödy's personality, to whom the piece was dedicated and who was suffering, apparently, from an incurable illness.

38. Act 3, shot 12: "Cut to close-up from above of cassette on stool, small grey rectangle on larger rectangle of seat. 5 seconds"; act 3, shot 24: "Cut to close-up of mirror reflecting nothing. Small grey rectangle (same dimensions as cassette) against larger rectangle of wall. 5 seconds."

39. Thus the key moment in *Ghost Trio*, the moment of recognition that I call the mirror moment, occurs in one form or another in just about all of Beckett's works. This is the point at which the story that the narrator tells is revealed to be his or her own. This happens at the end of *Film* when O is confronted by E and at the moment in *Ohio Impromptu* when the reader and the listener look into each other's eyes. It is implied in the Moran/Molloy relationship, explicitly stated in the Watt/Sam relationship, and so on.

40. This is also a central problematic of Thomas Mann's *Doktor Faustus*, in which the opposition between the impersonal, relational dimension of art and the personal, affective dimension is treated in terms of the opposition between melody and counterpoint.

5. MUSIC, METAPHYSICS, AND MORAL PURPOSE IN LITERATURE

1. This formulation, which clearly owes much to Heidegger, was first attributed to Beckett by Lawrence Harvey and has been widely quoted (see Bair; Pilling).

2. This approach to myth, which bears a close resemblance to the narrative strategy employed by Pinget in *Passacaille*, was given a more extensive description in chapter 2.

3. For a cogent critique of the musical metaphor in *The Raw and the Cooked*, see Winn, *The Pale of Words* (85–89).

4. For more on Lévi-Strauss's thought on the relationship between myth and fugue, see the long developments on this subject in *The Raw and the Cooked* (147–63, 240–55).

5. Of the other major intellectual currents that had a significant impact on the cultural life of the postwar years, psychoanalysis, Sartrian existentialism, and Marxism should also be mentioned. The former has been alluded to, albeit briefly, in the first part of this chapter; the latter two will be discussed in the following section.

6. Pinget and Beckett are, to my knowledge, entirely silent on the question of the political relevance of their literary work. Leiris does turn to this question from time to time but from a position of weakness: he is concerned about the apparent egoism of autobiography but never launches a full-fledged defense of the genre or of his particularly introverted practice of it.

7. As Britton points out, Robbe-Grillet has a tendency to conflate Sartre's doctrine of commitment with that of Socialist realism, no doubt because the latter makes an easier target. Britton's book offers an extremely useful history of the *nouveau roman*'s ongoing struggle with the problem of political commitment (and, more generally, the referential function of literature), as re-

vealed in the public debates of the new novelists with Sartre, the Tel Quel group, and others.

8. See Ricardou and Rossum-Guyon; this term is used on several occasions to refer to the first phase of the *nouveau roman*. Renato Barilli's essay, "Nouveau roman: Aboutissement du roman phénoménologique ou nouvelle aventure romanesque" (Ricardou and Rossum-Guyon 1:107–30), is central to this discussion.

9. Robbe-Grillet, in his second phase, turns away from phenomenological realism, but, as I suggested in chapter 2, the more extreme procedures of the so-called *nouveau nouveau roman* of the late sixties and seventies simply displace the initial concern with an *observing* mind onto the realm of the *imagining* mind.

10. These references are sprinkled throughout Robbe-Grillet's oeuvre. We've already considered (in chapter 1) the well-known "indigenous song" passage from *La Jalousie*. In his theoretical statements, Robbe-Grillet often refers to music, especially serial music, to explain the principles that govern the organization of narrative material in his films. See, for example, the interviews included in the *Édition vidéographique critique* of his films. Several of these interviews (which are transcribed in the accompanying booklet under headings like "La musicalisation du récit" and "La musique en lambeaux") focus on his interest in the musical deployment of material.

11. See my discussion of Ricoeur in the section "Music and Metaphor, Syntax and Semantics" in chapter 1.

12. Britton traces the evolution of this argument through Robbe-Grillet's career. In the early phases of his career, he tended to emphasize the complete autonomy of art and literature and then began a progressive shift toward a more properly instrumental view of literature.

13. The musical specificity of this problem is highlighted in Meyer's *Emotion and Meaning in Music*, which was considered in chapter 1. We also examined there Monroe Beardsley's attempt to overcome this problem.

14. A more common defense of music's utility in recent years has emphasized the neurological benefits of music. Developmental psychologists, for example, cite evidence suggesting that music stimulates the development of neural pathways in children that will, later in life, allow them to process information more intensively and store it more efficiently. Similarly, evolutionary psychologists have emphasized the competitive edge afforded by a highly discriminating sense of hearing (in escaping from predators, recognizing allies, attracting a mate, etc.). There is some debate as to whether musical skills

contribute directly to reproductive success and survival in the wild or if music is simply, as the cognitive scientist Steven Pinker has put it, a form of "auditory cheesecake" (534), that is, a pleasing but evolutionarily inconsequential by-product of the design of the relevant physiological systems. What all these arguments have in common is an emphasis on music as a form of play that helps to build perceptual acuity and improve cognitive skills. They do not directly address the question of music's *social* utility.

15. See Adorno's articles on Bach in *Prisms* and on Mahler and *musique concrète* in *Quasi una fantasia* and his monographs on Berg and Mahler.

16. Mahler makes an especially interesting test case for Adorno's historical theory of aesthetic value, because Adorno sees Mahler as a progressive composer, fully aware of his place in history, despite the fact that he composed in what Adorno considers to be an obsolete tonal idiom: "The scandal is that he . . . succeeded in expressing the truly unprecedented with a traditional vocabulary" (*Quasi una fantasia* 86).

17. Robbe-Grillet and Adorno display absolute confidence in the crucial historical role played by the new novel and the new music, respectively. Even if we agree with them on this point, however, and even if we accept their thesis about the social function of art, the passage of time has shown that the *nouveau roman* did not provide the only viable way forward for literary narrative any more than serialism provided the only way forward for music. Nevertheless, by problematizing the notion of content, just as serialism problematized the status of diatonic tonality, the literary avant-gardes of the postwar years have continued to exert their influence on subsequent generations. In the current postmodern era, writers have tended to recontextualize the techniques of the avant-garde, sometimes recycling them in more or less ironic ways, sometimes setting themselves up in opposition to them. It is not surprising, in this context, that the use of music as a formal model for narrative has fallen out of fashion in recent years. Postmodern writers like Pascal Quignard continue to invoke music as a model of expressive power and anagogic meaning, but, as Pautrot has remarked, they have tended to fall back on the more traditional use of music as subject matter, writing novels *about* music and musicians (See "De *La Leçon de musique* à *La Haine de la musique*"). Postmodern writers still show an interest in integrating musical values into their writing but tend to do so within the context of more traditional literary forms. Apart from Quignard, Pautrot also mentions the contemporary French-language writers Jean Echenoz, Antoine Volodine, Christian Gailly, Gilles Anquetil, and André Hodeir. Other writers that come to mind are Anthony Burgess, Thomas Bernhardt, Michael Ondaatje, Milan

Kundera, Toni Morrison, and Assia Djébar. This list is, needless to say, personal and makes no claim to exhaustivity.

18. See the discussion of Pavel in chapter 1.

19. See, for example, McClary, who succumbs to this temptation on numerous occasions. One thinks of Proust's Swann, who, in love, sees only that love reflected in the little phrase of Vinteuil.

Bibliography

Acheson, James. "Beckett, Proust and Schopenhauer." *Contemporary Literature* 19 (spring 1978): 165–79.

Adorno, Theodor. *Introduction to the Sociology of Music*. New York: Continuum, 1988.

——. *Philosophy of Modern Music*. New York: Seabury, 1973.

——. *Prisms*. Cambridge MA: MIT P, 1992.

——. *Quasi una Fantasia*. London: Verso, 1998.

——. "Trying to Understand *Endgame*." *Samuel Beckett's Endgame*. Ed. Harold Bloom. New York: Chelsea House, 1988. 9–40.

Aristotle. *Poetics*. Trans. Francis Fergusson. New York: Hill and Wang, 1961.

——. *La Poétique*. Texte, traduction, et notes par Roselyne Dupont-Roc et Jean Lallot. Paris: Seuil, 1980.

Aronson, Alex. *Music and the Novel*. Totowa NJ: Rowan and Littlefield, 1980.

Baetens, Jan. *Aux frontières du récit: Fable de Robert Pinget*. Leuven: Pers Leuven UP, 1987.

——. "Passacaille, ou la multiplication par zéro." *Littérature* May 1982: 93–104.

Bair, Deirdre. *Samuel Beckett: A Biography*. New York: Harcourt Brace Jovanovich, 1978.

Balzac, Honoré de. *Le chef-d'oeuvre inconnu*; *Gambara*; *Massimilla Doni*. Introductions, notes et documents par Marc Eigeldinger et Max Milner. Paris: Flammarion, 1981.

Barricelli, Jean-Pierre. *Melopoiesis: Approaches to the Study of Literature and Music*. New York: New York UP, 1988.

Barricelli, Jean-Pierre, Joseph Gibaldi, and Estella Lauter, eds. *Teaching Literature and Other Arts*. New York: Modern Language Association of America, 1990.

Barthes, Roland. *L'obvie et l'obtus*. Paris: Seuil, 1982.

Beardsley, Monroe. *Aesthetics: Problems in the Philosophy of Criticism*. New York: Harcourt Brace and World, 1958. 2nd ed. (with postface), Indianapolis: Hackett, 1981.

Beaujour, Michel. *Miroirs d'encre*. Paris: Seuil, 1980.

Beckett, Samuel. *Collected Shorter Prose*. London: Calder, 1984.

——. *Comédie et actes divers*. Paris: Minuit, 1972.

——. *Company*. New York: Grove, 1980.

——. *Complete Dramatic Works of Samuel Beckett*. London: Faber and Faber, 1986.

——. *Disjecta*. London: Calder, 1983.

——. *Dream of Fair to Middling Women*. London: Calder, 1993.

——. *How It Is*. New York: Grove, 1964.

——. *L'innommable*. Paris: Minuit, 1953.

——. *Malone meurt*. Paris: Minuit, 1951.

——. *Mercier and Camier*. New York: Grove, 1974.

——. *Molloy*. Paris: Minuit, 1951.

——. *More Pricks than Kicks*. London: Calder, 1993.

——. *Murphy*. London: Calder, 1957.

——. *Proust. Proust and Three Dialogues*. London: Calder, 1965.

——. *Quad et autres pièces pour la télévision*. Paris: Minuit, 1992.

——. *Three Novels by Samuel Beckett*. New York: Grove, 1965.

——. *Watt*. London: Calder, 1963 (for text quotations).

——. *Watt*. London: Olympia, 1953 (for musical quotations).

Benvéniste, Emile. "The Nature of the Linguistic Sign." *Problems in General Linguistics*. Trans. Mary Elizabeth Meek. Miami: Miami UP, 1971. 43–48.

Bergson, Henri. "The Idea of Duration." *Philosophers of Process*. Ed. Douglas Browning. New York: Random House, 1965. 6–43.

Bernhart, Walter, Steven Paul Scher, and Werner Wolf, eds. *Word and Music Studies: Defining the Field*. Amsterdam: Rodopi, 1999.

Bernold, André. *L'amitié de Beckett*. Paris: Hermann, 1992.

Bernstein, Susan. *Virtuosity of the Nineteenth Century*. Stanford CA: Stanford UP, 1998.

Blanchot, Maurice. *L'espace littéraire*. Paris: Gallimard, 1955.

——. *The Space of Literature*. Trans. Ann Smock. Lincoln: U of Nebraska P, 1982.

Brater, Enoch. *The Drama in the Text*. Oxford: Oxford UP, 1994.

Breton, André. *Nadja*. Trans. Richard Howard. New York: Grove P, 1960.

Britton, Celia. *The Nouveau Roman: Fiction, Theory and Politics*. New York: St. Martin's, 1992.

Brooks, Peter. *Reading for the Plot*. New York: Vintage, 1985.

Brown, Calvin S. *Music and Literature: A Comparison of the Arts*. Athens: U of Georgia P, 1948.

——. "Musico-Literary Research in the Last Two Decades." *Yearbook of Comparative and General Literature* 19 (1970): 5–27.

——. *Tones into Words: Musical Compositions as Subjects of Poetry*. Athens: U of Georgia P, 1953.

Bryden, Mary, ed. *Beckett and Music*. New York: Clarendon, 1998.

Bukofzer, Manfred F. *Music in the Baroque Era*. New York: Norton, 1947.

Burgess, Anthony. *Mozart and the Wolf Gang*. London: Vintage, 1991.

——. *Napoleon Symphony*. New York: Knopf, 1974.

——. *This Man and Music*. London: Hutchinson, 1982.

Butor, Michel. *Dialogue avec 33 variations de Ludwig van Beethoven sur une valse de Diabelli*. Paris: Gallimard, 1971.

——. *Improvisations on Butor: Transformation of Writing*. Ed. Lois Oppenheim. Trans. Elinor S. Miller. Tallahassee: UP of Florida, 1996.

——. "Michel Butor: Musique et littérature." Interview with Thierry Belleguic and Annick Desbizet. *Revue Frontenac* 8 (1991): 71–87.

——. "La musique, art réaliste." *Répertoire II*. Paris: Minuit, 1964. 27–41.

Calder, John, et al. *Beckett at 60: A Festschrift*. London: Calder and Boyars, 1967.

Cavell, Stanley. *Must We Mean What We Say?* Cambridge: Cambridge UP, 1969.

Chabert, Pierre, ed. *Samuel Beckett*. *Revue d'esthétique* (hors séries #01). Paris: Jean-Michel Place, 1990.

Cohn, Dorritt. *Transparent Minds*. Princeton NJ: Princeton UP, 1978.

Cohn, Ruby. *Just Play: Beckett's Theater*. Princeton NJ: Princeton UP, 1980.

Cometti, Jean-Pierre. "Activating Art." *Journal of Aesthetics and Art Criticism* 58.3 (summer 2000): 237–43.

Cupers, Jean-Louis. "Études comparatives: Les approches musico-littéraires. Essai de réflexion méthodologique." *La littérature et les autres arts*. Louvain: Université Catholique de Louvain, 1979. 63–103.

Dällenbach, Lucien. *Le récit spéculaire: Essai sur la mise en abyme*. Paris: Seuil, 1977.

Deguy, Michel. "A coeur et à chant." *Temps Modernes* 535 (1991): 13–19.

Deleuze, Gilles. *Difference and Repetition*. New York: Columbia UP, 1994.

——. *L'épuisé*. Samuel Beckett, *Quad et autres pièces pour la télévision*. Paris: Minuit, 1992. 55–106.

Derrida, Jacques. *De la grammatologie*. Paris: Minuit, 1967.

——. *La dissémination*. Paris: Seuil, 1972.

——. *Marges de la philosophie*. Paris: Minuit, 1972.

Descartes, René. *The Essential Descartes*. Ed. Margaret D. Wilson. New York: Meridian, 1969.

Dosse, François. *Histoire du structuralisme*. 2 vols. Paris: Livre de Poche, 1992.

Dujardin, Edouard. *Les lauriers sont coupés suivi de Le monologue intérieur*. Rome: Bulzoni, 1977.

Duvert, Tony. "La parole et la fiction." *Critique* May 1968: 540–55.

Edel, Leon. *The Modern Psychological Novel*. New York: Universal Library, Grosset and Dunlap, 1964.

Eliot, T. S. *Selected Prose of T. S. Eliot*. New York: Harcourt Brace Jovanovich, 1975.

Ellmann, Richard. *James Joyce*. New York: Oxford UP, 1959.

Escal, Françoise. *Contrepoints, musique et littérature*. Paris: Méridiens Klincksieck, 1990.

Fournier, Edith. "'Sans': Cantate et fugue pour un refuge." *Les Lettres Nouvelles* 3 (September–October 1970): 149–60.

Frege, Gottlob. "On Sense and Meaning." Trans. Max Black. *Translations from the Philosophical Writings of Gottlob Frege*. 3rd ed. Ed. Peter Geach and Max Black. Oxford: Blackwell, 1973. 56–78.

Freud, Sigmund. *Beyond the Pleasure Principle*. Trans. James Strachey. New York: Norton, 1961.

Frye, Northrop. *Anatomy of Criticism*. Princeton NJ: Princeton UP, 1957.

——. "Music in Poetry." *University of Toronto Quarterly* 11 (1941–42): 167–79.

Gardner, Howard. "Project Zero: Nelson Goodman's Legacy in Art Education." *Journal of Aesthetics and Art Criticism* 58.3 (summer 2000): 245–49.

Genette, Gérard. "L'autre du même." *Corps écrit* 15 (September 1985): 11–16.

——. *Figures III*. Paris: Seuil, 1972.

——. *Mimologiques*. Paris: Seuil, 1976.

Ghyka, Matila. *Le nombre d'or*. Paris: Gallimard, 1959.

Gide, Andre. *Les faux monnayeurs*. Paris: Folio, 1925.

Gilbert, Stuart. *James Joyce's* Ulysses. New York: Vintage Books, 1955.

Goodman, Nelson. *Languages of Art*. Indianapolis: Hackett, 1976.

Groupe Mu. *Rhétorique générale*. Paris: Larousse, 1970.

Guichard, Léon. *La musique et les lettres en France au temps du Wagnérisme*. Paris: PUF, 1963.

Hanslick, Eduard. *On the Musically Beautiful*. Trans. Geoffrey Payzant. Indianapolis: Hackett, 1986.

Helmholtz, Hermann. *On the Sensations of Tone*. New York: Dover, 1954.

Hoffmann, E. T. A. *E. T. A. Hoffmann's Musical Writings: Kreisleriana, The Poet and the Composer, Music Criticism*. Ed. David Charlton. Cambridge: Cambridge UP, 1989.

Hollander, John. *The Untuning of the Sky*. Princeton NJ: Princeton UP, 1961.

Homan, Sydney. *Filming Beckett's Television Plays: A Director's Experience*. Lewisburg: Bucknell UP, 1992.

Husserl, Edmund. "Phenomenology." *Critical Theory since 1965*. Ed. Hazard Adams and Leroy Searle. Tallahassee: Florida State UP, 1986. 658–63.

——. "The Phenomenology of Time Consciousness." *The Essential Husserl: Basic Writings in Transcendental Phenomenology*. Ed. Donn Welton. Bloomington: Indiana UP, 1999. 186–221.

Huxley, Aldous. *Point Counter Point*. New York: Harper and Row, 1928.

Jakobson, Roman. "Language in Relation to Other Communication Systems." *Ha-Sifrut/Literature: Theory—Poetics—Hebrew and Comparative Literature* 4 (1973): 612–17.

James, William. "The Stream of Thought." *Pragmatism, the Classic Writings.* Ed. H. S. Thayer. New York: Thayer, 1982. 142–50.

Jankélévitch, Vladimir. *La musique et l'ineffable.* Paris: Seuil, 1983.

Jaynes, Julian. *The Origin of Consciousness in the Breakdown of the Bicameral Mind.* Boston: Houghton Mifflin, 1977.

Johnson, Barbara. *Défigurations du langage poétique.* Paris: Flammarion, 1979.

Joyce, James. *Ulysses.* New York: Vintage, 1986.

Juarroz, Roberto. *Vertical Poetry.* Trans. W. S. Merwin. San Francisco: North Point, 1988.

Kandinsky, Wassily. *Du spirituel dans l'art et dans la peinture en particulier.* Paris: Denoël, 1989.

Kenner, Hugh. *Flaubert, Joyce, Beckett: The Stoic Comedians.* Boston: Beacon, 1962.

——. *A Reader's Guide to Samuel Beckett.* London: Thames and Hudson, 1973.

——. *Samuel Beckett: A Critical Study.* London: Calder, 1961.

Knowlson, James, ed. *As No Other Dare Fail.* London: Calder, 1986.

Knowlson, James, and John Pilling. *Frescoes of the Skull.* London: Calder, 1979.

Kundera, Milan. *The Art of the Novel.* New York: Grove, 1988.

Lacan, Jacques. *Ecrits I.* Paris: Seuil, 1966.

Lagerroth, Ulla-Britta, Hans Lund, and Erik Hedling. *Interart Poetics: Essays on the Interrelations of the Arts and Media.* Amsterdam: Rodopi, 1997.

Langer, Suzanne. *Philosophy in a New Key.* New York: Mentor, 1942.

Lawley, Paul. "Beckett's Dramatic Counterpoint: A Reading of *Play.*" *Journal of Beckett Studies* 9 (1984): 25–41.

Lees, Heath. "*Watt*: Music, Tuning and Tonality." *Journal of Beckett Studies* 9 (1984): 5–24.

Leiris, Michel. *A cor et à cri.* Paris: Gallimard, 1988.

——. *L'âge d'homme.* Paris: Folio, 1990.

——. *Biffures. La règle du jeu I.* Paris: Gallimard, 1991.

——. *Brisées.* Paris: Gallimard, 1992.

——. *Fibrilles: La règle du jeu III.* Paris: Gallimard Imaginaire, 1966.

——. *Fourbis: La règle du jeu II.* Paris: Gallimard Imaginaire, 1955.

——. *Frêle bruit: La règle du jeu IV.* Paris: Gallimard, 1976.

——. *Glossaire: J'y serre mes gloses. Mots sans mémoire.* Paris: Gallimard, 1969.

——. *Journal.* Paris: Gallimard, 1992.

——. *Manhood.* Trans. Richard Howard. New York: Grossman, 1963.

——. "Musique en texte et Musique anti-texte." *Langage tangage ou ce que les mots me disent*. Paris: Gallimard, 1985. 69–189.

——. *Operratiques*. Paris: POL, 1992.

——. *Le ruban au cou d'Olympia*. Paris: Gallimard, 1981.

——. *Scratches*. Trans. Lydia Davis. New York: Paragon House, 1991.

Lejeune, Philippe. *Lire Leiris*. Paris: Klincksieck, 1975.

——. *Le pacte autobiographique*. Paris: Seuil, 1975.

Lévi-Strauss, Claude. *The Naked Man*. New York: Harper and Row, 1981.

——. *The Raw and the Cooked*. New York: Harper and Row, 1969.

——. *Regarder, écouter, lire*. Paris: Plon, 1993.

——. *Structural Anthropology*. New York: Basic Books, 1963.

Lukàcs, Georg. "Art and Objective Truth." *Writer and Critic and Other Essays*. Ed. Arthur D. Kahn. London: Merlin P, 1970. 25–60.

——. *The Meaning of Contemporary Realism*. London: Merlin P, 1962.

Magee, Bryan. *The Philosophy of Schopenhauer*. Oxford: Clarendon, 1983.

Mallarmé, Stéphane. *Oeuvres complètes*. Paris: Pléiade, 1945.

Mann, Thomas. *Doctor Faustus*. New York: Modern Library, 1992.

Marx, Karl, and Friedrich Engels. *The Marx-Engels Reader*. 2nd ed. Ed. Robert C. Tucker. New York: W. W. Norton, 1978.

Matoré, Georges, and Irène Mecz. *Musique et structure romanesque dans* La recherche du temps perdu. Paris: Klincksieck, 1972.

Maubon, Catherine. *Michel Leiris au travail: Analyse et transcription d'un fragment manuscrit de "Fourbis."* Pisa: Pacini, 1987.

McClary, Susan. *Feminine Endings: Music, Gender, and Sexuality*. Minneapolis: U of Minnesota P, 1991.

McIver Lopes, Dominic. "From *Languages of Art* to Art in Mind." *Journal of Aesthetics and Art Criticism* 58.3 (summer 2000): 227–31.

McLuhan, Marshall. *Understanding Media: The Extensions of Man*. New York: Mentor, 1964.

Mehlman, Jeffrey. *A Structural Study of Autobiography: Proust, Leiris, Sartre, Lévi-Strauss*. Ithaca NY: Cornell UP, 1971.

Meyer, Leonard B. *Emotion and Meaning in Music*. Chicago: U of Chicago P, 1956.

Mihalovici, Marcel. "Ma collaboration avec Beckett." *ADAM: International Review* 25.337–39 (1970): 65–67.

Milly, Jean. *La phrase de Proust: Des phrases de Bergotte aux phrases de Vinteuil*. Paris: Larousse, 1975.

Mitchell, W. J. T. *Iconology: Image, Text, Ideology*. Chicago: U of Chicago P, 1986.

——. *Picture Theory*. Chicago: U of Chicago P, 1994.

Mood, John J. " 'The Personal System'—Samuel Beckett's *Watt*." *PMLA* 86 (March 1971): 255–65.

Morel, Renée. "Voix et moi." *Revue Romane* 23 (1988): 75–83.

Nadeau, Maurice. *Le roman français depuis la guerre*. Paris: Gallimard NRF, 1963.

Nattiez, Jean-Jacques. *Music and Discourse: Toward a Semiology of Music*. Princeton NJ: Princeton UP, 1990.

——. *Proust musicien*. Paris: Bourgeois, 1984.

Nietzsche, Friedrich. *The Birth of Tragedy and the Case of Wagner*. Trans. Walter Kaufmann. New York: Random House, 1967.

Ong, Walter. *Orality and Literacy: The Technologizing of the Word*. London: Methuen, 1981.

Oppenheim, Lois. *Samuel Beckett and the Arts*. New York: Garland (Border Crossings Series), 1999.

Park, Eric. "Fundamental Sounds: Music in Samuel Beckett's *Murphy* and *Watt*." *Modern Fiction Studies* 21 (summer 1975): 157–71.

Pater, Walter. *Essays on Literature and Art*. Ed. Jennifer Uglow. London: Everyman's Library, 1973.

Pautrot, Jean-Louis. "De *La Leçon de musique* à *La Haine de la musique*: Pascal Quignard, le structuralisme et le postmoderne." *French Forum* 22.3 (September 1997): 343–58.

——. "Musical Dimensions of Prose Narratives: *Musikant* by André Hodeir." *Mosaic* 33.2 (June 2000): 161–76.

——. *La musique oubliée*. Geneva: Droz, 1994.

Pavel, Thomas. *Fictional Worlds*. Cambridge MA: Harvard UP, 1986.

Perelman, Chaïm. *Rhétoriques*. Brussels: Éditions de l'Université de Bruxelles, 1989.

Pierce, John R. *The Science of Musical Sound*. Rev. ed. New York: W. H. Freeman, 1992.

Pinget, Robert. "Entretien avec Robert Pinget." Interview with Robert M. Henkels. *Études Littéraires* 19.3 (winter 1986–87): 173–82.

——. *L'inquisitoire*. Paris: Minuit, 1962.

——. "Une interview avec Robert Pinget." Interview with Bettina Knapp. *French Review* 42.4 (March 1969): 548–54.

——. *Passacaglia*. Trans. Barbara Wright. New York: Red Dust, 1978.

——. *Passacaille*. Paris: Minuit, 1969.

——. "Pseudo-principes d'esthétique." *Nouveau roman hier, aujourd'hui*. Ed. Jean Ricardou. Vol. 2. Paris: UGE, 1972. 311–50.

——. *Quelqu'un*. Paris: Minuit, 1965.

——. "Robert Pinget." NYU lecture. *Three Decades of the French New Novel*. Ed. Lois Oppenheim. Urbana: U of Illinois P, 1986. 143–51.

——. *Robert Pinget à la lettre: Entretiens avec Madeleine Renouard*. Paris: Belfond, 1993.

Pinker, Steven. *How the Mind Works*. New York: W. W. Norton, 1997.

Pound, Ezra. *Ezra Pound and Music: The Complete Criticism*. Ed. R. Murray Schafer. London: Faber and Faber, 1978.

Proust, Marcel. *Du côté de chez Swann*. Paris: Gallimard, 1954.

——. *Remembrance of Things Past*. Trans. C. K. Scott Moncrieff and Terence Kilmartin. 3 vols. New York: Vintage, 1982.

——. *Le temps retrouvé*. Ed. Bernard Brun. Paris: Gallimard, 1986.

Rabinovitz, Rubin. *The Development of Samuel Beckett's Fiction*. Urbana: U of Illinois P, 1984.

Ricardou, Jean. *Pour une théorie du nouveau roman*. Paris: Éditions du Seuil, 1971.

Ricardou, Jean, and Françoise van Rossum-Guyon, eds. *Nouveau roman: Hier aujourd'hui*. 2 vols. Paris: Union Générale d'Éditions, 1972.

Ricoeur, Paul. "Metaphor and the Central Problem of Hermeneutics." *Philosophy Looks at the Arts*. 3rd ed. Ed. Joseph Margolis. Philadelphia: Temple UP, 1987. 577–92.

——. *The Rule of Metaphor: Multi-disciplinary Studies of the Creation of Meaning in Language*. Trans. Robert Czerny. Toronto: U of Toronto P, 1977.

——. *Time and Narrative I*. Trans. Kathleen McLaughlin and David Pellauer. Chicago: U of Chicago P, 1984.

Robbe-Grillet, Alain. *Alain Robbe-Grillet, oeuvres cinématographiques: Édition vidéographique critique*. Ed. Pascal-Emmanuel Gallet. Paris: Ministère des Relations Extérieures, 1982.

——. "Entretien." Interview with Françoise Escal. *Revue des Sciences Humaines* 76.205 (January–March 1987): 97–109.

——. *For a New Novel*. Trans. Richard Howard. New York: Grove, 1965.

——. *La Jalousie*. Paris: Minuit, 1957.

——. *Pour un nouveau roman*. Paris: Minuit, 1961.

Robinson, Jenefer. "*Languages of Art* at the Turn of the Century." *Journal of Aesthetics and Art Criticism* 58.3 (summer 2000): 213–18.

Robinson, Michael. *The Long Sonata of the Dead: A Study of Samuel Beckett*. New York: Grove, 1969.

Roche, Maurice. *Compact*. Paris: Seuil, 1966.

——. *Maladie, mélodie*. Paris: Seuil, 1980.

Roche, Maurice. *Phenomenology, Language and the Social Sciences*. London: Routledge and Kegan Paul, 1973.

Rosen, Charles. *Sonata Forms*. Rev. ed. New York: Norton, 1998.

Rosmarin, Léonard A. *Robert Pinget*. New York: Twayne Publishers, 1995.

Roubaud, Jacques. *La fleur inverse: Essai sur l'art formel des troubadours*. Paris: Ramsay, 1986.

Rouget, Gilbert. *La musique et la transe*. Preface by Michel Leiris. Paris: Gallimard, NRF, 1980.

Rousseau, Jean-Jacques. *Discours sur l'origine des langues*. Ed. Jean Starobinski. Paris: Gallimard, 1990.

Russel, Catherine. "The Figure in the Monitor: Beckett, Lacan, and Video." *Cinema Journal* 28.4 (summer 1989): 20–37.

Ruwet, Nicolas. *Langage, musique, poésie*. Paris: Seuil, 1972.

Said, Edward. *Musical Elaborations*. New York: Columbia UP, 1992.

Sartre, Jean-Paul. *L'imaginaire, psychologie phénoménologique de l'imagination*. Paris: Gallimard, 1940.

——. *La nausée*. Paris: Gallimard, 1938.

——. *Qu'est-ce que la littérature?* Paris: Gallimard, 1948.

Saussure, Ferdinand de. *Les mots sous les mots*. Ed. Jean Starobinski. Paris: Gallimard, 1971.

Scher, Steven Paul. "How Meaningful Is 'Musical' in Literary Criticism?" *Yearbook of Comparative and General Literature* 21 (1972): 52–56.

——, ed. *Music and Text: Critical Inquiries*. Cambridge: Cambridge UP, 1992.

Schloezer, Boris de. *Introduction à J. S. Bach*. Paris: Idées Gallimard, 1947.

Schopenhauer, Arthur. *Philosophical Writings*. Ed. Wolfgang Schirmacher. New York: Continuum, 1994.

——. *The World as Will and Representation*. Trans. E. F. J. Payne. 2 vols. New York: Dover, 1969.

Senneff, Susan Field. "Song and Music in Samuel Beckett's *Watt*." *Modern Fiction Studies* 11.2 (summer 1964): 137–49.

Sieburth, Richard. "The Music of the Future." *A New History of French Literature*. Ed. Denis Hollier. Cambridge MA: Harvard UP, 1989. 789–98.

Sollers, Philippe, et al. *Tel Quel: Théorie d'ensemble*. Paris: Éditions du Seuil, 1968.

Stravinsky, Igor. *An Autobiography*. London: Calder and Boyars, 1975.

Strunk, Oliver. *Source Readings in Music History*. Vol. 2, *The Renaissance*. New York: Norton, 1965.

——. *Strunk's Source Readings in Music History*. Rev. and expanded ed. in one volume. Ed. Leo Treitler. New York: Norton, 1998.

Swain, Joseph P. *Musical Languages*. New York: Norton, 1997.

——. "The Range of Musical Semantics." *Journal of Aesthetics and Art Criticism* 54.2 (spring 1996): 135–52.

Thomas, Downing. *Music and the Origins of Language: Theories from the French Enlightenment*. New York: Cambridge, 1995.

Tooby, John, and Leda Cosmides. "Does Beauty Build Adapted Minds?" *SubStance* 30 (2001): 6–27.

Vidal, Jean-Pierre. "*Passacaille*: L'essaimage de la lettre envolée." *Études Littéraires* 19.3 (winter 1986–87): 98–118.

Walker, Jonathan "The Deconstruction of Musicology: Poison or Cure?" *Music Theory Online* 2.4 (May 1996).

Walton, Kendall L. *Mimesis as Make-Believe: On the Foundations of the Representational Arts*. Cambridge MA: Harvard UP, 1990.

Webern, Anton. *The Path to the New Music*. Ed. Willi Reich. Trans. Leo Black. New York: Theodore Presser, in association with Universal Edition, 1960.

Wilson, Edmund. *Axel's Castle*. New York: Charles Scribner's Sons, 1931.

Winn, James Anderson. *The Pale of Words: Reflections on the Humanities and Performance*. New Haven CT: Yale UP, 1998.

——. *Unsuspected Eloquence: A History of the Relations between Poetry and Music*. New Haven CT: Yale UP, 1981.

Wittgenstein, Ludwig. *Philosophical Investigations*. 3rd ed. Trans. G. E. M. Anscombe. New York: Macmillan, 1958.

——. *Tractatus Logico-Philosophicus*. Ithaca NY: Cornell UP, 1971.

Wolf, Werner. "Can Stories Be Read as Music? Possibilities and Limitations of Applying Musical Metaphors to Fiction." *Telling Stories: Studies in Honour of Ulrich Broich on the Occasion of His 60th Birthday*. Ed. Elmar Lehmann and Bernd Lenz. Amsterdam/Philadelphia: B. R. Grüner, 1992. 205–31.

——. *The Musicalization of Fiction: A Study in the Theory and History of Intermediality*. Amsterdam: Rodopi, 1999.

Yates, Frances. *The French Academies of the Renaissance*. New York: Routledge, 1988.

Zilliacus, Claus. *Beckett and Broadcasting*. Åbo: Åbo Academi, 1976.

Zukofsky, Louis. "*A*." Baltimore MD: Johns Hopkins UP, 1978.

Zumthor, Paul. *Oral Poetry: An Introduction*. Trans. Kathryn Murphy-Judy. Foreword by Walter J. Ong. Minneapolis: U of Minnesota P, 1990.

——. *La poésie et la voix dans la civilisation médiévale*. Paris: PUF, 1984.

Index

In the STAGES series